The Golden Age of Walt Disney Records 1933-1988

Murray's Collectors' Price Guide and Discography: LPs/45 rpm/78 rpm/EPs

R. Michael Murray

Antique Trader Books
A division of Landmark Specialty Publications

Dedication

To my wife, Claudia, and to my children Brian, Kathleen and Kelly, who have all kept smiling and have somehow managed to put up with "Recordman's" esoteric hobby these many years.

ISBN: 0-930625-70-6
Library of Congress Card Catalog Number: 97-72624

Editor: *Elizabeth Stephan*
Designer: *Sabine Beaupré*
Cover Design: *Jaro Sebek*
Design Assistants: *Lynn Bradshaw, Aaron Wilbers*

Cover photo credits:
Front cover: *(from top left, clockwise)*—Victor/RCA-224: "Who's Afraid of the Big Bad Wolf," 7" 78 rpm picture disc; Cadence CCS-1: "The Ballad of Davy Crockett," 10" 78 rpm; Disneyland WDL-4015: "Alice in Wonderland," 12" LP; Victor J-8: "Snow White and the Seven Dwarfs," 10", three 78 rpm set; Disneyland WDL-4013: "Dumbo," 12" LP; Disneyland WDL-4010: "Bambi," 12" LP; Disneyland WDL-4007: "Cinderella," 12" LP; Mickey Mouse Club MM-24: "Songs from Annette and Other Walt Disney Serials," 12" LP; Disneyland WDL-4002: "Pinocchio," 12" LP; Columbia MM-640: "The Whale Who Wanted to Sing at the Met," 10", three 78 rpm set; Decca A-369: "Saludos Amigos," 10", three 78 rpm set; Disneyland WDL-4001: "Song of the South," 12" LP.

Back cover: Mickey Mouse Club MM-12: "Musical Highlights from the Mickey Mouse Club TV Show," 12" LP.

Printed in the United States of America

To order additional copies of this book ar a catalog please contact:

Antique Trader Books
P.O. Box 1050
Dubuque, Iowa 52004
1-800-334-7165

Antique Trader Books
A division of Landmark Specialty Publications

Table of Contents

Section B: Disney-Related 33-1/3 LPs on Non-Disney Labels

Section C: Extended Play (EP) 7" Albums—45 rpm and 33-1/3 rpm

Section D: 78 rpm Records

Section E: The Disneyland and Buena Vista 45 rpm Recordings

Section F: "Little Golden" Records—All Sizes and Speeds

Section G: Other Non-Disney Label 45 rpm 7" Singles

Acknowledgments

Research for this book took me on a two and one-half year journey from New York City to Los Angeles and back. I've met some extremely warm and generous people along the way who have gone out of their way to assist me. I am especially indebted to Ken Sutak, fellow soundtrack collector and Disney fan, not only for his initial inspiration for this book ["Gee, it'd be nice to finally have a Disney Records guide...why don't *you* do one, Mike?"] but for his continued help, encouragement, and advice along the way. In addition to Ken's collection and mine, Peter Muldavin, Walter Mitchell, and Gary Brongo allowed me access to their own amazing Disney recordings collections from which the photos and some of the information in this book derive. Bill Cotter and Wayne Glenn provided a wealth of early information when I first began my research. Composer, author, and musicologist, Ross Care was especially helpful with Disney composer information, as was the invaluable research assistance of Paula Sigman Lowery in California.

This book would have been much less were it not for kindness and help of Dave Smith, Archives Director of the Walt Disney Archives, and his extremely helpful staff: Robert Tieman, Rebecca Cline and Collette Espino, who greatly assisted me via letters, and with on-site research during my visit to the Archives in Burbank, California.

Other major research facilities and personnel went out of their way to help out in this multi-year project: Sam Brylawski (Reference Librarian-Recorded Sound/Library of Congress); Gene DeAnna (Reference Librarian-Recorded Sound/Library of Congress); Claudia Depkin (Senior Archivist, BMG Entertainment [RCA]); and Susan Tyler Stinson (Curator, Belfer Audio Archive and Laboratory, Syracuse University).

Finally, the following people thankfully answered some of my pleas for "help" by letter and over the Internet, providing information which was gratefully incorporated into this book: Maurice Bichette; Julie M. Bohlander; Annette Bruno; Tom De Mary; Bill Emerson; Dan Hughes; John Keller; Peter Kelly; Lukas Kendall [Editor, *Film Score Monthly*]; Alfons A. Kowalski; Andrew Krieg; William Littman; Jonathan Motil; Phil Nohl [Editor, *The Soundtrack Collector*]; Lance Otto; Paul Scrabo; John Skoda; Dr. Robert Smith; and Ken Stigen. Disneyana collectors also owe a real thanks to Allan W. Miller, Elizabeth Stephan, and all the folks at Antique Trader Books for having provided the platform to finally get this first-time information out to collectors everywhere. Special thanks to you all and to my good friend "Recordman" and all of his vinyl buddies.

Manlius, New York
June 1997

Introduction

This book is a comprehensive chronicle of the recorded output of the Walt Disney film music and stories issued on shellac and later vinyl records in the United States, from the first records on the Victor and Bluebird labels in 1933 until approximately 1988, when Disney ceased production of "records" in favor of the compact disc format. In addition, as a long time record "collector," and with the help, input and advice of many other record, film, and Disneyana collectors, I have attempted to give current market pricing information on purchasing or selling now historical records such as these. Most of the information in this book has never before been made accessible to the general public.

Since 1929, the music of the films, scores, and records of the Walt Disney Company has formed a cross-generational backdrop to our lives. Most of us learned the major musical pieces at a young age and have retained them for life. Our mind often brings them forth in unusual circumstances: Humming "Some Day My Prince Will Come" in a business meeting, or unconsciously whistling "Bibbidi-Bobbidi-Boo" while jogging along a mountain road. Other film score composers have often successfully used Disney music "tag" references in their own works to not only provide immediate audience recognition, but to also invoke the awe of innocent childhood in us all. This technique was utilized with great effect by composer, John Williams, who referenced "When You Wish Upon a Star" from *Pinocchio* in the film *Close Encounters of the Third Kind*.

It is fair to say that Disney's music has been heard by more people around the world over the last sixty-five years than that of any other popular source. Indeed, by early on utilizing the musical talents of some of the best popular composers and musicians available at the time, the glorious Disney animated films and many of the live-action films are impossible to now imagine without the music we learned and passed on to our children. The successful Disney marketing strategy of periodically re-releasing its films for new generations, and the current availability of its films on videotape, has produced the modern day version of a society passing on its culture, music, and achievements to its children by way of oral history.

"Record collectors" such as myself have existed since the inception of the medium, from the early emphasis on collecting classical recordings of the 1920s and 1930s into the early jazz and "Big Band" sounds of the 1930s and 1940s. The 1950s were the heyday of the jazz collectors, and by the late 1960s and early 1970s, early rock and roll, rhythm and blues, and "doo-wop" recordings were (and still are) highly sought after. In the late 1960s and early 1970s the hobby of collecting film music soundtracks also gained recognition and many adherents.

As each of these areas of music collectibles became widespread, inevitably genre discographies and "price guides" appeared on the collector market as well to assist in the research and obtaining of the records. My own interest in film music in general resulted in my monthly column on soundtrack record collecting in *Film Score Monthly* magazine. This eventually led me to questions about the Disney recordings. Alas, my initial research showed that of all the music collectibles over the years, the Disney records had never been catalogued in depth, and most of the recordings were the subject of rumor only passed from collector to collector. This lack of general Disney collector reference material became especially surprising as I learned early on that there were several of the Disney vinyl long play (LP) albums and singles being bought in auction houses here and abroad for hundreds of dollars! Yet, with the exception of the Disney records recorded by Annette Funicello in the 1950s and early 1960s, the standard reference guides to popular and rock music, do not cover the Disney recordings at all! Moreover, while there are many "Disneyana" collectors around the world, the standard Disneyana reference works either refer only briefly to the recordings or don't mention them at all. What caused this lack of information?

Having now spent many uncountable hours researching this book, I have several different theories for the lack of Disney record information in the past. First, the Disneyland/Buena Vista output is a very large catalog of recordings in many different formats and various sizes within the individual formats: 78 rpm, 45 rpm, and 33-1/3 rpm. Second, the recordings were reissued many times over the years for new generations in various number sequences and changed cover formats, requiring specialized knowledge in order to determine and differentiate between the various pressings. Third, to cover the complete Disney music recordings issued prior to 1955 the cataloges of at least three other major record companies, Capitol, Decca, and RCA, have to be considered, along with over fifty other firms. Fourth, until within the last ten to fifteen years, many rock music collectors mistakenly thought of all Disney music as "kiddie" music. Finally, the issue of the difficulty of finding any Disney record in near mint condition has tended to frighten off all but the most dedicated and resourceful collectors.

This guide has now put together the information to satisfy the first three concerns listed above. With regard to the last concern, I can personally attest that collectors should be aware that near mint and mint copies of almost any record in the Disney-related catalog do exist, which any collector worth their name can eventually ferret out through his or her usual sources in "The Quest" for records in general. Some may be expensive, but this is true of any record category. This leaves us with the question as to why Disney records are collectible and should not be thought of as the normal "kiddie" collectible?

The Disney recordings are collectible to many different collecting specialties. They represent classic "Disneyana" as they derive from the films and stories made famous by Walt Disney. Indeed, this is Disneyana that can actually "talk" back to you if you wish, and doesn't have to just sit silently in a display case. For the animated artwork or cel collector, the covers to many of the Disneyland/Buena Vista albums, especially the "4000" series discussed, are absolutely gorgeous, high-quality framable reproductions of Disney art available in no other format. Many collectors buy and sell the albums for the art work alone. Many of the Disney "Story Teller" albums utilize original cel frames in the album booklets. Seeing a large collection of Disney record items for the first time is a vivid experience for collectors of any specialty. The intensely bright and colorful cartoon and live-action record covers and booklets provide a visual delight that cannot be matched in any other field.

The music from the Disney films and television shows are also collectible as soundtrack recordings, especially the first issue Disney pressings in any format featuring many of Disney's "Golden Age" composers. These albums can be enjoyable merely for the music, with the artwork considered as a bonus. There are collectors who specialize only in "Mickey Mouse Club" television items, or in "Davy Crockett" records of which there are abundant examples with fine photo covers. Rock music collectors have long sought out any of the recordings and great cover photos of Annette Funicello on singles and albums. Many of the albums qualify as highly sought after items for those who collect movie memorabilia in general. Some albums contain Broadway and "pop" music for those interested in those specialities. The list could go on and on. There is something in the Disney catalog to please any collector, and the era of the vinyl recordings has become one to be preserved as classic twentieth century Americana.

A Short History Of Recorded Disney Music

Prior to 1955, Walt Disney Productions (now the Walt Disney Company) did not produce and distribute its own music recordings from its films. It assigned or licensed out the rights to its music and recording rights to the major record corporations of the time, primarily RCA, Decca, and Capitol which released a few original Disney soundtracks, and many cast studio tracks to the films as well. Disney licensed not only its music, but cartoon drawings and/or photos, which usually appeared on these non-Disney album or singles covers making them true Disney collectibles as well. This was especially true in the 1930s through the early 1950s during the 78 rpm era (See separate non-Disney 78 rpm listings at Section D3).

In 1933, Saul Bourne, then the general manager of Irving Berlin, Inc. (Berlin), requested a Disney license for the music of *Who's Afraid of the Big Bad Wolf* and music from other Disney short cartoons. Disney agreed and, under the agreement with Berlin, it assigned the musical copyrights to the music produced by its staff composers for certain of its short subjects ("shorts") in return for a percentage of any licensing revenues produced. However, Disney retained the right to itself utilize the music in its motion pictures and, with amazing foresight, reserved television rights as well. This agreement was subsequently modified in 1935 and 1936 to include the music in additional cartoons.

After the original assignment, Berlin then licensed the music for *Who's Afraid of the Big Bad Wolf* to Victor Records, which produced immediate Depression-era hits of the song in September 1933 by The Don Bestor Orchestra on the Victor label, and Bill Scotti and Orchestra on the Bluebird label. Other "Silly Symphony" shorts original film music was licensed to Victor records in November 1933. In 1934, Victor released three 7", picture disc, 78 rpm singles featuring Frank Luther and Orchestra performing studio track versions of the music from the "Silly Symphonies" (See Section D3.31.1 below). In 1936, "H.M.V." records (the British RCA affiliate), released 78 rpm recordings of several of Disney's "Silly Symphonies" original soundtracks. These were released in the United States in October 1937 on RCA's "Bluebird" label as separate recordings (See Section D3.2.1).

In 1937, Disney was being financially pressured by the production costs of its first full-length, animated film, *Snow White and the Seven Dwarfs*, known around Hollywood as "Disney's Folly" at the time. Bourne, having seen that Disney's music could be successfully marketed, asked that Berlin also be assigned the musical rights to *Snow White* as well, promising to heavily promote the film through the music. At the time, it was a good business deal for the Disney studios and it assigned the rights to eight musical compositions from *Snow White and the Seven Dwarfs* to Berlin, in return for a share of the royalties from any licensees of the music.[1] Berlin used this arrangement to license the music from *Snow*

[1] Significantly, other than a right to royalties, Disney failed to reserve any rights to *Snow White*'s music, including its failure to allow Disney a license to use the music in any manner in the future. In 1994, Berlin's successor-in-interest, the Bourne Co. won a judgment of $420,000 against Disney for its use of music from *Snow White* and *Pinocchio* in paid television advertisements, a use not included in Disney's licenses. The court did find, however, that Disney's subsequent use of the music of *Snow White* and *Pinocchio* in their theatrical re-releases evinced an implied prior understanding and agreement between the parties regarding this use. Moreover, it was held that the 1930s agreements were sufficiently broad so as to allow Disney to incorporate its musical synchronization rights in the films for transfer to the new medium of videocassettes. See *Bourne Co. v The Walt Disney Company et al,* 31 U.S.P.Q. 2d 1858; 1994 WL 263482 (S.D.N.Y.); aff'd 68 F. 3d 621 (2nd Cir. 1995); *cert. den.*116 S.Ct.1890,135 L.Ed.2 184.

White to the Radio Corporation of America (RCA). This resulted in the first multi-record, original film soundtrack "album"—"Snow White and the Seven Dwarfs," released in the United States in January of 1938 on Victor Records (See Section 3.31.2). Walt and his older brother, Roy Disney, always later regretted this assignment, since they were never again to own the *Snow White* music outright. Even after Bourne's death in the mid-1950s, his widow refused to relinquish her rights to the music back to Disney. Notwithstanding its eventual second thoughts on these deals, in 1939 Disney entered into an agreement similar to the 1933 "shorts" agreement in which it assigned the music rights from *Pinocchio* to Berlin as well. Original soundtrack 78 rpm albums were then issued on Victor Records for both *Pinocchio* and *Dumbo* (see Section D.31.2).

In the early 1940s, Bourne left Berlin and formed a new company, "Bourne Music." He was able to keep control over all of the non-Berlin written music, to include many of the Disney shorts and the full-length animated features *Snow White*, *Pinocchio*, and *Dumbo*. Not having any other method of distribution of its music, Disney continued to license its music to third-party publishers throughout the 1940s.

The advent of World War II caused a general shortage of availability of Disney-related recordings for several reasons. Importation of shellac, which was used in the making of 78 rpm records, was greatly affected by the Japanese blockade of Malaya. This caused American manufacturers to step up experimentation in vinyl and plastic materials for the production of the records. The research resulted in the introduction of "vinylite" or "Bakelite" records in the later 1940s, especially useful in the making of children's "unbreakable" records.

However, other events in the early 1940s caused record production problems. Any recording of new Disney material was hampered when the American Federation of Musicians (AFM) sought to prevent unremunerated use of records on the radio, in clubs, and jukeboxes. To make matters worse, the American Society of Composers, Authors and Publishers (ASCAP) joined in the dispute with the radio industry over fees to be paid to ASCAP for the broadcast of its music over the airwaves. Not to be outdone, the radio industry formed its own rival organization, Broadcast Music Incorporated (BMI), with its own music publishing firm. As a result, no ASCAP music was played on the air for a year. Frustrated, the AFM declared a general musicians' strike against the record manufacturers, and no new records were recorded at all between August 1942 and November 1944. Any records which were released during that time period came from recordings made prior to the strike. Disney had previously utilized ASCAP services, however, in order to get air play for "Bambi," Disney used BMI. However, in the years after World War II, Disney considered BMI to be an inappropriate organization for the proper exploitation of the "Bambi" music. BMI agreed to give back the rights to "Bambi" and other songs only if Disney would form its own BMI-only publishing firm. Disney agreed, and thus was born the "Wonderland Music Company" in 1952.

In the meantime, the 1940s musical rights to the Disney films had been spread out among many different firms. The musical rights to *Saludos Amigos* and *The Three Caballeros* were assigned to Ralph Peer and Southern Music, and Peer International. Southern Music also got all the songs from *Make Mine Music* except "Johnny Fedora and Alice Blue Bonnet" which went to Leeds Music, and Regent Music got "All the Cats Join In" from the same film. Music from *The Adventures of Ichabod and Mr. Toad* were assigned to Edwin H. Morris & Co. Santly-Joy (later Anne Rachel Music) acquired the rights to the music from *Song of the South*, *Fun and Fancy Free*, *Melody Time*, and *So Dear to My Heart*, which Disney was finally able to regain in 1974.

Disney did not reap great profits from these deals. The usual arrangements with these third-party firms gave Disney 50% of the record royalties, out of which it usually had to pay its composers and writers approximately two-thirds of that amount. Moreover, Disney did not share at all in any ASCAP performing rights for the assigned music.

The year 1948 saw a major development occur which was to change the method of sound reproduction for the next forty years. Until that time all records produced after the early "cylinder" days of the industry, were 78 rpm recordings in various sizes in a flat "platter" style which proved not only very brittle, but very heavy and cumbersome to store. Its speed of revolution limited most 10" 78 rpm discs to very short playing times. In this watershed year, a record "format" war began between Columbia and RCA. Columbia had developed 10" and 12" 33-1/3 rpm long playing records which allowed greatly extended playing time for each record plus higher fidelity sound reproduction when compared to the earlier 78 rpm records. Moreover, as the records were vinyl based, they were lighter and virtually unbreakable.

Columbia originally offered the LP format to RCA, but RCA refused it, initially touting RCA's development of the 7" 45 rpm record as the wave of the future. Indeed, RCA initially sold 45 rpm record players at less than cost in order to push for that format's acceptance and dominance. RCA had originally developed a long play process in the 1930s which proved impractical. Eventually, Columbia's LP format won out for reproduction of multi-song collections or for lengthy compositions. However, RCA's "45" became the standard format for popular single recordings, and temporarily for multi-volume 45 rpm "albums."[2]

The "Walt Disney Music Company," an ASCAP firm, was established in August of 1949, at the suggestion of Fred Raphael, who had been Disney's Director of Music Exploitation for the three previous years. Its initial charge was to publish all music written for and used in Disney films, plus whatever "outside product" seemed appropriate. Its first published music was six songs from *Cinderella*, released in January of 1950. After 1949, all music Disney produced for any film, TV shows, stage shows, or theme park events was assigned to either the "Walt Disney Music Company" (ASCAP) or to the "Wonderland Music Company" (BMI) depending on the performing rights society membership of its composers. Similarly, Disney instituted a strong policy of insisting that when considering an artist for a new film, that it be made clear that all record rights to the music were to be reserved to Disney. If Disney had to use copyrighted, third-party music, the costs were usually considered prohibitive. The company was in the business of fantasy and entertainment, but it was also foremost a business.

With the introduction of the new record formats, record companies such as RCA and Decca, which had previously licensed Disney music from Berlin, Bourne, and others, then recycled many of their 78 rpm recordings onto the then "new" format 10" and 12" 33-1/3 long play (LP) record albums, and onto the smaller, 7" extended play (EP) 45 rpm record albums. These EPs allowed additional playing time in the 45 rpm format, typically allowing four songs to a disc (See non-Disney EP listings). From 1949 until approximately 1958, the industry continued to manufacture the older 78 rpm records as well, duplicating many titles with their smaller 45 rpm editions.

The format transition phase of the early 1950s is a collector's delight but an archivist's nightmare, as often the same score or composition could and did appear as separate releases in all formats: 78 rpm albums; 45 rpm albums; EP sets; and in 10" and

---

[2] Ironically, we still refer to the production and release of an artist's recorded music as a new "album," a term of the 78 rpm era when multi-volume records were actually released in hardbound, fold-open packaging sleeves resembling older picture albums or books. The term had essentially become dated during the LP era, yet has remained with us well into the CD age—a sentimental tie to our musical heritage.

12" LP versions. A similar occurrence began in 1958 and lasted through 1968 when stereophonic (stereo) records were introduced, replacing the decades-old, single-channel monaural (mono) recording process. Consumers and dealers often had mono and stereo copies of the same recording side by side. This is why you will see many records in this guide listed with both a mono and a stereo release. The stereo recordings eventually won out and even survived an ill-fated and brief attempt by the record manufacturers in the early 1970s to promote Quadraphonic (Quad), four-channel recordings. Disney never released Quad records during this time period, however. The record-buying public rebelled against this final attempt to foist upon it the third major and expensive format change in only a twenty-five year period. The new system never caught on and Quad records were an historical footnote by the mid-1970s.

While the Walt Disney Music Company had some earlier success in the late 1940s and early 1950s with popular music hits, such as Frankie Laine's "Mule Train" on Mercury, and Jo Stafford's "Shrimp Boats" on Columbia, it steadily lost money in 1950 through 1952. Fred Raphael left his position as General Professional Manager of Walt Disney Music in 1953 and James A. "Jimmy" Johnson became its General Manager and President.[3]

If any one event might be seen as the major impetus for Disney to have launched its own record label, that event was the world-wide success of over 200 different recorded versions of "The Ballad of Davy Crockett" in 1955! (See Section D3.7.2). The story of the music for "Davy Crockett" is as fascinating as its success. In the Spring of 1954, plans for the Disney three-part television series on the life and times of true life American legend Davy Crockett, were underway at the Disney Studios. It was felt that a common thread was needed to tie the three one hour segments together, as it covered over a twenty year span of Crockett's life. That thread proved to be a catchy theme song which provided a two minute plus overview of the Crockett legend. Composer George Bruns and lyrist Tom Blackwell were assigned the duties and came up with the song they titled, "The Ballad of Davy Crockett," with twenty written verses.

Inasmuch as Disney was still relegated to having others distribute records for it, Jimmy Johnson initially wanted Alan Livingston at Capitol Records to produce and handle its distribution. However, Capitol thought to request even more of the Disney music rights beyond what Capitol was already producing in its highly popular and attractive, children's record series. Capitol wanted to form a "Disney" or "Disneyland" label which it would own. Disney declined this offer however, inasmuch as it needed Capitol only for distribution purposes. Perhaps sensing the upcoming popularity of the TV show, Disney decided to cut its own master records with Fess Parker, the star of the show, and three "storyteller"-type records, one for each TV segment, featuring the original TV cast.

After the first segment in the TV Davy Crockett series aired on December 15, 1954 ("Davy Crockett—Indian Fighter"), Johnson went to New York City to hopefully conclude a deal with Columbia to distribute the records under license. While there, he was contacted by Archie Bleyer, head of Cadence Records, a man whom he greatly respected. Bleyer told Johnson that the public was clamoring for a record of the Davy Crockett TV theme. When informed that Johnson was to offer the recordings to Columbia, Bleyer requested that Cadence be allowed to immediately record its own version of the song and get it on the stands. Johnson readily agreed, reasoning that no other record could possibly compete

[3] The Disney Archives contains an unpublished manuscript by Jimmy Johnson entitled: *Inside the Whimsy-Works—My Thirty-seven Years with Walt Disney Productions* (1975), which contains some of the above factual information and a further fascinating account of his long service at the Disney studios. This and various company files proved invaluable in further understanding Disney's ultimate venture into the "record business."

with Fess Parker's original vocal version of the song. Within two weeks, Bleyer had "The Ballad of Davy Crockett" recorded by Bill Hayes, and a record of it out on Cadence Records. This record had originally reproduced a photo of Fess Parker as "Davy" on the its cover, but Bleyer destroyed all copies of the cover when Disney objected. What a collector's find that cover would be today! (See Sections D3.5 and G4)

Johnson completed his license of the original Davy Crockett masters to Columbia (See Section D3.7.2), but Fess Parker's Columbia record version of "The Ballad . . ." did not appear on the record stands until three weeks after Hayes' version on Cadence was climbing to the top of the popular music record charts. The Cadence version sold over 1-1/2 million copies in a very short time, while the Fess Parker rendition peaked at just short of a million records. The marketing of the music continued into the music publishing field, and "The Ballad . . ." sold over 3/4 million copies of the sheet music published by the Wonderland Music Company. The shows and theme for Disney's highly popular "Davy Crockett" television series spawned not only the sale of millions of records on non-Disney labels, but created a cultural and marketing phenomenon in the United States in the mid-1950s that has never since been matched. Anything related to "Davy Crockett" sold quickly, and the children of America briefly bedecked themselves in coonskin hats in the style of their TV hero.

The "Disneyland" TV show on the American Broadcasting Company Network (ABC) had commenced on October 27, 1954. Its early season touted not only the "Davy Crockett" series, but the creation of the original Disneyland theme park, which opened on July 17, 1955 in Anaheim, California, after heavy financial backing by ABC. Both creations proved a natural outlet for the promotion of Disney products, including Disney music. The concurrent success of TV's "The Mickey Mouse Club," also on ABC, gave anything Disney related overwhelming marketplace exposure.

In the Spring of 1955, ABC told Disney that it wanted to go into the record business. Johnson suggested that Sam Clarke from Cadence be hired to run the ABC operation in a joint deal with "Little Golden" records: Disney was to furnish the art and talent; Golden Records was to produce the record masters; and ABC was to distribute the records. Originally, eight 10" 78 rpm and 45 rpm records were produced and on the record stands within a week of the first airing of the "Mickey Mouse Club" TV show on October 3, 1955 (DBR Series 50 through 57. See Sections C8 and D1). While ABC also produced some Disney-related records on its own ABC-Paramount label, it initially could not get hit records or artists except for those on the "Mickey Mouse Club" label. Eventually producer Golden Records dropped out of the arrangement and Disney bought out ABC's interest. The Mickey Mouse Club records then became part of the Disney produced line in 1958.

It was the success of the Davy Crockett and the Mickey Mouse Club records which eventually convinced Walt Disney to start his own, full-time record production company. On January 31, 1956, Jimmy Johnson perceptively spelled out the business rationale. He first noted by analogy that Disney had earlier formed its own music publishing firms to, one: own the copyrights to Disney film music, and two: to be able to benefit the films by exploiting the music. Realizing that the publishing firms had little sway over record companies and radio disc jockeys, Johnson concluded that the reasons for in-house record production were similar, one: Disney should own any master records made with its talent and its music, and two: once the records were owned outright, Disney could better control the music to help the films even more. It was thought that this arrangement would greatly benefit the periodic re-release of Disney classic films by issuing older music to coincide with those releases, something other record companies would not do. Advantages were seen in producing and controlling Disney record releases in a growing foreign and educational market as well.

In 1955, Frances Archer and Beverly Gile were a singing duo discovered personally by Walt Disney who enjoyed their show in Palm Springs. The duo appeared on early episodes of "The Mickey Mouse Club" TV show, and recorded a very early, 1955 10" LP of "A Child's Garden of Verses" (See section A1) on a Charles Hansen distributed "Disneyland" label which was subsequently re-released many times in various formats.

Disneyland Records was officially founded in 1956 as a division of the Walt Disney Music Company, a wholly owned subsidiary of Walt Disney Productions. In its first year of recording, the records dealt exclusively with Disney films, subjects, and artists. This initial records venture was in cooperation with Hansen Publications, also headed by Charles Hansen, who had already been distributing Disney music, and who was to act as the Disney records distributor. This is why a few very early "Disneyland" LPs and singles are on a unique "pixie-dust" yellow label, with the "Disneyland" logo at the bottom, which often credited Hansen as distributor. With good distribution of the records thought assured, Tutti Camarata was hired as Musical Director of Disneyland Records. His initial production was the first 1956 LP original soundtrack recording to be on the official "Disneyland" designated series: "Song of the South" (WDL-4001), timed to coincide with the film's re-release. The "WDL-4000" series (See section A23) of LPs was launched with "sophisticated adult art covers" and priced at $4.98. It was felt that these quality pressings would "find their place in record stores alongside other Hollywood soundtracks and Broadway cast albums" and serve to promote reissues of classic animated films.

The Disneyland LP "WDL-3000" series (See section A14), selling at $3.98 was intended for use for Disneyland theme park music, including the "Disneyland Band," "The Player Piano," "Main Street," and the "Golden Horseshoe Review." The first record on the new label to be created entirely by the Disneyland Record company was "Walt Disney Takes You to Disneyland: A Musical Tour of Disneyland" (WDL-4004). "Westward Ho the Wagons" on LP WDL-4008, released on October 1, 1956, was the first soundtrack to be recorded for a new film release. Early non-Disney artists recorded include Mary Martin, Jan Clayton, and Stan Jones.

Unfortunately, Charlie Hansen's distribution of the records did not work out as Disney had hoped, and he was replaced by Al Latauska who organized independent distributors nationwide. Even this did not help, and by the Fall of 1957 into 1959 Disney Records was losing money. Considering the record business at the time, and given the nature of the music and records Disney was producing, that should have been no surprise. It was extremely difficult for music such as this to break into the record charts of the day. From 1955 onwards, "pop" music had begun to be dominated by the tidal wave of early rock and roll music which proved disastrous to all preconceived notions as to what would sell in the marketplace. Management personnel at Disney records had come of age with the sound of late 1930s and 1940s music. However, the 1940s sound of the "Big Bands," vocalist crooners and even most earlier jazz had become extremely dated by the mid-1950s. Disneyland was making such records as "Tutti's Trumpets" by Camarata (WDL/STER-3011) in 1957 while Elvis Presley and his peers were breaking all sorts of music sales records around the world. At the time, there was no doubt that Disney knew films, but it seemingly had no idea how, who or what to produce on records that would make money in the open marketplace. What chance then existed for high priced "children's records" and re-recordings of fifteen year old soundtracks?

In 1959, Disneyland Records retrenched in the face of dismal financial showings and almost folded its operations. The decision was made to abandon the "adult-style" WDL-4000 series of LPs, to drop most of the non-Disney musical talent, and to emphasize its children's line and "story-teller" series. Prices were dropped from $4.98 to a "DQ" line of budget LPs at $1.98 (See Section A6). Jimmy Johnson recognized that the children's record business was more closely akin to the children's book or toy business, rather than a "pop" record market. Let Disney do what Disney had always done best—concentrate on the children! Thus, the highly collectible "WDL-4000" series of beautifully produced record albums disappeared after only nineteen records.

Disney did establish the separate Buena Vista[4] record label in 1959 which was initially to produce whatever limited amount of "pop" recordings that Disney might make. In this regard, it is fair to say that Buena Vista Records could easily be called the label built by the recordings of ex-Mouseketeer, Annette Funicello, or simply "Annette" as she has been known over the years. Walt Disney had personally signed a future star when he hired Annette at the age of 12 in 1955 for the original cast of the "Mickey Mouse Club" TV show. There were plenty of Mouseketeers who could sing better than she, such as Darlene Gillespie, and others who could act and dance better, but Annette projected an aura of charm, innocence, and wholesomeness. She also had what Jimmy Johnson was later to call "identifiability" with her audience. These qualities, combined with her beauty and later sex appeal, catapulted her into early record chart recording success on Disneyland singles records. She was guided by Tutti Camarata with "pop-rock" hits such as "How Will I Know My Love," "Tall Paul," and "Pineapple Princess" penned by the Sherman brothers. Nine of the first twenty releases on the Buena Vista "3300" LP series (See Section A16) were Annette albums. She later had her own successful film and television career and has remained ever the classy woman, retained as a warm thought in the memories of her generation, a genuine cultural icon of the late 1950s and early 1960s.

Two other milestones in Disney record production later occurred in the 1960s and 1970s. The release of the Buena Vista original soundtrack to *Mary Poppins* in 1964, featuring Julie Andrews and Dick Van Dyke, sold 2.3 million albums in its first year of release and spawned many studio track recordings as well. This record tripled the gross for Disneyland Records and quadrupled its profit. The other major LP was the unexpected success of the "Mickey Mouse Disco" LP in 1979 which sold close to two million copies.

These two Disney record labels, Disneyland and Buena Vista, produced hundreds and hundreds of albums and singles in many different vinyl record formats, mono and stereo, from 1956 until 1988, when the advent of the compact disc medium took over at Disney and most other American record companies. All Disney record and tape labels were consolidated under the name "Walt Disney Records" in August of 1988. The "Touchstone" division was initially to distribute film soundtracks for Touchstone films. Disney Records was to issue family-fare records, and Disneyland Records was to continue its mission of appealing to the children. The musical legacy of Disney has continued to thrive on compact discs for future generations to enjoy, with great success with the film scores for *Beauty and the Beast*, *The Little Mermaid*, and *The Lion King*. Whatever new medium of sound reproduction appears in the future, you can be assured the sound of Disney music will be heard and loved. However, the glorious artwork and packaging of the early vinyl-era recordings will remain Disney's golden age for collectors of all ages.

[4] "Buena Vista" was named after the address of the Walt Disney Studios, 500 So. Buena Vista Drive, Burbank, CA 91521.

Condition and Pricing of the Records

I often see a potential record seller's advertisement in which the seller proclaims, for example, that a "Pinocchio" record is for sale: "Make me an offer!" First, the seller has not told you the format, label name, and number of the recording. Since Disney recordings were issued and reissued in so many different formats over the years, the lack of such information in the advertisement does not tell you which record is actually being offered for sale.

Initially, whether a seller or a buyer, you must inform or be informed of the details or pedigree of the particular record pressing under consideration. When such a recording is listed as, for example, "Pinocchio: LP/Disneyland WDL-4002," all parties are on notice as to the actual item being considered. You know the name of the album; its format (LP); its record label (Disneyland); and the particular record number (WDL-4002). For the record collecting novice, this release number usually appears on the outer cover or sleeve, and on the record label as well. There is now no doubt that both buyer and seller are talking about the same recording in negotiations and it avoids confusion and possible allegations of bad faith dealing at a later date. As you will discover below, there are many variations of "Pinocchio" and the difference in values may be several hundreds of dollars. Be sure what you're talking about before the money passes hands, especially if dealing by mail order.

As in any collectible's field, after the rarity per se, that is the overall availability and demand for the individual recording is considered,, the condition of the vinyl recording itself and the condition of the cardboard or paper outer cover, if any, are the primary considerations in setting the prices contained in this guide. In the example above, even if the seller has given you all the necessary details of the pressing under consideration, you still don't know what purported condition the record is in, unless you are considering the purchase in a retail store or record show where you can actually see the record yourself.

Why is knowing the condition of a recording so important? The simple answer is that, as with any antiques or collectibles, the condition affects the price or monetary worth of the recording, whether buying or selling. Why? While some hesitate to utilize the phraseology "Kiddie Records" when talking about the Disney line, it is a fact that many if not most of the Disney recordings were targeted at a youthful audience who, in most cases, would and did play and listen to the records. In the process, many of the records were subjected to the worst possible physical abuse only a young child could muster. Most records were not intentionally damaged, but were often regarded as playthings and were the victims of childhood negligence by those who simply didn't know any better.

In all fairness however, it should be noted that often the damage to a vinyl record was caused by the rather crude "record player" technology available at the time the records were made. This is especially so for the non-Disney label 78 rpm records produced from the 1930s into the early 1950s. Finding these 78 rpm recordings in anything near mint condition is a real coup, and they would command premium prices.

Many who collect Disney recordings may do so merely for the gorgeous artwork utilized on the album cover or singles sleeves. However, the "record collector" considers both the cover condition and that of the recording itself. This has resulted in various "record grading" standards utilized in the hobby over the years in an attempt to place seller and buyer on equal grounds when a purchase is considered. This system currently takes into consideration both the condition of the cover/sleeve and the condition of the vinyl record. In advertising the records, the grade for the record is usually given first, and then the grade for the cover. You will see a notation, for example: "M-/VG+." What does it all mean?

Current grading standards range from the ultimate collectible, a "still sealed (SS)" copy of the record, to those records graded "poor (P)," which are in terrible shape, suitable only as Frisbees or as a "filler" copy until you can obtain one of a higher grade. Reproduced in Appendix A, you will find the record grading standards utilized in the hobby. You should study them carefully before either buying or selling any record. In general, the grading system and the short-hand notation used in descending rank of collectibility, are as follows:

Still Sealed (SS)
Mint (M)
Mint Minus (M-); Sometimes noted as Near Mint (NM)
Very Good Plus (VG+); Sometimes noted as Excellent (EX or EXC)
Very Good (VG)
Good (G)
Poor (P)

In an effort to get even more specific, some dealers may add an extra "Plus" or "Minus" to a grade, e.g., "VG++," to indicate a record too good for the VG+ grade but not quite good enough for M- status. Variations on this exist, such as "strong VG+," etc. You should be aware that hardcore 78 rpm collectors use a different grading system. However, the above grades have been dominate in the record collecting hobby in general for last thirty years.

Thus, at a minimum when you place or see a record advertisement, you should see something like this: "Pinocchio; Disneyland WDL-4002; M-/VG+; (price)." However, even with the grading system you should also note any obvious defects in either the cover or the record. Defects include writing on the cover or label; albums with split seams; tape on the cover and various forms of "cut-out" record album cover holes or notches. Also listed in Appendix A, are various grading defect notations and other abbreviations commonly used in the record collecting hobby. If there is space, many ads also note the featured artists, color of the vinyl if other than black, whether or not the record is a promotional copy, has an attached booklet, and any other notable feature worth mentioning to the potential buyer.

Since the Disney records catalog is so large and came in so many formats, you should also include the size of the record and its speed as well, for example: 10" LP, 7" 45 rpm, etc. This will be helpful for the Disney novice who has not yet become familiar with the Disney numbering system as explained in this book.

The "guide" prices placed on the records in this book are based on many years of experience and were determined after consultation with other record and Disney collectors across the country. You may see them selling for less in some outlets, and for more in others. A brief word of advice learned from some hard-luck experiences: If you see a record you've been seeking for years at a nice price—buy it! It may disappear in the next ten minutes to another collector, and you may never run across another copy—if you do, it will be more expensive. This might be known as "Recordman's Law of Indecision."

Most importantly, please be aware that the estimated current values given in this book are for Mint Minus (M-) copies of the LP, EP and 45 rpm records only! The estimated values for the records are for both the record and its picture cover/sleeve together! The cover/sleeve is expected to be in approximately the same condition as the record. Variations in grade should be noted and will affect the overall selling price. If the record was produced with a picture cover/sleeve and has no cover/sleeve at the time of sale, approximately 40-45% should be deducted from the listed price. Many collectors will not buy a Disney record without its picture cover/sleeve. However, some may buy either separately to upgrade a lesser copy. If the record only came with a generic, non-picture cover/sleeve, the condition of the paper is not that important as it can always be replaced.

Please note that in pricing the 78 rpm records, the prices given are estimated prices for VG+ copies. In making a distinction between the formats, experience has shown that it is almost impossible to locate Mint or Mint Minus copies of 78 rpm records. The technology of the sound reproduction 78 rpm "record-players" virtually assured some damage to the records if they were played at all! So be aware that a true Mint or Mint Minus 78 rpm record would command at least a 50% premium over the price listed in this guide.

Any lesser grade copy of the record must have its price adjusted accordingly whether buying or selling. As a general rule "VG+" copies would be worth approximately 50% of the "M-" figure; "VG" copies at 25%; "G" copies at 10-20%; and "P" copies at 5-10% tops. Usually "P" copies are flea market dollar-a-record items, though some may pay more, especially if it is a rare item, even in this condition. Some collectors may buy low-grade, low-priced copies as "filler" copies in anticipation of finding later upgrades of the record for their collection. If any flea market dealer offers to sell you a "P" condition record at "M-" prices, telling you, "It's in the book," explain the difference to the "dealer," and if the price is not adjusted, just smile and walk on by. You can find it elsewhere for less, guaranteed. It may take some effort and time to search, but they are available for the right price and in the right condition. The word here is perseverance.

If the album is Still Sealed (SS), it will sell at a premium price over the guide price listed, ranging from 125% to 200%+ depending on the album's rarity. Please be aware that the use of manufacturer's plastic "shrink-wrap" on albums was a practice begun only in the late 1960s, and LPs or singles prior to that date, if sealed at all, were sealed in loose fitting, thin poly sleeves similar, but not identical to those available today which may be purchased by the collector to protect the albums. Be aware that some unscrupulous dealers may re-wrap albums, usually in "shrink-wrap," and try to sell them as new! Inspect the record carefully given the above information.

One interesting aspect that has become noticeable in record collecting is the market fluctuation between various regions of the country. As a general rule, if you live on either the East or West Coast you can expect to see records selling for higher prices, commensurate with the cost of living in these areas. Dealers in Heartland America tend to have somewhat lower prices. The source you buy from will also affect the price of a record. Real bargains, of course, may await those with the time and perseverance to prowl the flea markets, weekend garage sales and used-goods stores such as the Salvation Army and Goodwill outlets—but remember, condition of the item is paramount!

If you buy through mail-order from dealers advertising in record collector magazines, such as DIS*Coveries* or *Goldmine*, there are some bargains, but most ads are generally priced on-target for the more collectible items. However, the collector magazines provide one of the better sources for obtaining some of the rarer items, and you may advertise for your "wants" in them as well. Other sources would include local record/CD shows in your area. Antique "toy" shows often provide Disney record items, and any local "Disneyana" conventions are a must visit for those seeking Disney records.

Finally just to add a note of realism to those of you who think they will retire by selling their records. Many collectors will not pay guide prices for any record, unless it is extremely rare or sealed, and then it may sell quickly at a price well over that listed in this guide. Collectors generally expect to pay, and most would be happy with prices 20-25%

less than the values stated. You may not be able to sell "common" records, e.g., the umpteenth pressing of "Pinocchio," at anywhere near the price indicated because most other Disney collectors have it already. It's not that the record is not "worth" the stated value, it's just that the demand for it is less. If you try to sell your records to record dealers, the economics of their profession dictates that you will receive only a relatively small percentage of the record "guide" price, again, unless the record is very rare, or the demand for that record or artist is such that they can quickly re-sell it to waiting buyers. Be realistic in your expectations and remember it's just a very pleasurable hobby!

Understanding the Listings

Since Disney reissued most of its recordings many times over the years, the key to understanding and collecting them is in Disney's numbering system. There were over thirty different series of Disney records in its LP albums alone! Moreover, the EP and single recordings are a confusing hodgepodge unless you are aware of the numbering and the letter prefixes, if any, utilized.

In this book, for ease of use in checking out your Disney records, the Disney LP albums, EPs, and singles are listed in their ascending numerical sequence, without regard to the letter prefix of the number. For example, Disney's "Story Teller" LP numbered "ST-3904" will be found in the Disney Series "3900" LP listings, regardless of whether it appeared on either the Disneyland or Buena Vista record label. In any event, with only a few exceptions (e.g., the "1300" and "4000" LP series), the listed numerical series stayed within the designated label which is noted.

The listings are further broken down by their formats. The term "format" is used to denote what type of record, size, and speed, was issued. The listings you see contain "LP" albums (10" and 12" diameter listed together); "EP" recordings (various sizes and speeds); 78 rpm multi-record "albums" and single recordings; and 45 rpm single recordings. The Disney label formats are always listed first in the specific format, followed by known releases on other labels. So, for example, if you have a Disney EP numbered "DEP-4015," you will find it and all other Disney EPs of that "4000" series in the "EP" listings in its numerical sequence.

The records are all categorized, in numerical sequence within the named label formats. The album titles are then named after the numbers. In the case of the singles, the artists are listed first, if known, then the titles on the single. If only one side of the record title is known, you will see a "slash" mark after the known title and then a blank space, i.e., "Title of known song/ ." Information on records "N*ot issued*" and "possibly N*ot issued*" comes from the Disney Archives and my own research.

The prices listed are estimated "guide" prices for the individual records. The values are in U.S. dollars. These estimated prices are merely guide values. You will see some dealers selling for more, and some for less. It depends on a variety of factors, including the rarity and demand for a particular piece. As mentioned earlier, the values given are for Mint Minus (M-) copies of records to include sleeve/covers (if any) for LPs, EPs, and 45 rpm records. Values for 78 rpm records are for Very Good Plus (VG+) copies, to include sleeve/covers, if any. Values for lesser (or higher) grades must be adjusted accordingly!

Every attempt has been made to list the composer(s), if known, of a certain film score represented on most of the record albums. The composer(s) last name only is in parenthesis following the release date, if known. For a more detailed listing, see Appendix C for a separate major composer/lyrist section for further information on the named composer(s) of the films or TV show. The full name of the major featured artist(s) is listed on the record after the composer and record category. The exceptions to the "full name" artist listing are those recordings featuring "Annette" (Funicello) and (Tutti) "Camarata."

The dates given in this book are for the release of actual Disney label records and came mostly from Disney Archives files. This date may vary with the copyright date which sometimes, but not always, appears on the record cover or sleeve. Why is this? First, the copyright date often just refers to the cover photo or art, which may have been used in an earlier edition of the same record with a different number in a different series. A good example of this is "Black Beauty" on Disneyland DQ-1338, which was actually released in September of 1971. However, the only date of any kind which appears on its cover is "1966." That date however was the original copyright date for the art which first appeared on, or was produced for, its predecessor LP, "ST-3938" which was released in 1966.

Second, the Disney records were not always released in strict numerical and chronological order. Finally, the copyright date may be an advance date placed on the record at the time of its earlier release pending copyright approval. If a specific release date was not found, the date on the record cover, if any, was used sometimes interpolating it into what would be its approximate release date given its sequence in the series. Dates of some of the reissues and cover variations are given if known, in the same manner. You may be comforted to know that on occasion Disney's own official files are ambiguous or mistaken for some of these dates—they were producing and selling records, not compiling discographies for collectors. The dating you see below is likely not 100% accurate, but is the most accurate detailed research could make of it after all these many years.

Many artists recorded Disney music over the years. However to keep the listings manageable, and bearing in mind their desirability as Disney "collectibles," for either their cover art or music, the listings are limited, with a few exceptions (e.g., later Buena Vista, Touchstone or Hollywood distributed soundtracks), to non-Disney label listings in all formats dating from 1933 into the early 1960s/1970s, indicating some sample popular pressings. The non-Disney listing is undoubtedly not complete, but contains most of the major non-Disney recordings of the era described. Readers are especially encouraged to contact the author, in care of Antique Trader Books, with noted errors and to add other listings that may have been overlooked for inclusion in later editions of this guide.

The record listings contain certain abbreviations utilized to save space:

Book: Book or Booklet. The record contains a multi-page color booklet of Disney art and/or story or other information about the album, artist, or music on the record.

EP: Extended Play. Usually refers to a 7" 45 rpm record with a longer playing time than a standard 45 rpm record. They usually came in cardboard covers with pictures. Some had only picture sleeves ("P/S"). A very few "EPs" were recorded at 33-1/3 rpm and are noted as such. Note that "EP" records also came in 6" and 10" 78 rpm as well and are noted as such.

Date: Known or approximate dates of release of the record are listed after the title of the record.

G/F or GF: Gatefold Cover. The LP or EP cover opens up like a book.

LP: Long Play. Refers to either a 10" or 12" diameter 33-1/3 rpm record album. These came in cardboard covers with a cover picture depicting either a scene from the movie, animated characters, the artists, or music information. Note that these should not be confused with older 12" 78 rpm records which achieved a longer playing time by their enlarged size, and which, unfortunately at the time were also briefly known as "long play" records. Disney did not issue 12" 78 rpm records. However, at least one Disney related 12" 45 rpm record was made, e.g., the two record box-set of "Dragonslayer." This was included in the "LP" section as a matter of convenience as its appearance is that of an "LP" to the average buyer.

MST: Movie Soundtrack. The score is taken directly from the film. You should be aware that some film music was later re-recorded for an album, but unless noted as such by Disney, it is still known as the "MST" of the film.

P/S: Picture Sleeve. The record, usually a single recording, originally came with a paper cover with a picture of the artist(s) or scene from the movie. Often, the "P/S" is worth more than the record! They are difficult to find in excellent condition.

RPM: Revolutions Per Minute. Denotes the required rotation speed of the turntable to properly play back the record. The speeds were either 78 rpm, 45 rpm, or 33-1/3 rpm.

STK: Studio Track. The music or score has been recorded separately from that used in the film, though it may include the original artists. This was a common practice in the early pre-Disney label days for many of the 78 rpm albums listed on other non-Disney labels.

TVST/TV: Television Soundtrack Score or songs from a television show, series, or special.

Disney Records Valued Over $150

RCA 224: **"Who's Afraid of the Big Bad Wolf Parts I and II";** 1934; (Churchill); Frank Luther & Orch.; 7" 78 rpm Picture Disc **500***

RCA 225: **"In a Silly Symphony"/"Mickey Mouse and Minnie's In Town";** 1934; Frank Luther & Orch.; 7" 78 rpm Picture Disc **500***

RCA 226: **"Lullaby Land of Nowhere"/"Dance of the Bogey Men";** 1934; (Churchill/Harline); Frank Luther & Orch.; 7" 78 rpm Picture Disc **500***

*If accompanied by the original sleeve, add $100 per record!

Bluebird BC-2: **"Silly Symphony";** 1937; three record set; 78 rpm; with paper picture cover; Bluebird label; individual records numbered BK-5, BK-6, and BK-7 . . . . **500**

Bluebird BC-3: **"Mickey Mouse Presents Walt Disney's Silly Symphony Songs";** 1937; three record set; 78 rpm; with paper picture cover; Bluebird label; individual records numbered BK-8, BK-9, and BK-10 . . . . **500**

DL-3508: **"Annette and Hayley Mills (Singing 10 of Their Greatest All Time Hits)";** 1964; Disneyland LP; paper sleeve jacket **450**

WDL-4015: **"Alice in Wonderland";** 9/1957; (Fain/Livingston); STK; Camarata; Disneyland LP **350**

Victor J-8: **"Songs from Walt Disney's Snow White and the Seven Dwarfs";** 1937; MST; three record set; 78 rpm; with cover; Victor Records **300**

Victor P-18: **"Pinocchio";** recorded January 19, 1940, released in February 1940; MST; three record

set; 78 rpm; cover notes: "Recorded from the original sound track of the Walt Disney Production, *Pinocchio*; this was the first use of the term "original sound track"; individual records numbered 26477, 26478, and 26479
First issue: Light blue, die-cut front cover with eight color picture panels on the inner jacket and sleeves; internal sleeve artwork is beautiful; initially sold for $2.00 .... **150**

RCA Victor PMS-09898: **"Snow White and the Seven Dwarfs";** technically not an album, but more than a single; promotional 16" radio transcription record ... **300**

Buena Vista 414: Annette **"Teenage Wedding"/"Walkin' and Talkin'";** 1962; 45 rpm single with sleeve; P/S (extremely rare) **300**

WDL-4001: **"Song of the South";** 1956; (Wolcott/Amfitheatrof/Smith/others); MST; Disneyland LP; yellow label **300**

WDL-4001: **"Song of the South";** 1956; (Wolcott/Amfitheatrof/Smith/others); MST; Disneyland LP; second pressing with red label. **200**

WDL-4002: **"Pinocchio";** 1956; (Harline/Smith/others); MST; Disneyland LP; yellow label **225**

WDL-4007: **"Cinderella";** 1956; (David/Hoffman/Livingston/Wallace/Smith); MST; Disneyland LP .. **225**

WDL-4005: **"Snow White and the Seven Dwarfs";** 1956; (Churchill/Morey/Harline); Disneyland LP **200**

WDL-4010: **"Bambi";** 1957; (Churchill/Morey/Plumb); MST; Disneyland LP **200**

WDL-4013: **"Dumbo";** 1957; (Churchill/Wallace); MST; Disneyland LP **200**

CR2567-70: **"Merlin Jones";** 1963; radio spots and interview with Annette; promo **200**

RCA Y-6: **"Snow White and the Seven Dwarfs";** c. 1942; MST; three record set; 78 rpm; with cover **200**

ST-4901: **"The Sword in the Stone";** 1963; Disneyland "pop-up" figures LP **175**

ST-4903: **"101 Dalmatians";** 1963; Disneyland "pop-up" figures LP .. **175**

ST-4904: **"Dumbo";** 1963; Disneyland "pop-up" figures LP .. **175**

ST-4905: **"Pinocchio";** 1963; Disneyland "pop-up" figures LP .. **175**

RCA LBY-6700: **"The Walt Disney Omnibus";** five LP set; with hard cardboard, slip-in box. **175**

Unnumbered: **"A Child's Garden of Verses";** 1956; TVST; unnumbered 10" Disneyland LP **150**

ST-2001: **"Cinderella";** c. 1956-57; 10" LP; Disneyland LP **150**

(All LPs, 45 rpm or EPs in M-Condition. 78 rpm in VG+ Condition)

Disneyland and Buena Vista Record Labels and Inner Sleeves

In the Disneyland and Buena Vista record listings which follow, the labels are often described or referenced to distinguish them from other pressings. The photos below are a sample of representative Disney produced labels which may help you in determining original issues.

1. *Mickey Mouse Club "DBR" 78 rpm and 45 rpm yellow labels.*

2. *Mickey Mouse Club yellow LP labels.*

3. *Disneyland LPs "DQ" 1200-1300 series, original yellow labels.*

4. *Disneyland LPs "yellow rainbow" labels, e.g., reissues of "DQ" series and later pressings.*

5. Buena Vista LPs "1300" series, blue-green labels.

6. Disneyland LPs "1900" series, early aqua/green labels.

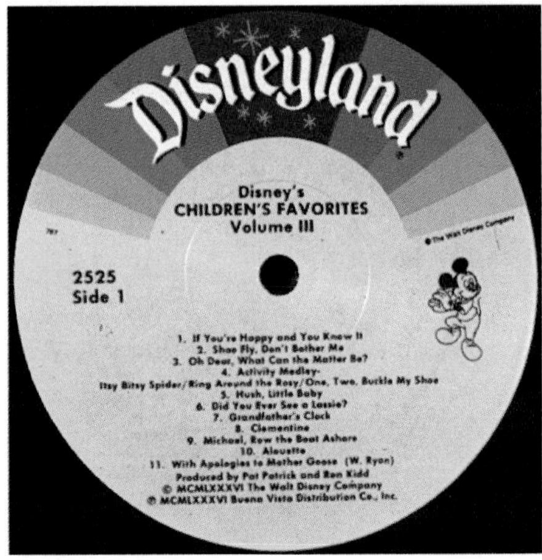

7. Disneyland LPs "2500" series, "yellow rainbow" labels.

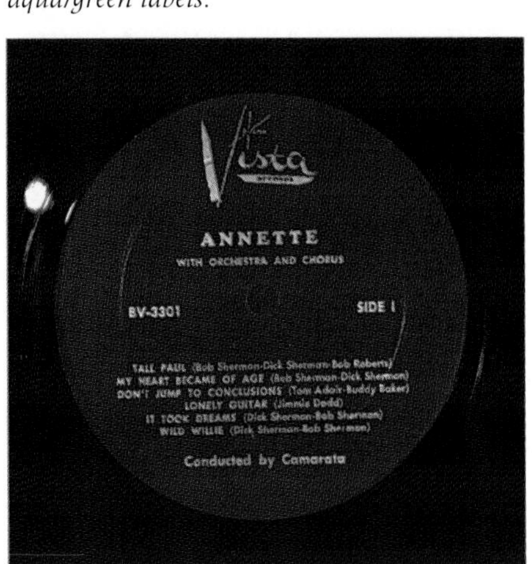

8. Buena Vista LPs "3300" series, early black labels.

9. Disneyland LPs ST "3800" and "3900" series, original purple labels.

10. Disneyland LPs "WDL-4000" series, early yellow labels used in the Hansen distributed records. Early "DEP" EPs were similar.

11. Disneyland LPs "WDL-4000" series, later red/maroon labels.

12. Buena Vista LPs "BV-4000" early black labels.

13. Buena Vista LPs "BV" series, later "black rainbow" labels.

14. Buena Vista LPs/EPs 1980s, red and gray labels.

Disney often utilized the inner record sleeves in its LP releases to advertise other releases in the series. Several are quite pretty and are also helpful to collectors who want to see pictures of others in the series. Many early LP releases also had back cover ads depicting photos of other albums as well.

15. Disneyland LPs, inner sleeve ad, version number 1; top rows depict many ST-3900 "Round covers."

16. Disneyland LPs, inner sleeve ad, version number 2; depicts many ST-3900 "Magic Mirror" covers.

17. Buena Vista LPs, inner sleeve ad, version number 1

18. Buena Vista LPs, inner sleeve ad, version number 2

Section A
33-1/3 rpm Long Play (LP) Recordings

All records in Section A are the standard 12" diameter LP format unless specifically noted as being early 10" releases or some other format. All listings in this book are for American records only. Be aware that any Disney record with "Spartan" listed on the cover or label is a Canadian pressing.

A1
The First Disneyland LP Record

Unnumbered: **"A Child's Garden of Verses";** 1955; (Conger); TVST; Frances Archer and Beverly Gile. This was the first "Disneyland" named LP label release, though it was actually produced and distributed by Hansen Records using Disney masters. Walt Disney had seen the artists performing at a local club and invited them to appear on the Mickey Mouse Club. It is an unnumbered 10" LP and one of only two of this size LP produced by Disney (See also "ST-2001"), since it was foreseen that 12" LPs were superseding the 10" LPs in popularity and convenience.

The front cover depicts umbrellas in a rainstorm, and inside one umbrella is a picture of children gathered around an organ grinder. It notes that the album is "from Walt Disney's Mickey Mouse Club Television Show on ABC-TV." The label is a light yellow with a drawing of Tinkerbell, "pixie dust," and the Disneyland logo at the bottom, similar to the early WDL-4000 LPs. The matrix/production numbers listed on the label are EB-1347/EB-1348. Extremely rare. Later released as WDL-3004, WDL-1008, DQ-1241 and ST-3802. . . . **150**

A2
Disneyland WDX "100" LP Series

WDX-101: **"Fantasia";** 3/1957; Leopold Stokowski and the Philadelphia Orchestra; MST; three LP set; GF; pastel cover; reprints original movie program booklet; squared off spine and a *maroon/red label* (See also Buena Vista "100 Series" below); Mono **60**

A3
Buena Vista "100" LP Series

WDX-101/STER-101: **"Fantasia";** Deluxe Edition—1961 reissue of original 1957 WDX-101 (see above); Leopold Stokowski and The Philadelphia Orchestra; MST;

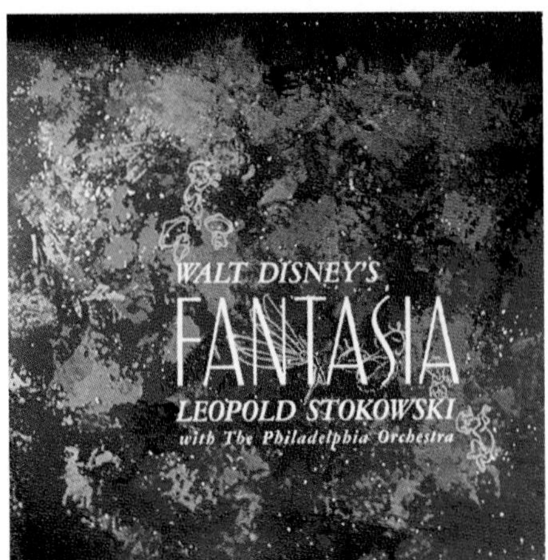

STER-101: ***"Fantasia"***

three LP set; pastels cover with reprint of original 24-page movie program; WDX edition has a *blue label* and squared off spine; STER edition has a black and yellow, rainbow label and a more rounded spine; Original Price: Mono $9.50/Stereo $11.50

Mono **30**

Stereo **40**

Also released as simply "101"; 4/1982; two LP album; GF with no inner book, but with eight interior pictures from the film; stereo **20**

102: **"Snow White and Seven Dwarfs";** 1975; MST; three LP box set; contains the complete movie with dialogue, music and effects, plus a poster book; "Commemorative Edition" with the "black rainbow" labels; TV promotional order; one hour and sixteen minutes in length **50**

103: **"The Hobbit";** 9/1977; (Laws/Bass); MST; two LP box set with special 16-page booklet **30**

Edition "103A"; sold through Sears, Roebuck stores; contains four iron-on transfer decals and poster; complete MST with dialogue, music, and effects; Original price: $9.98 . . . . **45**

V-104: **"Fantasia";** 1982; Irwin Kostal conducted version; STK; two LP set; digitally mastered; GF without inner booklet; Mickey as Sorcerer, high gloss cover **25**

A4
Disneyland "WDL-1000" LP Series

These were mostly cheaper reprints of some of the WDL "3000" Series, usually with the same picture covers, but with different color labels. There are some unique titles here though, so you should compare the "3000" series as well. Sometimes the cover art changed also. Generally, the last three numbers are the same for both series. These pressings did not have cover spine titles. Numbers with a suffix "M," were also part of Disney's "Magic Wipe-Off" series, which were sold with special wipe-off crayons and board. Original selling price: $1.98

WDL-1001: (*Not issued*)

WDL-1002[1] : (*Not issued*)

WDL-1003: (*Not issued*)

WDL-1004: **"16 Top Tunes of the Twenties";** 4/1959; Cliff Edwards; previously issued with title of "Ukulele Ike Sings Again" on WDL-3003; title was changed on the second WDL-3003 edition; later issued as "Ukulele Ike Happens Again" on BV-4043 . . . . **25**

[1] A 1960 Disneyland brochure mistakenly indicates that this number was assigned to "The Little Lame Lamb," however, that title appeared on Disneyland EP STEP-1002. See below.

WDL-1005: **"Songs of the National Parks";** 8/1958; (Jones); Stan Jones and the Ranger Chorus; Thurl Ravenscroft narrates; Jones had been a National Parks Service Ranger; album was sold only at Disneyland and at National Parks and Monuments **40**

WDL-1006: **"Folk Songs from the Far Corners";** 9/1959; Beverly Gile and Frances Archer **20**

WDL-1007: **"Yarns and Songs of the West";** 1959; Fess Parker **30**

WDL-1008M: **"A Child's Garden of Verses (and Other Songs for Children)";** Frances Archer and Beverly Gile; also appears as "WDL-1008," same price; later issued as DQ-1241 . . . . **20**

WDL-1009: (*Not issued*)

WDL-1010: **"Top Tunes of the 50's";** 4/1959; Darlene Gillespie; cover is different from original issue WDL-3010 where it was originally titled "Darlene of the Teens," it uses the second cover of the WDL-3010 edition (see below); Darlene sings cover versions of 1950s rock hits. **40**

WDL-1011: (*Not issued*)

WDL-1012: **"Meet Me Down on Main Street";** The Mellomen Barbershop Quartet **25**

WDL-1013: **"The Golden Horseshoe Review";** 1959; (Possibly *Not issued*) **25**

WDL-1014: **"Jimmie Dodd Sings His Favorite Hymns;"** later issued as DQ-1302 25

WDL-1015: (*Not issued*)

WDL-1016: **"Peter and the Wolf"/"The Sorcerer's Apprentice";** 1960; has a color "Peter and the Wolf" front cover, but a black and white Mickey Mouse back cover (compare with WDL-3016); later issued as DQ-1242 . . . . **30**

WDL-1005: "Songs of the National Parks"

WDL-1017: (*Not issued*)

WDL-1018: **"Parisian Life";** 11/1957; (Offenbach); Jany Sylvaire and Aime Doniat **35**

WDL-1019-1022: (*Not issued*)

WDL-1023: (*Not issued*)

WDL-1024: **"The Story of Old Yeller";** 1960; (Wallace) **40**

Reissued in 6/1974 with just the number; advertising "The Incredible Journey" on back cover; released in conjunction with Disney's re-release of a double-feature of these films; later issued as DQ-1258 . . . . **25**

WDL-1025: **"Waltzes of Vienna"** . . . **25**

WDL-1026-1029: (*Not issued*)

WDL-1030: **"Little Gems from Big Shows";** 5/7/1958; features Darlene Gillespie, Jerome Courtland, Henry Calvin, Cubby O'Brien, and Karen Pendleton; Pop Broadway songs **25**

WDL-1031-1037: (*Not issued*)

WDL-1038: **"Hi Ho—Mary Martin Sings and Swings Walt Disney Favorites";** Camarata conducts; later issued as ST-3943 . . . . **20**

WDL-1039: "**Saludos Amigos"** (Wolcott)/**"The Three Caballeros"** (Gilbert); 10/14/1958. As you will see below, these two 1940s films initially had 78 rpm albums on Decca in 1944. Decca never released LPs of these scores. As a result this studio track album and its earlier LP issue WDL-3039, are highly sought after. **50**

WDL-1040-1043: (*Not issued*)

WDL-1044: **"The Shaggy Dog";** 4/1959; (Smith); features Roberta Shore, Paul Frees, and "Moochie" (Kevin Corcoran); booklet insert; nice cover as there is no title information printed, only the picture of the dog; later issued as DQ-1243. **30**

A5
Disneyland "WDL-1101" LP Series (Fantasia)

These 1961 listings were later issues of the "Fantasia" albums on LP, which had been pressed earlier on the Disneyland "WDL-4100" Series (See below at Section A25) and in the three LP "100" Series set (See above at Section A2). All performed by Leopold Stokowski and the Philadelphia Orchestra.

WDL-1101A: **"Rite of Spring"/"Tocatta and Fugue"**
Mono **25**
Stereo **35**

WDL-1101B: **"The Nutcracker Suite"/"Dance of the Hours";** later issued as DQ-1243
Mono **25**
Stereo **35**

WDL-1101C: **"Night on Bald Mountain"/"Pastoral Symphony"/"Ave Maria"**
Mono **25**
Stereo **35**

A6
Disneyland "DQ" 1200 and 1300 LP Series

A6.1 *Disneyland* "DQ-1200" LP *Series*

All original 1200-1300 LPs had labels in varying shades of solid yellow. Reissues in this series appeared on yellow labels with a block "rainbow" at the top of the label. Early pressings had no spine titles on the covers. The original "DQ" 1200 series sold at $1.98.

When Disney phased out its WDL-4000 series, often times it used the remainder of its "4000" soundtrack vinyl to fill the early budget "DQ" albums until the separate "WDL" stock was exhausted. A "DQ" sticker was simply pasted over the "WDL" number on the label. Known examples include "Song of the South (Uncle Remus)," "Snow White," and "Alice in Wonderland."

Some of the record numbers in this series were also issued with an "M" suffix. These first "M" suffixes were what Disney referred to as "Magic Wipe-Off" series records for young children which came with wipe-off crayons and glossy back cover. I have indicated these by "(M)" after the "DQ" number.

Note however, that in later years, i.e., 1981, a number with an "M" suffix indicat-

DQ-1201: ***"Snow White and the Seven Dwarfs"*** *(First cover)*

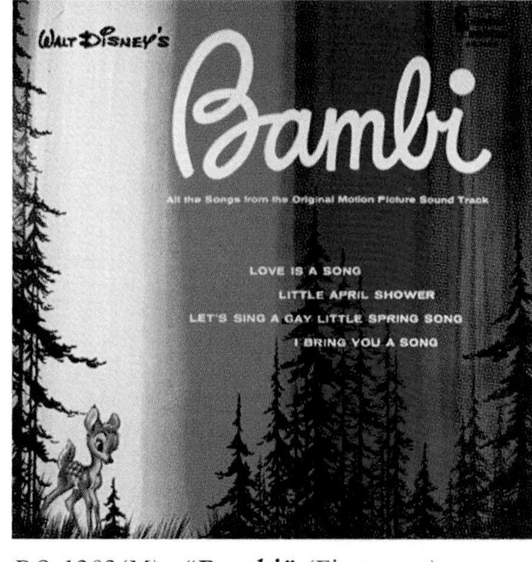

DQ-1203(M): ***"Bambi"*** *(First cover)*

ed a Spanish language edition of the record in this series. Where they exist, I have listed the "M" Spanish language editions after the English versions. The Spanish language editions were distributed in the United States on the "Disneylandia" label and often had different cover art than the English versions.

Some records in the DQ-1200 and 1300 series carry an "MO" suffix to the label number. It is believed this was a short-lived attempt by Disney to differentiate between stereo and mono pressings. The practice was not consistent, and some "DQ" records may appear both with, and without the "MO" suffix.

Those DQs which are stereo editions often just had a stereo sticker pasted on next to the regular DQ number.

DQ-1201: **"Snow White and the Seven Dwarfs";** 9/1959 and 1963; MST; all LPs derived from WDL-4005; original "whirlpool swirls" cover **50**

1968; with a reprint of the original WDL-4005 cover **25**

1987; beautiful high-gloss cover depicts Snow White standing, flanked by the Witch and the Queen, with Dwarfs at her feet; back cover film cel photos **30**

1201-M: **"Blanca Nieves Y Los 7 Enanos";** 6/1978 . . . . **30**

DQ-1202: **"Pinocchio";** 9/2/1959; MST; cover shows Gepetto with accordion; all LPs derived from WDL-4002. . . . . **30**

DQ-1202MO: 1963 . . . . **20**

1978; Pinocchio with cat **15**

1202-M: **"Pinocho";** 7/1978 . . . . . **30**

DQ-1203(M): **"Bambi";** 1959; forest scene cover with Bambi lower left corner; first edition has back cover ads for other "DQ" and "ST" releases; all Bambi LPs are derived from WDL-4010 . . . . **30**

Reissue with same cover has a yellow back cover with film pictures **15**

DQ-1203MO: 1963; cover shows Bambi running with bluebird flying over him and other characters **20**

7/1978; MST; "1203" number only; cover with Bambi and butterfly on tail **15**

*DQ-1208: **"Alice in Wonderland"** (First cover)*

1987; "1203" only; high gloss cover with butterfly on Bambi's tail, but different picture than 1978 edition **30**

1203-M: **"Bambi";** 7/1978 . . . . . . **30**

DQ-1204: **"Dumbo";** 9/8/1959; MST; red striped cover with Dumbo with mouse on trunk; first edition with nine back cover color photos of early "DQ" issues, yellow label; all Dumbo LPs derived from WDL-4013 . . . . **30**

1963; MST; second issue with four black and white back photos **15**

"1204" only; reissue on yellow-rainbow label; back cover of a flying Dumbo **10**

DQ-1205: **"Uncle Remus (Song of the South)";** 9/1959 and 1963; MST; yellow cover with Uncle Remus, and with Brer Rabbit dancing; back cover is white with pictures; all LPs derived from WDL-4001 . . . . **25**

"1205"; back cover is yellow with pictures. **15**

DQ-1206(M): **"Peter Pan";** 7/1959; cover has Peter and Tinker Bell looking through window **25**

1963; same front cover; back cover on first two pressings advertises other "DQs" at $1.89. . . **20**

Later issues with this front cover have a back cover with photos from film. **15**

1976; MST; cover has Peter and Captain Hook on cliff **15**

1206-M: **"Peter Pan y Wendy"** . . . **30**

DQ-1207: **"Cinderella";** 9/1959; Cinderella trying on slipper with white back cover; all LPs derive from WDL-4007; first pressing back cover has nine color photos of early "DQs" **35**

1963; MST; with pink back cover . . **20**

1987; MST; high gloss cover, Prince fits the slipper on Cinderella **30**

1207-M: **"La Cenicenta";** 7/1978 . . **30**

DQ-1208: **"Alice in Wonderland";** 1959 and 1963; MST; Darlene Gilespie; red cover with Alice centered and surrounded by Wonderland characters; derives from WDL-4015; first pressing back cover has nine color photos of early "DQs" **40**

Second pressing has five black and white photos on cover **30**

DQ-1208MO: 1968; blue or purple cover with a large Alice, the rabbit and the Cheshire Cat . . . **25**

1983; same cover **15**

1208-M: **"Alicia en el Pais de las Maravillas";** 7/1978 . . . . **30**

DQ-1209: **"Fun with Music—30 Favorite Disney Songs";** 10/1959; various Mickey Mouse Club cast members **25**

DQ-1210: **"Goofy's Dance Party (16 Easy Dances and How to Do Them)";** 10/7/1959 . . . . **20**

DQ-1211: **"Mother Goose Nursery Rhymes";** 2/4/1960; Sterling Holloway narrates; Camarata conducts **20**

DQ-1212: **"Donald Duck and His Friends";** 1/1960; Jiminy Cricket and other Disney characters **20**

1212-M: **"El Pato Donald y sus Amigos";** 7/1978 . . . . **30**

DQ-1213(M): **"Walt Disney's Most Beloved Songs from His Great Motion Pictures";** 6/1960 . . . .**25**

DQ-1214(M): **"Happy Birthday and Songs for Every Holiday";** 6/1960 . . **20**

DQ-1215(M): **"Musical Monkey Shines";** 6/1960; Western, circus and nonsense songs **30**

DQ-1216: **"Zoo Songs";** 6/24/60; Rica Moore **20**

DQ-1217: **"Songs of Our Heritage for Young Americans";** 1/1961; Disneyland Concert Band and Glee Club **25**

DQ-1218: **"Best Stories of Aesop";** 4/1961; Sterling Holloway narrates **20**

DQ-1219: **"Babes in Toyland";** 6/1961; (Herbert/Bruns) **20**

DQ-1220: **"Walt Disney's Dog Songs";** 7/1961; includes "Lady and the Tramp," "The Shaggy Dog," "Old Yeller," and "101 Dalmatians"; great cover with montage of the dog films **30**

DQ-1221: **"Animal Stories of Aesop";** 7/16/1961; Sterling Holloway narrates **20**

DQ-1222: **"Professor Ludwig Von Drake";** 7/24/1961; (Sherman); TV; from "Wonderful World of Color" **30**

DQ-1223: **"Acting Out the ABC's";** 1/1962; features Ginny Tyler, Terri York, Grey Johnson, and Children's Chorus **20**

*DQ-1219: **"Babes in Toyland"***

DQ-1224: **"Songs for Bedtime";** 6/1962; features Ilene Woods, Fess Parker, Marilyn Hooven, Terri York, Bob Grabeau, and Kathryn Beaumont **20**

DQ-1225: **"More Mother Goose";** 6/22/1962; features Ginny Tyler, and Robie Lester; Sterling Holloway narrates; Camarata conducts **20**

DQ-1226: **"Songs from All Around the World";** 6/22/1962; features Frances Archer and Beverly Gile with the Mouseketeers; first pressing back cover is in black and white **20**

Second pressing has color back cover **15**

DQ-1227: **"Musical Highlights from the Mickey Mouse Club";** 7/1962; same front cover (red, with Mickey) as the original MM-12 LP **30**

DQ-1228: **"Sleeping Beauty";** 6/22/1962; Darlene Gillespie and the Disneyland Chorus; first

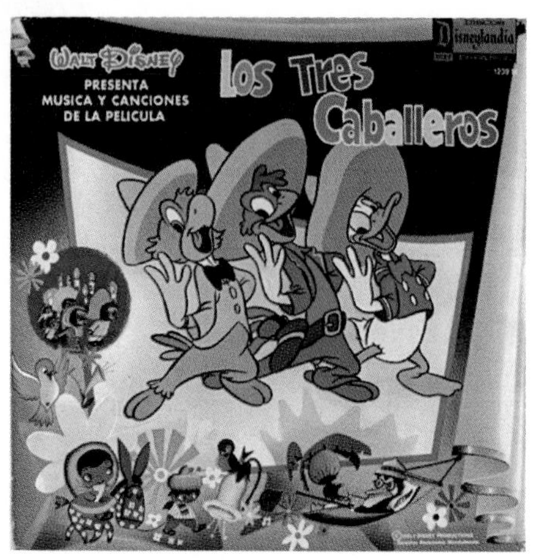

1239-M: "Los Tres Caballeros" (The Three Caballeros)

pressings read "Music from the Original Motion Picture Soundtrack" with black and white back cover pictures **20**

Later pressings read "All the Songs from the Motion Picture," with back cover pictures in shaded blue **15**

DQ-1229: **"Songs from the Mickey Mouse Club Serials";** 7/1962; includes "Annette," "Spin and Marty," "The Hardy Boys," "Corky and White Shadow"; reissue of Mickey Mouse Club LP MM-24; highly collectible cover . . **40**

DQ-1230: **"Original Chip 'n' Dale Chipmunk Fun";** 2/1963 . . . . **20**

DQ-1231: **"Lady and the Tramp";** 9/1962; (Burke/Lee); Teri York, Bob Grabeau; cover pictures dogs in a rainbow spiral **25**

"1231"; 1979; cover pictures dogs eating spaghetti **15**

1231-M: **"La Dama y el Vagabundo";** 7/1978 . . . . **30**

DQ-1232: **"A Child's Introduction to Melody and Instruments of the Orchestra";** 1/1963; Camarata conducts **20**

DQ-1233: **"Little Toot and Other Sailor Songs with Chip 'n' Dale";** 2/7/1963; Robie Lester; Thurl Ravenscroft narrates **20**

1969; same cover **15**

DQ-1234: **"Peter Cottontail (Plus Other Funny Bunnies and Their Friends)";** 1/1963 and 1969; features Vonnair Sisters, Robie Lester, Lucille Bliss, and Thurl Ravenscroft; green cover with Peter playing piano; five pictures on back cover **20**

1972; cover depicts Peter standing in front of a house; three pictures on back. **15**

DQ-1235: **"Sing Along with Jimmie Dodd";** 4/1963; cover picture of Dodd and Mickey Mouse Club cast; fairly rare **30**

DQ-1236: **"All the Songs from The Sword in the Stone";** 7/12/1963 . . **20**

DQ-1237: **"Songs from Snow White in French and English";** 9/1963; Dwarfs on cover with pictures of Eiffel Tower and Statue of Liberty; lyrics on the back cover **25**

DQ-1238: **"Summer Magic: Player Piano Sing Along";** 7/1963; all lyrics on the back cover **25**

DQ-1239: **"30 Favorite Songs of Christmas";** 8/1963; Santa Claus cover **20**

1239-M: **"Los Tres Caballeros" (The Three Caballeros);** 7/1978 . . . **30**

DQ-1240: **"A Rootin' Tootin' Hootenanny (Favorite Folk Songs)";** 7/1963; features Fess Parker, Frances Archer, and Beverly Gile **25**

DQ-1241: **"A Child's Garden of Verses";** 11/1964; Frances Archer and Beverly Gile; formerly WDL-1008, WDL-3004, ST-3802. . . . . . **20**

DQ-1242: **"Peter and the Wolf"/"The Sorcerer's Apprentice";** 11/1964; Stokowski and the Philadelphia Orchestra; Sterling Holloway narrates; same cover as former WDL-1016; also formerly WDL-3016, ST-3926 .... **20**

DQ-1243: **"Nutcracker Suite"/"Dance of the Hours"** 1/1964 and 1969; formerly WDL-1101B, WDL-4101B **20**

DQ-1244: **"Western Songs for Children (Winning of the West)";** 7/1963; features Fess Parker, Rex Allen, and Stan Jones **30**

DQ-1245: **"Walt Disney's Wonderful World of Color";** 11/1963; TV; features Annette, Hayley Mills, Fess Parker, and others; has a stunning, colorful, kaleidoscope cover; number was originally to be "The Happy Wanderer in Europe" **35**

DQ-1246: **"Story of The Littlest Outlaw";** 1/1964; MST; no music; number was originally to be "Christmas Carols" **20**

DQ-1247: **"Tales of Mother Goose (Vol. III)";** 12/1963; Rica Moore narrates; later reissued as ST-3949 .. **20**

DQ-1248: **"Mickey and the Beanstalk";** 12/1963; Robie Lester narrates; later reissued as ST-3974; first pressing has black and white back cover **25**

Second pressing has color back cover and blue and white pictures **15**

DQ-1249: **"Story of Robin Hood";** 1/1964; (Parker); MST (from live action film); features Richard Todd, Elton Hayes, Peter Finch, James Hayter, James Robertson Justice, Joan Rice, Patrick Barr, and Hubert Gregg; Dal McKennon narrates; later reissued as ST-3993 .... **20**

DQ-1245: "Walt Disney's Wonderful World of Color"

DQ-1250: **"Goldilocks and the Three Bears" (and "The Elves and the Shoemaker" and "The Twelve Brothers")**; 12/1963; Rica Moore narrates **20**

DQ-1251: **"The Story of Treasure Island";** 5/1964; (Parker); MST; later reissued as ST-3997 .... **20**

DQ-1252: **"Goofy's TV Spectacular"** (7/1964) **20**

DQ-1253: **"The Story of Hansel and Gretel";** 5/1964; (Humperdink); features Marni Nixon, Sally Sweetland, Ann Jillian, Martha Wentworth, Kathleen De Spain, and Michael Donahue; Laura Olsher narrates; Camarata conducts; later released as ST-3955. .... **20**

DQ-1254: **"Stories of the Great Composers, Vol. II";** 6/1964; R.C. Potter narrates; Camarata conducts **20**

DQ-1255: **"The Story of So Dear to My Heart"**; 7/1964; Bryan Russell; Carl Berg narrates **35**

DQ-1256: **"Ten Songs from Mary Poppins";** 5/1964; Marni Nixon and Richard Sherman; has original MST music with new vocals by Nixon and Sherman **20**

DQ-1257: **"Chilling, Thrilling Sounds of a Haunted House";** 5/1964; side one consists of ten stories with sound effects, side two is sound effects only **20**

DQ-1258: **"Legend of Lobo"/"Old Yeller";** 7/1964; Rex Allen; MST abridged **25**

DQ-1259: **"The Little Engine That Could, and Others";** 5/1964; includes "Casey Jones," "John Henry," "The Submarine Streetcar"; later released as ST-3958 .... **20**

DQ-1260: **"The Story of Johnny Appleseed";** 10/1964; Dennis Day; later released as ST-3996 ... **20**

DQ-1261: **"Let's Have a Parade";** 11/1964 .... **20**

DQ-1262: **"Emil and The Detectives";** 11/1964; Walter Slezak narrates **25**

DQ-1263: **"Learning to Tell Time is Fun";** 10/1964; (Camarata); Laura Olsher narrates; back cover features a smiling clock face, with special attachable clock hands included inside the cover; later released as ST-3959 .... **20**

DQ-1264: **"Professor Wonderful (Professor Julius Sumner Miller) Relating Stories of Sir Isaac Newton";** 11/1964; Great Men of Science Series; Professor Miller was a frequent guest on the Mickey Mouse Club TV Series **25**

DQ-1265: **"Famous Arias from Carmen (and Other Operas)";** 1/1965 .... **20**

DQ-1266: **"Famous Arias from Aida (and Other Operas)";** 1/1965 Marni Nixon and others; Camarata conducts **20**

DQ-1267: **"The Best of Broadway";** 1/1965; features Annette, Jerome Courtland, Henry Calvin, Darlene Gillespie, Cubby O'Brien, and Karen Pendleton; formerly WDL-3030 .... **25**

DQ-1268: **"Kipling's "Just So" Stories";** 1/1965; Sterling Holloway; features "The Cat That Walked by Himself" and "The Elephant's Child" **25**

DQ-1269: **"Pecos Bill and Other Stories in Song";** 8/1965; Fess Parker; includes "Noah's Ark" (Bruns—TVST); this has a very pretty, dark blue cover **30**

DQ-1270: **"These United States: Facts, Music and Folklore";** 6/1965; Dick Wittinghill narrates .. **20**

DQ-1271: **"Professor Julius Sumner Miller (Professor Wonderful) Relating Stories of Galileo";** 6/1965; Great Men of Science Series **25**

DQ-1272: **"Children's Riddles and Game Songs";** 5/1965; Camarata conducts **20**

DQ-1273: **"Professor Julius Sumner Miller Relating Stories of Ben Franklin, The Man and His Discoveries";** 1/1966; Great Men of Science Series **20**

DQ-1274: **"Further Adventures of Cinderella's Mice";** 6/1965; Robie Lester narrates **25**

DQ-1275: **"Rudyard Kipling's 'Just So' Stories Vol. II";** 6/1965; Sterling Holloway narrates **20**

DQ-1276: **"Stories of Hans Christian Andersen";** 8/1965; Robie Lester narrates; Camarata conducts; includes "The Steadfast Tin Soldier," "The Little Match Girl," "The Emperor's New Clothes," and "The Shepherdess and the Chimney Sweep"; later released as ST-3964 . . . . **20**

DQ-1277: **"All the Songs from Winnie the Pooh and The Honey Tree";** 5/1965; Sterling Holloway as Pooh, and others **20**

DQ-1278: **"Story of Goliath II";** 10/1965; (Bruns); formerly ST-1902 . . . . **20**

DQ-1279: **"The Grasshopper and the Ants";** 10/1965; (Harline); Sterling Holloway and Camarata; formerly ST-1905 . . . . **20**

DQ-1280: **"Story of the Swiss Family Robinson";** 10/1965; (Gilkyson); Kevin "Moochie" Corcoran narrates; no music; formerly ST-1907 and later ST-3977 . . . . **20**

DQ-1281: **"Story of Nikki—Wild Dog of the North";** 10/1965; (Smith); Thurl Ravenscroft narrates; formerly ST-1913 . . . . . . **25**

DQ-1282: **"Story of Hans Brinker";** 10/1965; formerly ST-1915 . . . . . . **20**

DQ-1283: **"Adventures of Little Hiawatha and His Friends, Elmer Elephant, The Ugly Duckling, The Flying Mouse";** 9/1965; Grey Johnson and Ginny Tyler narrate; first cover shows the title characters in a canoe; formerly ST-1917 . . . . **20**

1969; numbered only as "1283"; has a blue front cover featuring only "The Ugly Duckling"; back cover depicting the "canoe" scene from the earlier edition **15**

DQ-1284: **"Little Red Riding Hood and Other Best Loved Fairy Tales";** 9/1965; includes "Clytie," "Rapunzel," "Rumpelstiltskin," "Princess and the Pea," and "The Bremen Town Musicians"; formerly ST-1918, later ST-3965 . . **20**

*DQ-1287: **"Tubby the Tuba and Other Songs for Children About Music"***

DQ-1285: **"The Legend of Sleepy Hollow"/"Legend of Rip Van Winkle";** 9/1965; Billy Bletcher narrates; formerly ST-1920, later ST-3801 . . . . **20**

DQ-1286: **"Multiplication and Division";** 9/1965 and 1969; Jiminy Cricket and Rica Moore; formerly ST-1922 . . . . **20**

DQ-1287: **"Tubby the Tuba and Other Songs for Children About Music";** 9/1965; (Paul Tripp and George Kleinsinger); side one narrated by Annette; side two includes "Toot, Whistle, Plunk and Boom" with Jimmy Dodd; formerly ST-1928. . . . . **25**

DQ-1288: **"Marching Along with Mary Poppins";** 10/1965; members of the UCLA Marching Band play *Mary Poppins* songs; United Airlines ad on back cover . . **20**

DQ-1289/STER-1289: **"It's A Small World (18 Favorite Folk Songs)";** 10/1965; Disneyland Boys Choir
Mono **15**
Stereo **25**

DQ-1290: **"Story of The Ugly Dachshund"** (Sherman)/**"Songs of the Shaggy Dog"**; 1/1966 . . . . **25**

DQ-1291: **"Adventures of Bullwhip Griffin";** 2/1967; (Sherman/Leven/Bruns); Suzanne Pleshette; Bryan Russell narrates; story and songs; painted front cover **25**

DQ-1291-N: **"Necco Wafers Presents Soundtrack Songs and Dialogue from 'Bullwhip Griffin' ";** 2/1967; a Necco Wafer premium LP record with photo front cover and pink Disneyland label; rare **50**

DQ-1292/STER-1292: **"Carousel";** 9/1966; Jan Clayton; Camarata conducts; formerly STER-3317
Mono **15**
Stereo **20**

DQ-1293: **"State and College Songs";** 1/1967; with guest Cheerleader Annette; Stereo **40**

DQ-1294: **"Professor Julius Sumner Miller (Professor Wonderful) Relating Stories of Michael Faraday, Father of the Age of Electricity";** 2/1966; Great Men of Science Series; black and white cover **25**

DQ-1295: **"Story of Thumper's Great Race";** 4/1966; features Robie Lester, Dal McKennon, Junius Matthews, Bill Lee, and Sally Sweetland **20**

DQ-1296/STER-1296: **"Mary Martin Songs from Rodgers and Hammerstein's The Sound of Music";** 7/1966; released slightly earlier as STER-3936.

DQ Mono: green cover features children singing **15**

STER stereo: cover is white with title only **20**

DQ-1297: **"Story of the Seven Dwarfs and Their Diamond Mine";** 7/1966; features Thurl Ravenscroft, Bill Lee, and Bill Kanady; Robie Lester narrates **20**

DQ-1298: **"Follow Me Boys and Other Songs for the Campfire";** 1/1967; Fred MacMurray and Jack Halloran Singers **25**

DQ-1299/STER-1299: **"Songs from Brigadoon and Other Favorites";** 9/1966; Camarata conducts
Mono **15**
Stereo **20**

A6.2: *Disneyland* "DQ-1300" LP *Series*

See notes for the "1200" series above.

Note: The "Buena Vista" 1300 series appears below at Section A7

DQ-1300: **"A Nature Guide About Birds, Bees, Beavers and Bears";** 12/1966; from TV's "Wonderful World of Color" **15**

DQ-1301MO: **"All About Dragons: Puff the Magic Dragon"** (Yarrow)/**"The Reluctant Dragon"** (Wolcott); 5/1966; Thurl Ravenscroft narrates; includes "Mad Madam Mim" and "The Loch Ness Monster"; later released as ST-3817 . . . . **20**

DQ-1302: **"Favorite Hymns for Family Singing";** 1/1967; Jimmie Dodd; formerly WDL-1014 and WDL-3014 . . . . **15**

DQ-1303/STER-1303: **"Songs from the Happiest Millionaire";** 10/1967; MST; features Richard Sherman, Bill Kanady, Joseph Pryor, Bill Lee, and Carol Lombard
Mono **15**
Stereo **20**

DQ-1304MO/STER-1304: **"Songs from The Jungle Book and Other Jungle Favorites";** 9/1967; (Sherman/Gilkyson/others); The Jungle V.I.P.'s; back cover pictures are in color
Mono **15**
Stereo **20**
DQ-1304: Back cover pictures in black and white **15**
1304-M: **"El Libro de la Selva";** 7/1978 . . . . **30**

DQ-1305: **"Blackbeard's Ghost";** 1967; Peter Ustinov narrates; no music; later released as ST-3978 . . **20**

DQ-1306: **"The Country Cousin";** 1/1967; (Baker); formerly ST-1903 . . **15**

DQ-1307: **"Pollyanna";** 1/1967; MST; Hayley Mills; formerly ST-1906 . . . . **25**

DQ-1308: **"101 Dalmatians: In Story and Songs";** 12/1966; formerly ST-1908 . . . . **20**

DQ-1309: **"Perri";** 1/1967; Darlene Gillespie; Jimmie Dodd narrates; formerly ST-3902 (same cover) and ST-1909 . . . . **20**

DQ-1310: **"The Three Little Pigs";** 12/1966; Sterling Holloway narrates; formerly ST-1910 . . . . . . **15**

DQ-1311: **"The Prince and the Pauper";** 1/1967; formerly ST-1912 . . . . **15**

DQ-1312: **"Great Composers, Vol. I";** 1/1967; formerly ST-1919 . . . . **15**

DQ-1308: ***"101 Dalmatians: In Story and Songs"***

DQ-1313: **"Addition and Subtraction";** 12/1966 and 1969; Jiminy Cricket and Rica Moore; formerly ST-1922 . . . . **15**

DQ-1314: **"Story of 20,000 Leagues Under the Sea";** 12/1966; song and dialogue; formerly ST-1924 . . **20**

DQ-1315: **"Three Adventures of Davy Crockett";** 1968; (Bruns); TVST; Fess Parker and Buddy Ebsen; white bordered cover; formerly ST-1926 . . . . **25**

DQ-1316/STER-1316: **"Songs from The One and Only, Genuine, Original Family Band";** 5/1968; (Sherman)
Mono **15**
Stereo **20**

DQ-1317/STER-1317: **"Songs About Winnie the Pooh and Tigger";** 5/1968; (Sherman); includes all the songs from *Winnie the Pooh and the Blustery Day*
Mono **15**
Stereo **20**

DQ-1318: **"Music from Three Walt Disney Motion Pictures";** 6/1968;

Hayley Mills, Annette and others; Camarata conducts; includes "In Search of the Castaways," "The Parent Trap," "Summer Magic" . . . **25**

DQ-1319: **"Favorite Songs of Christmas";** 11/1968; Mickey Mouse conducts the "All Mouse Chorus" . . . **15**

DQ-1320: **"The Little Drummer Boy and Other Songs of Christmas";** 11/1968 . . . **15**

DQ-1321: **"Mickey Mouse and His Friends";** 8/1968 . . . **15**

STER-1322: **"Man of La Mancha";** 7/1967; Mike Sammes Singers; Camarata conducts . . . **15**

DQ-1323: **"The Absent Minded Professor"/"The Shaggy Dog";** 4/1967; Kevin Corcoran narrates; cover features the flying car over Washington D.C. . . . **20**

DQ-1324: **"Further Adventures of Jiminy Cricket";** 8/1967; four songs . . . **15**

DQ-1325/STER-1325: **"Dr. Dolittle";** 12/1967; Mike Sammes Singers; Camarata conducts
Mono . . . **15**
Stereo . . . **20**

DQ-1326/STER-1325: **"Songs from Bedknobs and Broomsticks";** 7/1971; Mike Sammes Singers
Mono . . . **15**
Stereo . . . **20**

DQ-1327: **"Songs from Heidi"** (Camarata)/**"Switzerland"** (Smith); 12/1968; MST . . . **20**

DQ-1328MO: **"Songs from the Wizard of Oz"/"The Cowardly Lion of Oz";** 1/1969 . . . **20**

DQ-1329MO: **"The Gingerbread Man and Other Stories and Songs";** 6/1969; Robie Lester narrates; includes "The Little Red Hen," "Mickey Mouse, The Brave Little Tailor," and "Babes in Toyland" . . . **20**

DQ-1330: **"21 Short Stories for Little People";** 1969; (Alfred Stern); Frances Archer and Beverly Gile . . . **15**

DQ-1331: **"Songs from Oliver!"/"Chitty Chitty Bang Bang";** 7/1969; Mike Sammes Singers; Camarata conducts . . . **15**

DQ-1332: **"Hang Your Hat on the Wind";** 7/1969; Randy Sparks . . . **20**

DQ-1333: **"The Aristocats and Other Cat Songs";** 8/1970; features Phil Harris, Robie Lester, Mike Sammes Singers, The Wellingtons, and Louis Prima; this was originally planned to be "Songs of the National Parks" . . . **15**

DQ-1334: **"Rubber Duckie and Other Songs from Sesame Street";** 8/1970; TV; produced by the Children's Television Workshop; this was originally planned to be "The Living Desert"/"The Vanishing Prairie" . . . **15**

DQ-1335: **"Silly Symphonies";** 12/1970; eight stories in song: "The Bremen Town Musicians," "Rapunzel," "Susie, the Little Blue Coupe," "Gingerbread Man," "Lambert, the Sheepish Lion," "Little House, Little House," "Willie the Whale," "Johnny Fedora," and "Alice Blue Bonnet"; this was originally planned to be "True Life Adventures" . . . **20**

DQ-1336: **"Cowboy and Indian Songs";** 12/1969; Fess Parker; yellow and brown line-drawn cover of Parker as Davy Crockett; stereo . . . **30**

DQ-1337: **"Up, Down All Around—24 More Songs for Little People";** 4/1972; (Stern); features Frances Archer, Beverly Gile, and Alfred Stern **15**

DQ-1338: **"The Story of Black Beauty";** 9/1971; Robie Lester narrates; Camarata conducts; formerly ST-3938; this was originally planned to be "Sounds Funny." **15**

DQ-1339: **"Camarata Conducts Fiddler on the Roof";** 9/1971; Mike Sammes Singers; formerly ST-4033 . . . . **15**

DQ-1340: **"Man of La Mancha";** 9/1971; Mike Sammes Singers; formerly ST-4027 . . . . **15**

DQ-1341/STER-1341: **"Louis Armstrong: The Wonderful World of Walt Disney";** 9/1971; formerly STER-4044
Mono **15**
Stereo **20**

DQ-1342: **"The Mouse Factory Presents Mickey and His Friends";** 12/1971; includes "The Ballad of Davy Crockett by 'Four Mosquitoes from Jersey Marsh' " . . **20**

DQ-1343/STER-1343: **"Songs from Sesame Street 2";** 12/1971; TV; produced by the Children's Television Workshop
Mono **15**
Stereo **20**

STER-1344: **"The New Zoo Revue";** 10/1972; music and lyrics by Douglas R. Momary; "A Funco Corp. Presentation" **15**

DQ-1345/STER-1345: **"Candy Man and Other Sweet Songs";** 7/1972
Mono **15**
Stereo **20**

DQ-1342: "The Mouse Factory Presents Mickey and His Friends"

DQ-1346: **"America the Beautiful";** 7/1972; Disneyland Concert Band and Glee Club; traditional American songs **20**

DQ-1347: **"A Day at the Zoo with Burl Ives";** 8/1972 . . . . **15**

DQ-1348: **"The Sounds of Christmas";** 9/1973; Pete Renoudet narrates; side one is "Story, Songs and Sounds of Christmas"; side two is "Christmas sound effects" **15**

DQ-1349/STER-1349: **"What a Wonderful Thing Is Me!";** 12/1972; (Baker); Frances and Tom Adair wrote the songs; features Jerry Whitman, Ida Sue McCune, and Diana Lee
Mono **15**
Stereo **20**

STER-1350: **"Songs from The Electric Company TV Show";** 1/1973; (Baker) **15**

DQ-1351/STER-1351: **"Songs from the Mister Rogers TV Show";** 1/1973 Jerry Whitman with

DQ-1358: "Trick or Treat-Stories and Songs of Halloween"

DQ-1362/STER-1362: "Mickey Mouse Club Mousekedances and Other Mouseketeer Favorites"

Orchestra conducted by Buddy Baker
Mono **15**
Stereo **20**

DQ-1352/STER-1352: **"The World Is a Circle from *Lost Horizon* (and Others)";** 2/1973; arranged and conducted by Buddy Baker and Camarata
Mono **15**
Stereo **20**

DQ-1353: **"Story and Songs from Robin Hood";** 8/1973; (Bruns); Pete Renoudet narrates; Roger Miller songs **15**

DQ-1354: **"Christmas Carols from All of Us to All of You";** 5/1973 . . **15**

DQ-1355: **"A Christmas Adventure in Disneyland";** 4/1973; Gloria Wood narrates; Camarata conducts; formerly ST-3912 . . . . . . **15**

DQ-1356: **"Disney Christmas Favorites";** 4/1973; features Ludwig Mousensky and the All-Mouse Symphony Orchestra **20**

DQ-1357/STER-1357: **"Bob McGrath Sings for All the Boys and Girls";** 12/1973; McGrath was featured on TV's "Sesame Street"
Mono **15**
Stereo **20**

DQ-1358: **"Trick or Treat-Stories and Songs of Halloween"** (Livingston)/**"The Story and Song from The Haunted Mansion"** (Baker); 4/1974; cast of "Mansion" includes Ron(ny) Howard; Thurl Ravenscroft narrates; the inner sleeve contains two cut-out Halloween masks **25**

DQ-1359/STER-1359: **"Little Red Caboose and Other Childrens' Hits—Chip 'n' Dale";** 1/1973; features Burl Ives; Jimmie Dodd, and Disneyland Boys' Chorus
Mono **15**
Stereo **20**

DQ-1360: **"Sing and Other Sunny Songs";** 2/1974 . . . . **15**

DQ-1361: **"I Love a Parade: Favorite Marches for Children";** 1974; The Disneyland Band **15**

DQ-1362/STER-1362: **"Mickey Mouse Club Mousekedances and Other Mouseketeer Favorites";** 12/1974; has fifteen-page insert (Mickey Mouse Club Mouseketeer cast photo album); issued originally as a gatefold booklet in ST-3815
Mono **20**
Stereo **25**

DQ-1363: *(Not issued)*

DQ-1364: *(Not issued)*

DQ-1365: *(Not issued)*

DQ-1366: **"America Sings";** 7/1974; (Baker); Burl Ives; from the Disneyland theme attraction **15**

DQ-1367: **"T'was the Night Before Christmas";** 9/1976; (Laws/Bass); TVST; Joel Grey narrates **20**

DQ-1368: **"Frosty's Winter Wonderland";** 12/1976; TV; features Andy Griffith, Shelly Winters, Dennis Day, Jackie Vernon, and Paul Frees **25**

DQ-1369: **"Story of The Rescuers";** 5/1977; (Butler); MST; cast includes: Bob Newhart, Eva Gabor, Joe Flynn, and Geraldine Page; Shelby Flint songs; Bob Holt narrates; music and dialogue **15**

DQ-1370: *(Not issued)*—1981 Disney sales brochures advertised this as "Dragonslayer" but it was never issued by Disney. The film was a joint production with Paramount Pictures. See the 12" 45 rpm release on "Label X" noted below in the non-Disney "LP" section.

BV-1301: "Musical Kaleidoscope (17 Selections from 17 Fabulous Albums)"

A7
Buena Vista "1300" LP Series

BV-1301: **"Musical Kaleidoscope (17 Selections from 17 Fabulous Albums)";** 9/1959; aqua colored label. This album's first back cover notes the creation of the Buena Vista label, stating that certain previous "WDL" titles will be made available through Buena Vista. The back cover of the second issue of this album contains the new "phantom" assigned numbers of certain of the "WDL" line to the BV numbering system discussed below in section A16. Original price: $1.98 . . . . **30**

BV-1302: **"Say One for Me";** 6/1959; (Van Heusen/Cahn); contains cover versions of the film musical by Rex Allen, Roberta Shore, and Tony Paris; original price: $1.98 . . . . **20**

BV-1303: **"Life of the Party (The Wonderland Player Piano)";** 9/1959; attractive cover features dance hall girls around a

ST-1901: "Story of Darby O'Gill and the Little People"

mustached gentleman at a player piano; original price: $1.98; formerly WDL-3001 . . . . **30**

A8
Disneyland "ST-1900" LP Series

The labels for this series began with a solid aqua color, shifted to solid blue and eventually most were issued in solid green color. Any number with an "M" suffix was a Spanish language issue on the "Disneylandia" label. Original price: $1.98.

ST-1901: **"Story of Darby O'Gill and the Little People";** 7/1959; (Wallace); features Arthur Shields and Pat O'Malley and a Sean Connery song; Sterling Holloway narrates **50**

1901M: **"Vamos a Cantar";** 11/1981 . . . . **30**

ST-1902: **"Story of Walt Disney's Goliath II";** 10/1959; (Bruns); Sterling Holloway narrates; later released as DQ-1278. . . . . **30**

ST-1903: **"Story of the Country Cousin";** 9/3/1959; (Baker); Henry Calvin narrates; later released as DQ-1306 . . . . **30**

1973; released as "1903" by Walt Disney Educational Materials Co. **15**

ST-1904: **"Story of Toby Tyler in the Circus";** 2/1960; (Baker); features Henry Calvin, Brian Corcoran, Sam Treat, and Dal McKennon; back cover photos from film **35**

ST-1905: **"Story of the Grasshopper and The Ants";** 3/24/1960; (Harline); Sterling Holloway narrates; Camarata conducts; later released as DQ-1279 . . . . **30**

ST-1906: **"Story of Pollyanna";** 6/1960; (Smith); MST; Hayley Mills; Kevin Corcoran narrates; later released as DQ-1307 . . . . **50**

ST-1907: **"Story of the Swiss Family Robinson";** 11/1960; Kevin Corcoran narrates; no music; later DQ-1280 . . . . **20**

ST-1908: **"101 Dalmatians in Story and Song";** 11/1960; (Bruns/Leven); later released as DQ-1308 . . . . **25**

ST-1909: **"Story of Perri";** 3/22/1961; (Smith/Bruns); Jimmie Dodd narrates; formerly ST-3902 with same cover; later released as DQ-1309 . . . . **25**

ST-1910: **"Story and Songs About Walt Disney's Three Little Pigs";** 1961; (Churchill); also with "Magic Wipe-off" back cover; later released as DQ-1310 . . . . **20**

ST-1911: **"Story of the Absent Minded Professor";** 3/22/1961; (Sherman); narrated by Sterling Holloway; later released as DQ-1323 . . . . **25**

ST-1912: **"Story of the Prince and the Pauper";** 7/1961; later released as DQ-1311 . . . . **20**

ST-1913: **"Story of Nikki, Wild Dog of the North";** 7/1961; (Smith); later released as DQ-1281 . . . . **30**

ST-1914: **"Story of Greyfriars Bobby";** 11/1961; (Sherman); back cover has four photos from film **30**

ST-1915: **"Story of Hans Brinker and the Silver Skates";** 2/1962; TV; later released as DQ-1282 . . . . **20**

ST-1916: **"Story of Big Red";** 6/1962; (Sherman); music and dialogue **30**

ST-1917: **"Adventures of Little Hiawatha and His Friends";** 7/1962; Ginny Tyler narrates; includes "Elmer Elephant"; "The Ugly Duckling"; "The Flying Mouse"; later released as DQ-1283 . . . . **25**

ST-1918: **"Best Loved Fairy Tales";** 7/1962; later released as DQ-1284 and ST-3965 . . . . **25**

ST-1919: **"Stories of the Great Composers (Vol. 1)";** 2/1963; Russell C. Potter narrates; Camarata conducts; later released as DQ-1312 . . . . **20**

ST-1920: **"The Legend of Sleepy Hollow"/"Rip Van Winkle";** 2/4/1963; Later released as DQ-1285 . . . . **25**

ST-1921: **"Story of Hector the Stowaway Pup";** 9/1963; (Sherman); TV **30**

ST-1922: **"Addition and Subtraction";** 7/1963; Rica Moore and Jiminy Cricket; later released as DQ-1313 . . . . **20**

*BV-2000: **"The Music of Walt Disney: From Snow White to Mary Poppins"***

ST-1923: **"Multiplication and Division";** 1963; Rica Moore and Jiminy Cricket; later DQ-1286 . . . . **20**

ST-1924: **"Story of 20,000 Leagues Under the Sea";** 9/1963; includes one song and dialogue; later released as DQ-1314 . . . . **25**

ST-1925: **"The Story of Savage Sam";** 6/1963; (Gilkyson); features original movie cast **30**

ST-1926: **"Three Adventures of Davy Crockett";** 8/1963; (Bruns); later released as DQ-1315 . . . . **30**

ST-1927: **"Story of An Incredible Journey";** 9/1963; (Wallace); back cover with four pictures; later released as part of DDF-2 . . . **30**

1974; back cover also advertises "Old Yeller"; issued on re-release of double-feature of these films . . . **20**

ST-1928: **"Musical Story of Tubby the Tuba";** 10/1963; (Kleinsinger); Annette narrates; later released as DQ-1287 . . . . **30**

ST-2001: ***"Cinderella"***

A9
Buena Vista "2000" LP Issue

BV-2000: **"The Music of Walt Disney: From Snow White to Mary Poppins";** 1967; commemorative album with Walt Disney (1901-1966) picture on white cover; it is the only album in this Buena Vista series **40**

A10
Disneyland "ST-2000" LP Series

ST-2001: **"Cinderella";** 1957; Jiminy Cricket narrates; one 10" LP; triple GF cover with color photos; a "Jiminy Cricket Story Teller." Archives' files indicate Disney had planned in 1956 to issue a series of triple gatefold "Silly Symphonies" LPs. That never happened, but this one triple gatefold issue was produced **150**

ST-2002: **"The Little Lame Lamb";** 1958; (Camarata); Mary Martin; 12" LP; purple label **50**

A11
Buena Vista "2100" Series

(See "BV-62100" Series below)

A12
Disneyland "2500" LP Series

This same series was also released in part as the Buena Vista "62500" Series (See "62500" Series below). Series labels were of the yellow rainbow variety. Numbers with an "M" suffix were Spanish language editions released on the "Disneylandia" label.

2501: **"The All New Mickey Mouse Club (Original TV Cast)";** 1/1977; includes poster and song lyrics on inner sleeve **15**

2502: **"The Best of Disney Vol. 1";** 7/1978; this has a great cover with a multitude of Disney characters and a printed "film strip" depicting film cels from various Disney films; white background cover **25**

2503: **"The Best of Disney Vol. II";** 7/1978 . . . . **25**

Same cover as above except it has a yellow background and the characters in the film strip on the cover are different; this and 2502 were also sold as a set; set price . . **40**

2504: **"Mickey Mouse Disco";** 7/1979; this album sold almost two million copies! **15**

2504M: **"Mickey Mouse Disco";** 10/1980; Spanish language edition **25**

2505: **"Disney's Children's Favorites Vol. I"**[2]**;** 6/1979; Larry Groce and the Disneyland Children's Sing-a-long Chorus **15**

2506: **"Disney's Christmas Favorites";** 9/1979; features Larry Groce, Mike Sammes Singers, and Disneyland Children's Sing Along Chorus **15**

2507: **"Chilling, Thrilling Sounds of the Haunted House";** 8/1979; spooky sound effects **15**

2508: **"Disney's Children's Favorites, Vol. II";** 8/1979; Larry Groce and the Disneyland Children's Sing Along Chorus **15**

2509: **"The Sounds of Outer Space";** 8/1981; science fiction-type sound effects **15**

2510: **"The Official Album of Disneyland"/"Walt Disney World";** 5/1980 . . . . **15**

2511: **"Yankee Doodle Mickey";** 7/1980; features Molly Ringwald, The Disneyland Children's Sing Along Chorus, and others; with very colorful cover of Mickey **25**

2512: **"Pardners—14 Great Cowboy Songs";** 9/1980; Larry Groce and the Disneyland Children's Sing Along Chorus **15**

2513: **"Disney's Goin' Quackers—Wacky Songs to Quack You Up";** 9/1980; features Donald Duck, Larry Groce, and the Disneyland Children's Sing Along Chorus **15**

2514: **"Disney's Merry Christmas Carols";** 9/1980; Larry Groce and the Disneyland Children's Sing Along Chorus; includes eleven songs; lyrics on back cover; see also Disneyland 1V-8150 below . . **15**

[2] Albums 2505, 2508, and 2525 were also sold together as a three LP package set entitled **"Disney's Children's Favorites."** Guide price: $45

2515: (*Not issued*)

2516: **"Mousercise";** 2/1982; with insert booklet **15**

2516-M: **"Ejercicos con Mickey Mouse";** 12/1982 . . . . **30**

2517: **"The Story of Tron";** 8/1982; includes music, dialogue, and sound effects from film **30**

2518: **"Flashbeagle";** 3/1984; TVST ("Peanuts" Special); Desiree Goyette and Ed Bogus **20**

2519: **"The Official Album of Walt Disney World Epcot Center";** 2/1983 . . . . **15**

2520: **"Splashdance";** 10/1983 . . . . . **15**

2521: **"Totally Minnie";** 1/1986; featuring electronic synthesizer music **15**

2522: (*Not issued*)

2523: **"Rainbow Brite—Paint a Rainbow in Your Heart";** 10/1984 . . . . **15**

2524: **"Voices of Liberty";** 12/1984; acappella singing group featured at Epcot attraction **25**

2525: **"Disney's Children's Favorites, Vol. III";** 6/1986 . . . . . . **15**

2526: **"The Chipmunk Adventure";** 9/1988; MST **15**

2527: **"Rock Around the Mouse";** 9/1987 . . . . **20**

2528: **"Children's Favorite Silly Songs";** 1988; lyrics included **15**

2529: **"Solid Gold Chipmunks—Buena Vista presents 'Special Anniversary Collection—30 Years of Great Hits' ";** 1988 . . . . . **15**

2530: **"Solid Gold Chipmunks";** 1988; 30th Anniversary Collection **15**

2531: **"The Official Album of Walt Disney World";** 6/1988; theme attraction music **15**

A13
Buena Vista "2600" LP Series ("Charlie Brown Records")

This is a cheaper pressing release of the BV "3700" "Peanuts" series with different covers (See below). This series did not have gatefold covers or booklets!

2601: *(Not issued)*

2602: **"Charlie Brown's All-Stars";** 3/1979; yellow cover with team photo snapshots **15**

2603: **"He's Your Dog, Charlie Brown";** 3/1979; cover of Charlie bringing bowl to a dancing Snoopy **15**

2604: **"It's the Great Pumpkin, Charlie Brown";** 10/1978; Linus and Sally in pumpkin patch **15**

2605: **"You're in Love, Charlie Brown"** **15**

A14
Disneyland "WDL-3000" LP Series, and the "Disneylandia en Espanol" 3000 issue

Many of these were reprinted in the cheaper WDL "1000" Series (See A4 above). Note that some of these listings were later proposed to have certain duplicate BV-3300 numbers by Disney which were never actually issued. (See note for 3300 series below at Section A16). The unused numbers are listed in the footnote below for historical purposes only.[3] The early "3000s" sold for $3.98.

One addition to the listing is the PA-ST-3000 edition on a "Disneylandia" Spanish language label. The Disneylandia label editions were produced and distributed in the United States and often had different art work covers than English language counterparts. Most of these are listed in the "3900" series below.

PA-ST-3000: **"Los Tres Caballeros" (The Three Caballeros);** Spanish language "Story Teller" album **30**

WDL-3001: **"Life of the Party";** 1956; The Wonderland Player Piano; includes postcard size lyrics booklet; yellow label with Disneyland logo at bottom; hard to find **40**

Second pressing is on purple label with lyrics booklet approx. 9" x 5"; later released as BV-1303 . . . . **30**

Third pressing with logo at top; purple label **20**

WDL-3002: **"Disneyland Band Concert";** 1956; Vesey Walker

Yellow label **30**

Purple label **25**

---

[3]

WDL-3000 Number	Proposed, but not used, New Number
WDL-3006	BV-3316
WDL-3011	BV-4047
WDL-3015	BV-3314
WDL-3017	BV-3310
WDL-3021	BV-3306
WDL-3022	BV-3311
WDL-3026	BV-3304
WDL-3029	BV-3315
WDL-3030	BV-3309
WDL-3031	BV-3317
WDL-3032	BV-3305
WDL-3034	BV-3302
WDL-3035	BV-3308
WDL-3036	BV-3307
WDL-3038	BV-3318
WDL-3039	BV-3312

WDL-3003: **"Ukulele Ike Sings Again";** 1956; Cliff Edwards and the Wonderland Jazz Band; orange cover features a cartoon of Edwards playing a ukulele with musicians; yellow label **45**

WDL-3003: **"16 Top Tunes of the Twenties";** second edition retitled; cover features a multi-scene film-strip down the right side. "Ukulele Ike" was Edwards' stage name prior to his Disney work. In the 1920s and 1930s, Edwards sold over 70 million records. The Wonderland Jazz Band was conducted by George Bruns, featuring Bruns (trombone & tuba), and Disney associates Marvin Ash (piano); Jess Bourgeois (bass); Nick Fatool (drums); Don Kinch (trumpet); and George Probert (clarinet). Re-released as "Ukulele Ike Happens Again" on BV-4043. . . . . **35**

WDL-3004: **"A Child's Garden of Verses";** 1956; Frances Archer and Beverly Gile; later released as WDL-1008, DQ-1241 and ST-3802; see also Section A1 . . . . **25**

WDL-3005: **"Echoes of Disneyland";** 1957; Dee Fisher plays the Disneyland Wurlitzer Electronic Organ; cover photo of "Main Street" at Disneyland at night **30**

WDL-3006: **"Folk Songs from the Far Corners";** 1/1957; Frances Archer and Beverly Gile **25**

WDL-3007: **"Yarns and Songs";** 3/1957; Fess Parker; cover photo of Parker with guitar **40**

WDL-3008: **"Life of the Party Vol. II";** 1/1957; Wonderland Player Piano; with lyric sheet booklet **25**

WDL-3009: **"George Bruns and the Wonderland Jazz Band 'Deep in the Heart of Dixieland' ";**

*WDL-3009: **"George Bruns and the Wonderland Jazz Band 'Deep in the Heart of Dixieland' "***

4/30/1957; colorful animation cover **30**

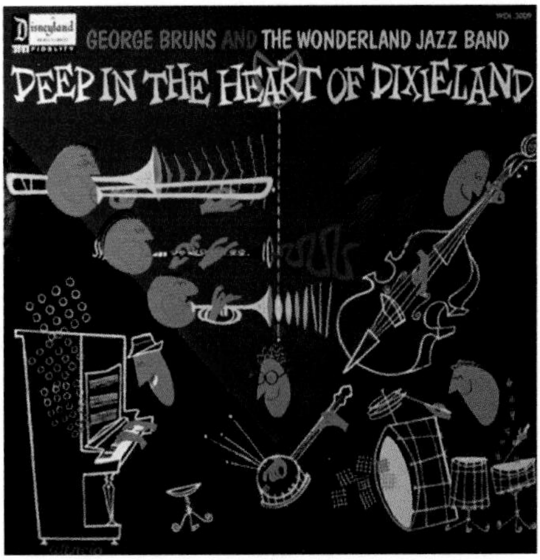

WDL-3010: **"Darlene of the Teens";** 5/1957; Darlene Gillespie; album consists of cover versions of '50s rock songs; first cover is yellow with a large photo of Darlene in front of a microphone, with cartoon kids dancing; back cover has pictures of Darlene and Tutti Camarata; this cover was also used in her "DEP-3010" EPS below at Section C2 . . . . **75**

Second pressing: **"Top Tunes of the '50's—Darlene Gillespie Sings TV Favorites";** 1958. This cover is completely different,with overall black background with a right side strip with five photos in TV screen designs. Darlene was an original Mouseketeer on the Mickey Mouse Club TV show and had the best singing voice of any of the cast. Unfortunately she never caught on as did Annette Funicello, who soon vastly eclipsed her in popularity and in record sales. **50**

WDL-3016 ***"The Sorcerer's Apprentice"/"Peter and the Wolf"***

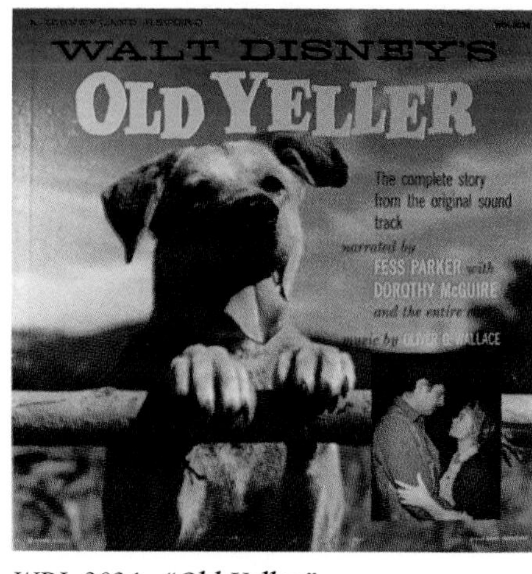

WDL-3024: ***"Old Yeller"***

WDL-3011/STER-3011: **"Tutti's Trumpets";** 1957 mono/1959 stereo; Camarata conducts; cover features abstract trumpet
Mono **20**
Stereo **30**

WDL-3012: **"Meet Me Down on Main Street";** 1957; The Mellomen Barbershop Quartet **30**

WDL-3013: **"Slue Foot Sue's Golden Horseshoe Review";** 1957; features Betty Taylor, Donald Novis, The Mellomen, The Strawhatters, and Wally Boag; "Slue Foot Slue" was Pecos Bill's girlfriend in *Melody Time*; cover is a colorful one, from the stage at the Disneyland attraction **30**

WDL-3014: **"Jimmie Dodd Sings His Favorite Hymns";** 1958; Jimmie Dodd Cover features a mosaic church; later released as DQ-1302 . . . . **25**

WDL-3015: **"Creakin' Leather";** 1958; (Jones); Stan Jones sings his songs; the cover is purple with a photo of cowboys at dusk; renamed "Ghost Riders in the Sky" on BV-3306 . . . . **45**

WDL-3016-R **"The Sorcerer's Apprentice"/"Peter and the Wolf";** 4/3/1958; first edition has high gloss covers, front and back; Mickey as the "Sorcerer's Apprentice" is on the front cover; and "Peter and the Wolf" on the back; the cover is of near cel quality and is highly sought after . . **75**

Second pressing as "WDL-3016"; Sterling Holloway narrates; has a glossy cover photo of Mickey Mouse on the front cover; and a non-glossy back cover for "Peter and the Wolf"; compare with WDL-1016 where the titles and photos are reversed **50**

WDL-3017: **"All the King's Saxes";** 1958; Hymie Shertzer; Big Band saxes; Saxophone cover **30**

WDL-3018: **"Parisian Life";** 1958; (Offenbach); Jany Sylvaire and Aime Doniat; highlights from Offenbach operettas **30**

WDL-3019: (*Not issued*)

WDL-3020: (*Not issued*)

WDL-3021/STER-3021: **"Autumn";** 1958 mono/1959 stereo; Camarata conducts
Mono **20**
Stereo **25**
This album was also packaged together in a four LP set, titled "Music of the Seasons" with numbers 3026/3037/3032 below; the set was issued in both mono and stereo sound; original price: $11.95
Mono Set **40**
Stereo Set **80**

WDL-3022: **"Dancing in Peacock Alley";** 12/1958; Bernie Leighton on piano; very pretty peacock cover **30**

WDL-3023: **"Community Concert";** 1958; Frances Archer and Beverly Gile; pink cover photo of Archer and Gile **30**

WDL-3024: **"Old Yeller";** 12/1957; (Wallace); features Fess Parker, Dorothy McGuire, Tommy Kirk, Kevin Corcoran, and Chuck Connors; four color pictures on back cover **50**

WDL-3025: **"Waltzes of Vienna";** 1958; arranged and conducted by Frederick Stark **25**

WDL-3026/STER-3026: **"Winter";** 10/1958 mono/1959 stereo; (Camarata)
Mono **20**
Stereo **25**

WDL-3027/STER-3027: **"Summer";** 1958 mono/3/1959 stereo; (Camarata)
Mono **20**
Stereo **25**

WDL-3028: (*Not issued*)

WDL-3029: **"Melodies for Midnight";** 8/1959; Johnny La Padula on accordion; dark purple cover depicting a couple by the seaside at night **30**

WDL-3030: **"Little Gems from Big Shows";** 6/1958; features Darlene Gillespie, Jerome Courtland, Henry Calvin, Cubby O'Brien, and Karen Pendleton; Pop Broadway songs; later released as DQ-1267 . . . . **30**

WDL-3031/STER-3031: **"Mary Martin Sings A Musical Love Story";** 10/1958 mono/1959 stereo
Mono **20**
Stereo **25**

WDL-3032/STER-3032: **"Spring";** 10/1958 mono/1959 stereo; (Camarata)
Mono **20**
Stereo **25**

WDL-3033: **"This Was the West—The Story and the Songs";** 9/1958; Stan Jones; introduction by Thurl Ravenscroft; uncredited background vocals by the "Sons of the Pioneers"; GF with booklet . . **45**

WDL-3034/STER-3034: **"The Happy Wanderer in Europe";** 10/1958 mono/1959 stereo; Camarata with Gloria Wood; Pop folk songs
Mono **20**
Stereo **25**

WDL-3035: **"Date Nite in Disneyland";** 6/1958; Elliott Brothers and Tony Paris; colorful cover photo of this pop dance band **30**

WDL-3036/STER-3036 **"Jan Clayton in Rodgers and Hammerstein's Carousel";** 6/1958 mono/1959 stereo; Jan Clayton Sings: Brussels World's Fair; Camarata conducts
Mono **20**
Stereo **25**

WDL-3037: (*Not issued*)

WDL-3038/STER-3038: **"Hi Ho!";** 3/1958 mono/1959 stereo; (Mary Martin); it has a different cover than its later release on WDL-4016, but same album; later released as ST-3943
Mono **20**
Stereo **25**

WDL-3039: **"Saludos Amigos"/"The Three Caballeros";** 10/1958; STK. As you will see below in Section 3.10.1, these two 1940s films initially had 78 rpm albums on Decca in 1944. Decca never released LPs of these scores. As a result this later studiotrack album and its later LP reissue, WDL-1039, are highly sought after. . . . **100**

WDL-3040: (*Not issued*)—The Disney Archives carries a file listing of this as "Camarata Plays Disney" (1959), but the actual record is unconfirmed, the Archives does not have a copy and believes it was never issued.

WDL-3041: **"Westward Ho the Wagons";** 1959; (Bruns/Jones/Smith); MST; Fess Parker; reissue of WDL-4008; some issues just had a "WDL-3041" sticker pasted over the WDL-4008 number on the cover, utilizing the 4008 vinyl **30**

3102: "Pinocchio"

WDL-3042: **"Walt Disney Takes You to Disneyland (Musical Tour of Disneyland)";** 1959; formerly WDL-4004 . . . . **25**

WDL-3043: (*Not issued*)—Was listed as "Sounds Liberty (1959)" in a 1963 company memo, but believed to be unissued.

WDL-3044: **"The Shaggy Dog and His Friends";** 1959; (Smith); features Roberta Shore, Paul Frees, and "Moochie"; with booklet **30**

WDL-3045: **"Childhood Memories";** 1959; Rica Moore; yellow cartoon cover of young boy in a garden **25**

A15

Disneyland 12" LP Picture Discs, Including the "3100" Series and the Theme Park "Souvenir" LPs

The "3100" series LP's[4] came in die-cut covers which revealed the inner pic-

[4] In 1980, the first three of the "3100" LP picture discs (**"Snow White," "Pinocchio," and "The Lady and the Tramp"**) were also sold as a "Picture Disc Collection" package box set numbered 3V-8139. Guide price: $90

In 1981, the above titles, plus **"The Fox and the Hound"** were sold as a mail order for $19.95 as a four LP "Picture Disc Collection" set through Book Club Associates in Garden City, New York. Guide price: $120

3103: ***"Lady and the Tramp"***

3110: ***"Peter Pan"***

ture disc. The back cover was a photo of side two of the LP. These discs originally sold for $5.98. Issues with a suffix "M" are Spanish language issues on the Disneylandia label. The other picture discs were "souvenir" LP's usually purchased on-site at either Disneyland or Walt Disney World.[5]

3101: **"Snow White and The Seven Dwarfs";** 2/1981; MST **30**

3101-M: **"Blanca Nieves Y los 7 Enanos"** **40**

3102: **"Pinocchio";** 2/1981; MST **30**

3102-M: **"Pinocho"** **40**

3103: **"Lady and the Tramp";** 2/1981; MST **30**

3103-M: **"La Dama Y el Vagabundo"** **40**

3104: **"Mary Poppins";** 1981; MST **30**

3105: **"The Jungle Book";** 1981; MST **30**

3106: **"The Fox and the Hound";** 1981; MST **30**

3106-M: **"El Zorro el Sabueso"** . . **40**

3107: **"Cinderella";** 1981; MST **30**

3108: **"Stories and Songs of Bambi";** 1982; MST **30**

3109: **"Mickey's Christmas Carol in Story and Song";** 1982 . . . . **30**

3110: **"Peter Pan";** 1982; MST **30**

3111: **"Mickey Mouse Disco";** 1982 . . . . **30**

3112: (*Not issued*)—Was scheduled to be "The Black Cauldron"

(End of the "3100" Series)

WE-2: **"A Musical Souvenir of Walt Disney World's Magic Kingdom";** 1973; 5,000 copies pressed **100**

WE-3: **"A Musical Souvenir of America on Parade";** 1975; 5,000 copies pressed **100**

---

[5] See also: Buena Vista LP Picture Disc Series "63100" at Section A29.4 below; the Disneyland "Souvenir" EP Picture Discs below in EP Section C7; the MCA disc at Sec. B32; the Rhino disc at Sec. B44; and the Victor 78rpm discs at Sec. D3.31.1. Other "one-sided" 78 rpm picture discs are found at Sections D3.19, D3.20, D3.21, and D3.30.

WE-3: **"Walt Disney World Adventureland Steel Band";** 1976; issued with the same number as the preceding LP but this is NOT a picture disc **15**

A16
Buena Vista "3300" LP Series

Original prices: Mono-$3.98/Stereo $4.98

In 1961, the back cover to Buena Vista 1301 ("Musical Kaleidoscope") indicated Disney's apparent plans to reassign certain of its Disneyland WDL "3000" number series to the Buena Vista "BV-3300" series, and listed the proposed new numbers. This would have resulted in certain BV "3300" releases having two differently named albums with the same number! This number reassignment never took place, and records with these "reassigned" WDL-3000 numbers were never actually released with the new Buena Vista numbers.

In the past, this caused confusion amongst collectors of Disney recordings who often looked for recordings with numbers that never really existed. Indeed, some previous listings of a few Disney records actually put prices on these non-existent records! Listed in the footnote below, for historical purposes only, are the purported reassignment of numbers was to have been.[6]

This "3300" series, and many of the 45 rpm singles deriving from it, can fairly depict "Buena Vista" as the Disney label initially built by Annette Funicello. As a former "Mouseketeer" on the "Mickey Mouse Club" TV show, Annette had become "America's Sweetheart" and her recording career blossomed as she developed into a beautiful and curvaceous young woman. She starred in many of the "surf" movies of the early 1960s and was featured in many later TV commercials. Over the years, "Annette" has remained one of the most fondly remembered and classiest women of her era. Her records on Buena Vista, and her very early ones on Disneyland have long been sought out by rock record collectors, who have boosted their values beyond what straight Disney collectors might otherwise expect. The covers to Annette's albums are collectible in themselves! Hayley Mills collectors seek out all of her albums and singles on the Buena Vista label as well.

BV-3301: **"Annette";** 2/1960; Annette Funicello; black label **90**

BV-3302: **"Annette Sings Anka";** 2/1960; Annette Funicello; with enclosed photo; black label; rare
With Picture **120**
Without Picture **80**

BV-3303: **"Hawaiiannette";** 6/1960; Annette Funicello; black label **60**

BV-3304: **"Italiannette";** 10/1960; Annette Funicello; black label **60**

---

[6] The proposed renumbering system, which was not implemented, would have had the following results:

OLD NUMBER	NEW NUMBER
WDL-3034	BV-3302
WDL-3011	BV-3303
WDL-3026	BV-3304
WDL-3032	BV-3305
WDL-3021	BV-3306
WDL-3036	BV-3307
WDL-3035	BV-3308
WDL-3030	BV-3309
WDL-3017	BV-3310
WDL-3022	BV-3311
WDL-3039	BV-3312
WDL-3033	BV-3313
WDL-3015	BV-3314
WDL-3029	BV-3315
WDL-3006	BV-3316
WDL-3031	BV-3317
WDL-3038	BV-3318

BV-3305: **"Dance Annette";** 1961; Annette Funicello **60**

BV-3306: **"Ghost Riders in the Sky";** 1/1961; (Jones); renamed from former WDL-3015, with the same cover **30**

BV-3307: **"Rex Allen Sings: 16 Favorite Songs (16 Golden Hits)";** 2/1961 . . . . **40**

BV-3308/STER-3308 **"Tutti's Trumpets";** 12/1961 mono/1962 stereo; Camarata conducts; formerly WDL-3011; later released as BV-4047
Mono **20**
Stereo **30**

BV-3309/STER-3309: **"The Parent Trap"** (Sherman)/**"Intermezzo and Others"** (Camarata); 6/1961; MST; features Hayley Mills with Annette Funicello and Tommy Sands; black label
Mono **40**
Stereo **60**

BV-3310: **"High and Dry with the Yachtsmen";** 12/1961; The Yachtsmen were: Carl Berg, Ray Gordon, Jay Huling, and Bill Reed; folk songs; cover features the group in a boat in the desert; black label **30**

BV-3311/STER-3311: **"Let's Get Together";** 1962; Hayley Mills; black label
Mono **20**
Stereo **45**

BV-3312: **"Annette—The Story of My Teens . . . and the Sixteen Songs That Tell It";** 1962; Annette Funicello; GF with booklet; black label. **60**

BV-3313/STER-3313: **"Teen Street (Maurice Chevalier and Hayley Mills Take You to Teen Street)";** 1/1963; has three Annette Funicello songs; Black label
Mono **40**
Stereo **60**

*STER-3314: **"Muscle Beach Party"/"Merlin Jones and The Scrambled Egghead";***

BV-3314/STER-3314: **"Muscle Beach Party"/"Merlin Jones and The Scrambled Egghead";** 4/1964; MST; Annette Funicello and Frankie Avalon; number originally scheduled to be for "Picture Themes" LP which actually became 3319 below
Mono **50**
Stereo **120**

BV-3315/STER-3315: **"Billy Storm";** 4/1963; white photo cover; number was originally scheduled for an LP to be titled "Lover Come Back" (*Not issued*)
Mono **25**
Stereo **35**

BV-3316/STER-3316: **"Annette's Beach Party";** 7/1963; MST; Annette Funicello; non-GF; front cover has Annette roasting hot dogs, with back cover of her with surfboard
Mono **50**
Stereo **100**

BV-3323: "The Moon Spinners"

BV-3317/STER-3317: **"Carousel";** 7/1963; Jan Clayton and Gloria Wood Chorus; non-GF with cover portrait of Clayton; later released as BV-3939 and DQ-1292
Mono **25**
Stereo **35**

BV-3318/STER-3318: **"The Famous Ward Gospel Singers";** 7/1963; non-GF black cover featuring a tambourine
Mono **25**
Stereo **35**

BV-3319/STER-3319: **"33 Great Walt Disney Motion Picture Melodies";** 11/1963; Camarata conducts; abstract cover; number was originally to be "Disneyland After Dark" (canceled)
Mono **25**
Stereo **35**

BV-3320/STER-3320: **"Annette On Campus";** 1/1964; with The Wellingtons; one of the most famous Annette covers
Mono **50**
Stereo **100**

BV-3321/STER-2231: **"The Changing Seasons";** 1964; Camarata Stereophonic Strings
Mono **20**
Stereo **30**

BV-3322/STER-3322: **"In the Still of the Night";** 12/1959 mono/1960 stereo; Camarata Stereophonic Strings; cover depicts a painting of the beach at night; original title was to have been "All the Things You Are" for the mono issue
Mono **20**
Stereo **30**

BV-3323: **"The Moon Spinners";** 7/1964; (Grainer); MST; title song by Terry Gilkyson **40**

BV-3324/STER-3324: **"Annette at Bikini Beach";** 9/1964; MST; Annette Funicello; contains a Beach Boys track; GF cover featuring Annette in a bathing suit
Mono **40**
Stereo **80**

BV-3325/STER-3325: **"Annette's Pajama Party";** 11/1964; (Styner); Annette Funicello; GF cover of Annette in various regular and shorty pajamas
Mono **40**
Stereo **80**

BV-3326: **"Original Music from The Living Desert"/"The Vanishing Prairie";** 11/1964; (Smith); MST; the original releases were on RCA EP# ERAS-1 and Columbia 10" LP CL-6332 below **50**

BV-3327/STER-3327 **"Annette Sings Golden Surfin' Hits (and Just for Fun 'The Monkey's Uncle')";** 7/1965; Annette Funicello; cover depicts Annette looking at a skateboard, with a small insert of her with surfboard
Mono **80**
Stereo **120**

BV-3328/STER-3328: **"Something Borrowed, Something Blue";** 1/1965; Annette Funicello; portrait painting on cover
Mono **50**
Stereo **100**

BV-3329: (*Not issued*)

BV-3330: **"Tinpanorama";** 8/1965; (Richard and Robert Sherman); Camarata conducting special Sherman songs done in styles ranging from ragtime music to the early 1960s **30**

BV-3331: (*Not issued*)

BV-3332: (*Not issued*)

BV-3333/STER-3333: **"Let's Fly with Mary Poppins";** 8/1965; Sam Butera and The Witnesses and Louis Prima and Gia Maione
Mono **20**
Stereo **30**

BV-3334/STER-3334: **"That Darn Cat";** 11/1965; (Bruns/Sherman); MST; Louis Prima and Bobby Troup
Mono **15**
Stereo **25**

BV-3335/STER-3335: **"Mary Poppins En Francais" (in French);** 12/1966; Christiane Legrand and Bob Martin; all liner notes are in French
Mono **20**
Stereo **30**

BV-3336: **"Concert in the Park";** 3/1966; Durand Area High School Band; they were the winner of the First Annual Disneyland Marching Band contest **20**

BV-3337/STER-3337: **"Walt Disney World Band";** 4/1972; James Christenson as band director; cover shows the band in front of Cinderella's castle
Mono **15**
Stereo **25**

BV-3338: (*Not issued*)

BV-3339: **"Robin Hood";** 1974; Louis Prima with Sam Butera and the Witnesses; stereo **25**

A17
Disneyland "DL-3500" LP Series

Many of these LPs had non-Disney commercial tie-ins to other companies, and were special orders, premiums or give-away records from the companies. Other companies associated with the individual pressing is listed (if known) after the date.

DL-3501: **"Treasury of Dog Stories";** 8/1963; three LP box-set; includes "The Incredible Journey," "Savage Sam," "Big Red," "Old Yeller," "Greyfriars Bobby," and "Nikki" . . **50**

DL-3502: **"Western Songs and Stories";** 10/1964 . . . . **30**

DL-3503: **"Famous Dog Stories";** 10/1964 . . . . **30**

DL-3504: **"Snow White in French and English"/"The Happy Wanderer in Europe";** 10/1964 . . . **30**

DL-3505: **"Folk Songs from Around the World"/"Christmas Folk Songs";** 10/1964 . . . . **30**

DL-3506: **"Zoo Songs"/"Goofy's Dance Party";** 10/1964; paper sleeve **50**

DL-3507: **"Stories of Aesop"/"Stories of Mother Goose";** 10/1964; paper sleeve . . . **50**

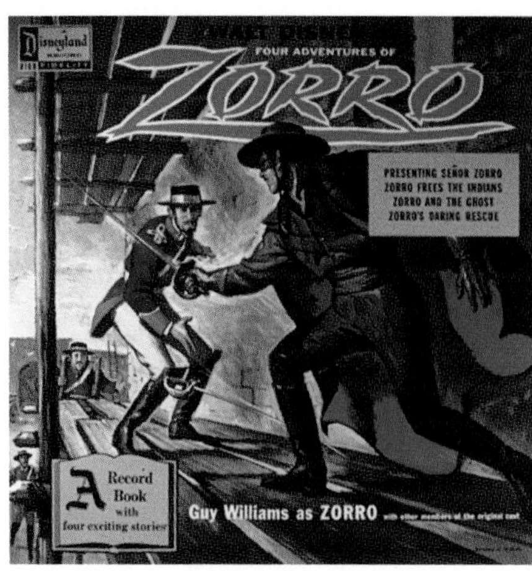

WDA-3601: "Four Adventures of Zorro"

DL-3508: **"Annette and Hayley Mills (Singing 10 of Their Greatest All Time Hits)";** 10/1964; five songs by each artist on separate sides; cover pictures small photos of each artist; TV offer record; paper sleeve; very rare. In the past this record has been erroneously listed in some "rock" albums price guides as "BV-3508 Annette and Hayley." Walt Disney Archives confirms this was never released with a Buena Vista number. The confusion arises from the outer sleeve which notes: "Buena Vista Records Presents . . . ." However, the vinyl album itself is actually on Disneyland DL-3508 . . . . **450**

DL-3509: **"Walt Disney's Happiest Songs";** 9/1967; Gulf Oil **15**

DL-3510: **"Walt Disney's Merriest Songs";** 7/1968; Gulf Oil **15**

DL-3511: **"Goldilocks";** 1/1970; Armstrong Floor Covering; features Mary Frances Crosby as Goldilocks, Bing Crosby, Katherine Crosby, and Nathaniel Crosby; later released as ST-3998. . . . . **25**

DL-3512: **"Pinocchio";** 3/1971; Shasta Soft Drink; MST; cover with Pinocchio dancing with Figaro **25**

STER-3513: **"50 Happy Years of Disney Favorites (1923-1973)";** 12/1972; two LP set; stereo **30**

DL-3514: **"Walt Disney's Greatest Songs";** 3/1974; two LP set **20**

DL-3515: **"The Best of Disney";** 3/1976; Kellogg's cereal Premium; MST; two LP set; GF, no book **30**

DL-3516: **"Family Reunion";** 11/1979; Kraft Food Products; Kraft logo on cover and label; has Sing-Along book with lyrics; Disneyland's 25th Anniversary. **25**

DL-3517: **"The Fox and the Hound";** 1981; promo album **25**

DL-3518: **"The Disney Family Christmas Album";** 7/1981; issued through Radio Shack only; Larry Groce and the Disneyland Children's Sing Along Chorus; ten songs; has twelve-page booklet insert; catalog number 51-3041 on front of album **25**

DL-3519: **"Disney's Christmas All-Time Favorites";** 12/1984; mail order only; also released with the number "1V-8150" on the back cover **25**

A18
Disneyland "WDA-3600" LP Series

This was a short-lived series devoted to TV music. Original price: $3.98

WDA-3601: **"Four Adventures of Zorro";** 2/1958; (Lava/Bruns); Guy Williams and Cast perform: "Presenting Senor Zorro," "Zorro Frees the Indians," "Zorro and the Ghost," and "Zorro's Daring Rescue"; GF with booklet **80**

WDA-3602: **"Three Adventures of Davy Crockett";** 9/1958; (Bruns); features Fess Parker and cast; GF with black and white picture booklet; first reissue of Columbia CL-666 after Columbia's license of the Disney master recordings expired on Feb. 6, 1958 .... **50**

A19
Buena Vista "3700" LP Series ("Charlie Brown Records")

This series was issued with gatefold covers with booklets. Compare with the cheaper "2600" series above. It derives from the "Peanuts" comic strip characters created by Charles Schultz. Several TV animated specials featured these shows as well.

3701: **"A Charlie Brown Christmas";** 10/78; red cover with Christmas bulbs and the kids around a Christmas tree; this TV special is repeated year after year **20**

3702: **"Charlie Brown's All-Stars";** 3/1979; white cover features kids on a pitcher's mound **20**

3703: **"He's Your Dog, Charlie Brown";** 3/1979; cover shows Snoopy on his doghouse **20**

3704: **"It's the Great Pumpkin, Charlie Brown";** 10/78; cover shows Snoopy jumping over a pumpkin **20**

3705: **"You're in Love, Charlie Brown";** 6/1979; cover shows Charlie spraying a hose on Snoopy **20**

A20
Disneyland "Story Teller" "ST" 3800-3900 LP Series

You should not interpret a Disney "ST" prefix as meaning "stereo." It stands for "Story Teller" and most of this line are in fact mono recordings unless noted. This is why Disney was later forced to use the prefix "STER" on its later "WDL" and "BV" pressings when stereo recordings were released. Most of the "ST's" had gatefold (GF) covers with an inner multi-page booklet. The recordings are usually studio tracks, though many feature original soundtrack music and/or songs behind the narrative. Over 40 of the scripts to the early "ST's" were written by James A. "Jimmy" Johnson, the General Manager and President of the Walt Disney Music Division. As these "ST's" were targeted for very young children ("kiddie records"), finding these albums in Mint (M) or Mint Minus (M-) condition is very difficult—this is actually true of any Disney recording and children's records in general!

The first two pressings of some of the early "ST" numbers in the "3900" series are the most collectible. The first issue "ST's" of the first ten named titles have what collectors call "Round" painted covers, where the design on the cover is circular. The second issue "ST's" of these (except Dumbo), and a few first issues of later titles, are known as "Magic Mirror" pressings, where a portion of the cover is die-cut in an oval to reveal a portion of the inner booklet. Some early pressings of the "Magic Mirror" editions also had a

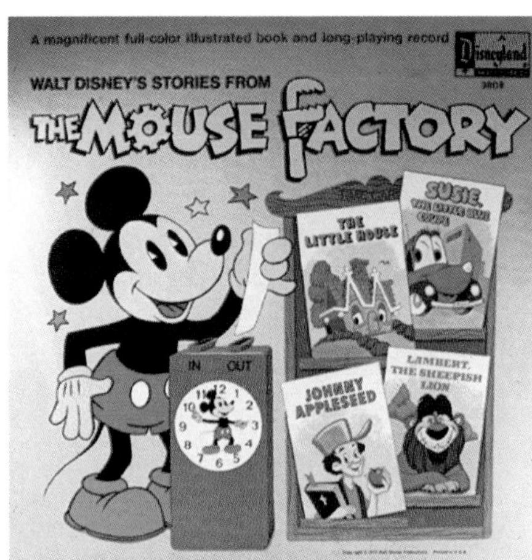

STER-3808: ***"Stories from the Mouse Factory"***

hard, clear plastic covering under the die-cut opening, e.g., "Cinderella" and "Pinocchio." The "3900" "Round" and "Magic Mirror" covers are identified

The covers and sometimes the contents and/or booklets often changed many times over the years as they were continuously re-released for new generations. Generally, the "Round" and "Magic Mirror" and other early "ST" pressings contained glossy-page booklets which utilized movie cel artwork. When the "ST" prefix was dropped in the later reissues, often the booklets changed text and utilized painted artwork. If known reissue dates are listed, the covers may have changed as well. The original label color for the "3900" series, and the first few issues in the "3800" was purple. Aberrant red, and black labels exist and reissues were on the yellow rainbow labels

Finally, while most of the albums had an "ST" prefix, later pressings just gave only the number itself on the cover. So, if you see just a number in this series listed, it is usually really a later Story Teller from the 1970s or 1980s, or a later reissue of the earlier numbered "ST's."

A20.1: *Disneyland* "ST-3800" *Series*

This "3800" Series may, or may not have the prefix "ST" on the cover, especially the later editions. This series was actually produced later than the "3900" series, to avoid a numbering conflict with the WDL/Buena Vista "4000" Series. The records were originally priced at $5.98.

ST-3801: **"The Legend of Sleepy Hollow—The Story and Songs"/"The Legend of Rip Van Wrinkle";** 1/1971; formerly DQ-1285 . . . . **25**

ST-3802: **"A Child's Garden of Verses";** 1/1971; Frances Archer and Beverly Gile; formerly released as WDL-1008, DQ-1241, and WDL-3004; see also Section A1 . . . . **25**

STER-3803: **"The Story and Songs of Born Free"** (Barry)/**"Living Free"** (Kaplan); 4/1972; Lois Lane narrates; with original film dialogue and music; includes poster of "Elsa's Cubs" **20**

STER-3804: **"The Story and Songs from Bedknobs and Broomsticks";** 8/1971; (Sherman); Dal McKennon narrates **20**

ST-3805: **"Mickey Mouse—'This Is My Life' ";** 8/1971; eleven-page booklet of history of Mickey **30**

STER-3806: **"Hall of Presidents";** 8/1972; (Baker); features Royal Dano as Lincoln; Lawrence Dobkin narrates; eleven-page booklet; this is a Walt Disney World attraction **25**

STER-3807: **"New Zoo Revue";** 10/1972; cover marked "A Presentation of Funco Corp." **25**

STER-3808: **"Stories from the Mouse Factory";** 8/1972; includes "The Little House," "Susie, the Little Blue Coupe," "Johnny Appleseed," and "Lambert, the Sheepish Lion" **25**

ST-3809: **"Escape to Witch Mountain";** 3/1975; (Mandel); Eddie Albert narrates; stereo **25**

ST-3810: **"Story and Songs from Robin Hood";** 8/1973; (Bruns/others); MST; Roger Miller narrates; animated version; stereo **25**

ST-3811: **"An Adaption of Dickens' Christmas Carol";** 9/1975; (Baker); Walt Disney Players; GF with slip-in booklet; stereo; also appears as "D-3811" **25**

ST-3812: **"America Sings";** 6/1974; Burl Ives; soundtrack for the Disneyland attraction **25**

ST-3813: **"Winnie the Pooh and Tigger Too";** 7/1974; Sterling Holloway and Paul Winchell; Sebastian Cabot narrates **25**

ST-3814: **"The Island at the Top of the World";** 10/1974; (Jarre); Thurl Ravenscroft narrates; with cast; stereo **25**

ST-3815: **"Mickey Mouse Club Song Hits";** 7/1975; sixteen-page Mouseketeer photo album; very collectible; stereo **35**

ST-3816: **"Story of The Rescuers";** 5/1977; (Butler); MST; features Bob Newhart, Eva Gabor, Geraldine Page, and Joe Flynn; includes songs and dialogue **25**

ST-3817: **"Dragons and Dinosaurs"**; 1977; Thurl Ravenscroft narrates; includes "The Reluctant Dragon," "Puff the Magic Dragon," "Mad Madam Mim," and "The Loch Ness Monster" **25**

ST-3818: **"Pete's Dragon";** 11/1978; Bob Holt narrates; includes songs and dialogue **25**

ST-3819: **"The Hobbit";** 10/1978; (Laws); MST; includes songs and dialogue **30**

ST-3820: **"The Small One";** 12/1978; (Brunner); MST; features Sean Marshall, Olan Soulé, Joe Higgins, William Woodson, Hal Smith, and Gordon Jump; includes songs and dialogue **25**

ST-3821: **"The Story of the Black Hole";** 11/1979; (Barry) **30**

ST-3822: **"The Return of the King";** 3/1980; (Laws/Bass); MST; includes songs and dialogue **30**

ST-3823: **"The Fox and the Hound";** 6/1981; MST; Lance Legault narrates **20**

ST-3824 (*Not issued*)—A 1981 Disney catalog lists this as available as "Dragonslayer," however, it was never issued by Disney. See the "Label X" 12" 45 rpm issue in the LP section below.

ST-3825: **"Mickey's Christmas Carol";** 8/1982; (Baker); MST; issued through Radio Shack only; based on Dickens' *Christmas Carol*; not a GF but does have a slip-in, twelve-page booklet; with additional "Realistic" logo/number on label: "Realistic Cat. No. 51-3004" and "Custom manufactured in U.S.A. for Radio Shack..." **35**

Note: Numbers 3881-3899 were assigned to French pressings

*ST-3904: **"Story of Dumbo"** (Round cover)*

A20.2: *Disneyland* "ST-3900," *and the* "*Disneylandia en* Espanol" 3900 LP *Series*

This English language American series was actually produced prior to the "3800" series above. See introductory statement at Section A20. All original pressing "3900" series had purple labels. Reissues in this series appeared with yellow rainbow labels. Original Price: $3.98.

Many in this series also had early 1970s Spanish language "PA" prefix editions which often had different artwork covers. These were American Spanish language editions, made and distributed on the "Disneylandia" label in the United States, and are noted after the English edition if issued (See also the "3000" series LPs above).

ST-3901: **"A Day at Disneyland";** 1957; features Walt Disney and Jiminy Cricket; round cover **70**

ST-3902: **"Perri";** 3/1958; (Smith/Bruns); features Jimmie Dodd and Darlene Gillespie; Camarata conducts; GF cover does not have booklet but opens up to reveal a two page map of the forest, keyed to adventures in the story; round cover has the circle formed by leaves and forest plants around Perri the squirrel; rare; later released as DQ-1309 with same front cover; see also ST-1909 . . . . **50**

ST-3903: **"Story of Bambi";** 10/1957; Jimmie Dodd; round cover **50**

"Story of Bambi"; 1960; Magic Mirror cover **30**

"Story and Songs from Bambi"; 1969; covers with both inner and outer record pockets **20**

1980; cover of Bambi lying down with butterfly on his nose **15**

PA-ST-3903: **"Bambi"** **30**

ST-3904: **"Story of Dumbo";** 10/15/1957; Timothy Mouse and original cast; round cover; for reasons unknown, no Magic Mirror cover was released for Dumbo **50**

"Story and Songs from Dumbo"; 1965; orange cover **25**

ST-3905: **"Story of Pinocchio";** 10/1957; Jiminy Cricket and original cast; round cover; movie cel artwork **50**

"Story of Pinocchio"; 1960; Magic Mirror cover; same interior artwork as above but reproportioned; text differs from round cover **30**

"Story and Songs from Pinocchio"; 1969; cover of Pinocchio with apple; booklet same as Magic Mirror **20**

"3905"; 1978; with different painted booklet art and text cover with Pinocchio on workbench; yellow rainbow label **15**

PA-ST-3905: **"Pinocho";** 1974 . . . **30**

ST-3906: **"Story of Snow White and the Seven Dwarfs";** 11/22/1957; Annette narrates; round cover **75**

*ST-3907: **"Stories of Uncle Remus (Song of the South)"** (Round cover)*

*ST-3909: **"Story of Alice in Wonderland"** (Round cover)*

"Story of Snow White and the Seven Dwarfs"; 1960; Magic Mirror cover; booklet of movie cel art work **30**

"Story and Songs from Snow White and Seven Dwarfs"; 1969; cover of Snow White sweeping; painted booklet art **20**

1980; Hal Smith narrates; cover of Snow White dancing with "Doc" **15**

PA-ST-3906: **"Blanca Nieves y los 7 Enanos"** **30**

ST-3907: **"Stories of Uncle Remus (Song of the South)";** 1/1958; features James Baskett and cast; Dal McKennon narrates; round cover; eight-page, glossy paper movie cel booklet; GF cover with back cover depicting ten of the original "round" cover "STs" plus "Sleeping Beauty" **50**

1967; same as 1957 but back cover depicts photos from the inner booklet **30**

"Songs and Stories of Uncle Remus"; 1970 as "3907"; includes "Brer Rabbit," etc; with twelve-page matte booklet with different text than above **25**

1980; same cover **15**

ST-3908: **"Cinderella";** 1/1958; features Jiminy Cricket and original cast; round cover **50**

"Cinderella"; 1960; Magic Mirror cover **30**

"Cinderella"; 1969; pink cover with mice sewing dress; eleven-page movie cel booklet **25**

Also appears as "3908" with same cover but with painted picture booklet **15**

1980; blue cover depicts Cinderella, Fairy Godmother, and carriage **15**

PA-ST-3908: **"La Cenicienta"** **30**

ST-3909: **"Story of Alice in Wonderland";** 5/1958; (Fain); Darlene Gillespie; round cover . . . **50**

"Alice in Wonderland"; 1962 and 1967; Magic Mirror cover with eleven-page booklet with glossy movie cel art **30**

"Alice in Wonderland"; 1969; green psychedelic cover with same booklet as above; purple label **25**

Also appears as "3909" with eleven-page painted art work booklet; red label **15**

ST-3910: "Story of Peter Pan" (Magic Mirror cover)

PA-ST-3909: **"Alicia en el Pais de las Maravillas"** **30**

ST-3910: **"Story of Peter Pan";** 5/1958; (Fain); Jimmie Dodd and original cast; round cover **50**

"Story of Peter Pan"; 1962; features Bobbie Driscoll, Kathy Beaumont, Paul Collins, Tommy Luske, Hans Conreid, and Bill Thompson; Magic Mirror cover . . . **30**

"Story and Songs from Peter Pan"; 1969 . . . . **20**

1982 . . . . **15**

"Story and Songs from Peter Pan"; 1989; cover shows group flying over island **10**

PA-ST-3910: **"Peter Pan y Wendy"** **30**

ST-3911: **"Story of Sleeping Beauty";** 10/1958; Mary Martin; glossy cover with back cover art (color or black and white) of the Prince and Sleeping Beauty **30**

1969; with back cover art showing pictures of inner booklet pages **20**

ST-3912: **"A Christmas Adventure in Disneyland";** 11/2/59; Camarata conducts; later DQ-1355; later DQ-1355 . . . . **30**

ST-3913: **"Babes in Toyland";** 7/1961; Magic Mirror cover **30**

"Babes in Toyland"; 1969 . . . . **20**

ST-3914: **"A Child's Primer—Music, How It's Made and Played";** 8/17/61; (Based on shorts *Melody* and *Toot, Whistle, Plunk and Boom*) **35**

ST-3915/STER-3915: **"The Great Composers";** 9/1961; Russell C. Potter narrates; Camarata conducts; later released as ST-3968

Mono **20**

Stereo **30**

ST-3916: **"In Search of the Castaways";** 10/1962; (Alwyn/Sherman); MST; Hayley Mills and Maurice Chevalier; John Mills narrates; Mathieson conducts **75**

ST-3917: **"Story of Lady and the Tramp";** 8/15/1962; Ginny Tyler narrates; Magic Mirror cover **30**

"Story and Songs from Lady and the Tramp"; 1969; back cover is green with pictures of inner picture booklet **20**

1980; front cover advertises twelve-page "read-along" book; yellow back cover **15**

PA-ST-3917: **"La Dama y el Vagabundo"** **30**

ST-3918: **"How to Be a Mouseketeer";** 8/1962; 36 songs; fourteen-page booklet; Mickey Mouse Club logo on cover **40**

ST-3919-2/STER-3919-2: **"Great Operatic Composers and Their Stories";** 11/1962; two LP set; original price: $5.98; see also ST-3969 and ST-3970 below

Mono 20
Stereo 30

ST-3920: **"Animal Folk";** 9/1963; Burl Ives 30

ST-3921: **"Walt Disney Presents Folk Heroes";** 9/1963; TV (Bruns/Jones/Baker/others); features The Wellingtons, Rex Allen, Fess Parker, and Stan Jones; Westerns theme songs; number was originally scheduled to be "The Sword and the Stone," which went instead to the "pop-up" series at ST-4901 30

WDEMCO-3921: Walt Disney Educational Media Company release; 1974 20

ST-3922: **"Story and Songs from Walt Disney's Mary Poppins";** 5/1964 ; features Marni Nixon, Richard Sherman, and Dal McKennon; red label 20

1969 15

ST-3922-N: Necco Wafer premium LP with pink label and green and pink cover 40

ST-3923: **"20,000 Leagues Under the Sea" (French edition only);** 1964; contains a studiotrack score by Maurice Jarre 30

ST-3924: **"Folk Lullabies";** 7/1964; Burl Ives 30

ST-3925: **"Walt Disney Presents It's A Small World";** 5/1964; from Pepsi-Cola New York World's Fair Exhibit; Winston Hibler narrates; white, abstract cover; eleven-page, glossy paper booklet; purple label 40

Second issue has yellow cover with photo of the attraction 20

Third issue numbered "3925" only; has same yellow cover; purple label 15

*ST-3925: **"Walt Disney Presents It's A Small World"** (First cover)*

Fourth issue numbered "3925"; with rainbow label and matte photo booklet 10

ST-3926: **"Walt Disney Presents Peter and the Wolf"/"The Sorcerer's Apprentice";** 5/1964; Sterling Holloway narrates; Magic Mirror cover 30

1969; regular issue 20

ST-3927/STER-3927: **"Chim Chim Cheree and Other Children's Choices";** 12/1964; Burl Ives; non-gatefold 20

ST-3928: **"Walt Disney Presents Winnie the Pooh and Honey Tree";** 5/1965; (Sherman); Sterling Holloway as Winnie the Pooh; Sebastian Cabot narrates; based on A.A. Milne books; first pressing has black and white back cover 25

Second issue has color back cover with booklet pictures 15

Issue only numbered "3928" has rainbow label 15

PA-ST-3928 **"Winnie Puh y el Arbol de Miel";** 1973 30

ST-3929: (*Not issued*)

ST-3930: **"Story of the Scarecrow of Oz";** 5/1965; Ray Bolger narrates . . 30

ST-3931/STER-3931: **"National Anthems and Their Stories";** 7/1965; Dick Wittingham narrates; Camarata conducts
Mono 20
Stereo 30

ST-3932/STER-3932: **"Great Ballets and Their Stories";** 1/1966; Orchestra of the Royal Opera House Covent Garden; Edward Downes conducts
Mono 20
Stereo 30

ST-3933/STER-3933: **"Great Piano Concertos and Their Composers";** 1/1966
Mono 20
Stereo 30

ST-3934: **"Story and Songs of Walt Disney's 101 Dalmatians";** 9/1965; great cover of the dogs in a park with Cruella lurking nearby 40

ST-3935: **"A Treasury of Mother Goose Nursery Rhymes"/"More Mother Goose";** 1965; music by Camarata; side one narrated by Sterling Holloway; side two features and Ginny Tyler and Robie Lester; formerly ST-4902 . . . 25

ST-3936/STER-3936: **"The Sound of Music";** 4/1966; Mary Martin; formerly DQ/STER-1296
Mono 15
Stereo 25

ST-3937: **"Pirates of the Caribbean";** 1966; (Bruns); Thurl Ravenscroft narrates; music for Disneyland adventure attraction 30

ST-3938: **"The Story and Songs of Black Beauty";** 5/1966; Jack Halloran Singers; Robie Lester narrates; later released as DQ-1338 20

ST-3939: **"Carousel";** 7/1966; Jan Clayton; Camarata conducts; formerly WDL-3036 and BV-3317; later released as BV-4029 . . 20

ST-3940/STER-3940: **"A Musical Tour of France with Maurice Chevalier";** 9/1966; includes "Joie de Vivre" from short *Monkeys Go Home*
Mono 20
Stereo 30

ST-3941/STER-3941: **"The Story of California";** 4/1967; Frances Archer and Beverly Gile; Dick Whittinghill narrates
Mono 20
Stereo 30

ST-3942: **"Happy Birthday Party with Winnie the Pooh";** 6/1966; Sterling Holloway narrates 25

ST-3943/STER-3943: **"Mary Martin Sings Walt Disney Favorites";** 8/1966; formerly WDL-3038 and WDL-4016
Mono 15
Stereo 20

ST-3944/STER-3944: **"Great Violin Concertos and Their Composers";** 8/1967; Kurt Graunke conducts
Mono 20
Stereo 30

ST-3945: **"Acting Out the ABC's";** 1/1968; includes Ginny Tyler, Terri York, and Grey Johnson 20

ST-3946: **"Story of the Gnome** Mobile"; 5/1967; (Baker); MST; Tom Lowell narrates 30

ST-3947/STER-3947: **"Story and Song of The Haunted Mansion";** 9/1969; (Baker); MST; features Ronny Howard, Robie Lester,

Pete Renoudet, and Eleanor Audley; Thurl Ravenscroft narrates
Mono **15**
Stereo **25**

ST-3948/STER-3948: **"The Story and Songs of The Jungle Book";** 8/1967; with glossy booklet and outside record pocket with black and white back cover pictures; purple label
Mono **15**
Stereo **25**
1978; has a matte booklet with inner pocket and color back cover pictures; yellow rainbow label **15**
PA-ST-3948: **"El Libro de la Selva"** **30**

ST-3949: **"Mother Goose Rhymes and Their Stories";** 2/1969; Rica Moore narrates; Camarata conducts **20**

ST-3950: **"Rudyard Kipling's Just So Stories";** 1/1968; Sterling Holloway narrates **25**

ST-3951: (*Not issued*)

ST-3952/STER-3952: **"Story of George and the Happiest Millionaire";** 1968; Mike Sammes Singers
Mono **20**
Stereo **30**

ST-3953: **"Winnie the Pooh and the Blustery Day";** 1/1968; (Sherman); Sterling Holloway as Pooh; back cover shows inside booklet panels **20**
Issue numbered only "3953"; back cover shows contents of record; black label **15**

ST-3954: (*Not issued*)

ST-3955/STER-3955: **"Story of Hansel and Gretel";** 12/1968; Marni Nixon, Sally Sweetland; Laura Olsher narrates; Camarata conducts; formerly DQ-1253
Mono **15**
Stereo **25**

ST-3956: **"The Cowardly Lion of Oz" (8/1969) Mike Sammes Singers;** Camarata conducts **20**

ST-3957: **"Story and Songs of the Wizard of Oz";** 4/1969 . . . . **25**

ST-3958: **"The Little Engine That Could"/"The Submarine Streetcar";** 12/1968; formerly DQ-1259 . . . . **20**

ST-3959: **"Learning to Tell Time Is Fun";** 12/1968; narrated by Laura Olsher; formerly DQ-1263 . . . . . . **15**

ST-3960/STER-3960: **"More Jungle Book: Further Adventures of Baloo and Mowgli";** 3/1969; Phil Harris and Louis Prima
Mono **20**
Stereo **30**

ST-3961/STER-3961: **"Story of The One and Only, Genuine, Original Family Band";** Sherman; 6/1968
Mono **15**
Stereo **20**

ST-3962: (*Not issued*)—This was to be "Music of Walt Disney" which became BV-2000.

ST-3963: **"Stories and Songs of Walt Disney's Three Little Pigs—How They Fooled the Big Bad Wolf and the Three Little Wolves and Invented a Wolf-Spanking Machine";** 7/1967; (Churchill/Camarata); Sterling Holloway narrates **25**
PA-ST-3963: **"Los Tres Cochinitos"** **30**

ST-3964: **"The Stories of Hans Christian Andersen";** 7/1967; Robie Lester narrates; Camarata conducts; formerly DQ-1276 . . . . . **20**

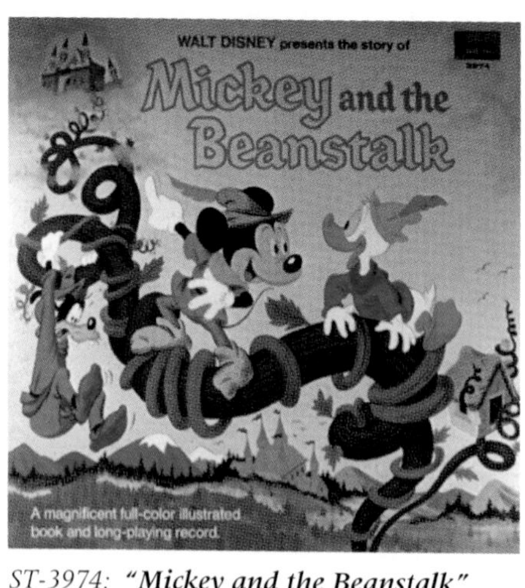

ST-3974: "Mickey and the Beanstalk"

PA-ST-3964: **"Hans Christian Anderson"** 30

ST-3965: **"Treasury of Mother Goose"/"More Mother Goose";** 7/1967; Rica Moore narrates; formerly DQ-1284 and ST-1918 .. 20

ST-3966: **"The Enchanted Tiki Room"** (Bruns)/**"The Adventurous Jungle Cruise";** (5/1968) conducted by Bruns and Camarata; outside record pocket 40

Issue numbered only "3966" has rainbow label and inner record pocket. 15

ST-3967/STER-3967: **"The Story of Heidi";** 8/1968
Mono 15
Stereo 20

ST-3968/STER-3968: **"The Great Composers";** 2/1968; R.C. Potter narrates; Camarata conducts; formerly ST-3915.
Mono 15
Stereo 25

ST-3969/STER-3969: **"Great Operas and Their Stories, Vol. I";** 2/1968; Carl Princi narrates; formerly ST-3919-2
Mono 15
Stereo 25

ST-3970/STER-3970: **"Great Operas and Their Stories, Vol. II";** 2/1968; Marni Nixon and others, Orchestra of the Royal Opera House Covent Garden; Edward Downes conducts; formerly ST-3919-2
Mono 15
Stereo 25

ST-3971: **"Winnie the Pooh and the Heffalumps";** 11/1968; Sterling Holloway narrates 20

ST-3972: **"Winnie the Pooh and the North Pole Expotition" (sic);** 9/1968; Sterling Holloway as Pooh; also features Dallas McKennon, Robie Lester, Thurl Ravenscroft, Sam Edwards, and Jonathan Walmsley 25

ST-3973: **"Now We Are Six";** 11/1968; (Camarata); Joan Brown and Mike Sammes Singers; Sterling Holloway narrates; A.A. Milne poems 20

ST-3974: **"Mickey and the Beanstalk";** 7/1968; Robie Lester narrates; first pressing has black and white inner cover picture of the giant 25

Second pressing numbered "3974" has color inner cover of Mickey 15

ST-3975: **"The Stories and the Songs of Winnie the Pooh and Tigger";** 8/1968 20

ST-3976/STER-3976: **"When We Were Very Young";** 6/1968
Mono 15
Stereo 20

ST-3977: **"Story of the Swiss Family Robinson";** 6/1968; no music **20**

ST-3978: **"Story of Blackbeard's Ghost";** 2/1968; Peter Ustinov narrates; no music; formerly DQ-1305 . . . . **25**

ST-3979/STER-3979: **"Story of Doctor Dolittle";** 9/1968; Camarata conducts; Mike Sammes Singers
Mono **15**
Stereo **20**

ST-3980: (*Not issued*)

(ST-3981): **"Great Moments with Mr. Lincoln";** Note: This was only released as a Buena Vista record on BV-3981/STER-3981 (See below). It is, however, actually a "Story Teller" album but without a "ST" noted!

ST-3982: **"Misty the Mischievous Mermaid";** 6/1969; features Carole Lorrimer, Tony Brandon, Sally Milner, Peter Hawkins, Ysanne Churchman, and Roland Pickering **30**

ST-3983/STER-3983: **"Peer Gynt Suite";** 6/1969; Graunke Symphony Orchestra
Mono **20**
Stereo **30**

ST-3984/STER-3984: **"Mother Goose Suite"/"Children's Corner";** 1969; Camarata conducts
Mono **20**
Stereo **30**

ST-3985: **"Children's Games"** (Bizet)/**"Woodland Sketches"** (MacDowell); 6/1969; Camarata conducts **25**

ST-3986: **"Story of The Love Bug";** 3/1969; Gerry Hoff, Robie Lester, and Dallas McKennon; Buddy Hackett narrates; no music **30**

ST-3987: **"Highlights from Scheherazade";** 4/1970; Symphonie-Orchester Graunke **25**

ST-3988: **"Arabian Nights" (The Voyages of Sinbad the Sailor);** 12/1969 . . . . **20**

ST-3989: **"Aladdin and His Wonderful Lamp";** 4/1970; David Gell narrates **20**

PA-ST-3989: **"Aladino y la Lampara Maravillosa"** **30**

ST-3990/STER-3990: **"The Nutcracker Suite"/"Dance of the Hours";** 1970; Graunke Symphony Orchestra; from STER-101
Mono **15**
Stereo **25**

STER-3991: **"The Orange Bird";** 3/1971; Anita Bryant and Mike Sammes Singers **20**

ST-3992: **"Story and Songs of the Tin Woodsman of Oz";** 1/1970 . . . . **25**

ST-3993: **"Story of Robin Hood";** 1/1970; (Parker); MST; Dallas McKennon narrates; features the original cast; formerly DQ-1249 . . **20**

ST-3994: **"Walt Disney World's Country Bear Jamboree"** (Bruns)/**"Mile Long Bar";** 9/1971; (Bruns) **35**

STER-3995: **"Story of The Aristocats";** 8/1970; features Robie Lester, Phil Harris, and Mike Sammes Singers; Sterling Holloway narrates **20**

PA-ST-3995: **"Los Aristogatos"** . . . **30**

ST-3996: **"Story of Johnny Appleseed";** 1/1970; Dennis Day narrates **25**

ST-3997: **"Story of Treasure Island";** 6/1970; (Parker); features original

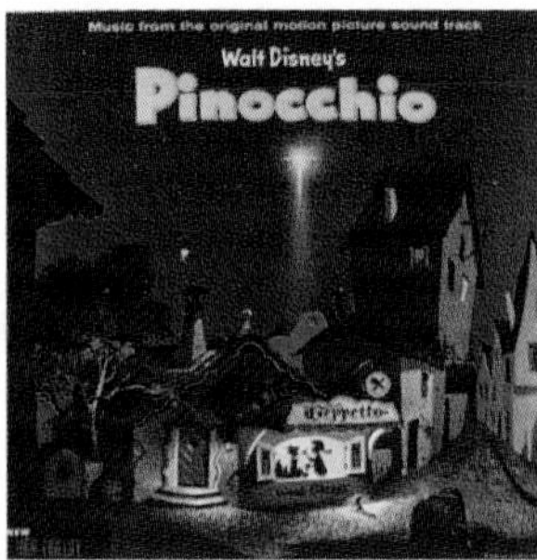

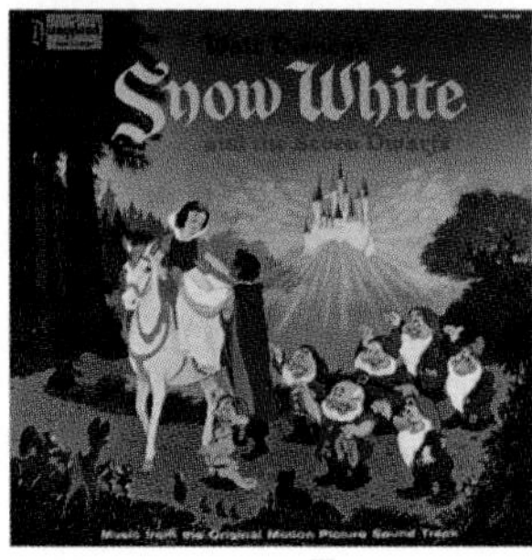

Top to bottom, left to right: WDL-4001: ***"Song of the South"****; WDL-4002:* ***"Pinocchio"****; WDL-4003:* ***"Switzerland"/"Samoa"****; WDL-4004:* ***"Walt Disney Takes You to Disneyland—A Musical Tour of the Magic Kingdom"****; WDL-4005:* ***"Snow White and the Seven Dwarfs"****; WDL-4006:* ***"Secrets of Life"***

cast; Dal McKennon narrates; formerly DQ-1251 . . . . **20**

ST-3998: **"Goldilocks";** 6/1970; Mary Frances Crosby as Goldilocks; features Bing Crosby, Katherine Crosby, and Nathaniel Crosby; later released as DL-3511 . . . . **25**

ST-3999: **"The Boatniks";** 6/1970 . . . **30**

A21
Buena Vista "3981" LP Issue

BV-3981/STER-3981: **"Great Moments with Mr. Lincoln";** 1/1968; (Baker); Royal Dano as Lincoln; narrated by Paul Frees; based on the theme park attraction. This number and pressing appear to be an anomaly—it is actually a "Story Teller" album with Buena Vista logos. It is probably due to an overall production error. See above note for ST-3981 listing.
Mono **20**
Stereo **30**

A22
Disneyland "4000" Stereo Issue

STER-X 4000: **"Disneyland Stereophonic Highlights";** 1959; side one consists of original film music from Fantasia; side two is

"Presenting Tutti Camarata—Mr. Stereo," consisting of music from his other Disney stereo LPs; text only cover with gold background without artwork; gray label; original price: $2.98. Technically this is not one of the "WDL-4000" series below, but is a "stereo sampler" LP. It mentions on the jacket that WDL-4018/STER-4018, "Sleeping Beauty," is due out on "November 1st." **30**

A23
Disneyland "WDL-4000" Series (Disney's First In-House Record Label 12" Albums)

This is the most collectible Disney series! These were quality produced albums, initially targeted at the "adult" market buyers, but they did not sell well. They had vibrant cover graphics and colors, substantial cardboard covers and were excellent vinyl pressings. Many animation film collectors have bought some of these titles at auction as substitutes for near cel quality artwork. They originally sold for $4.98 each.

WDL-4001: **"Song of the South";** 1956; (Wolcott/Amfitheatrof/Smith/others); MST; gorgeous live-action/cartoon, yellow-orange sunset cover; yellow label **300**

Also appears on a second pressing red/maroon label edition **200**

WDL-4002: **"Pinocchio";** 5/19/1956; (Harline/Smith/others); MST; cover depicts a night scene of Pinocchio's village; yellow label **225**

Note: WDL-4003-WDL-4020 have maroon/red labels.

WDL-4003: **"Switzerland"/"Samoa";** 7/15/1956; (Smith/Wallace); MST; from two *People and Places* documentary shorts **50**

WDL-4004: **"Walt Disney Takes You to Disneyland—A Musical Tour of the Magic Kingdom";** 5/1/1956; (Wallace/Bruns/Camarata); Walt Disney narrates; cover shows photo of Walt Disney and the Disneyland train station; early GF issue; first record on the Disneyland record label created entirely by Disneyland Records **75**

WDL-4005: **"Snow White and the Seven Dwarfs";** 1956; (Churchill/Morey/Harline/Smith); MST; classic cover depicting Snow White, the Prince, and the Dwarfs was reissued with less vibrant colors on the 1968 "DQ-1201" **200**

WDL-4006: **"Secrets of Life";** 7/15/1956; (Smith); MST; from the *True Life Adventure Film Series* with segments on Nature's Secrets, Growing Things, Bees, Ants, and others **75**

WDL-4007: **"Cinderella";** 1956; (David/Hoffman/Livingston/Wallace/Smith); MST; one of the prettiest Disney covers done in shades of blue, white, and pink, showing Cinderella's carriage racing through the nighttime village **225**

WDL-4008: **"Westward Ho the Wagons!";** 10/1/1956; (Bruns/Jones/Smith); MST; features Fess Parker and original cast; nice wagon-trains-in-the-sunset cover **70**

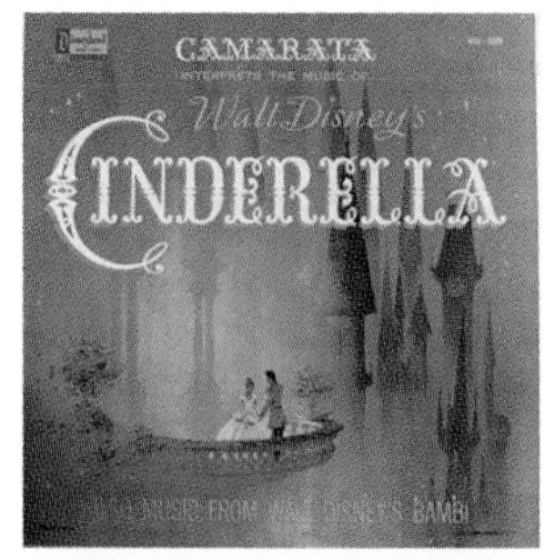

Top to bottom, left to right: WDL-4007: ***"Cinderella"****; WDL-4008:* ***"Westward Ho the Wagons!"****; WDL-4009:* ***"Camarata Interprets Music from Cinderella and Bambi"*** *(front cover), WDL-4009:* ***"Camarata Interprets Music from Cinderella and Bambi"*** *(back cover); WDL-4010:* ***"Bambi"****; WDL-4011:* ***"True Life Adventures"***

WDL-4009: **"Camarata Interprets Music from Cinderella and Bambi";** 2/1957; pink Cinderella front cover and blue Bambi back cover (different cover art than either 4007 or 4010); recorded at the American Legion Hall in Hollywood, after Camarata discovered that it had excellent acoustics **60**

WDL-4010: **"Bambi";** 3/1957; (Churchill/Morey/Plumb); MST; cover with Bambi, Thumper, and friends is stunning and colorful; release was timed to coincide with a re-release of the film **200**

WDL-4011: **"True Life Adventures";** 1957; (Smith); MST; music from five documentary shorts: *Bear Country, Beaver Valley, Nature's Half Acre, Olympic Elk,* and *Prowlers of the Everglades*; cover depicts a small bear lounging on a tree **75**

WDL-4012: (*Not issued*)—While unconfirmed, early Disney files indicate a possibility that this unissued record was initially a planned release of "The Littlest Outlaw" Cf. Disneyland 45 rpm singles in WD-4000 series below.

WDL-4013: **"Dumbo";** 1957; (Churchill/Wallace); MST; pastel spotlights on flying Dumbo give cover a beautiful art deco appearance. This record was originally planned by Disney to be coupled with "Bongo" (the Circus Bear). "Bongo" had been earlier leased to Columbia, and later ABC-Paramount, whose lease was to expire on 9/30/56.

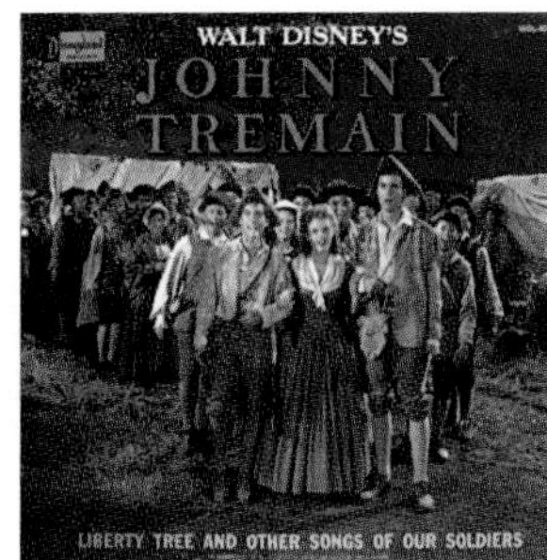

Top to bottom, left to right: WDL-4013: ***"Dumbo"****; WDL-4014:* ***"Johnny Tremain"/"Songs of Our Soldiers"****; WDL-4015:* ***"Alice in Wonderland"****; WDL-4018/STER-4018:* ***"Sleeping Beauty"****; WDL-4019/STER-4019:* ***"Grand Canyon"****; WDL-4021/STER-4021:* ***"Walt Disney's Music Cavalcade (From Mickey Mouse to Sleeping Beauty—Music from the Soundtracks of Thirty Years of Walt Disney Films)"***

For whatever reason, "Bongo" never made it into the WDL-4000 series. **200**

WDL-4014: **"Johnny Tremain"/"Songs of Our Soldiers";** 1957; (Bruns); MST; photo cover of cast members **50**

WDL-4015: **"Alice in Wonderland";** 9/1957; (Fain; Livingston) STK Camarata conducts; colorful cover depicts Alice, with the Cheshire cat in a tree; extremely rare. This LP was long thought to be non-issued as it appeared near the time Disney was thinking of phasing out this more expensive "WDL" LP series in favor of its "DQ" line. The cover art never appeared again on a Disney LP, although some of the remaining red label "WDL" vinyl records were used as fillers for the early "DQ-1208" red cover pressings. It is one of the rarest Disney records. Its price is expected to rise significantly. **350**

WDL-4016/STER-4016: **"Mary Martin—Hi Ho!";** 1958 mono/1959 stereo; different cover than WDL-4038; formerly WDL-3038, WDL-1038; also later released as ST-3943
Mono **20**
Stereo **30**

WDL-4017: *(Not issued)*

WDL-4018/STER-4018: **"Sleeping Beauty";** 1/5/1959; (Tchaikovsky/Bruns); MST
Mono **30**
Stereo **45**

BV-4028/STER-4028: ***"The Carnival of the Animals"***

WDL-4019/STER-4019: **"Grand Canyon";** 12/1958; (Grofe); MST; Symphonic Orchester Graunke, Frederick Stark conductor; GF with seven-page booklet; beautiful graphics and booklet; from "Music Mural" series
Mono **30**
Stereo **60**

WDL-4020/STER-4020: **"America the Beautiful";** 9/1959; The Disneyland Chorus and Brass Band; traditional American songs; from a "Circarama" short; GF with eight-page booklet; blue cover with a mirror-type photo of a New England town in the Fall; from "Music Mural" series; hard to find
Mono **40**
Stereo **80**

WDL-4021/STER-4021: **"Walt Disney's Music Cavalcade (From Mickey Mouse to Sleeping Beauty—Music from the Soundtracks of Thirty Years of Walt Disney Films)";** 10/6/1959; two LP set; GF with twelve-page booklet; side one has "Silly Symphony" excerpts by Harline Churchill, and others; brilliant multi-color abstract cover; gray label; from "Music Mural" series; original price: $5.98
Mono **40**
Stereo **80**

Note: The consecutive "4000" numbering continued under the Buena Vista label in 1961. See Buena Vista "4000" LP section below

A24
Buena Vista "4000" LP Series

These albums continued the numerical sequence from the Disneyland WDL "4000" series. They were quality produced, top-of-the-line issues with gatefold covers and booklets unless otherwise indicated. Original selling price: Mono: $4.79/Stereo: $5.79

BV-4022/STER-4022: **"Babes In Toyland";** 11/1961; (Herbert/Bruns); MST; features Annette, Tommy Sands, Ed Wynn, and Ray Bolger; GF but no booklet
Mono **40**
Stereo **60**

BV-4023/STER-4023: **"Camarata Conducts A Modern Interpretation of Snow White and the Seven Dwarfs";** 6/1963; issued in GF with a first cover with a black band and a red rose
Mono **30**
Stereo **40**

1967; issued in a later non-GF cover with cover line drawing of Camarata and Seven Dwarfs cartoon; without booklet
Mono **20**
Stereo **30**

BV-4024/STER-4024: (*Not issued*)
This was scheduled to be "Savage Sam"; see ST-1925

BV-4025/STER-4025: **"Summer Magic";** 6/1963; (Sherman); MST; features Hayley Mills, Burl Ives, and Eddie Hodges; GF without booklet
Mono **40**
Stereo **60**

BV-4026/STER-4026: **"Mary Poppins";** 3/1964; (Sherman); MST; Julie Andrews and Dick Van Dyke; no booklet; sold over 2.3 million copies in its first year of release; the exact same album was released through RCA's record club the same year, which augmented its distribution; see RCA LP section below
Mono **15**
Stereo **25**
BV-4026L: 6/1964; "limited edition" preview album **50**
BV-4026: commercial albums have a black border with painting of Andrews and Van Dyke; this edition has white background with the actual photos of the stars used as a model for the painting on other issues **40**

BV-4027/STER-4027: **"Camarata Conducts Man of La Mancha";** 6/1967; STK; with Mike Sammes Singers; later released as DQ-1340
Mono **20**
Stereo **30**

STER-4039: ***"Papa Haydn's Surprise and Toy Symphonies"***

BV-4028/STER-4028: **"The Carnival of the Animals";** 7/1967; (Saint-Saens/Camarata); verses by Ogden Nash
Mono **20**
Stereo **30**

BV-4029/STER-4029: **"Carousel";** 6/1967; Jan Clayton and Gloria Wood Choir; formerly ST-3939, WDL-3036, and BV-3317
Mono **15**
Stereo **25**

BV-4030/STER-4030: **"Camarata Conducts The Happiest Millionaire";** 11/1967; STK; Mike Sammes Singers
Mono **20**
Stereo **30**

STER-4031: **"Selections from Fantasia";** 6/1970; MST[7]; Stokowski and the Philadelphia Orchestra; formerly STER-101 . . . . **25**

BV-4032/STER-4032: **"Camarata Conducts Brigadoon";** 1/1968; STK; Jerome Courtland and Gloria Wood Choir
Mono **20**
Stereo **30**

[7] Note, inasmuch as "Selections from Fantasia" was issued in 1970, the possibility exists that a different title number "4031" was planned earlier in 1968. This is unconfirmed. The front cover to this album reproduces that of WDL-3016 but with muted colors and less of a gloss.

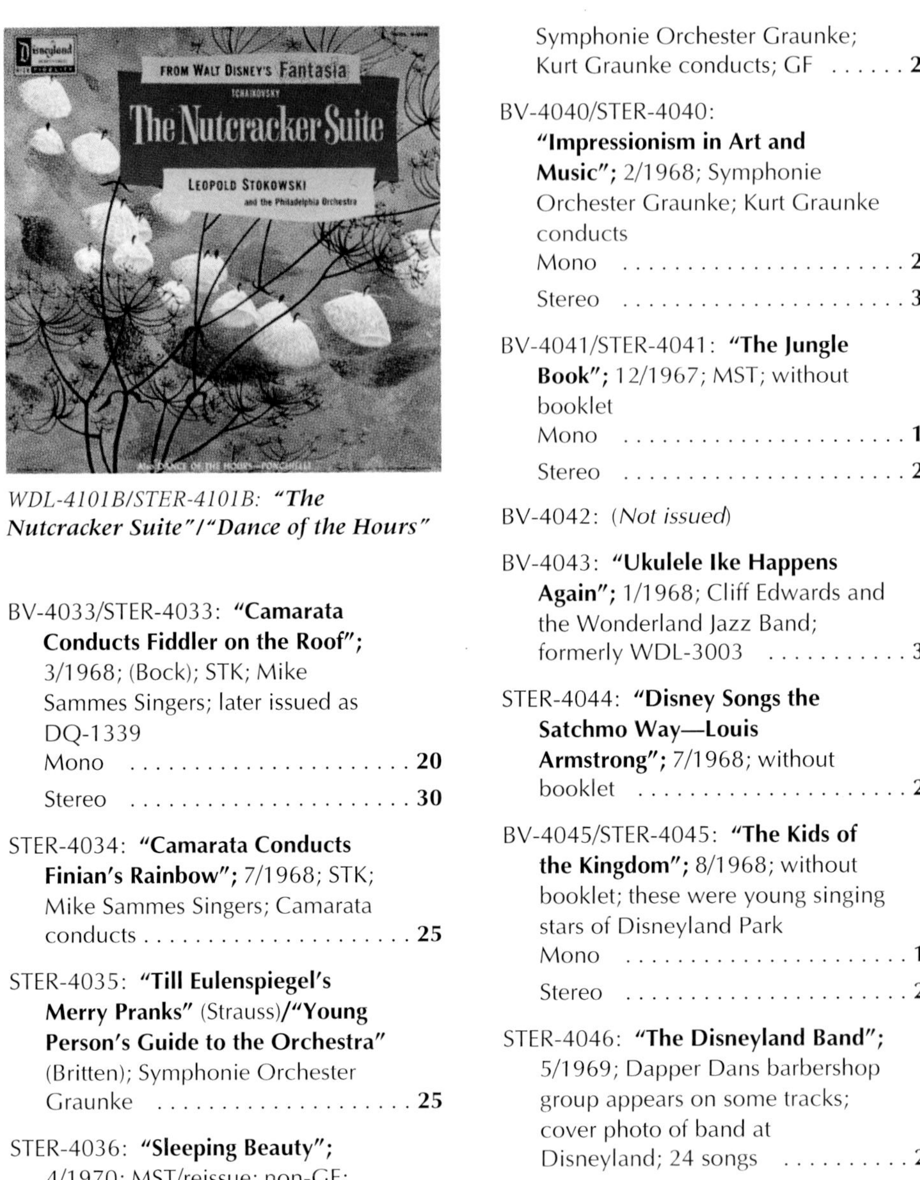

WDL-4101B/STER-4101B: "The Nutcracker Suite"/"Dance of the Hours"

BV-4033/STER-4033: **"Camarata Conducts Fiddler on the Roof";** 3/1968; (Bock); STK; Mike Sammes Singers; later issued as DQ-1339
Mono **20**
Stereo **30**

STER-4034: **"Camarata Conducts Finian's Rainbow";** 7/1968; STK; Mike Sammes Singers; Camarata conducts **25**

STER-4035: **"Till Eulenspiegel's Merry Pranks"** (Strauss)/**"Young Person's Guide to the Orchestra"** (Britten); Symphonie Orchester Graunke **25**

STER-4036: **"Sleeping Beauty";** 4/1970; MST/reissue; non-GF; formerly BV-4018. .... **20**

BV-4037: **"Annette Funicello";** 7/1972; front cover shows Annette in 1972; back cover shows her as Mousketeer **40**

BV-4038: (*Not issued*)

STER-4039: **"Papa Haydn's Surprise and Toy Symphonies";** 8/1968; Symphonie Orchester Graunke; Kurt Graunke conducts; GF **25**

BV-4040/STER-4040: **"Impressionism in Art and Music";** 2/1968; Symphonie Orchester Graunke; Kurt Graunke conducts
Mono **20**
Stereo **30**

BV-4041/STER-4041: **"The Jungle Book";** 12/1967; MST; without booklet
Mono **15**
Stereo **25**

BV-4042: (*Not issued*)

BV-4043: **"Ukulele Ike Happens Again";** 1/1968; Cliff Edwards and the Wonderland Jazz Band; formerly WDL-3003 .... **30**

STER-4044: **"Disney Songs the Satchmo Way—Louis Armstrong";** 7/1968; without booklet **25**

BV-4045/STER-4045: **"The Kids of the Kingdom";** 8/1968; without booklet; these were young singing stars of Disneyland Park
Mono **15**
Stereo **20**

STER-4046: **"The Disneyland Band";** 5/1969; Dapper Dans barbershop group appears on some tracks; cover photo of band at Disneyland; 24 songs **20**

BV-4047: **"Camarata Featuring Tutti's Trumpets";** 8/1970; Camarata conducts; colorful cover; formerly WDL-3011 ...... **20**

BV-4048: **"Camarata Featuring Tutti's Trombones";** 8/1970; Camarata conducts; colorful cover **20**

ST-4901: "The Sword in the Stone"

ST-4903: "101 Dalmatians"

A25
Disneyland "WDL-4100" Series (Fantasia)

Mono editions sold at $3.98; stereo editions at $4.98. All were combined in the three LP "101" series release above (See also STER-X 4000). Early mono issues had maroon labels, with the later monos and stereos switching to gray labels. The mono recordings were issued in 1958—the stereo recordings in 1959. Original soundtrack recordings by Leopold Stokowski and the Philadelphia Orchestra.

WDL-4101A/STER-4101A: **"Rite of Spring"/"Tocatta and Fugue"**
Mono **20**
Stereo **30**

WDL-4101B/STER-4101B: **"The Nutcracker Suite"/"Dance of the Hours";** comes in two covers: one with back cover notes and Nutcracker cover (folded back cover flap); other with Nutcracker cover and Dance of the Hours cartoon on back
Mono **20**
Stereo **30**

WDL-4101C/STER-4101C: **"Night on Bald Mountain"/"Pastoral Symphony/"Ave Maria"**
Mono; cover has "Pastoral" only, back cover folded flap **20**
Stereo; "Night" front cover; "Pastoral" back cover **30**

A26
Disneyland "ST-4900" Disneyrama "Pop-up" Gatefold LP Series

These are rare and highly collectible in top condition as the cover opens up to reveal a six-page "pop-up" figures, accordion-type, foldout. Purple labels. These are difficult to find in nice condition as young children tended to improperly fold or rip apart the pop-up figures. Original selling price: $4.79

ST-4901: **"The Sword in the Stone";** 1963 . . . . **175**

ST-4902: **"Mother Goose Nursery Rhymes";** 1963; later issued as ST-3935 . . . . **125**

ST-4903: **"101 Dalmatians";** 1963; cover later issued on ST-3934 . . . **175**

ST-4904: **"Dumbo";** 1963; orange, flying Dumbo cover to this edition became the cover to ST-3904 in 1965; see Section A20.2 above . . . **175**

ST-4905: **"Pinocchio";** 1963; cover features Pinocchio, the cat, and the fox, followed by Jiminy Cricket walking through the village (cover is unique to this album) . . . **175**

A27
Buena Vista "5000" LP Series

Label colors were of the black and yellow rainbow-type.

BV-5001/STER-5001: **"The Happiest Millionaire";** 6/1967; (Sherman); MST
Mono . . . **15**
Stereo . . . **20**

BV-5002/STER-5002: **"The One and Only, Genuine, Original Family Band";** 4/1968; (Sherman); MST; Buddy Ebsen and Leslie Ann Warren
Mono . . . **15**
Stereo . . . **20**

STER-5003: **"Bedknobs and Broomsticks";** 5/1971; (Sherman); MST; Angela Lansbury and David Tomlinson . . . **15**

STER-5004: **"Scandalous John";** 7/1971; (McKuen); MST . . . **30**

STER-5005: **"Mary Poppins";** 3/1973; (Sherman); MST; non-GF; formerly BV-4026 . . . **15**

STER-5006: **"It's A Small World"/"Walt Disney's Greatest Hits";** 11/1973; Mike Curb Congregation; white photo cover of group . . . **20**

STER-5007: **"The Hobbit";** 10/1977; (Laws/Bass); MST; Glen Yarbrough singing; single LP with songs and instrumentals without narration or dialogue; green cover; compare with slightly earlier box set on Buena Vista 103 above . . . **25**

STER-5008: **"The Black Hole";** 11/1979; (Barry); MST; first digitally recorded soundtrack . . . **50**

STER-5009: **"Snow White and the Seven Dwarfs";** 11/1979; Radio City Music Hall Productions, Inc.; stage show cast: Snow White—Mary Jo Salerno, Prince Charming—Richard Bowne, and The Queen—Anne Francine . . . **30**

A28
Disneyland "8100" LP Series

This series of albums may have been specially packaged sets for premiums, mail orders, etc. It is also possible that they were specially pressed "record club" editions. They are renumbered albums derived from others in the Disney catalogue. Others probably exist.

2V-8105: **"Walt Disney Presents Merry Christmas Songs: 29 All-Time Favorites";** 1978; two LP set . . . **20**

1V-8120: **"Disney's Children's Favorites Vol. I";** 1979; Larry Groce and the Disneyland Children's Sing Along Chorus . . . **15**

1V-8121: **"Disney's Children's Favorites Vol. II";** 1979; Larry Groce and the Disneyland Children's Sing Along Chorus **15**

1V-8122: **"Mickey Mouse Disco";** 1979 .... **15**

3V-8139: **"The Disney Picture Disc Collection";** 1980; includes "Lady and the Tramp"; "Pinocchio"; "Snow White and the Seven Dwarfs"; package of three early "3100" series LP picture discs **90**

1V-8150: **"Disney's Christmas All-Time Favorites";** 1981; except for the title, this has the same front cover as Disneyland 2514 above; 20 songs **15**

A29
Buena Vista 60000 LP Series

A29.1: *The Buena Vista* "60600" *Series*

BV-60605: **"Oliver and Company";** 1988; released in November, 1988 and was the last vinyl Disney record; also the first and last record released on the then new "Walt Disney Records" label .. **25**

A29.2: *Buena Vista* "62100" ("2100") *Series*:

These were well-produced albums containing the stories and dialog from mostly non-Disney produced movies. They contained photo booklets with actual movie scenes. Some in this series were released without the initial number "6," and are indicated in the listings preceded by "(6)."

BV-62112: "The Story of Who Framed Roger Rabbit"

BV-62101: **"The Story of Star Wars";** 6/1983; sixteen-page book **20**

BV-62102: **"The Story of The Empire Strikes Back";** 6/1983; sixteen-page book **20**

BV-62103: **"The Story of Return of the Jedi";** 1983; sixteen-page book **20**

BV-(6)2104: **"Rebel Mission to Ord Mantell";** 1983 .... **20**

BV-(6)2105: **"War Games";** 1983 ... **20**

BV-62106: (*Not issued*) Was scheduled to be "How the Ewoks Saved the Trees."

BV-62107: **"The Story of Indiana Jones and the Temple of Doom";** 7/1984; sixteen-page book **20**

BV-62108: (*Not issued*)

BV-62109: **"The Story of The Black Cauldron";** 7/1985 .... **20**

BV-(6)2110: (*Not issued*)

BV-(6)2111: **"Rainbow Brite Christmas";** 9/1985 .... **20**

BV-62112: **"The Story of Who Framed Roger Rabbit"**; 6/1988; (Silvestri); twelve-page book **20**

BV-62113: **"The Story of Willow"**; 4/1988; sixteen-page book **20**

A29.3: *Buena Vista* "62500" *Series*

Note that this series is, in part, the same as the Disneyland "2500" series above at Section "A12" except it is on Buena Vista.

62501: **"Mickey Mouse Club—All New from 1977—Original TV Cast"** **20**

62502: **"Walt Disney's Magic Kingdom—Best of Disney"** **20**

62503: **"Best of Disney Vol. II"** **20**

62504: **"Mickey Mouse Disco"**; 1979; sold almost two million copies **15**

62505: **"Disney's Children's Favorites Vol. I"**; 1979 . . . . **15**

62506: **"Disney's Christmas Favorites"**; 1979 . . . . **15**

62507: **"Chilling Thrilling Sounds of the Haunted House"**; 1979 . . . . . . **15**

62508: **"Disney's Children's Favorites, Vol. II"**; 1979 . . . . **15**

62509: **"The Sounds of Outerspace"**; 1981 . . . . **15**

62510: **"The Official Album of Disneyland"/"Walt Disney World"**; 1980 . . . . **15**

62511: **"Yankee Doodle Mickey"**; 1980; features Molly Ringwald and others; great Mickey Mouse cover **25**

62512: **"Pardners—14 Great Cowboy Songs"**; 1980 . . . . **15**

62513: **"Disney's Goin' Quackers"**; 1980 . . . . **15**

62514: **"Merry Christmas Carols"**; 1980 . . . . **15**

62515: (*Not issued*)

62516: **"Mousercise"**; 1982; with booklet **15**

62517: **"The Story of Tron"** (1982) . . **20**

62518: **"Flashbeagle"**; TVST; "Peanuts" special **20**

62519: **"Official Album of Walt Disney World Epcot Center"**; 1983 . . . . **15**

62520: **"Splashdance"**; 1983 . . . . **15**

62521: **"Totally Minnie"**; 1986 . . . . . **15**

62522: (*Not issued*)

62523: **"Rainbow Brite-Paint a Rainbow in Your Heart"**; 1984; Jim Andron **15**

62524: **"Voices of Liberty"**; 1984; Epcot Center theme attraction. **20**

62525: **"Disney's Children's Favorites, Vol. III"**; 1986 . . . . **15**

62526: **"The Chipmunk Adventure"**; 1988; (Edleman); MST; non-Disney film with the Chipmunks: Alvin, Simon, and Theodore **20**

62527: **"Mickey's Rock Around the Mouse"**; 1988; features Little Richard, The Jordanaires, and Buzz Cason **15**

62528: **"Children's Favorite Silly Songs"**; 1988 . . . . **15**

62529: (*Not issued*)

62530: **"Solid Gold Chipmunks—Buena Vista presents 'Special Anniversary Collection—30 Years of Great Hits' "**; (1988) **15**

62531: **"The Official Album of Walt Disney World"**; 1988 . . . . **15**

62532: **"Oliver and Company";** 1988 . . . . **20**

A29.4: Buena Vista "63100" Picture Disc Series

63155: **"The Story of Return of the Jedi";** 6/1983; (Williams); photos of an Ewok and Luke Skywalker; picture disc **30**

63156: **"Rainbow Brite: Paint a Rainbow in Your Heart";** 11/1984; photos of Rainbow Brite, and of children playing ring around rosy; picture disc **30**

Note: See also Section A15, A28 Picture Discs, and the EPs in Section C3.

A29.5: Buena Vista "64100" Series

64100: **"Who Framed Roger Rabbit?";** 6/1988; (Silvestri); MST . . **25**

64101: **"Oliver and Company";** 1988; (Redford/others); MST **25**

A30 Mickey Mouse Club Label "MM" LP Album Series

These were generally compilations off of the 78 rpm and 45 rpm Mickey Mouse Club EPs and the Disneyland "DBR" singles. Highly collectible cover photos and artwork. Original price: $1.98.

MM-12: **"Musical Highlights from the Mickey Mouse Club TV Show";** 1/22/1958[8]; later issued as DQ-1227 . . . . **75**

MM-14: **"27 New Songs from the Mickey Mouse Club TV Show";** 10/1958 . . . . **50**

MM-16: **"Mouseketeers Talent Roundup";** 1958; inludes songs from Zorro, Andy Burnett, and Perri **40**

MM-18: **"We're the Mouseketeers";** 12/1957 . . . . **40**

MM-20: **"A Walt Disney Song Fest";** 2/1958; Mouseketeers sing **40**

MM-22: **"Holidays with the Mouseketeers (A Song for Every Holiday)";** 6/1958; features Darlene Gillespie, Jimmie Dodd, Karen Pendleton, Cubby O'Brien, and Jiminy Cricket **40**

MM-24: **"Songs from Annette and Other Walt Disney Serials";** 5/1958; (Bruns/Lava/Jones); features Annette, Darlene Gillespie, and others; highly sought after LP **125**

[8] The original Mouseketeers were: Nancy Abate, Sharon Baird, Billie Jean Beanblossom, Bobby Burgess, Lonnie Burr, Tommy Cole, Dennis Day, Mary Espinosa, Annette Funicello, Darlene Gillespie, Bonnie Lou Kern, Carl "Cubby" O'Brien, Karen Pendleton, Mary Sartori, Bronson Scott, Michael Smith, and Mark Sutherland. Additions that year included Johnny Crawford, Dickie Dodd, Judy Harriet, John Lee Johann, Ronnie Steiner, and Doreen Tracey. Paul Peterson and Tim and Mickey Rooney, Jr. also appeared briefly in the first season.

Many left after the first season, and the following were added: Sherry Allen, Eileen Diamond, Cheryl Holdridge, Charles Laney, Larry Larsen, Jay-Jay Solari, and Margene Storey. In its third and final season, the club also included Don Agrati (Don Grady), Bonnie Lynn Fields, Linda Hughes and Lynn Ready.

Only Sharon, Bobby, Lonnie, Tommy, Annette, Darlene, Cubby, Karen, and Doreen remained with the show over its three year run.

MM-24: "Songs from Annette and Other Walt Disney Serials"

MM-26: **"The Littlest Outlaw (Lava) and Three Other Stories";** 7/1958; includes "Bongo," "The Three Little Pigs," and "Johnny Appleseed" **50**

MM-28: **"Songs About Zorro and Other TV Heroes";** 7/1958; (Bruns/Lava/Jones); includes "Andy Burnett," "Davy Crockett," "Mike Fink," "Cheyenne," and Sheriff of Cochise **90**

MM-30: **"Mickey Mouse's Christmas Surprises";** 11/1958 . . . . **40**

MM-32: **"Walt Disney's Sleeping Beauty";** 11/28/1959; Darlene Gillespie **40**

MM-34: (*Not issued*) This was scheduled to be "The Shaggy Dog," but it was canceled.

A31
Disneyland Disney Double Feature "DDF" LP Series

These were two LP gatefold albums, without booklets, which combined previously issued "DQ" and "ST" recordings under separate "DDF" numbering. All albums were issued in June of 1971. The previous albums used are listed in parenthesis. "DDF" stands for "Disney Double Feature."

DDF-1: **"Animal Stories of Aesop"** (DQ-1221)/**"The Best Stories of Aesop"** (DQ-1218) **25**

DDF-2: **"Walt Disney's Dog Stories"** (DQ-1220)/**"The Incredible Journey"** (ST-1927) **35**

DDF-3: **"The Sword in the Stone"** (DQ-1236)/**"The Prince and the Pauper"** (DQ-1311) **25**

DDF-4: **"Pecos Bill"** (DQ-1269)/**"The Littlest Outlaw"** (DQ-1246) **25**

DDF-5: **"Hans Brinker and the Silver Skates"** (DQ-1282)/**"Toby Tyler in the Circus"** (ST-1904) **25**

A32
Disneyland "DMK" Educational LP Kits

In 1977, Walt Disney Educational Media Company issued a series of albums of Disneyland "Language Arts and Skills Builder" kits, which combined an LP and photo slides. There are others currently unknown. Prices include slides!

DMK-1002: **"The Haunted Mansion";** slides #69-0101 . . . . . . **50**

DMK-1003: **"The Jungle River Cruise";** music and sound effects for the Jungle River Cruise; slides #69-0103 . . . . **50**

DMK-1006: **"The Pirates of the Caribbean";** slides #69-0102 . . . . . **50**

DMK-1007: **"Journey Into Space";** slides #69-0104 . . . . **50**

A33
Other Miscellaneous Disney Radio, Promos, and Demo Records (LP/EP)

Prior to the release of a new film, it was a common practice for Disney and other film studios to issue special, promotional radio spot advertising records in radio markets around the country. These albums generally featured various timed advertisements to be broadcast, and sometimes included "open-ended" interviews with a film's stars, in which a station's disc jockey, utilizing a prepared script, was able to do a voice-over, fake "interview" with the star. These are fairly rare, and especially difficult to find with a "script," if any, still packaged with the record. Disney issued these albums for many of its feature films, and the albums that can currently be verified have been included. Many others may exist. Unless noted otherwise, these records usually came in plain sleeves. Those with a "CR" number prefix were pressed by "Custom Recorders." If a label name is in parenthesis, the name does not appear on the label. "No label" means that the name of the manufacturer making the record for Disney is unknown. Often there were no identifying numbers on these records, in which case "no number" is stated. These were not commercial recordings meant to be released to the general public, but they are out there now for collectors to track down.

RCA Victor PMS-09898: **"Snow White and the Seven Dwarfs";** 1937 film; 78 rpm 16" radio transcription record; promotional release; total time: 13:45; describes the movie and contains portions of most of the songs **300**

Walt Disney Productions A2580A: **"(Adventures of) Ichabod";** 6/24/1949; Mickey on typed label **100**

WOR Recording 54656: **"Robin Hood (Story of Robin Hood and His Merry Men)";** 1952; radio spot and story; light blue label **50**

WOR Recording 61968: **"Peter Pan";** 11/13/1952; one-sided three hole LP; light blue label **100**

WOR Recording 109066: **"Peter Pan";** 1953 film; one-sided; light blue label; issued on film's rerelease in 1958 .... **40**

WOR Recording 109915: **"The Light in the Forest";** 1958; 6 radio spots; light blue label **40**

WOR Recording 110511: **"The Light in the Forest";** 1958; 6 radio spots; light blue label **40**

Carlton Productions 111518: **"White Wilderness";** 1958; radio spots; one sided LP; light blue label **30**

Capitol Custom DSP-102: **"Grand Canyon";** 1958; two-sided 8" record; yellow label indicating "Theater Use Only with Announcer" **40**

Buena Vista ZOR-1: **"The Sign of Zorro";** 1958; 12" blue vinyl LP; picture sleeve depicting Zorro on a horse, and the star, Guy Williams **60**

[Buena Vista] JC-1: **"Jungle Cat";** 1959; one-sided red vinyl LP **50**

[Buena Vista] SHD-1: **"The Shaggy Dog";** 1959; 11 radio spots include Annette tracks; one-sided red vinyl, yellow label; Matrix number V8811 .... **100**

Kal-Kan KKVS-101REV: **"The Shaggy Dog";** 1959; radio commercial spots for dog food company; one-sided LP **45**

Walt Disney Productions B8423A: **"Toby Tyler";** 1960; 12" 78 rpm with 7 radio spots; label is white and green with Mickey Mouse **40**

[Buena Vista] TD-1: **"Ten Who Dared";** 9/6/1960; two tracks; white typed label **50**

David and Coe, Inc. No Number: **"Pollyanna";** 5/9/1960; 7 radio spots; one sided three-hole disc; typed label **40**

Universal Recorders [Buena Vista]: **"Pollyanna";** 1960. This is possibly a five record, 12" red vinyl, radio spots set; each with a paper sleeve with drawings of the film's stars, of which only the following have been confirmed:

POL3—**"Voices of the Stars"** **30**

POL4—**" 'Who Am I?' Contest"** . . **30**

POL5—One-sided record with radio spots **30**

[Buena Vista] DAL-1 (UR-716): **"101 Dalmatians";** 1961; one-sided LP; picture label **45**

[Buena Vista] BT-1: **"Babes in Toyland";** 1961; side one has 13 spots ranging from 10 to 55 seconds; side two contains 5 multiple song tracks from the film; label shows Annette dancing with Tommy Sands; released by Buena Vista Distributing Company **100**

Walt Disney Productions B92584A: **"The Absent-Minded Professor";** 1961; Mickey on typed label **50**

[Custom Recorders] No Number: **"Greyfriars Bobby";** 1961; radio spots; contains 12 tracks ranging from 55 to 10 seconds; one-sided disc pressed by Custom Recorders; tan 5" picture label depicts the movie dog **40**

CR-2308: **"The Parent Trap";** 1961; 5 tracks, including Tommy Sands and Annette; paper picture sleeve; issued with same number as below **50**

Disney Demo #1: **"The Parent Trap";** 1961; side 1A inlcudes "The Parent Trap" (1:48)/"For Now, For Always (Maggie's Theme)" (2:34); side 1B includes "Let's Get Together" (1:18)/ "Whistling at the Boys" (1:33); 7" EP; black label, no cover; very rare Hayley Mills collectible **100**

CR-2308: **"Nikki, Wild Dog of the North";** 1961; 11 radio spots; one-sided LP; issued with same number as above **30**

[Buena Vista] MP-1: **"Moon Pilot";** 1962; 9 radio spots; one-sided; blue vinyl LP; blue picture label . . **50**

[Buena Vista] BV-1: **"Bon Voyage";** 1962; 10 radio spots and songs; white picture label **30**

[Buena Vista] BR-1: **"Big Red";** 1962; 12 radio spots; white picture label **30**

CR-2462: **"Almost Angels";** 1962; 4 radio spots; one-sided LP; green label **30**

CR-2470: **"The Legend of Lobo";** 1962; 6 radio spots; one-sided LP; light brown label **30**

[Buena Vista] CAS-1: **"In Search of the Castaways";** 1962; 13 radio spots; one-sided LP **30**

Buena Vista No Number: **"Savage Sam";** 1963; 7 radio spots; one-sided LP; yellow picture label **30**

CR-2494: **"Son of Flubber";** 1963; 10 radio spots; one-sided LP; light blue label **40**

CR-2535: **"Summer Magic";** 1963; radio spots with 14 tracks; oversize yellow picture label of Hayley Mills and Eddie Hodges (?) **75**

CR-2539: **"20,000 Leagues Under the Sea";** 1954 film; LP radio spots for film's 1963 reissue; orange picture label. **40**

CR-2541: **"The Incredible Journey";** 1963; 8 radio spots; one-sided LP **40**

CR-2554: **"Thomasina (Three Lives of)";** 1963; 7 tracks; one-sided LP; orange label with picture of the cat **30**

CR-2555: **"The Sword in the Stone";** 1963; 14 radio spots; white and green picture label **30**

CR-2568: **"The Misadventures of Merlin Jones";** 1963; 12 radio spots; fuschia colored label **45**

CR-2569: **"The Misadventures of Merlin Jones";** 1963; interview with Annette and Annette sings "Merlin Jones"; yellow picture label; highly sought after **200**

American International 810: **"Beach Party";** 1963; disc jockey open-ended interview with Annette . . . **100**

Buena Vista No Number: **"Miracle of the White Stallions";** 1963; one-sided; red vinyl LP; black and white picture label **50**

CR-2594: **"Mary Poppins";** 1964; interviews with stars of film **30**

CR-2598: **"Mary Poppins";** 1964; interviews with stars of film **30**

CR-2599: **"Mary Poppins";** 1964; interviews with stars of film **30**

CR-2603: **"The Moon-Spinners";** 1964; 10 radio spots; light blue label **35**

CR-2607/2608: **"Mary Poppins";** 1964; one record; aqua picture label **30**

American International 1064: **"Pajama Party";** 1964; disc jockey open-ended interview with Annette **100**

CR-2630: **"So Dear to My Heart";** 1949 film; one-sided LP; yellow label; issued for the rerelease of the film in 1964 . . . . **40**

CR-2647: **"Mary Poppins";** 1965; two LP set; one has yellow label, the other a blue label; regular commercially released outer picture cardboard cover, which is modified to name the radio spots on the records **50**

CR-2668: **"Emil and the Detectives";** 1964; 10 radio spots; one-sided LP; green picture label **30**

CR-2687: **"The Monkey's Uncle";** 1965; 10 radio spots; one-sided LP; yellow picture label **30**

[Walt Disney Productions] B11310A: **"The Monkey's Uncle";** 1965; one-sided 12" 78 rpm record; Mickey picture label. **30**

Famous American Stars 378: **"The Monkey's Uncle";** 1965; disc jockey open-ended interview with Annette; EP **75**

CR-2700: **"Old Yeller";** 1957 film; 11 radio spots; one-sided LP; oversized picture label featuring the dog and family; issued for the rerelease of the film in 1965 . . . . . **40**

No Label S4RG-0278/0279: **"Those Calloways";** 1965; radio spots inlcude 20 tracks; blue and white label **40**

CR-2733: **"That Darn Cat";** 1965; 14 radio spots; LP; yellow picture label **30**

Famous American Stars Series 547: **"That Darn Cat";** 1965; includes open-ended interviews with Hayley Mills, Roddy McDowell, Dean Jones, and Dorothy Provine; 10" LP; green label **50**

CR-2738: **"The Ugly Dachshund";** 1965; radio spots; orange and green labels **30**

CR-2748: **"Bambi";** 1942 film; radio spots include 9 tracks; one-sided disc; green picture label; issued for the rerelease of film in 1963 . . . **40**

Famous American Celebrity Series 662: **"Bambi";** 1942 film; blue vinyl 7" EP; issued on film's rerelease in 1963 . . . . **50**

CR-2756: **"Mary Poppins";** 1965; 9 radio spots; one-sided LP; green picture label **30**

[Buena Vista WOND-1]: **"The Music of Mary Poppins"**; 4/1966; MST/STK; includes various tracks from Buena Vista, Reprise, and Columbia recordings of Disney music; DJ/Promo pressing by "The Wonderland Music Company, Inc."; white cover with gold print; indicates that "This is a collector's LP especially prepared for Radio" and "Citation Edition"; the "WOND-1" number does not appear on album **30**

[Buena Vista] No Number: **"Lt. Robin Crusoe U.S.N.";** 1966; 13 radio spots ranging from 10 to 55 seconds; white label with Mickey at radio **30**

Famous American Stars Series 663: **"Lt. Robin Crusoe, U.S.N.";** 1966; includes interviews with Dick Van Dyke, Nancy Kwan, and Akim Tamiroff; one-sided LP; blue label **40**

CR-2753: **"The Jungle Book";** 1967; 10 radio spots; green and white picture label; Note: this may mistakenly show a number of "2953" **30**

CR-2801: **"Follow Me, Boys!";** 1966; radio spots; one-sided LP; yellow picture label **35**

Famous American Stars Series 759: **"Follow Me, Boys!";** 1966; includes interviews with Fred MacMurray, Vera Miles, and Kurt Russell **35**

CR-2773: **"The Fighting Prince of Donegal";** 1966; 10 radio spots; one-sided LP; green picture label . . **30**

CR-2807: **"Monkeys, Go Home!";** 1967; 13 radio spots; picture label **30**

CR-2809: **"Adventures of Bullwhip Griffin";** 1967; 12 radio spots; yellow picture label **30**

Famous American Star Series 845: **"Adventures of Bullwhip Griffin";** 1967; includes interviews; blue vinyl LP **50**

CR-2818: **"Snow White and the Seven Dwarfs";** 1937 film; 7 radio spots; one-sided LP; white picture label of the Seven Dwarfs; issued for the 1967 rerelease of the film **50**

CR-2823/2824: **"The Gnome-Mobile";** 1967; radio spots; side one has 5 55-second spots; side two has 8 spots varying from 10 to 25 seconds; green picture label **30**

Famous American Stars Series 923: **"The Gnome-Mobile";** 1967; includes interviews with Tom Lowell, Karen Doreice, and Cami Sebring; orange label **30**

CR-2833/2834: **"The Happiest Millionaire";** 1967; side one has 6 55-second spots; side two has 10 tracks ranging from 10 to 55 seconds; pink and white picture label **30**

Famous American Stars Series 939: **"The Happiest Millionaire";** 1967; interview with Lesley Ann Warren **30**

CR-2860: **"Blackbeard's Ghost";** 1968; 10 radio spots; one-sided LP; purple picture label **30**

Famous American Stars Series 1074: **"Blackbeard's Ghost";** 1968; includes interviews with Peter Ustinov, Dean Jones, and Suzanne Pleshette **30**

[Buena Vista] No number: **"Blackbeard's Ghost";** 1968; one-sided LP; label with Mickey at radio **30**

Famous American Stars Series 1124: **"The One and Only, Genuine, Original Family Band";** 1968; includes interviews with John Davidson, Walter Brennan, and Lesley Ann Warren; blue label **30**

Famous American Stars Series 1126: **"The One and Only, Genuine, Original Family Band";** 1968 includes interviews with Buddy Ebsen and Janet Blair; blue label **30**

CR-2871: **"The One and Only, Genuine, Original Family Band";** 1968; 8 radio spots ranging from 10 to 55 seconds; pink picture label **25**

CR-2872: **"Never a Dull Moment";** 1968; radio spots include 10 tracks ranging from 55 to 10 seconds; one-sided disc; white label depicting Dick Van Dyke leaning against a tommy-gun **30**

CR-2879: **"The Parent Trap";** 1961 film; one-sided LP; orange and white label; issued for the rerelease the film 1968 . . . . **30**

CR-2887/2888: **"The Horse in the Gray Flannel Suit"/"Winnie the Pooh and the Blustery Day";** 1968; side one has 6 tracks ranging from 55 to 10 seconds; side two has the first 4 tracks for "Horse", tracks 5 through 8 are for "Winnie" **30**

Famous American Star Series 1338-Re-1: **"The Horse in the Gray Flannel Suit";** 1968; includes interviews with Dean Jones, Diane Baker, Morey Amsterdam, Paul Winchell, and Sterling Holloway; blue vinyl LP **40**

CR-2889: **"Winnie the Pooh [and the Blustery Day]";** 1968; 14 radio spots; yellow and white, and green and white picture labels **30**

CR-2894: **"The Swiss Family Robinson";** 1960 film; one-sided LP; with green and white picture label; issued for the rerelease of the film in 1969 . . . . **30**

CR-2953: **"The Love Bug";** 1969; 18 radio spots; green and white label **30**

CR-2957: **"The Love Bug";** 1969; 7 radio spots; one-sided LP; typed label may mistakenly indicate the number as "2597" **30**

CR-2977: **"Peter Pan";** 1953 film; 5 tracks; one-sided LP; oversized green picture label featuring Peter Pan; issued for the rerelease film in 1969 . . . . **35**

CR-2995/2996: **"Rascal"/"Hang Your Hat on the Wind";** 1969; radio spots; side one has 5 spot promos and the soundtrack song "Summer Sweet" (composer:

Bobby Russell) 2:28; side two has two more spots and the songs "Hang Your Hat on the Wind" (composer/artist: Randy Sparks) 1:18; white label depicts Billy Mumy with a raccoon on his head and a dog by his side **30**

Garrison System Inc. 1546: **"Rascal";** 1969; 6 tracks include interviews with Steve Forrest and Billy Mumy; black label **30**

Disneyland, No Number **"[Rascal] 'Summer Sweet' ";** 1969; 3 tracks including song from film; one-sided 12" record; white label **25**

CR-3036: **"101 Dalmatians";** 1961 film; 6 radio spots; one-sided LP; green picture label; issued for the rerelease of film in 1969 .... **30**

CR-3043: **"Fantasia";** 1940 film; 4 radio spots; one-sided LP; green and white picture label; issued for the film's 1969 rerelease **45**

CR-3048: **"The Computer Wore Tennis Shoes";** 1969; radio spots; one-sided LP; blue and white picture label **25**

No Label 1762: **"The Computer Wore Tennis Shoes";** 1969; radio spots; 10" LP; blue label **30**

CR-3053: **"King of the Grizzlies";** 1970; 6 radio spots; one-sided LP; picture label **30**

CR-3055: **"The Swiss Family Robinson"** (1960 film)/**"101 Dalmatians"** (1961 film); 6 radio spots; one-sided LP; orange and white label; issued for the rerelease of these two films in 1969; see same number below ... **30**

CR-3055: **"In Search of the Castaways";** 1963 film; 13 radio spots; one-sided LP; issued for the rerelease fo the film in 1969; Note: same number as above **30**

Famous American Star Series 1475: **"Smith!";** 1969; includes interviews with Glenn Ford and Nancy Olson; clear yellow vinyl 12" LP; pale yellow label **40**

CR-3064: **"Sleeping Beauty";** 1959 film; 10 radio spots; one-sided LP; oversized white and green picture label; issued for the rerelease of the film 1970 .... **30**

CR-3070: **"The Boatniks";** 1970; 11 radio spots; white picture label ... **30**

CR-3082: **"The Aristocats";** 1970; 7 radio spots; one-sided LP; black and yellow picture label **30**

Garrison Systems Inc. 2079: **"The Aristocats";** includes interviews with Hermione Baddeley, Phil Harris, Sterling Holloway, and Eva Gabor 1970; 10" LP **40**

CR-3083: **"The Wild Country";** 1971; radio spots; one-sided LP; oversize orange label **25**

CR-3093: **"The Barefoot Executive";** 1971; radio spots; one-side LP; yellow and white picture label ... **30**

Famous American Stars Series 2203: **"The Barefoot Executive";** 1971; includes interviews with Wally Cox, Heather North, Joe Flynn, and Kurt Russell; 10" LP **30**

CR-3094: **"Pinocchio";** 1940 film; one-sided LP; orange and gray picture label of Pinocchio and Jiminy Cricket; issued for the rerelease of film the in 1971 ..... **40**

CR-3256: **"Scandalous John";** 1971; four radio spots and the song "Pastures Green" plus interview with McKuen; one-sided LP; orange picture label of Rod McKuen sitting of stool **25**

CR-3257: **"Scandalous John";** 1971; 11 radio spots; one-sided; orange picture label **25**

No Label 571-USA: **"Scandalous John";** 1971; interview with McKuen; green picture labels of Rod McKuen sitting of stool **35**

CR-3258: **"$1,000,000 Duck";** 1971; radio spots; one-sided LP; picture label **25**

[Garrison?] 2126: **"The Wild Country";** 1971; side one is interview with Vera Miles, and a "featurette"; side two has interviews with Clint Howard and Ron(ny) Howard; 10" 33-1/3 rpm; blue label **30**

[Garrison?] 2205/2206: **"$1,000,000 Duck";** 1971; includes 4 interviews with Dean Jones, Sandy Duncan, and Tony Roberts; 10" LP **40**

CR-3267: **"The Living Desert" (1953 film)/"The Vanishing Prairie" (1954 film);** 4 radio spots; one-sided LP; yellow picture label; apparently issued for the rerelease of these films 1971 . . . . **30**

CR-3270/3271: **"Bedknobs and Broomsticks";** 1971; radio spots; side one features 8 55-second spots with Angela Lansbury; side two features Lansbury in 5 other spots ranging from 25 to 10 seconds; yellow and white picture label **25**

Garrison Systems Radio Network WDP-100: **"Bedknobs and Broomsticks";** 1971; one hour radio special with script and cues; dramatic program in 4 acts, Pete Renoudet narrates; features Angela Lansbury, David Tomlinson, Sam Jaffe, and John Ericson; abstract cover with figures and title; yellow label **50**

WOND-2: **"Songs from Bedknobs and Broomsticks";** 4/1971; WLP; GF includes separate complete written music folios for each song . . **50**

CR-3276: **"Lady and the Tramp";** 1955 film; 8 radio spots; one-sided LP; issued for the rerelease of the film in 1971 . . . . **30**

[Garrison?] 2393/2394: **"Lady and the Tramp";** 1955 film; songs by Peggy Lee and Sonny Burke; one LP; probably issued for the rerelease of film in 1971 . . . . **30**

CR-3277: **"Song of the South";** 1946 film; 6 radio spots; one-sided LP; orange and white picture label; issued for rerelease of the film in 1972 . . . . **100**

CR-3281: **"The Biscuit Eater";** 1972; 10 radio spots; orange and white picture label **25**

CR-3298: **"Napoleon and Samantha";** 1972; 13 radio spots; one-sided LP; blue and white picture label **25**

CR-3300: **"Dumbo";** 1941 film; 10 radio spots; gray picture label; issued for the 1972 rerelease of the film **40**

CR-3360: **"The Sword in the Stone";** 1963 film; 10 radio spots; one-sided LP; oversized yellow picture label; issued for 1972 rerelease of the film **25**

No Label SMDS-200: **"Snowball Express";** 1972; radio spots and star quotes; LP; cardboard picture cover; picture labels in red and white/green and white **40**

Garrison System Radio Network 2599/2600: **"Napoleon and Samantha";** 1972; 10" LP; blue cover **25**

[Garrison?] DS-2687/2688: **"The World's Greatest Athlete";** 1972; side one includes 8 promo spots, the theme from the film, and the "Teeny-Weeny Theme" (Marvin Hamlisch); side two, track 1 features Tim Conway, tracks 2 through 5 consist of open-ended interviews with Jan Michael Vincent, John Amos, and Dayle Haddon; picture label; mono recording. **40**

Garrison Radio Network 872 USA: **"Run, Cougar Run";** 1972; 4 radio spots and one track by James Agar; orange picture label . . **25**

No Label DIS-72-1: **"Now You See Him, Now You Don't";** 1972; radio spots and interviews; cardboard cover with picture **40**

CR-3388: **"One Little Indian";** 1973; 8 radio spots; one-sided LP; picture label **25**

CR-3391: **"That Darn Cat";** 1965 film; 9 tracks ranging from 10 to 60 seconds; one-sided disc; orange label depicting that cat and four of the stars; released by Buena Vista Distributing Company; issued for 1973 rerelease of the film **25**

Buena Vista DS-2724/2725: **"Charley and the Angel"/"Cinderella";** 1973; side one, tracks 1 through 6 promotes the double billing of the two films (including the rerelease of Cinderella), tracks 7 through 10 promote "Charley"; side two has four tracks with open-ended interviews with Fred MacMurray, Cloris Leachman, and Harry Morgan; red and white picture label **25**

[Buena Vista] 2919: **"Robin Hood";** 1973; for the animated film; includes songs, interviews and radio spots; issued with a cardboard cartoon cover; green and white picture label **40**

Buena Vista 2940: **"Superdad";** 1973; radio interviews and spots **30**

[Walt Disney Productions?] Audiodisc A8333A: **"Summer Magic";** 1963 film; 6/17/1973; radio spots; green label with Mickey; probably issued for the 1973 rerelease of the film **25**

[Garrison?] DS-2812/2813: **"The Shaggy Dog";** 1959 film; 12 radio spots; red vinyl LP; picture label; numbering indicates LP was released in 1973 or later, possibly for a rerelease of the film **75**

CR-3406: **"Walt Disney's Alice in Wonderland";** 1951 film; 7" EP; "Youth Radio Spots", tracks 1-4: 50- , 30- , 20- , 10-second spots, tracks 4-7: 30-second tracks; art work label; issued for rerelease of the film in 1974 . . . . **50**

CR-3423: **"Old Yeller";** 1957 film; 6 radio spots; one-sided LP; yellow and white picture label; issued on the rerelease of the film in 1974 . . . . **30**

[Buena Vista] No Number: **"The Island at the Top of the World";** 1974; 8 radio spots; label shows Mickey at radio **25**

[Buena Vista] No Number: **"Herbie Rides Again";** 1974; 11 radio spots; label shows Mickey at radio **30**

[Buena Vista] No number: **"The Castaway Cowboy"/"The Absent-Minded Professor";** 1974; 8 radio spots; label shows Mickey at radio **30**

[Buena Vista] No Number: **"The Bears and I"/"The Shaggy Dog";** 1974; label shows Mickey at radio **30**

WOND-3: **"America Sings";** 7/1974; no booklet; WLP with red, white, and blue cover; this was a special promo for LP ST-3812 . . . . **35**

Buena Vista No Number **"Treasure Island" (1954)/"Dr. Syn, Alias the Scarecrow" (1975);** radio spots for 1975 coupling of these films; one-sided LP; white label features Mickey Mouse tuning in an old radio with the words "Radio Spots" coming out of radio **30**

[Buena Vista] No number **"Snow White and the Seven Dwarfs";** 1937 film; one-sided LP; white label shows Mickey at radio; issued for 1975 rerelease of the film **30**

[Buena Vista] No Number: **"The Strongest Man in the World";** 1975; 8 tracks of varying length; one-sided disc; white label features Mickey Mouse tuning in an old radio with the words "Radio Spots" coming out of radio **30**

[Buena Vista] No Number: **"One of Our Dinosaurs Is Missing";** 1975; one-sided LP; label shows Mickey at the radio **25**

[Buena Vista] No Number: **"The Apple Dumpling Gang";** 1975; 6 radio spots; one-sided LP; white label shows Mickey at radio **25**

[Buena Vista] No number: **"Best of Walt Disney's True-Life Adventures";** 1975; 4 radio spots; one-sided LP; label shows Mickey at radio **25**

[Buena Vista] No Number: **"Escape to Witch Mountain";** 1975; 3 radio spots; one-sided LP; label shows Mickey at radio **30**

[Buena Vista] No Number: **"Fantasia";** 1940 film; 4 radio spots; one-sided LP; label shows Mickey at radio; issued for one of the many rereleases of this film, probably 1977 . . . . **30**

CR-3473: **"Bambi";** 1942 film; radio spots, 6 tracks; one-sided disc; green picture label; issued for the rerelease of the film in 1977 . . . . . **40**

[Walt Disney Productions?] C-17941-B: **"The Fox and the Hound";** 1981 film; 7/12/1978; unknown contents; Mickey on label; this and the two records below are dated three years before the actual release of the film **30**

[Walt Disney Productions?] C-17942: **"The Fox and the Hound";** 1981 film; 7/12/1978; unknown contents; Mickey on label; this and the record above and below are dated three years before the actual release of the film **30**

[Walt Disney Productions?] C-17943: **"The Fox and the Hound";** 1981 film; 7/12/1978; unknown contents; Mickey on label; this and the two records above are dated three years before the actual release of the film **30**

Section B
Disney-Related 33-1/3 LPs on Non-Disney Labels

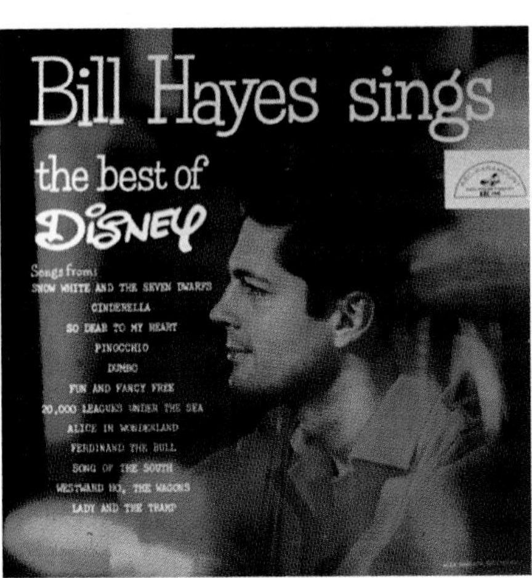

ABC-194: ***"Bill Hayes Sings the Best of Disney"***

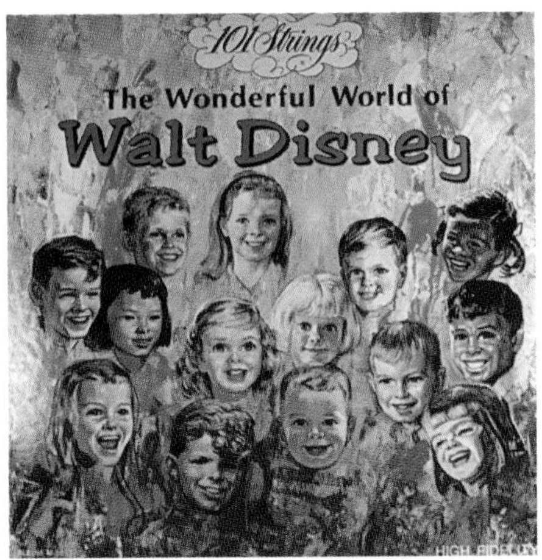

S-5057/M-5057: ***"The Wonderful World of Walt Disney"***

Note: Songs marked with * are non-Disney selections.

B1
A&M Records 33-1/3 rpm LPs

SP-3913: **"Good Morning, Vietnam";** 1987; various artists; Disney distributed film **15**

SP-3918: **"Stay Awake—Various Interpretations of Music from Vintage Disney Films";** 1988; unusually arranged album with various artists: Betty Carter, Bill Frisell & Wayne Horvitz, Garth Hudson, Los Lobos, Natalie Merchant, Michael Stipe, Mark Bingham and the Roches, Aaron Neville, Harry Nilsson, Ken Nordine, NBRQ, Sinead O'Connor, Buster Poindexter and the Banshees of Blue, Bonnie Raitt and Was (Not Was), Ringo Starr, Sun Ra and His Arkestra, Syd Straw, Yma Sumac, James Taylor, Suzanne Vega, and Tom Waits **20**

B2
ABC-Paramount 33-1/3 rpm LPs

ABC-194: **"Bill Hayes Sings the Best of Disney";** 1957; Bill Hayes and Don Costa Orchestra **45**

B3
Alshire (Budget Sound Inc.) 33-1/3 rpm LPs

S-5057/M-5057: **"The Wonderful World of Walt Disney";** 101 Strings
Mono 15
Stereo 20

B4
Atlantic 33-1/3 rpm LPs

81933-1: **"Beaches";** 1988; (DeLerue); Bette Midler vocals and one DeLerue track 15

B5
AVL Records 33-1/3 rpm LPs

AVL-6017: **"When You Wish Upon a Star";** 1977; Disney Jazz musical arrangements by the group Carnival 15

B6
Boardwalk 33-1/3 rpm LPs

SW-36880: **"Popeye";** 1980; Harry Nilsson 20

L-6960: "The Grasshopper and the Ants"/"Rusty in Orchestraville"

B7
Capitol 33-1/3 rpm LPs

The Capitol LP series was a repackage of its very popular 78 rpm singles and albums released under Disney license in the 1940s and early 1950s (See 78 rpm Section D3.6). All incorporate beautiful Disney cover artwork, and are "adaptions," i.e., studio tracks, often featuring members of the original movie cast and the Billy May Orchestra. Many are narrated by Don Wilson. There are many other non-Disney titles in the complete Capitol series incorporating many of the Warner Brothers characters as well.

HX-3061: **"The Three Little Pigs"/"Mr. Toad";** 10" LP 50

HX-3062: **"The Grasshopper and the Ants"/"Tales of Uncle Remus";** 10" LP 50

H-3069: **"Walt Disney Songs";** Happy Jack Smith; 10" LP 30

JAO-3252: **"Walt Disney's 'The Three Little Pigs' and Other Disney Selections";** 1961; songs by Happy Jack Smith; Don

Wilson narrates; Billy May Orchestra; A Capitol 'Record Reader' 30

J-3253: **"The Sorcerer's Apprentice"/"Pinocchio"/"Ferdin and the Bull"/"The Flying Mouse";** 1961; Don Wilson narrates; Mickey on cover 30

J-3256: **"Little Toot and Other Walt Disney Favorites";** 1961; includes: "The Country Cousin," "Little Hiawatha," "Elmer Elephant," "Three Orphan Kittens," and "Bongo the Circus Bear" 30

J-3260: **"Walt Disney's Lady and the Tramp"/"Ichabod and Mr. Toad"/"Rob Roy (The Highland Rogue)";** 1962; Basil Rathbone and Cast on Ichabod and Toad; original cast on "Lady and the Tramp" 40

J-3264: **"The Grasshopper and the Ants"** (Don Wilson & Original Cast)/**"Mickey Mouse's Birthday Party"** (Stan Freeberg); 1962 30

J-3265: **"Song of the South and Other Disney Productions"** features Johnny Mercer, Pied Pipers, James Baskett and original cast, Billy May Orchestra, Happy Jack Smith, and Frank De Vol Orchestra; includes "Dumbo," "Pinocchio," and "Snow White" . . 30

L-6956: **"Three Little Pigs"** (Don Wilson)/**"Sparky's Magic Piano"*;** 1975; Wonderland Records Series; Note: this and all "L" prefix records below were manufactured for "ZIV International" 20

L-6960: **"The Grasshopper and the Ants"** (Don Wilson & Original Cast)/**"Rusty in Orchestraville"*;** 1975; Wonderland Records Series 20

L-6986: **"Walt Disney's Tales of Uncle Remus"** (Original Cast)/**"Tickety Tock"*;** 1975; Wonderland Records Series 20

L-6987: **"Walt Disney's Little Toot"/"The Three Orphan Kittens"** (Don Wilson)/**"Bozo and the Birds"*;** 1975; Wonderland Records Series 20

L-8109: **"Mickey and the Beanstalk"** (Billy May Orch.)/**"Mickey Mouse's Birthday Party"** (Stan Freeberg); 1978; Wonderland Records Series 20

L-8110: **"The Sorcerer's Apprentice"** . . 20

SW-11704: **"Pete's Dragon";** 1977; (Hirshhorn); MST 20

B8
Casablanca 33-1/3 rpm LPs

NBLP-7196: **"Music from Star Trek and The Black Hole";** 1980; Meco 20

B9
Cathedral 33-1/3 rpm LPs

No Number: **"Tales of Jiminy Cricket";** c. early 1950s; STK; includes "Legend of Johnny Appleseed" (Cliff Edwards) and " 'R' Coon Dog" (Jimmy MacDonald); spaced tone cues throughout the stories ("automatic signal") indicating it was used in conjunction with either a book or slides; noted as "Series 3," there may have been others in this series; red vinyl; master numbers JC-159/520 35

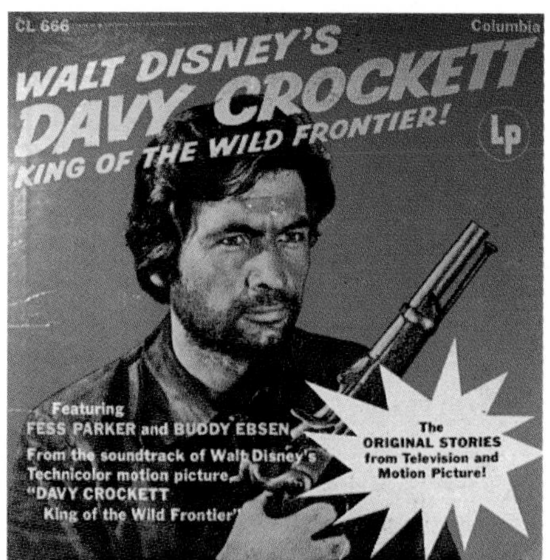

CL-666: "Davy Crockett—King of the Wild Frontier"

B10
CBS 33-1/3 rpm LPs

IM-37232: **"When You Wish Upon a Star: A Tribute to Walt Disney";** 1981; The Mormon Tabernacle Choir and Columbia Symphony Orchestra; also appeared with a listed number of "FM-37200" **15**

SM-37782: **"Tron";** 1982; (Carlos); MST **25**

B11
Cherry Lane Records 33-1/3 LPs

00301: **"Splash";** 1984; (Holdridge); Royal Philharmonic Orchestra; Digital recording; Daryl Hannah mermaid cover **25**

CL-672: "Songs from Walt Disney's Magic Kingdom"

B12
Columbia/Harmony 33-1/3 rpm LPs

CL-666: **"Davy Crockett—King of the Wild Frontier";** 1955; (Bruns); TVST; Fess Parker. This is the rare first edition release on an LP. (See also Columbia EPs and 78 rpm section.) Disney leased the master recordings to Columbia in late December, 1954. The lease expired on February 6, 1958 and Disney then released it on LP WDA-3602. . . . . **100**

CL-672: **"Songs from Walt Disney's Magic Kingdom";** 1955; Dottie Evans and Johnny Anderson and Merry Makers; Ray Carter conducts; GF cover opens from the left; first pressings have a back cover with six small color pictures of other Columbia albums **40**

Second pressings do not have back cover color pictures **30**

CL-1059/CS-8090: ***"Dave Digs Disney"***

CL-1059/CS-8090: **"Dave Digs Disney";** Dave Brubeck Quartet; Disney characters on cover
Mono; 1957 . . . . **35**
Stereo; 1959 . . . . **55**

CL-1966/CS-8766: **"The Dukes at Disneyland";** 1962; The Dukes of Dixieland at the 1962 Dixieland Jazz Festival at Disneyland
Mono **15**
Stereo **25**

CL-6332: **"The Vanishing Prairie";** 1954; (Smith); MST; 10" LP; contains 7:30 more music than the reissue on Buena Vista BV-3326 above; rare **80**

JL-8503: **"Bongo"/"Land of the Lost";** 10" LP; Dinah Shore **60**

(Columbia) Harmony HL-9503: **"All Time Favorite Walt Disney Songs";** 1959 . . . . **20**

CL-2366/CS-9166: **"Music from Mary Poppins, The Sound of Music, My Fair Lady and Other Great Movie Themes";** 1965; Ray Conniff Singers
Mono **10**
Stereo **15**

CRL-57094: ***"Lawrence Welk and His Champagne Music Play the Music of Walt Disney"***

B13
Coral 33-1/3 rpm LPs

CRL-57094: **"Lawrence Welk and His Champagne Music Play the Music of Walt Disney";** 1957 . . . . .**35**

B14
Decca 33-1/3 rpm LPs

DLP-5015: **"Snow White and the Seven Dwarfs";** 1949; Lyn Murray Orchestra; 10" LP **75**

DLP-5040: **"Alice in Wonderland";** STK; 10" LP; Ginger Rogers & Victor Young Orchestra; non-Disney music; Disney art cover . . . **40**

DL-5125: **"Treasure Island"** (Thomas Mitchell)/**"Alice in Wonderland";** 10" LP **75**

DL-5151: **"Song Hits from Pinocchio";** 1950; 10" LP; Cliff Edwards & Victor Young Orchestra; cover has Pinocchio in a circle; original price: $2.85 . . . . . **65**

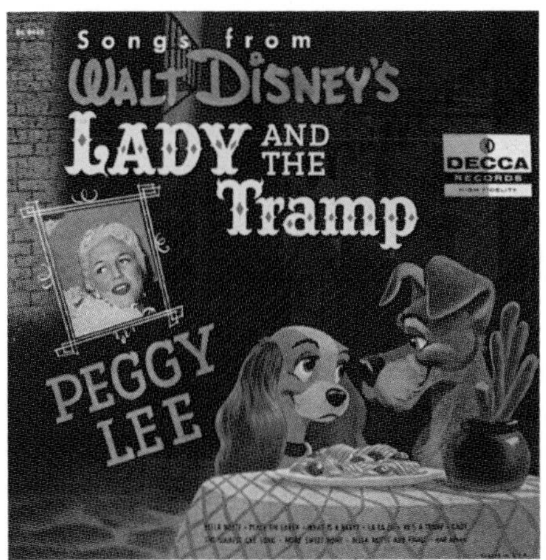

Songs from
Walt Disney's
Lady and the Tramp
Decca
Peggy Lee

DL-5557: ***"Lady and the Tramp"***

DL-8105: ***"Music from Disneyland"***

Also issued in a 12" LP; great cover featuring Pinocchio and the Blue Fairy **60**

DL-5557: **"Lady and the Tramp";** 1955; MST; 10" LP; Peggy Lee with Victor Young Orchestra and Oliver Wallace Orchestra **70**

DLP-6000: **"The Happy Prince"/"The Small One";** 10" LP; STK; Bing Crosby; non-Disney music; Disney art cover; original price: $2.75 . . . . **40**

DLP-6001: **"Ichabod—The Legend of Sleepy Hollow** (Bing Crosby) **and Rip Van Winkle"** (Walter Huston); 1949; 10" LP; original price: $3.35 . . . . **60**

DL-8105: **"Music from Disneyland";** 1955; Jack Pleis & Orchestra **40**

DL-8221: **"A Visit to Disneyland";** 1956; Fred Waring and the Pennsylvanians **40**

DL-8387/DL-78387: **"Song Hits from Walt Disney's Pinocchio"/"Wizard of Oz"*;** 1956; STK; Victor Young Orchestra, Judy Garland on "Wizard" side; see MCA picture-disc LP of this below

Mono **25**

Stereo; electronic stereo **15**

DL-8462: **"Lady and the Tramp";** 1957; MST; features Peggy Lee, Victor Young Orchestra, Oliver Wallace Orchestra, and Disney Studio Orchestra **100**

DL-9106: **"Ichabod and Mr. Toad"/"Rip Van Winkle";** 1961 . . **40**

DL-74283: **"The Happy Prince"** (Bing Crosby/Orson Welles)/**"The Small One"** (Bing Crosby); Victor Young score on "Prince" and Bernard Herrmann score on "Small One"; electronic stereo **20**

B15
Delos 33-1/3 rpm LPs

DEL/F 25412: **"Voices from the Hollywood Past"** (1975) Delos Film Buff Series; this album contains a 7:46 Terry Thomas interview with Walt Disney, and also includes interviews with Basil Rathbone, Buster Keaton, Harold Lloyd, and Stan Laurel **35**

B16
Design Records 33-1/3 rpm LPs

DLP-49: **"Musical Festival of Walt Disney Favorites";** c. 1957; The Cricketones; Warren Vincent conducts **20**

B17
Dunhill Records 33-1/3 rpm LPs

DS-50016: **"The Best of Walt Disney";** 1969; Trousdale Strings and the Dawn Chorale **20**

B18
Elektra/ Musician Records 33-1/3 rpm LPs

60806-1: **"Cocktail";** 1988; various artists **15**

60857-1: **"New York Stories";** 1988; various artists **15**

B19
EMI Records 33-1/3 rpm LPs

F1-93492: **"Pretty Woman";** 1990 . . .**15**

B20
Epic Records 33-1/3 rpm LPs

SE-40398: **"Ruthless People";** 1986; various artists **15**

B21
Everest Records 33-1/3 rpm LPs

CBR-1011: **"When You Wish Upon a Star: 16 Disney Favorites"** **20**

B22
Goodtime Jazz 33-1/3 rpm LPs— "Firehouse Five Plus Two"

The Dixieland group, "The Firehouse Five Plus Two," changed personnel over the years but it was comprised of Disney employees, animators, etc. Walt Kelly, who would later earn fame for his "Pogo" comic strip, was a very early member of the group before it began to record records. The group appeared on several of the Disney TV shows. It was led by Ward Kimball on trombone, and in its early incantation featured: Danny Alguire—trumpet; Frank Thomas—piano; Harper Goff—banjo; Ed Penner—tuba; Monte Mountofy—drums; George Probert—clarinet/alto sax; and Eddie Forrest. It finally disbanded in 1971. "L-1 to L-26" below are 10" mono LPs; "L-12000" records are 12" mono; and "L-10000" records are 12" stereo.

L-1: **"Firehouse Five Plus Two Vol. 1";** 1953; 10" LP **50**

L-2: **"Firehouse Five Plus Two Vol. 2";** 1953; 10" LP **50**

L-6: **"Firehouse Five Plus Two Vol. 3";** 1953; 10" LP **50**

L-16: **"Firehouse Five Plus Two Vol. 4";**1953; 10" LP **50**

L-23: **"Firehouse Five Plus Two Goes South! Vol. 5";** 1954; 10" LP **50**

L-12010: **"Firehouse Five Plus Two Vol. 1"**; 1955 . . . . **30**

L-12011: **"Firehouse Five Plus Two Vol. 2"**; 1955 . . . . **30**

L-12013: **"Firehouse Five Plus Two Vol. 3"**; 1955 . . . . **30**

L-12014: **"Firehouse Five Plus Two Plays for Lovers"**; 1955 . . . . **30**

L-12018: **"Firehouse Five Plus Two Goes South!"**; 1955 . . . . **30**

L-12028: **"Firehouse Five Plus Two Goes to Sea"**; 1956 . . . . **30**

L-12038: **"Firehouse Five Plus Two Crashes a Party"**; 1957 . . . . **30**

L-12040: **"Firehouse Five Plus Two Dixieland Favorites"**; 1957 . . . . . . **30**

L-12044: **"Firehouse Five Plus Two Around the World"**; 1958 . . . . **30**

L-12049: **"Firehouse Five Plus Two at Disneyland"**; 1958 . . . . **30**

L-12052: **"Firehouse Five Plus Two Goes to a Fire"**; 1959 . . . . **25**

L-12054: **"Firehouse Five Plus Two Twenty Years Later"**; 1959 . . . . . . **25**

S-10028: **"Firehouse Five Plus Two Goes to Sea"**; 1960 . . . . **25**

S-10038: **"Firehouse Five Plus Two Crashes a Party"**; 1960 . . . . **25**

S-10040: **"Firehouse Five Plus Two Dixieland Favorites"**; 1960 . . . . . . **25**

S-10044: **"Firehouse Five Plus Two Around the World"**; 1960 . . . . **25**

S-10049: **"Firehouse Five Plus Two at Disneyland"**; 1960 . . . . **25**

S-10052: **"Firehouse Five Plus Two Goes to a Fire"**; 1960 . . . . **25**

S-10054: **"Firehouse Five Plus Two Twenty Years Later"**; 1960 . . . . . . **25**

B23
Hamilton Records 33-1/3 rpm LPs

HLP-152/HLP-12152: **"Mary Poppins: Songs from the Walt Disney Production"**; c. 1965; Lawrence Welk Singers
Mono **15**
Stereo **20**

B24
Hanna-Barbera 33-1/3 rpm LPs

HLP-2035: **"Fred Flintstone and Barney Rubble in 'Songs from Mary Poppins' "**; 1965 . . . . **40**

B25
Happy Time 33-1/3 rpm LPs

HT-1004: **"Songs from Walt Disney and Others"** **20**

HT-1022: **"Davy Crockett and Other Western Favorites"** **40**

HT-1034: **"Songs from Walt Disney's Mary Poppins"** **20**

HT-1038: **"Songs from Walt Disney's Pinocchio"** **20**

HY-1039: **"Songs from Snow White and the Seven Dwarfs"** **20**

HT-1055: **"More Walt Disney Favorites and Others"** **20**

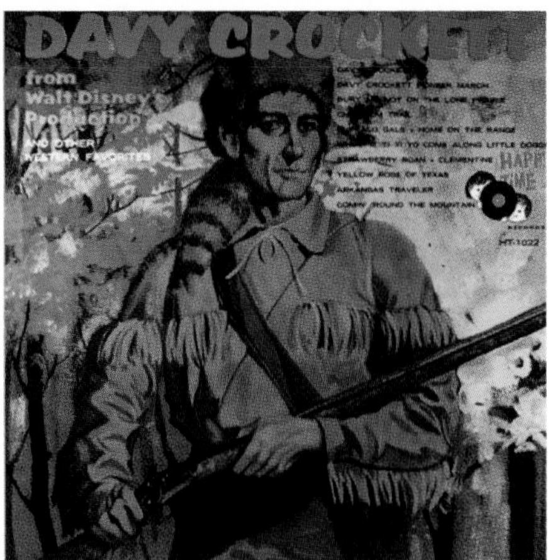

HT-1022: "Davy Crockett and Other Western Favorites"

B26

International Award 33-1/3 rpm LPs

KIA-1004: **"Walt Disney Favorites and Others"** **20**

B27

Intrada 33-1/3 rpm LPs

RVF-6004: **"Night Crossing";** 1987; (Goldsmith) **25**

B28

JMI 33-1/3 rpm LPs

JMI-4005: **"Nashville Coyote";** 1973; (Baker); Walter Forbes sings **45**

B29

Kapp 33-1/3 rpm LPs

KL-1419/KS-3419: **"Songs from Mary Poppins and Other Favorites";** The Do-Re-Mi Children's Chorus with Mary Martin
Mono **15**
Stereo **20**

B30

Label X 45 rpm "LP"

LXSE 2-001: **"Dragonslayer";** 1983; (North); "audiophile" recording box-set contains an hour of music on two "12" 45 rpm records; 2,500 copies were produced; rare; Note: it is included in the LP section because of its 12" size (the average buyer may mistakenly identify it as a 33-1/3 rpm LP set) . . **150**

B31

MGM (Leo the Lion) 33-1/3 rpm LPs

CH-515: **"Story of Snow White and the Seven Dwarfs and Other Walt Disney Songs";** The MGM Players and the Prides of Leo **30**

CH-1021: **"Story of Snow White and the Seven Dwarfs and Other Walt Disney Songs";** The MGM Players and the Prides of Leo; formerly MGM CH-515 . . . . **20**

CH-1022: **"Story and Songs of Pinocchio";** The MGM Players and the Prides of Leo **25**

*MCAP-13301: "Song Hits from Walt Disney's Pinocchio"/"The Musical Score of the Wizard of Oz"**

OV-5000: "The Magical Music of Walt Disney: 50 Years of Original Motion Picture Soundtracks"

B32
MCA 33-1/3 rpm LPs

MCA-6160: **"Down and Out in Beverly Hills";** (Summers); MST; various artists **20**

MCA-6189: **"The Color of Money";** (Robertson); MST; various artists . . **20**

MCA-6244: **"The Disney Album";** 1988; Barbara Cook; Disney characters on cover; An "MCA Classics" release **20**

MCAP-13301: **"Song Hits from Walt Disney's Pinocchio"/"The Musical Score of the Wizard of Oz"*;** 1983; features Ken Darby Singers, Cliff Edwards, The Kings Men, Julietta Novis, and Victor Young Orchestra; Judy Garland and Victor Young Orchestra on "Wizard" side; picture disc edition of the older Decca LP DL-8387 above **50**

B33
Monument 33-1/3 rpm LPs

MLP-8034/SLP-18034: **"The Swingers' Guide to Mary Poppins";** The Tupper Saussy Quartet with Charlie McCoy

Mono **15**

Stereo **20**

B34
Ovation 33-1/3 rpm LPs

OV-5000: **"The Magical Music of Walt Disney: 50 Years of Original Motion Picture Soundtracks";** 1978; 4 LP box set; 52-page book; records numbered 5000-1, -2, -3, -4 . . . . **60**

1P-6887: **"Mickey Mouse's 50th";** 1978; Side one includes "I Grew Up on Mickey Mouse" and "The Mickey Mouse Club March"; side

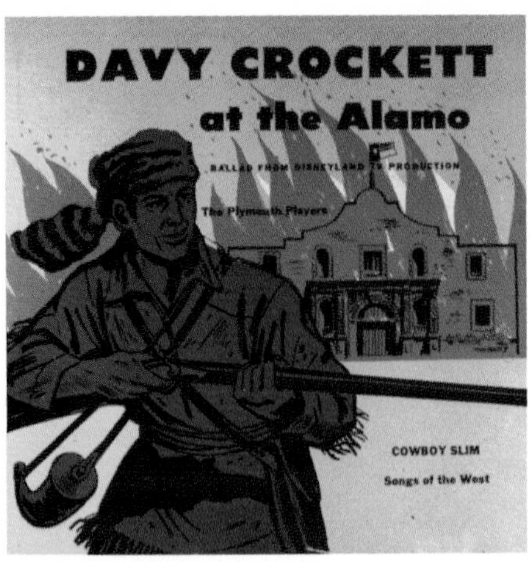

M-763: "Davy Crockett at the Alamo"/"Songs of the West"

two includes Medley-Suite from Bedknobs and Broomsticks **25**

B35
Palace 33-1/3 rpm LPs

M-763: **"Davy Crockett at the Alamo"/"Songs of the West";** c. 1955; features Cowboy Slim, Scotty MacGregor, and the Plymouth Players; includes "Ballad of Davy Crockett," story, and western songs; line-drawn yellow cover shows Davy together with the Alamo in flames **40**

M-764: **"Davy Crockett in Congress";** c. 1955; Cowboy Slim and The Plymouth Players; includes "Ballad of Davy Crockett," story, and western songs; line-drawn yellow cover shows Davy in front of the Capitol; also appears on a Plymouth LP #P12-133 with the same cover picture except the cover is in red, white, and blue ... **40**

B36
Peter Pan 33-1/3 rpm LPs

8053: **"Peter Pan Players Present The Best of Walt Disney";** 1972 .. **20**

B37
Pickwick/Pickwick International/ Mr. Pickwick 33-1/3 rpm LPs

PDA-029: **"Walt Disney Original Soundtrack Parade Vol. 1";** two LP set **25**

PDA-030: **"Walt Disney Original Soundtrack Parade Vol. 2";** two LP set **25**

50 DA-318: **"50 Playtime Walt Disney Favorites";** two LP set **25**

SHM-938: **"Walt Disney's Mary Poppins";** c. 1965 .... **15**

HM-969: **"Walt Disney's Pinocchio"** **20**

SHM-3428: **"Barbara Cook—The Disney Album"** **15**

PLD-8010: **"40 Walt Disney Originals";** 1978; two LP set **20**

Mr. Pickwick SPC-5107: **"Pinocchio";** 1974; non-Disney cover; stereo **15**

Mr. Pickwick SPC-5117: **"Snow White and the Seven Dwarfs";** 1974; non-Disney cover **15**

Mr. Pickwick SPC-5119: **"15 Walt Disney Favorites";** 1974; electronic stereo **10**

B38
Polydor
33-1/3 rpm LPs

PD-6021: **"Salute to Disney";** 1973; Arthur Fiedler & the Boston Pops . . 25

B39
Premier Records Ltd.
33-1/3 rpm LPs

CBR-1011: **"When You Wish Upon a Star: 16 Disney Favorites";** 1984; appears to be the same LP as Everest LP above 15

B40
RCA 33-1/3 rpm LPs

LY-1: **"Treasure Island"/"Alice in Wonderland";** 1951; STK; 10" LP; "Treasure" side features Bobby Driscoll and Cast, non-Disney Music by Henri Rene; "Alice" side features Kathryn Beaumont, Ed Wynn, Jerry Colonna, and Sterling Holloway; original cost: $4.00 75

COP/CSO-11: **"Mary Poppins"** MST; 1964; GF cover with same graphics as the Buena Vista 4026 release; issued by the RCA Record Club
Mono 15
Stereo 25

RCA/NKS 2-76: **"The Wonderful Fantasy of Walt Disney";** 1976; two LP set; features Joe Reisman Orchestra, Rosemary Rice Children's Chorus, Fontane Sisters, Richard Wolfe Children's Chorus, Ethel Ennis, Fess Parker, Living Voices, and Bunny Berrigan Orchestra with Gail Reese; RCA Records Educational Department; electronic stereo 25

LPM-1119: ***"Walt Disney Song Carousel"***

RCA/NKS 3-76: **"Pinocchio"** (Cliff Edwards)/**"Peter and the Wolf"** (Sterling Holloway); 1976; RCA Records Educational Department . . 20

DEL-1-0140: **"The Aristocats and Other Favorite Songs About Cats";** 1976; Richard Wolfe Children's Chorus; RCA Educational Records 20

DEL-1-1068: **"Walt Disney's Peter Pan"/"Alice in Wonderland";** 1976; Joe Reisman Orchestra and Chorus; RCA Educational Records . . 20

DPL-2-0165(e): **"The Wonderful Fantasy of Walt Disney";** 1976; STK; two LP set; features Joe Reisman Orchestra, Rosemary Rice Children's Chorus, Fontane Sisters, Richard Wolfe Children's Chorus, Ethel Ennis, Fess Parker, Living Voices, and Bunny Berrigan Orchestra with Gail Reese; non-GF cover with front and back cover Disney character montage; produced for Candelite Music Inc.; electronic stereo 25

LPM-1119: **"Walt Disney Song Carousel";** 1955; Joe Reisman Orchestra; front cover opens in the center to reveal a GF drawing of Disneyland castle and cartoon characters **35**

LPM-3101: **"Song Hits from Peter Pan and Hans Christian Anderson";** Hugo Winterhalter & Orchestra; 10" LP **45**

AYL1-4449(e): **"Cinderella"** **15**

AYL1-4450(e): **"Make Mine Music"/"Pinocchio"/"Peter and the Wolf";** 1983; Walt Disney Song Carousel **15**

8533-1-R: **"Heartbreak Hotel";** 1988; (Delerue); various artists; released by Disney **15**

R220262: **"Snow White and the Seven Dwarfs"/"Peter and the Wolf"/"Pinocchio"/"Long-Name-No-Can-Say"*;** 1976; two LP set; features Dennis Day, Ilene Woods, Sterling Holloway, and Cliff Edwards. This "R" prefix record, and those below were RCA "Music Service" records which had a generic LP cover with a label hole in it. Probably releases for disc jockies. They were recycled versions of the licensed studio tracks RCA had earlier released on RCA, Camden, and Bluebird. **20**

R223234: **"Walt Disney's Bambi"/"The Wizard of Oz"*;** 1976; two LP set; Shirley Temple and The Tootlepiper's Zoo **20**

R224032: **"Walt Disney's Peter Pan"/"Alice in Wonderland"/"Johnny Appleseed"/"Pecos Bill";** 1976; two LP set; features Ken Darby Singers, Joe Reisman Orchestra, Roy Rogers, and Sons of the Pioneers **25**

R233565: **"Walt Disney's Dumbo"/"The Tootlepiper's Circus"/"Walt Disney's Bambi"/"20,000 Leagues Under the Sea";** 1976; two LP set **20**

B41
RCA
"Bluebird" Children's 33-1/3 rpm LPs

These were budget label LP issues of previous RCA 78 rpm and 45 rpm recordings.

RCA LBY-1009: **"Peter Pan"/"Alice In Wonderland";** 1958; original cast **40**

RCA LBY-1012: **"Bambi"** (Shirley Temple)**/"The Tootlepiper's Zoo";** 1958 . . . . **40**

RCA LBY-1026: **"Dumbo"** (Shirley Temple)**/"The Tootlepiper's Circus";** 1959 . . . . **40**

RCA LBY-1044: **"Snow White and the Seven Dwarfs";** Dennis Day . . **40**

RCA LBY-6700: **"The Walt Disney Omnibus";** five LP set in a hard cardboard, slip-in box; beautiful maroon cover features a punch-out set of 10 Disney characters; high quality, inner 24-page, slip-in booklet duplicates the cover figures' position; contains all of the RCA/Bluebird/Camden studio tracks of the Disney films: *Bambi, Peter and the Wolf, Pinocchio, Cinderella, Dumbo, 20,000 Leagues Under the Sea, Johnny Appleseed, Alice in Wonderland,*

Snow White and the Seven Dwarfs, and *Peter Pan*; deduct $75 if cover characters are punched out, but included; deduct $100 if missing any of the punch-out cover characters; rare **175**

B42
RCA-CAMDEN 33-1/3 rpm LPs

These were 1960s budget LP issues of recordings previously available in the RCA 78 rpm and 45 rpm equivalents. The "stereo" pressings with the "(e)" suffix are electronic, fake stereo.

CAL-881/CAS-881: **"Mary Poppins"**; 1965; STK; The Living Voices
Mono **10**
Stereo **20**

ACL1-0379: **"Mary Poppins"**; 1973; STK; Living Voices; reissue of CAL-881 above **10**

CAL-1009/CAS-1009(e): **"Walt Disney's Peter Pan and Alice in Wonderland"**; 1960; STK; features Bobby Driscoll, Kathryn Beaumont, and Ed Wynn
Mono **25**
Stereo **10**

CAL-1012/CAS-1012(e): **"Walt Disney's Bambi"/"The Tootlepiper's Zoo";** 1962; STK; Shirley Temple
Mono **25**
Stereo **10**

CAL-1026/CAS-1026(e): **"Dumbo"** (Shirley Temple)**/"The Tootlepiper's Circus";** 1959
Mono **25**
Stereo **10**

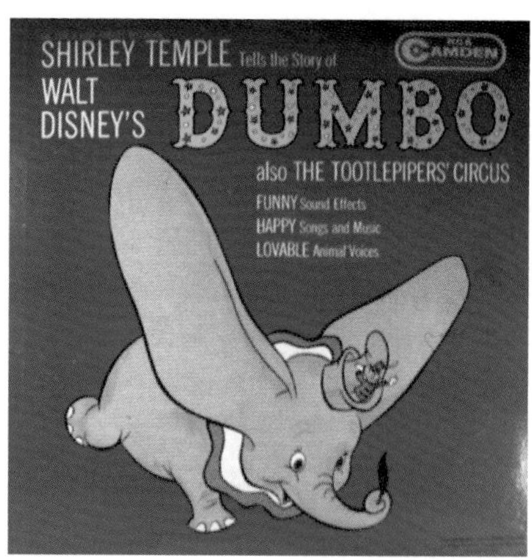

CAL-1026/CAS-1026(e): ***"Dumbo"***

CAL-1044/CAS-1044(e): **"Walt Disney's Snow White and the Seven Dwarfs"** (Dennis Day and Ilene Woods)**/"Long-Name-No-Can-Say"*/"Nicki Nicki Tembo" (A Chinese Fable)*;** 1960; STK; Paul Wing performs on all songs
Mono **25**
Stereo **10**

CAL-1054/CAS-1054(e): **"Johnny Appleseed"** (Dennis Day)**/"Pecos Bill"** (Roy Rogers and The Sons of the Pioneers); 1964; STK
Mono **25**
Stereo **10**

CAL-1057/CAS-1057(e): **"Cinderella"** (Leyden)**/"20,000 Leagues Under the Sea"** (Leyden); 1965; STK; "Cinderella" cast: Ilene Wood, James MacDonald, Eleanor Audley, Helene Stanley, Lucille Bliss, Verna Felton, John Brown, Clarence Nash, and Verne Smith narrates; "20,000" cast: William Redfield, Ian Martin, Bernard Lenrow, Sandy Fussell, and Arthur Anderson; songs by William Clauson

Mono 25

Stereo 10

CAL-1067/CAS-1067(e): **"Walt Disney's Pinocchio"** (Cliff Edwards)/**"Peter and the Wolf"** (Sterling Holloway); 1965; STK

Mono 25

Stereo 10

CAL-1085/CAS-1085(e): **"Cinderella";** 1966; STK; Paul Tripp narrates

Mono 25

Stereo 10

CAL-1087/CAS-1087(e): **"The Big Bad Wolf";** 1966; STK; Paul Tripp narrates

Mono 25

Stereo 10

CAL-1102/CAS-1102: **"Songs from Walt Disney's The Jungle Book";** 1968; Charles Grean conducts

Mono 10

Stereo 25

CAL-2146/CAS-2146: **"Music from 'The Happiest Millionaire' ";** 1967; The Living Voices

Mono 10

Stereo 20

CXS-9014: **"The Wonderful Fantasy of Walt Disney";** 1972; STK; two LP set; features Joe Reisman Orchestra, Rosemary Rice Children's Chorus, Fontane Sisters, Richard Wolfe Children's Chorus, Ethel Ennis, Fess Parker, Living Voices, and Bunny Berrigan Orchestra with Gail Reese; GF; electronic stereo 20

B43
Reprise 33-1/3 rpm LPs

R-6141/RS-6141: **"Duke Ellington Plays Walt Disney's 'Mary Poppins' ";** STK; cover photo of the rooftop dance scene from film

Mono 15

Stereo 25

B44
Rhino Records 33-1/3 rpm LPs

RNDF-204: **"Annette's Beach Party";** 1984; MST; cover reproduces BV-3316 20

RNDF-205: **"Annette Muscle Beach Party";** 1984; MST; cover reproduces BV-3314 20

RNDF-206: **"The Best of Annette";** 1984; Annette Funicello hits; cover reproduces a smaller version of the BV-3320 "On Campus" album 20

RNLP-702: **"The Best of Annette";** 1984; Annette Funicello hits; picture disc 50

B45
Richmond (London) 33-1/3 rpm LPs

RPS-39005: **"Disney Meets the Wizard";** STK; Roger Ericson and His Men; seven Disney songs and five from *The Wizard of Oz*; "Percussive Stereo Series" 20

B46
Ronco 33-1/3 rpm LPs

R2100: **"Walt Disney's Greatest Hits—24 Original Motion Picture Themes";** 1976; two LP set; includes 8 cut-out pictures and song lyrics; Canadian pressing is CSPS-1068
With pictures un-cut **30**
Has pictures, but cut **20**
LPs but no pictures **10**

B47
Royale 33-1/3 rpm LPs

LP81: **"Alice in Wonderland";** 10" LP; Bob Dale and Nadia Dore **30**

B48
Sears Roebuck 33-1/3 rpm LPs

KIA-1004: **"Songs from Walt Disney and Others"** **20**

B49
Somerset 33-1/3 rpm LPs

P-23100: **"Favorite Songs from Walt Disney's Mary Poppins";** c. 1965; The Sound Stage Chorus **20**

B50
Sonic Atmospheres 33-1/3 rpm LPs

S-113: **"Return to Oz";** 1985; (Shire); MST; nicely produced album with audiophile sound **40**

S-113: "Return to Oz"

B51
Til Records 33-1/3 rpm LPs

Til 488: **"It's a Small World: Songs of Walt Disney: Vol. 1";** 1977; Terrytowne Players **15**

Til 502: **"It's a Small World: Songs of Walt Disney: Vol. 2";** 1977; Terrytowne Players **15**

B52
Varese Sarabande 33-1/3 rpm LPs

VS-5219: **"Three Fugitives";** 1989; (McHugh); MST **20**

STV-81253: **"The Black Cauldron";** 1985; (E. Bernstein); MST **30**

704.510: **"Return to Snowy River, Part II";** 1988; (Rowland) **20**

704.610: **"D.O.A.";** 1988; (Jankel); MST **20**

B53
VeeJay 33-1/3 rpm LPs

VJ-1110/SR-1110: **"My Favorite Songs from Mary Poppins and Other Songs to Delight";** Ray Walston and His Favorite Children's Chorus; Walston was the star of the TV program, "My Favorite Martian"
Mono **15**
Stereo **25**

B54
Waldorf Music Hall 33-1/3 rpm LPs

MH-33-137: **"Songs from Walt Disney Films (& Others)";** 10" LP; comes in both yellow and red covers with picture of what appears to be either Davy Crockett or Daniel Boone on cover **40**

B55
Windham Hill 33-1/3 rpm LPs

WH-1039: **"Country";** 1984; (Gross); MST **20**

WH-1041: **"Film Music";** 1985; (Isham); includes music from Disney film *Never Cry Wolf*; also *Mrs. Soffer*, and *The Times of Harvey Milk* **20**

B56
Win Mil 33-1/3 rpm LPs

206: **"Lowery [Organ] Presents Disney Magic";** various Disney music played on organ; cover is a picture of Disneyland **30**

B57
Wonderland 33-1/3 rpm LPs[1]

LP-77: **"Pinocchio";** 1974; The Sandpipers; John Allen narrates . . . **20**

LP-107: **"Favorite Songs from Walt Disney Motion Picture Hits";** 1974; Mitch Miller and the Sandpipers **20**

B58
Wyncote 33-1/3 rpm LPs

W-9049/SW-9049: **"Mary Poppins";** STK; Cheltenham Orchestra and Chorus
Mono **10**
Stereo **15**

W-9198/SW-9198: **"A Tribute to Walt Disney";** Hollywood Studio Orchestra; mono version is attributed to the Cheltenham Orchestra and Chorus
Mono **10**
Stereo **20**

---

[1] This is a different "Wonderland" Records than that on the Capitol LPs above. This series was produced by A.A. Records, Inc., which controlled the "Little Golden" recording rights at the time. See footnote 9 in Section D below.

Section C
Extended-Play (EP) 7" Albums—45 rpm and 33-1/3 rpm

Extended Play (EP) records were hybrids, half-way between the LPs and the standard 45 rpm records. Generally, they were 7" 45 rpm records, though as you will see below, some 10" 78 rpm EPs were produced also. The narrower groove allowed more than two songs to be reproduced on the disc—usually four songs. Some later EPs were produced in 33-1/3 rpm editions as well, allowing up to six songs per disc. They usually had cardboard covers reproducing the original artwork as also appeared on the LP edition. Often a complete LP would be reproduced in multi-volume EP sets, either as fold-out albums or in separate covers. Sometimes just a few songs, usually the "hits" from the LP, would be released as an EP.

Generally, pop/rock EPs were phased out by other record companies in the late 1950s. After issuing several records in its "DEP" series, Disney also became convinced that the "LP" was to be the "more convenient" wave of the future for more popular and serious music in its line. However, Disney continued to release children-oriented EPs well into the 1980s, many with booklets. As with the other series, the early releases are the more collectible.

Please take note that Disneyland and Buena Vista later had some 7" 33-1/3 rpm records in the "500" (non-"LLP" series), "600," "700," and "800" numbered record series, which are included in the 45 rpm section below (see Section "E") to keep them numerically correct for ease of use and review in this guide. These special EPs are noted as such in the individual listings in those series.

Note: Songs marked with * are non-Disney selections.

C1
Disneyland Label "STEP-1000/2000" EPs

E-1001: **"Player Piano Music";** 1955; was used as a test project by Disney when it was considering entering the record field[1] **80**

STEP-1002: **"The Little Lame Lamb";** 1956; Mary Martin; two EP set

---

[1] There are two "orphan" EPs. They are noted here as they were listed in the Archives files but not available for viewing or further information:

OEP-77: **"Four Songs from Song of the South";** 1956

OEP-78 **"Railroadin' Man"/"Sons of Old Aunt Dinah"/"Autumn Way"/"Summer Love";** 1956; all from *The Great Locomotive Chase*

These songs are likely the same in sequence as were issued in Disney's early "F" Series 45 rpm/78 rpm at "F-034" and "F-035" and "F-037" and "F-038" (See Section E1.2 below). The songs themselves were mentioned in an early 1956 Disney memo as scheduled for production that year. It is possible that the record prefixes were actually "DEP" and not "OEP" as was typed on Archives' file cards. Guide values for each: $50.

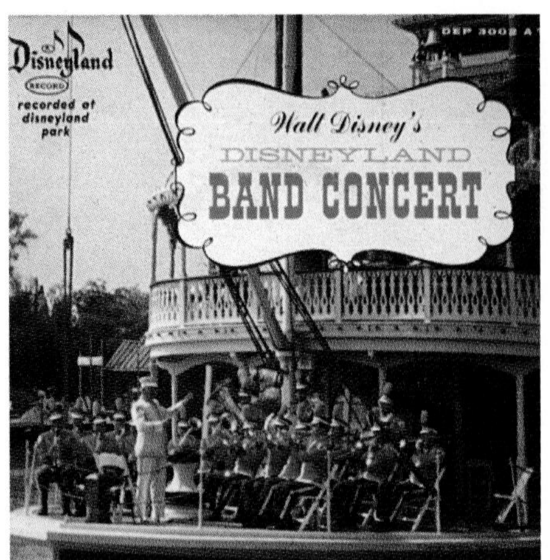

DEP-3002A: "Disneyland Band Concert"

with heavy paper booklet; purple label **40**

STEP-1003: **"Walt Disney's Christmas Concert";** 1957; The All-Mouse Symphony; purple label **30**

STEP 2001A: **"Cinderella";** Jiminy Cricket narrates; was listed in Archives, but no copy was available for inspection **80**

STEP-2002A (and STEP-1002): **"The Little Lame Lamb";** two EP set; Mary Martin; with twelve-page booklet; original cost: .98¢ **50**

C2
Disneyland Label "DEP" 3000 Series EPs

Any of the original Disneyland "DEP" Series EPs are difficult to find in nice condition. When they appear at record shows, flea markets and the like, they sell quickly. Original cost: .98¢

3001: (*Not issued*)

DEP-3002A: **"Disneyland Band Concert";** 1956; Vesey Walker; yellow label **25**

3003-3009: (*Not issued*)

DEP-3010: **"Darlene of the Teens" (Part I)";** 1957; Darlene Gillespie; this EP and the two below use the yellow cover showing Darlene at a microphone as was used on the LP WDL-3010 . . . . **50**

DEP-3010: **"Darlene of the Teens (Part II)";** 1957; Darlene Gillespie **50**

DEP-3010: **"Darlene of the Teens (Part III)";** 1957; Darlene Gillespie **50**

DEP-3011A: **"Tutti's Trumpets"** (Camarata) **20**

3012: (*Not issued*)

DEP-3013A: **"Dixieland at Disneyland";** The Strawhatters **25**

3014-3015: (*Not issued*)

DEP-3016A: **"Peter and the Wolf";** MST; Sterling Holloway narrates **30**

DEP-3016B: **"The Sorcerer's Apprentice";** MST; from Fantasia; Sterling Holloway narrates **50**

C3
Buena Vista "3300" EPs

BVEP-3301A: **"Annette (Lonely Guitar + 3)";** 1959; Annette; includes "Jo-Jo, the Dog-faced Boy," "Love Me Forever," "My Heart Became of Age," and "Lonely Guitar"; black label with the pink cover as used on WDL-3301; rare **75**

BVEP-3302A: **"Rex Allen (4 Songs)";** 1959; includes the songs "No One to Cry To," "Gotta Travel On," Streets of Laredo," and "Bronco Boogie"; P/S; green label; original price: .98¢ **40**

C4
Disneyland Label "DEP" 3600 Series

Both of these EPs come in brilliant, colorful, paper covers with a cloth-like feel and purple labels. Original cost: .98¢

DEP-3601A: **"Presenting Señor Zorro"/"Zorro Frees the Indians";** 2/1958; P/S **40**

DEP-3601B: **"Zorro and the Ghost"/"Zorro's Daring Rescue";** 2/1958; P/S **40**

C5
The Disneyland Label "DEP" 3900 Series EPs

Original cost: .98¢

3901: *(Not issued)*

DEP-3902A: **"Perri (Four Songs)";** 3/1958; purple label; cover same as ST-3902 .... **30**

3903-3909: *(Not issued)*

DEP-3910A: **"Peter Pan (Four Songs)";** 7/1958 .... **30**

C6
Disneyland Label "DEP" 4000 Series LPs

These are highly sought after as they reproduce the original beautiful "WDL-4000" LP animated covers in a smaller format. All of the animated cover films, except "Alice in Wonderland" also include a back cover with six brilliant reproductions of the other animated film covers. Original cost: .98¢

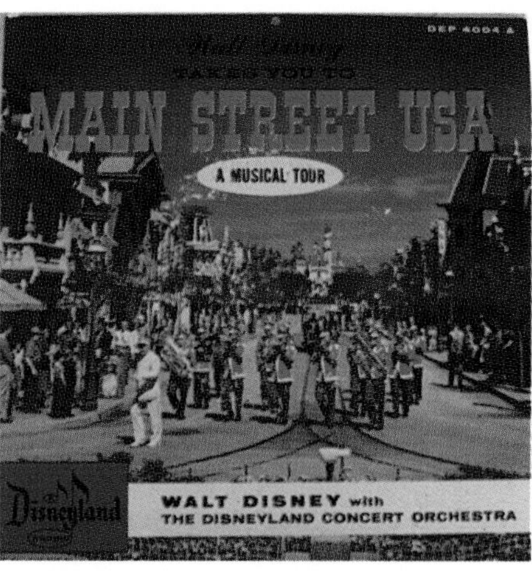

DEP-4004A: ***"Walt Disney Takes You to Main Street USA"***

DEP-4001A: **"Song of the South";** 1956; MST; same cover as WDL-4001 .... **90**

DEP-4002A: **"Pinocchio";** 5/14/1956; MST; same cover as WDL-4002 .... **50**

DEP-4003A: *(Not issued)*

DEP-4004A: **"Walt Disney Takes You to Main Street USA";** 1956 .. **45**

DEP-4004B: **"Walt Disney Takes You to Adventureland";** 1956 .... **45**

DEP-4004C: **"Walt Disney Takes You to Frontierland";** 1956 ...... **45**

DEP-4004D: **"Walt Disney Takes You to Tomorrowland";** 1956 .... **45**

RD-4004: **"A Rocket Trip to the Moon";** 1958; taken from the Tomorrowland sequence from LP WDL-4004 "Walt Disney Takes You to Disneyland"; same

DEP-4004D: ***"Walt Disney Takes You to Tomorrowland"***

WD-4: ***"Main Street Electrical Parade"***

contents as DEP-4004D but with different cover, depicting an adult and child astronaut looking out of a spaceship window at the moon **30**

DEP-4004E: **"Walt Disney Takes You to Fantasyland";** 1956 . . . . . . **45**

DEP-4005A: **"Snow White and the Seven Dwarfs";** 1956; MST; same cover as WDL-4005 . . . . **50**

DEP-4006A: (*Not issued*)

DEP-4007A: **"Cinderella";** 1956; MST; same cover as WDL-4007 . . **50**

DEP-4008A: (*Not issued*)

DEP-4009A: (*Not issued*)

DEP-4010A: **"Bambi";** 1957; MST; same cover as WDL-4010 . . . . **50**

DEP-4011A: (*Not issued*)

DEP-4012A: (*Not issued*)

DEP-4013A: **"Dumbo";** 1957; MST; has same cover as WDL-4013 . . . . **50**

DEP-4014A: (*Not issued*)

DEP-4015A: **"Alice in Wonderland";** 1958; has same cover as rare WDL-4015 . . . . **140**

DEP-4016A: **"Hi Ho";** 1959; STK; Mary Martin **25**

DEP-4016B: **"Snow White";** 1959; STK; Mary Martin **25**

C7
Disneyland Picture Disc "Souvenir" EPs

These 7", 45 rpm picture disc EPs were available at Disneyland and Walt Disney World as "souvenirs" of a visit to the theme park. Other than WD-1, they came in clear vinyl covers with backer cards. They are very collectible.

WD-1: **"The Walt Disney Character Parade";** 33-1/3 rpm "flexidisc" of pliable plastic; includes "The Character Parade"/"Mickey Mouse March"; GF cover with a mailer envelope **50**

WE-1: **"Electrical Water Pageant";** 1973 . . . . **50**

DE-1: **"Main Street Electrical Parade";** 6/1973 . . . . **50**

WD-2: **"It's a Small World";** 1975; with insert; 10,000 copies issued . . **75**

DE-4: **"Main Street Electrical Parade";** 1973 . . . . **50**

WE-4: **"Main Street Electrical Parade";** 1977 . . . . **50**

WD-4: **"Main Street Electrical Parade";** 6/1977; Stereo **50**

WD-5: **"Main Street Electrical Parade";** 1977; with insert **50**

C8
Disneyland "DBR" EPs (Including the Mickey Mouse Club "DBR" EP Series)

"DBR" stands for "Disney Big Record," so-called at the time because it was an EP which could hold four songs/stories. All had very colorful covers containing animated art or photos of the artists. There were 78 rpm counterparts for some of these (See Section D1). They were initially produced pursuant to a three-way arrangement with Disney, Golden Records, and ABC (See "A Short History of Recorded Disney Music"). Though dates appear on many covers, you cannot always rely on those dates for the release date as it referred to the copyright date for the art or photo (See "Understanding the Listings"). Some covers opened at the top, and others opened at the side. Issues numbered DBR-50 to DBR-61 were initially produced in orange vinyl, with second pressings on black vinyl. There are some in the series which had only ink-printed labels, i.e., no paper label on the record.

Golden Records' original 1955 license to produce these records was to have expired on September 30, 1956, however it was apparently extended until 1958 when Disney took back control, production, and distribution of the series. All issues actually released by Golden will have indications on the cover and/or the label that the record was distributed by "AM-PAR" (ABC's distribution division). Those without such notations were issued by Disney in 1958 and thereafter. The Disney Archives files on release dating for these records are somewhat misleading to collectors and discographers inasmuch as, for its purposes, Disney recognizes that the series only began when it took back control in 1958.

The Disney DBR's commenced their number sequence at number "DBR-20" through "DBR-97" however, chronologically they are out of order. They began production in 1955 at DBR-50 and ceased at DBR-20 in 1964. Confused? See the footnote below for their yearly production sequence and the individual listings for the date of release of a specific record.[2]

DBR-20: **"Songs from Mary Poppins (Four Songs)";** 6/1964; MST **20**

DBR-21: **"Ballad of Davy Crockett"/"Farewell";** 8/1963; Fess Parker **25**

---

[2] 1955: DBR 50-57 (AM-PAR releases)
1956: DBR 58 to 67 (AM-PAR releases)
1957: DBR-68 to 70 (AM-PAR releases)
1958: DBR 71 to 92
(Disneyland releases hereafter)
1959: DBR 38-49
1960: DBR 93-94
1961: DBR 29-37 and 95-97
1962: DBR 24-28
1963: DBR 21-23
1964: DBR 20

Note that Little Golden Records had also earlier produced a series of 10" 78 rpm EPs known as "Big Golden Records" in which its Disney-related titles were also numbered as "DBR" (Disney Big Record) numbered 1 to 7, 13, 16, 20, and 29. Thus there is a numbering overlap with Disney DBRs 20 and 29. See Section F below.

DBR-22: **"Songs from Sword in the Stone";** 7/1963; MST **20**

DBR-23: **"Savage Sam"/"Old Yeller";** 6/1963 . . . . **25**

DBR-24: **"Pinocchio";** 1/1962; MST; contains original front and back cover art from DEP-4002A; this and the similarly-marked animated MSTs below simply used the plates from covers of the "DEP" series with a restamped "DBR" number on it; the only other difference is that these are paper sleeves. **30**

DBR-25: **"Sorcerer's Apprentice";** 1/1962; MST **20**

DBR-26: **"Dumbo (Four Songs)";** 1/1962; MST; contains original front and back cover art from DEP-4013A **30**

DBR-27: **"Bambi";** 1/1962; MST; contains original front and back cover art from DEP-4010A **30**

DBR-28: **"Uncle Remus (Song of the South)";** 1/1962; MST; contains original front and back cover art from DEP-4001A **30**

DBR-29: **"Peter and the Wolf";** 8/1961 . . . . **20**

DBR-30: **"Alice in Wonderland (Four Songs)";** 8/1961; Darlene Gillespie; contains original front and back cover art from DEP-4015A **50**

DBR-31: **"Perri (Four Songs)";** 8/1961; Jimmie Dodd and Darlene Gillespie; same original front cover from DEP-3902A **25**

DBR-32: **"Babes in Toyland (Four Songs)";** 7/1961; **20**

DBR-33: **"Babes in Toyland (Four More Songs)";** 7/1961 . . . . **20**

DBR-34: **"Colorful World of Professor Ludwig Von Drake (I'm Ludwig Von Drake)";** 7/1961 . . . . **15**

DBR-35: **"Lady and the Tramp (Four Songs)";** 7/1961 . . . . **15**

Note: "6 Big Songs Records" begin here. Disney advertised these as "Disney Big 6" records.

DBR-36: **"Six Mother Goose Songs";** 7/1961; Sterling Holloway **15**

DBR-37: **"Androcles and the Lion"/"The Hare and the Hound";** 7/1961 . . . . **15**

DBR-38: **"Walt Disney's Game Songs";** 11/1959 . . . . **20**

DBR-39: **"Walt Disney Presents The Swamp Fox: Six songs of the Revolutionary War";** 11/1959 . . . . **25**

DBR-40: **"Stories in Song of the West";** 10/1959; Fess Parker **25**

DBR-41: **"Walt Disney's A Cowboy Need a Song";** 10/1959; Fess Parker **25**

DBR-42: **"Walt Disney Presents Folk Songs for Small Folks";** 11/1959 . . **20**

DBR-43: **"Walt Disney's Shaggy Dog Stories";** 8/1959 . . . . **25**

DBR-44: **"Walt Disney Presents Goofy's Dance Party";** 10/1959 . . **20**

DBR-45: **"Sing a Song with Mickey";** 10/1959 . . . . **20**

DBR-46: **"Walt Disney's Happy Birthday to You";** 10/1959 . . . . . . **20**

DBR-47: **"Walt Disney's Christmas Concert"/"Jiminy Cricket Sings 'From All of Us to All of You' ";** 11/1959 . . . . **20**

DBR-48: **"Walt Disney's Donald Duck and His Chipmunk Friends";** 10/1959 . . . . **20**

DBR-49: "Songs from Walt Disney's Toby Tyler

DBR-58: "Spin and Marty—The Triple 'R' Song"

DBR-49: **"Songs from Walt Disney's Toby Tyler—Featuring the Amazing Mr. Stubbs";** 10/1959 . . . **25**

Note: The "Mickey Mouse Club" 45 rpm 7" EPs begin here

DBR-50: **"Mickey Mouse Club March"/"Merry Mouseketeers March"/"Monday Through Friday Songs";** 1955
Orange vinyl **40**
Black vinyl **30**

DBR-51: **"Fun with Music—Vol. I";** 1955; Jimmie Dodd and Mouseketeers
Orange vinyl **25**
Black vinyl **20**

DBR-52: **"Fun with Music—Vol. II";** 1955
Orange vinyl **25**
Black vinyl **20**

DBR-53: **"Fun with Music from Many Lands";** 1955; featuring Jimmy Dodd, Frances Archer, and Beverly Gile
Orange vinyl **25**
Black vinyl **20**

DBR-54: **"Mousekedances: 6 Dances and How to Do Them";** 1955; featuring Jimmy Dodd, Ruth Carrell, and Mouseketeers
Orange vinyl **25**
Black vinyl **20**

DBR-55: **"Mouseketunes";** 1955; Jimmie Dodd and Mouseketeers
Orange vinyl **25**
Black vinyl **20**

DBR-56: **"Jiminy Cricket Sings 5 Mickey Mouse Club Songs";** 1955; Cliff Edwards
Orange vinyl **25**
Black vinyl **20**

DBR-57: **"Jiminy Cricket Presents Bongo";** 1955; Cliff Edwards
Orange vinyl **30**
Black vinyl **25**

DBR-58: **"Spin and Marty—The Triple 'R' Song";** 1956; (Jones); Tim Considine
Orange vinyl **25**
Black vinyl **20**

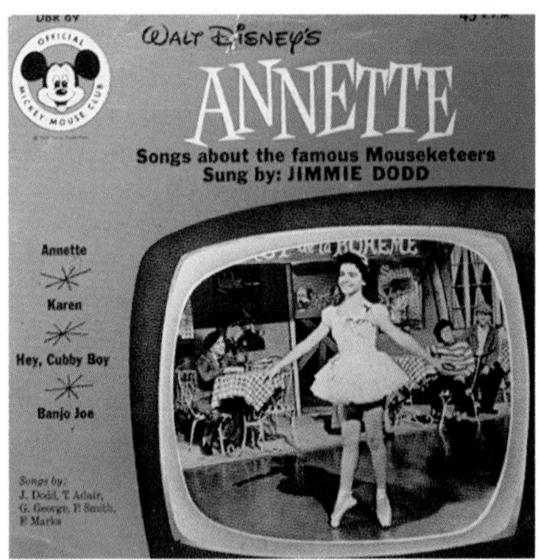

DBR-69: "Songs About Annette and Famous Mousketeers"

DBR-76: "Old Yeller"

DBR-59: **"Corky and White Shadow";** 1956; Darlene Gillespie and Buddy Ebsen
Orange vinyl **25**
Black vinyl **20**

DBR-60: **"Story of Johnny Appleseed";** 1956; Buddy Ebsen
Orange vinyl **30**
Black vinyl **25**

DBR-61: **"Story of The Littlest Outlaw";** 1956; (Lava); Cliff Edwards
Orange vinyl **30**
Black vinyl **25**

Note: Issues below only appeared on black vinyl and with paper sleeves

DBR-62: **"Mousekethoughts";** 1956; Jimmie Dodd **20**

DBR-63: **"Roll Up the Rug for More Mousekedances";** 1956; Mouseketeers **20**

DBR-64: **"Mousekemusicals";** 1956; Darlene Gillespie **20**

DBR-65: **"Safety First";** 1956; Jiminy Cricket **20**

DBR-66: **"Uncle Remus (4 Songs from Song of the South)";** 1956 . . **35**

DBR-67: **"Westward Ho the Wagons";** 1956; Jimmie Dodd and the Mouseketeers; four songs **25**

DBR-68: **"Mousekartoon Time";** 1957; Jimmie Dodd **20**

DBR-69: **"Songs About Annette and Famous Mousketeers";** 1957; Jimmie Dodd; cover photo of Annette in ballerina costume; highly sought after **60**

DBR-70: **"Four Songs from Cinderella";** 1957; Jimmie Dodd and Darlene Gillespie **25**

Note: AM-PAR releases end at DBR-70. Remaining issued by Disneyland

DBR-71: **"We're the Mouseketeers";** 1958; Mouseketeers **20**

DBR-72: **"Songs from 'Perri' ";** 1958; Jimmie Dodd and Darlene Gillespie **20**

DBR-73: **"The Saga of Andy Burnett"**; 1958; Jerome Courtland . . 20

DBR-74: **"Mickey's Big Show"**; 1958; Darlene Gillespie 25

DBR-75: **"Karen and Cubby"**; 1958; Karen Pendleton and Cubby O'Brien 20

DBR-76: **"Old Yeller"**; 1958; Jerome Courtland and Kevin Corcoran 25

DBR-77: **"Songs from Walt Disney's Zorro"**; 1958; Henry Calvin 25

DBR-78: **"Four Songs from Walt Disney's Snow White"**; 1958; Mouseketeers 25

DBR-79: **"Words to Grow By"**; 1958; features Annette, Jimmie Dodd, and Darlene Gillespie 30

DBR-80: **"Song and Story of The Three Little Pigs"**; 1958 20

DBR-81: **"Songs from Walt Disney's Peter Pan"**; 1958; Jimmie Dodd . . 20

DBR-82: **"Songs from Walt Disney's TV Serials"**; 10/1958 30

DBR-83: **"Moochie and Three Other Songs from TV Show"**; 10/1958 . . 20

DBR-84: **"Many Happy Returns"**; 10/1958; Darlene Gillespie and Jimmie Dodd 25

DBR-85: **"Holidays with the Mouseketeers—Part I (4 Holiday Songs)"**; 1958; Mouseketeers 20

DBR-86: **"Holidays with the Mouseketeers—Part II (4 Holiday Songs)"**; 1958; Mouseketeers 20

DBR-87: **"Holidays with the Mouseketeers—Part III"**; 10/1958; Mouseketeers 20

DBR-88: **"Sleeping Beauty-Songs and Story"/"Once Upon a Dream"/"I Wonder"**; 1958; Darlene Gillespie 20

DBR-89: **"Four Songs from Walt Disney's Sleeping Beauty"**; 1958; Disneyland Chorus 20

DBR-90: **"Story and Song of Paul Bunyan (Parts I and II)"**; 11/1958; (Bruns); Thurl Ravenscroft narrates 20

DBR-91: **"Christmas Trees of Disneyland"**; 10/1958; Camarata and Chorus; includes "Jingle Bones," "Adventureland Christmas Tree," "Fantasyland Story Book Tree," and "Tomorrowland Fantastic Christmas Tree" 20

DBR-92: **"The Shaggy Dog"**; 1958; Moochie and Roberta Shore 25

DBR-93: **"Songs from Walt Disney's Pollyanna"**; 1960; Hayley Mills . . . 25

DBR-94: **"Songs from Swiss Family** Robinson"; 1960; photo cover 20

DBR-95: **"Songs from 101 Dalmatians"**; 1961 25

DBR-96: **"Donald Duck in Six Fun Stories"**; 1961 20

DBR-97: **"Daniel Boone and Songs of Other Heroes"**; 1961 20

C9
Disneyland "Little Golden Book and Records" and Other "200" Series 33-1/3 rpm EPs

These gatefold EPs were similar to Disney's "300" series below, with gatefold booklets, but appear to have been issues of non-Disney related Little Golden "fairy tales" through #255. The later numbers were assigned to "The Getalong Gang," "Rainbow Brite," and "Chipmunk" series.

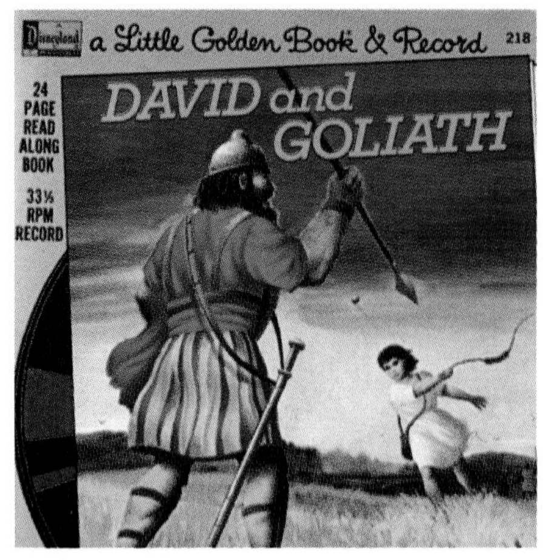

218: "David and Goliath"

201: **"The Saggy Baggy Elephant";** 9/1976 . . . . **10**

202: **"Tawny Scrawny Lion";** 9/1976 . . . . **10**

203: **"The Pokey Little Puppy";** 9/1976 . . . . **10**

204: **"Rumpelstiltskin";** 9/1976 . . . . . **10**

205: **"Scuffy the Tugboat";** 9/1976 . . **10**

206: **"Story and Song of Thumbelina";** 9/1976 . . . . **10**

207: **"Little Boy with a Big Horn";** 9/1976 . . . . **10**

208: **"Story and Song of Puss in Boots";** 9/1976 . . . . **10**

209: **"Chicken Little";** 9/1976 . . . . . . **10**

210: **"The Large and Growly Bear";** 9/1976 . . . . **10**

211: **"Tootle";** 9/1976 . . . . **10**

212: **"The Color Kittens";** 9/1976 . . . . **10**

213: **"The Happy Man and His Dump Truck";** 9/1976 . . . . **10**

214: **"The Taxi That Hurried";** 9/1976 . . . . **10**

215: **"Smokey the Bear";** 9/1976 . . . . **10**

216: **"The Little Engine That Could";** 9/1976 . . . . **10**

217: **"The Pussycat Tiger";** 9/1976 . . **10**

218: **"David and Goliath";** 9/1976 . . . **10**

219: **"Noah's Ark";** 9/1976 . . . . **10**

220: **"The Lively Little Rabbit";** 9/1976 . . . . **10**

221: **"Circus Time";** 9/1976 . . . . **10**

222: **"Seven Little Postmen";** 9/1976 . . . . **10**

223: **"There's No Such Thing as a Dragon";** 9/1976 . . . . **10**

224: **"The Little Fat Policeman";** 9/1976 . . . . **10**

225: **"Just for You";** 11/1983 . . . . **10**

226: **"Merry Christmas, Mom and Dad";** 7/1984 . . . . **10**

227: **"Just Me and My Dad";** 11/1983 . . . . **10**

228: **"Just Grandma and Me";** 10/1983 . . . . **10**

229-250: *(Not issued)*

251: **"The Night Before Christmas";** 10/1976 . . . . **10**

252: **"Rudolph the Red-Nose Reindeer";** 10/1976 . . . . **10**

253: **"Story and Song of Frosty the Snow Man";** 10/1976 . . . . **10**

254: **"Story and Song of The Twelve Days of Christmas";** 10/1976 . . . . **10**

255: **"Story and Song of Jingle Bells";** 10/1976 . . . . **10**

256-259: *(Not issued)*

260: **"Here Comes Garfield";** 10/1984 . . . . **10**

261: **"Garfield on the Town";** 10/1984 . . . . **10**

262: **"Garfield in the Rough";** 5/1985 . . . . **10**

263-269: (*Not issued*)

270: **"The Getalong Gang and the Missing Caboose";** 10/1984 . . . . . . **10**

271: **"The Getalong Gang and the Bad Loser";** 10/1984 . . . . **10**

272: **"The Getalong Gang and the Big Bully";** 10/1984 . . . . **10**

273: **"The Getalong Gang and the New Neighbor";** 10/1984 . . . . **10**

274-279: (*Not issued*)

280: **"Rainbow Brite Saves Spring";** 9/1984 . . . . **10**

281: **"Rainbow Brite and the Brook Meadow Deer";** 9/1984 . . . . **10**

282: **"Rainbow Brite and the Big Color Mixup";** 1/1985 . . . . **10**

283: **"Happy Birthday, Buddy Blue";** 1/1985 . . . . **10**

284: **"The Chipmunk Adventure";** 3/1987 . . . . **10**

285: **"The Chipmunks Join the Circus";** 3/1987 . . . . **10**

C10

Disneyland "Book and Record" "LLP" "300" EP Series 33-1/3 rpm

This series for young children commenced in the early 1960s, and consists of gatefold, 7" albums with "read-along," multi-page inner booklets and EP record, noting: "SEE the pictures—HEAR the record—READ the book." The original issues of these had lime colored labels and were prefixed with "LLP" through at least number 367. Reissues of these early numbers without the "LLP" prefix are worth about two-thirds of the original listed price. Later editions and earlier reprints just had the numbers. Most of the later issues and some reprints of the earlier numbers had yellow labels with a Disney logo in a blocked rainbow at top. I have noted the reissue dates where available. This "300" series appeared prior to the "200" series above.

Spanish language versions of some of the "300" series were also produced and distributed in the United States on the "Disneylandia" label. They had color booklets as well. Disney noted these with an "M" suffix, and they are listed in their numerical position with their English counterparts.

301: **"Story of Sleeping Beauty";** 11/1965; green cover **15**

1977 reissue: dark blue cover with different graphics **10**

301M: **"La Bella Durmiente";** 4/1978 . . . . **20**

302: **"Mary Poppins";** 11/1965; light blue cover **15**

1968 reissue: dark blue cover with different graphics **10**

302M: **"Mary Poppins";** 4/1978 . . . . **20**

303: **"Three Little Pigs";** 11/1965; red cover **15**

1978 reissue: green cover with different graphics **10**

303M: **"Los Tres Cochinitos";** 4/1978 . . . . **20**

304: **"Peter Pan and Wendy";** 11/1965; green cover **15**

1977 reissue: blue cover with different graphics **10**

304M: **"Peter Pan y Wendy";** 4/1978 . . . . **20**

305: **"Story of 101 Dalmatians" /"Songs from 101 Dalmatians";** 11/1965; red cover **15**

1977 reissue: brown cover with different graphics **10**

305M: **"La Noche De Las Narices Frias";** 4/1978 . . . . **20**

309: "Bambi (Parts I and II)"

306: **"Story of Alice in Wonderland" /"Alice in Wonderland"/"I'm Late";** 11/1965; yellow cover **15**

1979 reissue: replaces song "Alice in Wonderland" with "The Unbirthday Song"; green cover; different graphics **10**

306M: **"Alicia en el Pais de las Maravillas";** 4/1978 . . . . **20**

307: **"Story of Lady and the Tramp"/"Belle Notte"/"Siamese Cat Song";** 11/1965; blue cover . . **15**

1979 reissue: green cover; different graphics **10**

307M: **"La Dama y el Vagabundo";** 4/1978 . . . . **20**

308: **"Story of Cinderella"/"Songs from Cinderella";** 11/1965; blue cover **15**

1977 reissue: orange cover; different graphics **10**

308M: **"La Cenicienta";** 4/1978 . . . . **20**

309: **"Bambi (Parts I and II)";** 4/1966; Robie Lester **15**

1977 reissue **10**

309M: **"Bambi";** 4/1978 . . . .**20**

310: **"Story of Snow White and the Seven Dwarfs"/"Heigh Ho"/"Whistle While You Work";** 4/1966; Robie Lester **15**

1977 reissue **10**

310M: **"Bianca Nieves y Los Siete Enanos";** 4/1978 . . . . **20**

311: **"Story of Pinocchio"/"When You Wish Upon a Star"/"Give a Little Whistle";** 4/1966 . . . . **15**

1977 reissue; Robie Lester **10**

311M: **"Pinocho";** 4/1978 . . . . . . **20**

312: **"Mother Goose Rhymes Part I and II";** 4/1966; Sterling Holloway **15**

1979 reissue **10**

313: **"Story of Winnie the Pooh and the Honey Tree"/"Songs from Winnie the Pooh and the Honey Tree";** 1/1967 . . . . **15**

1979 reissue **10**

313M: **"Winnie Puh y el Arbol de Miel";** 4/1978 . . . . **20**

314: **"The Seven Dwarf's and Their Diamond Mine";** 3/1967 . . . . **15**

315: **"Story of Goldilocks and the Three Bears"/"Goldilocks Songs";** 3/1967 . . . . **15**

315M: **"Ricitos De Oro y Los Tres Osos";** 4/1978 . . . . **20**

316: **"The Gnome Mobile";** 3/1967 . . . . **20**

317: **"The Story of Hansel and Gretel";** 4/1967 . . . . **15**

317M: **"Hansel y Gretel";** 4/1978 . . . . **20**

318: **"Black Beauty";** 3/1967 . . . . **15**

319: **"Story of The Jungle Book";** 1967 . . . . **15**

1977 reissue **10**

319M: **"El Libro Selva";** 4/1978 . . . . **20**

320: **"The Happiest Millionaire";** 10/1967; Robie Lester **15**

321: **"Peter and the Wolf";** 10/1968 . . . . **15**

1978 reissue **10**

322: **"Heidi";** 1968 . . . . **15**

323: **"It's a Small World";** 10/1968 . . . . **15**

323M: **"Que Pequeno es el Mundo";** 4/1978 . . . . **20**

324: **"Story of Dumbo/"Casey Jr."/"When I See an Elephant Fly";** 3/1968; Robie Lester **15**

1978 reissue **10**

324M: **"Dumbo";** 4/1978 . . . . **20**

325: **"How the Camel Got Its Hump";** 1968; from "Just So Stories" **15**

326: **"Acting Out the ABC's";** 3/1968; Robie Lester **15**

327: **"Story of Winnie the Pooh and the Blustery Day";** 6/1969; Sterling Holloway **15**

1978 reissue **10**

328: **"Little Red Riding Hood";** 10/1968 . . . . **15**

328M: **"Caperucita Roja";** 4/1978 . . . . **20**

329: **"Babes in Toyland";** 10/1968 . . . **15**

330: **"Little Hiawatha";** 10/1968 . . . . **15**

331: **"Story of the Grasshopper and the Ants";** 10/1968 . . . . **15**

332: **"Little Red Hen";** 10/1968 . . . . . **15**

333: **"Winnie the Pooh and Tigger";** 6/1968 . . . . **15**

333M: **"Winnie Puh y Tigger";** 4/1978 . . . . **20**

334: **"Mickey Mouse As the Brave Little Tailor";** 10/1968 . . . . **20**

334M: **"Mickey Mouse, el Sastrecillo Valiente";** 4/1978 . . . . . **20**

334: "Mickey Mouse As the Brave Little Tailor"

335: **"Johnny Appleseed";** 9/1969 . . . **15**

336: **"Pirates of the Caribbean";** 1969 . . . . **15**

337: **"The Gingerbread Man";** 8/1969 . . . . **15**

338: **"Story of More Jungle Book";** 6/1969; Robie Lester **15**

339: **"The Haunted Mansion" /"Sound Effects";** 1970 . . . . **15**

340: **"The Ugly Duckling";** 4/1970 . . . . **15**

340M: **"El Patito Feo";** 2/1973 . . . **20**

341: **"The Emperor's New Clothes";** 4/1970 . . . . **15**

342: **"Story of Robin Hood Part I and II";** 5/1970 . . . . **15**

343: **"Story of Thumper's Race";** 5/1970 . . . . **15**

344: **"The Night Before Christmas";** 9/1970 . . . . **15**

345: **"Story of The Bremen Town Musicians"/"The Bremen Town Musicians Band";** 5/1970 . . . . **15**

346: **"Rapunzel";** 10/1970 . . . . **15**

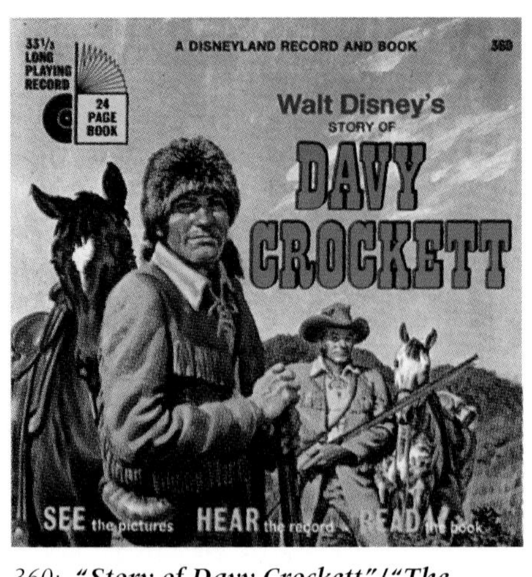

360: "Story of Davy Crockett"/"The Ballad of Davy Crockett"

347: **"The Story of The Wizard of Oz"/"Over the Rainbow" /"Follow the Yellow Brick Road";** 5/1970 . . . . **15**

1978 reissue **10**

347M: **"El Mago de Oz";** 2/1973 . . . . **20**

348: **"Story of Mickey and the Beanstalk";** 5/1970 . . . . **20**

348M: **"Mickey y Las Habichuelas";** 2/1973 . . . . **20**

349: **"Story of The Aristocats";** 9/1970 . . . . **15**

349M: **"Los Aristogatos";** 4/1971 . . . . **20**

350: **"Pecos Bill";** 12/1970 . . . . **15**

351: **"Lambert, the Sheepish Lion";** 12/1970 . . . . **20**

352: **"Susie, the Little Blue Coupe";** 12/1970 . . . . **20**

353: **"The Little House";** 12/1970 . . . **20**

354: **"Johnny Fedora and Alice Blue Bonnet";** 12/1970 . . . . **20**

355: **"The Whale Who Wanted to Sing at the Met";** 12/1970 . . . . **20**

356: **"Aladdin and His Lamp";** 5/1971 . . . . **15**

356M: **"Aladino y La Lampara Maravillosa";** 2/1973 . . . . **20**

357: **"Story of the Swiss Family Robinson"/"Animals and Clowns";** 5/1971 . . . . **10**

357M: **"La Familia Robinson";** 2/1973 . . . . **20**

358: **"20,000 Leagues Under the Sea" (Lois Lane narrates)/"A Whale of a Tale" (The Wellingtons);** 5/1971 . . . . **10**

358M: **Veinte Mil Leguas de Submarino;** 2/1973 . . . . **20**

359: **"Voyages of Sinbad the Sailor";** 5/1971 . . . . **10**

359M: **"Sinbad el Marino";** 2/1973 . . . . **20**

360: **"Story of Davy Crockett"/"The Ballad of Davy Crockett";** 5/1971 . . **25**

361: **"Treasure Island";** 5/1971 . . . . . **10**

361M: **"La Isla del Tesoro";** 2/1973 . . . . **20**

362: **"More Mother Goose";** 5/1971 . . **10**

363: **"Story of Brer Rabbit and the Tar Baby"/"Zip-A-Dee-Doo Dah";** 5/1971 . . . . **10**

363M: **"El Hermano Rabito y el Muneco de Brea";** 2/1973 . . . . **20**

364: **"Bedknobs and Broomsticks";** 5/1971 . . . . **10**

365: **"Story of Robin Hood";** 7/1973 . . . . **10**

365M: **"Robin Hood";** 4/1978 . . . . **20**

366: **"Story and Songs of Winnie the Pooh and Tigger Too";** 8/1974 . . . **10**

367: **"Story of The Rescuers";** 6/1977 . . . . **10**

367M **"Bernardo y Bianca";** 4/1978 . . . . **20**

368: **"The Hobbit";** 8/1977 15

369: **"Pete's Dragon";** 11/1977 10

369M: **"Mi Amigo el Dragon";** 7/1979 20

370-380: (*Not issued*)—French issue numbers only.

381: **"The Black Hole";** 11/1979 15

381M: **"El Abismo Negro";** 8/1980 20

382: **"The Return of the King";** 3/1980 15

383: **"The Fox and the Hound";** 6/1981 10

383M: **"El Zorro el Sabueso";** 5/1982 20

384: **"Tron";** 7/1982; Note: this was originally listed in Disney sales brochures as "Dragonslayer" but Disney never released any format recording of that film in any series. 20

384M: (*Not issued*)

385: **"Return to Oz";** 5/1985 15

386: **"Mickey's Christmas Carol";** 8/1982 10

387: **"Counting Fun";** 8/1984; Disney Discovery Series 10

388: **"Baby Animals";** 8/1984; Disney Discovery Series 10

389: **"The Black Cauldron";** 6/1985 . . 15

389M: Issued but name unknown 20

390: **"Manners";** 8/1985; Disney Discovery Series 10

391: **"ABC's";** 8/1985; Disney Discovery Series 10

392: **"Things That Go";** 8/1985; Disney Discovery Series 10

393: **"People at Work";** 8/1985; Disney Discovery Series 10

394: **"Hoppopotamus Goes to Hollywuz";** 9/1985 10

395: **"Bumbelion's Funny Money";** 9/1985 10

396: **"Butterbear's Surprise Guest";** 9/1985 10

397: **"Elerro and the Brahma Bullfinch";** 9/1985 10

C11
Buena Vista "400" Series 33-1/3 EPs

C11.1 *Charlie Brown* EPs

These 33-1/3 EPs are 7" in diameter and continued the "LLP" concept with 24-page booklets. They were based on the popular comic strip "Peanuts" by Charles Schultz.

401: **"A Charlie Brown Christmas";** 10/1977 10

402: **"Charlie Brown's All-Stars";** 7/1978 10

403: **"He's Your Dog, Charlie Brown";** 7/1978 10

404: **"It's the Great Pumpkin, Charlie Brown";** 10/1978 10

405: **"You're In Love, Charlie Brown";** 10/1978 10

406: **"Snoopy Come Home";** 1/1980 10

407: **"It's Your First Kiss, Charlie Brown";** 7/1980 10

408: **"You're A Good Sport, Charlie Brown";** 7/1980 10

409: **"It's a Mystery, Charlie Brown";** 7/1980 10

457: "The Dark Crystal"

410: **"It Was a Short Summer, Charlie Brown"**; 7/1980 .... **10**

411: **"You're the Greatest, Charlie Brown"**; 7/1980 .... **10**

412-449: (*Not issued*)

C11.2: *Star Wars/Star Trek and Other Film EPs*

This series is Disney related only by the Buena Vista label. It consists of tie-ins with the *Star Wars*; *Indiana Jones*; *Star Trek* and other movie series. These are 7" 33-1/3 rpm gatefold "read-along" Adventure Series records with 24-page booklets featuring story and original photos from these movies.

Some were also produced and distributed in the United States in Spanish language editions with an "M" suffix to the record number. I have has listed those I am aware of in their numerical sequence with their English language counterparts.

450: **"Star Wars"**; 4/1979 .... **10**

450M: **"La Guerra De Las Galaxias"**; 9/1980 .... **15**

451: **"The Empire Strikes Back"**; 1980 .... **10**

451M: **"El Imperio Contraataca"** **15**

452: **"Raiders of the Lost Ark"**; 11/1981 .... **10**

452M: (*Not issued*)—Was to be "Los Cazadores del Area Perdide."

453: **"Droid World"**; 4/1983 .... **10**

454: **"Planet of the Hoojibs"**; 4/1983 .... **10**

455: **"Return of the Jedi"**; 4/1983 ... **10**

456: **"E.T., The Extra-Terrestrial"**; 12/1982; Drew Barrymore **10**

457: **"The Dark Crystal"**; 2/1983 .... **10**

458: **"The Black Stallion"**; 2/1983 ... **10**

459: **"The Black Stallion Returns"**; 12/1982 .... **10**

460: **"The Ewoks Join the Fight"**; 4/1983 .... **10**

461: **"Star Trek I—The Motion Picture"**; 8/1983 .... **15**

462: **"Star Trek II—The Wrath of Khan"**; 8/1983 .... **15**

463: **"Star Trek III—The Search for Spock"**; 4/1984 .... **15**

464: **"The Last Starfighter"**; 9/1984 .... **15**

465: **"Indiana Jones and the Temple of Doom"**; 6/1984 .... **10**

466: **"Gremlins"**; 4/1984 .... **10**

467: **"The Ewok Adventure"**; 10/1984 .... **10**

468: **"Robo Force—The Battle at the Fortress of Steele"**; 1/1985 ...... **10**

469: **"Goonies"**; 7/1985 .... **10**

470: **"Ewoks—Battle for Endor"**; 10/1985 .... **10**

471: **"Star Trek IV—The Voyage Home"**; 11/1986 .... **15**

472-479: (*Not issued*)

480: **"Adventures in Colors and Shapes (Star Wars)"** **15**

481: **"Adventures in ABC (Star Wars)"** **15**

LLP-482: **"Labyrinth"** **15**

LLP-483-500: (*Not issued*)

C12
Disneyland Other "LLP" "500" Series EPs

The "LLP" series continued for a short time in a "500" series also. "Disney's Adventures of The Gummi Bears" was a Disney TV series from 1985-1990. "Disney's Fluppy Dogs" was a TV special from November 27, 1986. All with booklets as in the above "LLP" style. Note: There is a much earlier "F-501 to F-504" series of 45 rpm "Zorro" records which appears at Section E3 below in a separate "500" number records listing in which some of these numbers are duplicated.

LLP-501: **"Gummies to the Rescue";** 11/1985 . . . . **10**

LLP-502: **"Zummi's Magic Spell";** 11/1985 . . . . **10**

LLP-503: **"The Great Mouse Detective";** 7/1986 . . . . **15**

LLP-504-505: (*Not issued*)

LLP-506: **"Totally Minnie";** 1/1986; single 33-1/3 record; features "Totally Minnie" and "Hey Mickey"; no booklet; Note: other special issue "500" numbered records, 45 rpm and 33-1/3, 7" singles appear in the 45 rpm section E3 below. **15**

LLP-507: **"Safety First";** 7/1986; Disney Discovery Series **10**

LLP-508: **"Colors and Shapes";** 7/1986; Disney Discovery Series . . **10**

LLP-509: **"Fluppy Dogs I: The** Happiest Fluppy"; 9/1986 . . . . **10**

LLP-510: **"Fluppy Dogs II: Lost and Found Fluppy";** 9/1986 . . . . **10**

C13
Disneyland "700" Series EPs

LLP-700-704: LLPs not issued on vinyl, but see separate Special Promo 45 rpm 700 section below at Section E5.

LLP-705: **"Photon I—The Adventure Begins";** 12/1986 . . . . **10**

LLP-706: **"Photon II—Tunnels of Danger";** 12/1986 . . . . **10**

C14
Disneyland "FS-900" Series EPs

The "FS" stands for "Four Complete Songs." These had picture sleeves. Later issues dropped the "FS" prefix.

FS-901: **"Bedknobs and Broomsticks"/"The Age of Not Believing"/"A Step in the Right Direction";** 1/1972 . . . . **15**

FS-902: **"Bedknobs and Broomsticks"/"Beautiful Briny";** 1/1972 . . . . **15**

FS-903: **"The Aristocats";** 1/1972 . . . **15**

FS-904: **"Mary Poppins"/ "Supercalifragilisticexpialidocious" /"One Man Band";** 1/1972 . . . . **15**

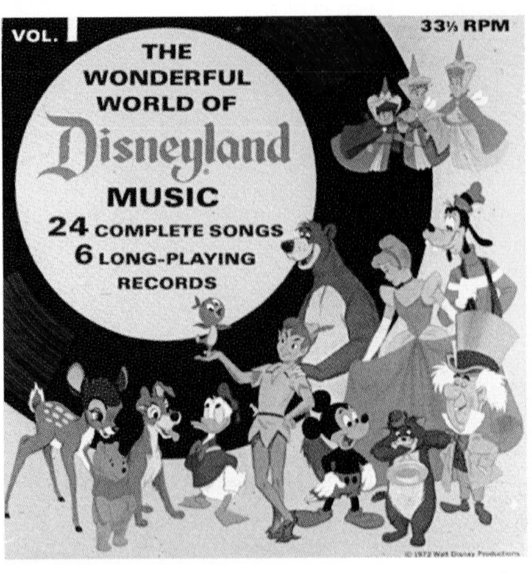

Vol. 1: "Wonderful World of Disneyland Music"

FS-905: **"Mary Poppins"/"Chim Chim Cheree"/"I Love to Laugh"/"Step in Time"/"Let's Go Fly a Kite"**; 1/1972 . . . . **15**

FS-906: **"Walt Disney Presents The Jungle Book"**; 1/1972 . . . . **15**

FS-907: **"Winnie the Pooh and the Honey Tree"**; 1/1972 . . . . **15**

FS-908: **"Lady and the Tramp"**; 1/1972 . . . . **15**

FS-909: **"It's a Small World"**; 1/1972; Disneyland Boys' Choir . . **15**

FS-910: **"Acting Out the ABC's"**; 1/1972 . . . . **15**

FS-911: **"Babes in Toyland"**; 1/1972 . . . . **15**

FS-912: **"Alice In Wonderland"**; 1/1972 . . . . **15**

FS-913: **"Walt Disney's Cinderella"**; 1/1972 . . . . **15**

FS-914: **"Happy Birthday"**; 1/1972 . . . . **15**

FS-915: **"Peter Pan"/"What Made the Red Man Red"/"The Elegant Captain Hook"/"You Can Fly"**; 1/1972; includes **15**

FS-916: **"Bambi"**; 1/1972 . . . . **15**

FS-917: **"Sleeping Beauty"/"Once Upon a Dream"/"I Wonder"**; 1/1972 . . . . **15**

FS-918: **"Walt Disney Presents Hansel and Gretel"**; 1/1972 . . . . . **15**

FS-919: **"Mickey Mouse and the Mouse Factory"**; 1/1972 . . . . **15**

FS-920: **"Donald Duck and the Mouse Factory"**; 1/1972 . . . . **15**

FS-921: **"Winnie the Pooh and the Blustery Day"**; 1/1972 . . . . **15**

FS-922: **"The Orange Bird"**; 1/1972 . . . . **15**

FS-923: **"Goofy and the Mouse Factory"**; 1/1972 . . . . **15**

FS-924: **"Heidi"**; 1/1972 . . . . **15**

FS-925: **"Mother Goose Rhymes and Their Stories"**; 1/1972 . . . . **15**

FS-926: **"Robin Hood"**; 6/1973 . . . . . **15**

FS-927: **"Snow White"**; 6/1973 . . . . . **15**

FS-928: **"Pinocchio"**; 6/1973 . . . . **15**

Vol. 1: **"Wonderful World of Disneyland Music"**; 1972; 24 songs; six EP box set; contains the following "FS" EPs: 901, 904, 907, 908, 915, 917; with specially designed, individual art work paper sleeves for each record; cover on box is the same multi-Disney character drawing as appeared on the back cover of the early "FS" single issue EPs **50**

Disneyland CD-334: ***"Little Man of Disneyland"***

C15
Miscellaneous Disneyland 45 rpm EP Records

C15.1: *Mickey Mouse Club Little Golden Book and Record Sets*

These 7" Disney records came in three separate sets consisting of a Mickey Mouse Club "Little Golden" Book ("Little Golden Books That Read Themselves") and a Disneyland record. The book and the record were packaged in a slip-in cardboard picture sleeve with an opening at the top. Prices include the sleeve, book, and record.

Disneyland CD-334: **"Little Man of Disneyland";** 1955; Mitch Miller Orchestra; narrated by Gilbert Mack; book #D46 by the same name **40**

Disneyland CD-429: **"Walt Disney's Bambi"** **40**

Disneyland CD-433: **"The Seven Dwarfs Find a House"** **40**

C15.2: *Hardees Restaurant Premium* "Gremlins" EPs

4041H: **"The Gift of the Mogwai";** 5/1984 . . . . **10**

4042H: **"Gizmo and the Gremlins";** 5/1984 . . . . **10**

4043H: **"Escape from the Gremlins";** 5/1984 . . . . **10**

4044H: **"Gremlins—Trapped";** 5/1984 . . . . **10**

4045H: **"The Last Gremlin";** 5/1984 . . . . **10**

C15.3: *Other Miscellaneous Disneyland* EPs

04: **"Tall Paul + 3";** 1959; Annette; unconfirmed as an American release **50**

C16
Non-Disney Label EPs

C16.1: ABC-*Paramount* EPs

194 (A): **"Bill Hayes Sings the Best of Disney";** EP from the LP of same name listed above **15**

194 (B): **"Bill Hayes Sings the Best of Disney";** EP from the LP of same name listed above **15**

194 (C): **"Bill Hayes Sings the Best of Disney";** EP from the LP of same name listed above **15**

C16.2: *Capitol* EPs

Capitol EPs had original Disney cover art taken from the equivalent 78 rpm albums. The "EAP" series sold for $1.40.

EAP-1-3182: **"The Ugly Duckling"** (Stan Freeberg)/**"Woody Woodpecker & the Animal Crackers"** (Mel Blanc) **30**

EAP-1-3183: **"Ferdinand the Bull"/"Little Hiawatha"** (Don Wilson) **30**

EAP-1-3184: **"Three Orphan Kittens"/"The Country Cousin"** (Don Wilson) **30**

EAP-1-3185: **"Elmer Elephant"/"Bongo the Circus Bear"** (Don Wilson) **30**

DAP-1-3235: **"Tales of Davy Crockett, Parts 1 and 2";** Tennessee Ernie Ford; includes the "Ballad of Davy Crockett" and "Farewell" **35**

C16.3: *Columbia* EPs

C16.3.1: Davy Crockett TV Series

See introduction for Columbia 78 rpm section D3.7.2 and "A Short History of Recorded Disney Music."

Columbia B-2031: **"Davy Crockett—Indian Fighter";** 1955 . . **40**

Columbia B-2032: **"Davy Crockett—Goes to Congress";** 1955 . . . . **40**

Columbia B-2033: **"Davy Crockett—At the Alamo";** 1955 . . **40**

Columbia B-2073: **"Davy Crockett and Mike Fink";** 1956; EP; includes "Their Great Keelboat Race" and "Their Fight with the River Pirates"; record numbered 37156/37157; Columbia's lease of the Disney masters expired on August 15, 1958 . . . . **90**

C16.3.2: Other Columbia EPs

Columbia B-1926: **"The Vanishing Prairie";** (Smith) **50**

Columbia B-6723: **"Songs from Walt Disney's Magic Kingdom (Vol. 1)";** 1955; features Dottie Evans, Johnny Anderson and Merry Makers; Ray Carter conducts **15**

Columbia B-6724: **"Songs from Walt Disney's Magic Kingdom (Vol. 2)";** 1955; features Dottie Evans, Johnny Anderson and Merry Makers; Ray Carter conducts **15**

Columbia B-6725: **"Songs from Walt Disney's Magic Kingdom (Vol. 3)";** 1955; features Dottie Evans, Johnny Anderson and Merry Makers; Ray Carter conducts **15**

Columbia B-10591: **"Dave Digs Disney (Vol. 1)";** Dave Brubeck Quartet **20**

Columbia B-10592: **"Dave Digs Disney (Vol. 2)";** Dave Brubeck Quartet **20**

Columbia ???: **"Happy Birthday";** 6" 33-1/3 rpm flexidisc; features Donald, Mickey, Goofy, and Pluto **15**

C16.4: *Decca* EPs

Decca ED-719: **"Pinocchio";** 1950; Cliff Edwards and Victor Young Orchestra **30**

Decca ED-728: **"Songs from Lady and the Tramp";** two EP set; Peggy Lee; GF album **45**

Decca ED-778: **"A Visit to Disneyland";** 1956; Fred Waring and the Pennsylvanians **25**

Decca ED-834: **"Music from Disneyland";** 1955; two record set; Jack Pleis Orchestra and Chorus; GF; (See LP Decca 8105) . . **25**

Decca ED-1011: **"The Ballad of Davy Crockett";** Fred Waring and the Pennsylvanians; back cover contains 20 verses of the song **30**

Decca ED-2210: **"Songs from Disneyland";** Cliff Edwards; orchestra conducted by Sonny Burke **25**

Decca ED-2448: **"Songs from Westward Ho the Wagons";** Rex Allen **30**

C16.5: *Fisher-Price* EPs

These included a 24-page booklet.

3160: **"Mother Goose Rhymes";** 1/1985 . . . . **10**

3161: **"The Story of the Ugly Duckling";** 1/1985 . . . . **10**

3162: **"Little Red Riding Hood";** 1/1985 . . . . **10**

3163: **"The Story of Hansel and Gretel";** 1/1985 . . . . **10**

3164: **"Story of Goldilocks and the Three Bears";** 1/1985 . . . . **10**

3165: **"The Story of the Little Red Hen";** 1/1985 . . . . **10**

C16.6: *General Electric* EPs

WD-101: **"3 Little Pigs"** **20**

WD-102: **"Pinocchio"** **20**

WD-103: **"Cinderella"** **20**

WD-104: **"Peter Pan"** **20**

WD-105: **"Snow White"** **20**

WD-106: **"Alice in Wonderland"** . . . **20**

WD-107: **"Lady and the Tramp"** **20**

WD-108: **"101 Dalmations"** **20**

WD-109: **"Mickey Mouse"** **20**

WD-110: **"Bambi"** **20**

WD-111: **"Dumbo"/"When I See an Elephant Fly";** 1969 . . . . **20**

WD-112: **"Sleeping Beauty"** **20**

WD-113: **"Donald Duck"** **20**

WD-114: **"Mary Poppins"** **20**

WD-115: **"Winnie the Pooh"** **20**

WD-116: **"Jungle Book"** **20**

WD-117: **"Aristocats"** **20**

WD-118: **"The Sword in the Stone"** . . **20**

WD-119: **"Swiss Family Robinson"** . . **20**

WD-120: **"Pluto"** **20**

WD-121: **"It's a Small World"** **20**

WD-122: **"Minnie Mouse's Suprise"** **20**

WD-123: **"Goofy"** **20**

WD-124: **"Walt Disney World"** **20**

General Electric issued these 7" "Picturesound Program" records to be used with its "Show 'n Tell Phono-Viewer." Others likely exist. See also a separate G.E. "Carousel of Progress" record DL-559 at Section E3 below.

CBS Records continued to issue "picturesound" EPs for the G.E. Player during 1978-1983. The following are the CBS EP records confirmed to date:

51221: **"Pinocchio"** 15

51223: **"Peter Pan"** 15

51224: **"Mickey and the Beanstalk"** 15

51225: **"Alice in Wonderland"** 15

51226: **"The Sorcerer's Apprentice"** 15

51230: **"Dumbo Learns to FLy"** 15

51232: **"Donald Duck at the Zoo"** . . 15

51241: **"Minnie Mouse's Suprise Birthday Party"** 15

51405: **"Snow White"** 15

51408: **"Mickey Mouse's Undersea Treasure"** 15

51410: **"Sleeping Beauty"** 15

C16.7: MGM EPs

X1145: **"Lady and the Tramp";** 1955; features Kay Armen, The Marion Sisters, Joe Lipman and His Orchestra 35

C16.8: RCA 45 *rpm* EP *Recordings*

C16.8.1: RCA 45 rpm "EYA" Series

These EPs, issued c. 1954-55, derived from the earlier issues of these titles on the RCA 78 rpm albums.

EYA-2: **"Three Little Pigs"** (MST)/**"The Orphan's Benefit"** (MST)/**"The What-zis and the Who-zis"** (Mickey and Pluto) 40

EYA-4: **"Dumbo";** Shirley Temple and cast 25

EYA-5: **"Pecos Bill";** from *Melody Time*; Roy Rogers & Sons of the Pioneers; same cover as Y-389 (78 rpm) below 25

EYA-6: **"Johnny Appleseed";** Dennis Day 25

EYA-7: **"Bambi";** Shirley Temple and cast 25

EYA-17: **"Treasure Island";** Bobby Driscoll 25

EYA-26: **"Snow White and Sneezy"/"Snow White and Dopey";** Dennis Day 25

EYA-46: **"Alice in Wonderland"** 25

EYA-407: **"Song Hits from Peter Pan";** 1952; features Hugo Winterhalter and Orchestra, Stuart Foster, and Judy Valentine 20

C16.8.2: Other RCA EPs of Note

EPC-1119: **"Walt Disney Songs for the Family";** 1955; Joe Reisman Orchestra 25

ERAS-1: **"The Living Desert [Suite]";** 1953; (Smith); MST; GF with book; reissued on Buena Vista BV-3326; Rare 100

C16.9: *Waldorf Music Hall* EPs

MH-45-158: **"Songs from Walt Disney Films";** yellow cover 20

MH-45-159: **"Songs from Walt Disney Films";** red cover 20

Section D
78 RPM Records

Note: Price estimates for all 78 rpm records are for VG+ condition copies. Grades higher than VG+ will command premium prices above those listed. See "Condition and Pricing of the Records."

78 rpm records were the industry standard until they began their fade-out in 1948 with the introduction of Columbia's then new LP format and RCA's introduction of the 45 rpm 7" disc in 1949. During the 1950s, singles were often pressed on both 45 rpm records and in the 10" 78 rpm format. Smaller 7" and 6" 78 rpm records were often produced for the children's market, i.e., "Kiddie" records, as early as the 1930s, often with special colorful labels and some picture discs. Disney series singles from the 1950s, e.g., the "DBR" and "LG" records had the records in both formats.

Other than its very short playing time, the initial biggest drawback to 78 rpm children's records was the fragility of the early shellac/wax based record itself, which often seemed as if it would break and shatter if you looked at it the wrong way! This problem was solved in the 1940s with the introduction of vinyl, plastic and or "Bakelite" process records, deemed as "unbreakable" in the children's market. This new material was used extensively in the non-Disney label recordings of the 1940s and early 1950s. When Disney began to issue its own recordings in the mid-1950s, vinyl had become standard, and the records have survived in varying conditions. As noted above, Disney-related recordings in 78 rpm format are difficult (but not impossible) to find above VG+ condition due to handling by children and the playback medium of the time.

DBR-50: ***"Mickey Mouse Club March"/"Merry Mouseketeers March"/"Monday Through Friday Songs"***

Note: Songs marked with * are non-Disney selections.

D1
Disney 10" 78 rpm "EP" Recordings—The Mickey Mouse Club "DBR" Records

These were initially released by Golden Records and distributed by AMPAR under an arrangement with Disney in 1955. You should review the prior notes above at Section C8. However many of

DBR-51: ***"Fun with Music—Vol. I"***

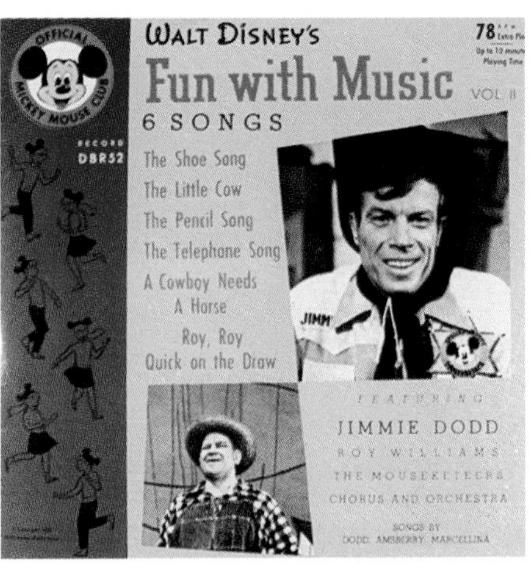

DBR-52: ***"Fun with Music—Vol. II";***

the records bore the familiar Mickey Mouse Club emblem on the label, so most people think of them as "Disney" releases. Some pressings bore Cinderella's castle as a logo on the record. Early editions in the series exist in orange vinyl and some in black vinyl editions. Originals up to DBR-61 were first issued in orange vinyl, and thereafter black vinyl. Numbers DBR-50 to DBR-61 on black vinyl are second pressings. These originally had cardboard covers which switched to paper sleeves at DBR-62. While these are technically 78 rpm "EPs" ("Extra Play"—"Up to 10 minutes playing time"), due to their 10" size, they facially appear to be standard "78's," hence they are included here.[1]

Numbers 50 through at least 92 appeared as the same numbers and titles on the Mickey Mouse Club 45 rpm "DBR" EP series also (See above at Section C8). While the 45 rpm EP editions sequenced through DBR-97, these 78 rpm editions ended with DBR-92. Their larger cover size makes them more collectible than the 45 DBRs.

Disney took back control of the record series in 1958. Original issues up to and including DBR-70 will bear the "AM-PAR" distribution notice on the cover and/or the record label.

Note: DBR-50 through DBR-61 were issued with cardboard covers.

DBR-50: **"Mickey Mouse Club March"/"Merry Mouseketeers March"/"Monday Through Friday Songs";** 1955
- Orange vinyl **50**
- Black vinyl **30**

DBR-51: Jimmie Dodd and the Mouseketeers **"Fun with Music—Vol. I";** 1955
- Orange vinyl **30**
- Black vinyl **25**

DBR-52: **"Fun with Music—Vol. II";** 1955
- Orange vinyl **30**
- Black vinyl **25**

DBR-53: Jimmy Dodd, Frances Archer, and Beverly Gile **"Fun with Music from Many Lands";** 1955

[1] Note that Little Golden Records had also earlier produced a series of 10" 78 rpm EPs known as "Big Golden Records" in which its Disney related titles were also numbered as "DBR" (Disney Big Record). Do not confuse them with these Disney issues. See Section F below.

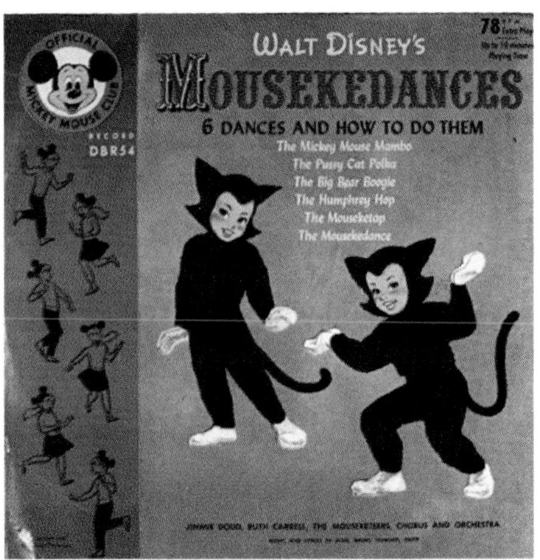

*DBR-54: **"Mousekedances: 6 Dances and How to Do Them"***

Orange vinyl **30**
Black vinyl **25**

DBR-54: Jimmy Dodd, Ruth Carrell, and the Mouseketeers **"Mousekedances: 6 Dances and How to Do Them"**; 1955
Orange vinyl **30**
Black vinyl **25**

DBR-55: Jimmie Dodd and the Mouseketeers "**Mouseketunes"**; 1955
Orange vinyl **30**
Black vinyl **25**

DBR-56: Cliff Edwards **"Jiminy Cricket Sings 5 Mickey Mouse Club Songs"**; 1955
Orange vinyl **30**
Black vinyl **25**

DBR-57: Cliff Edwards **"Jiminy Cricket Presents Bongo"**; 1955
Orange vinyl **30**
Black vinyl **25**

DBR-58: Tim Considine **"Spin and Marty—The Triple 'R' Song"**; 1956; (Jones)
Orange vinyl **30**
Black vinyl **25**

*DBR-57: Cliff Edwards **"Jiminy Cricket Presents Bongo"***

DBR-59: Darlene Gillespie and Buddy Ebsen **"Corky and White Shadow"**; 1956
Orange vinyl **30**
Black vinyl **25**

DBR-60: Buddy Ebsen **"Story of Johnny Appleseed"**; 1956
Orange vinyl **35**
Black vinyl **25**

DBR-61: Cliff Edwards **"Story of The Littlest Outlaw"**; 1956; (Lava)
Orange vinyl **40**
Black vinyl **30**

Note: Issues below only appeared on black vinyl and with paper sleeves.

DBR-62: Jimmie Dodd **"Mousekethoughts"**; 1956 ...... **30**

DBR-63: Mouseketeers **"Roll Up the Rug for More Mousekedances"**; 1956 .... **30**

DBR-64: Darlene Gillespie **"Mousekemusicals"**; 1956 .... **30**

DBR-65: Jiminy Cricket **"Safety First"**; 1956 .... **30**

DBR-68: *"Mousekartoon Time"*

DBR-70: *"Four Songs from Cinderella"*

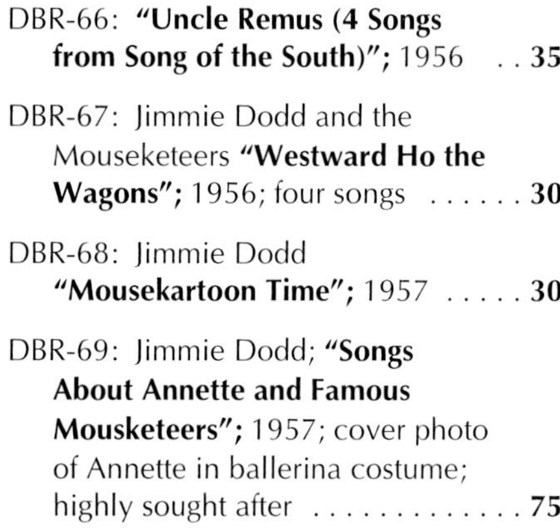

DBR-66: **"Uncle Remus (4 Songs from Song of the South)"**; 1956 . . 35

DBR-67: Jimmie Dodd and the Mouseketeers **"Westward Ho the Wagons"**; 1956; four songs 30

DBR-68: Jimmie Dodd **"Mousekartoon Time"**; 1957 30

DBR-69: Jimmie Dodd; **"Songs About Annette and Famous Mousketeers"**; 1957; cover photo of Annette in ballerina costume; highly sought after 75

DBR-75: *"Karen and Cubby"*

DBR-70: Jimmie Dodd and Darlene Gillespie **"Four Songs from Cinderella"**; 1957 30

Note: AM-PAR releases end at DBR-70. Remaining issued by Disneyland.

DBR-71: Mouseketeers **"We're the Mouseketeers"**; 1958 30

DBR-72: Jimmie Dodd and Darlene Gillespie **"Songs from 'Perri' "**; 1958 30

DBR-73: Jerome Courtland **"The Saga of Andy Burnett"**; 1958 35

DBR-74: Darlene Gillespie **"Mickey's Big Show"**; 1958 30

DBR-75: Karen Pendleton and Cubby O'Brien **"Karen and Cubby"**; 1958 30

DBR-76: Jerome Courtland and Kevin Corcoran **"Old Yeller"**; 1958 35

DBR-77: Henry Calvin **"Songs from Walt Disney's Zorro"**; 1958 40

DBR-78: Mouseketeers **"Four Songs from Walt Disney's Snow White"**; 1958 30

DBR 77
78 RPM
WALT DISNEY'S
ZORRO
Songs
from the exciting
TV Series

DBR-77: "Songs from Walt Disney's Zorro"

DBR 78
FOUR SONGS FROM
Walt Disney's
Snow White
and
The Seven
Dwarfs
featuring the
MOUSEKETEERS
78 RPM

DBR-78: "Four Songs from Walt Disney's Snow White"

DBR-79: Annette, Jimmie Dodd, and Darlene Gillespie **"Words to Grow By"**; 1958 . . . . **35**

DBR-80: **"Song and Story of The Three Little Pigs"**; 1958 . . . . **30**

DBR-81: Jimmie Dodd **"Songs from Walt Disney's Peter Pan"**; 1958 . . **35**

DBR-82: **"Songs from Walt Disney's TV Serials"**; 10/1958 . . . . **40**

DBR-83: **"Moochie and Three Other Songs from TV Show"**; 10/1958 . . **30**

DBR-84: Darlene Gillespie and Jimmie Dodd **"Many Happy Returns"**; 10/1958 . . . . **30**

DBR-85: **"Holidays with the Mouseketeers—Part I (4 Holiday Songs)"**; 1958; Mouseketeers **30**

DBR-86: **"Holidays with the Mouseketeers—Part II (4 Holiday Songs)"**; 1958; Mouseketeers **30**

DBR-87: Mouseketeers **"Holidays with the Mouseketeers—Part III"**; 10/1958 . . . . **30**

DBR-88: Darlene Gillespie **"Sleeping Beauty—Songs and Story"/"Once Upon a Dream"/"I Wonder"**; 1958 . . . . **30**

DBR-89: Disneyland Chorus **"Four Songs from Walt Disney's Sleeping Beauty"**; 1958 . . . . **30**

DBR-90: **"Story and Song of Paul Bunyan (Parts I and II)"**; 11/1958; (Bruns); Thurl Ravenscroft narrates **30**

DBR-91: Camarata and Chorus **"Christmas Trees of Disneyland"**; 10/1958; includes "Jingle Bones," "Adventureland Christmas Tree," "Fantasyland Story Book Tree,"

78 RPM
MORE PLAYING TIME
MORE SONGS
"Many Happy Returns"
Happy Birthday
from
the Mouseketeers
Especially for you
The Unbirthday Song

DBR-84: "Many Happy Returns"

and "Tomorrowland Fantastic Christmas Tree" **30**

DBR-92: Moochie and Roberta Shore **"The Shaggy Dog";** 1958 . . . **30**

D2
Disneyland "LG" 6" 78 rpm Series

These were 6", single 78 rpm records with an aqua color label and picture sleeve. Some have no paper label, with the information printed directly in ink in the label area. They tracked the 45 rpm "LG" (Little Gem) Series at least through LG-782 (See also Section "E6" below). They are very difficult to locate in near mint condition. As noted above, values listed are for records, with their sleeves, in VG+ condition.

LG-701: **"Donald Duck and His Nephews Sing Clementine"/"We Boys Will Shine Tonight";** 6/1960 . . . . **20**

LG-702: **"Donald Duck and Uncle Scrooge's Money Rocket (A Fun Story)";** 6/1960 . . . . **20**

LG-703: **"Mickey's Band Concert"/"While Walking Through the Park One Day"/"The Band Played On"/"In the Good Old Summertime";** 6/1960 . . . . **20**

LG-704: **"Chipmunk Fun with Chip 'n' Dale";** 6/1960 . . . . **20**

LG-705: **"Walt Disney's Mother Goose Rhymes"/"London Bridge Is Falling Down"/"Here We Go 'Round the Mulberry Bush Disneyland Children's Chorus";** 6/1960 . . . . **20**

LG-706: **"Walt Disney's Bear Went Over the Mountain"/"Sing A Song of Six Pence"/"Hey Diddle Diddle"/"Misty Moisty Morning Disneyland Children's Chorus";** 6/1960 . . . . **20**

LG-707: **"Walt Disney's Lullabies: Rockabye Baby"/"Brahms' Lullaby";** 6/1960 . . . . **20**

LG-708: **"Walt Disney's Frog Went A-Courtin' "/"Fiddle Dee Dee";** 6/1960; Frances Archer and Beverly Gile **20**

LG-709: **"America the Beautiful"** (Hayley Mills)/**"Yankee Doodle"** (Disneyland Chorus); 6/1960 . . . . . **30**

LG-710: **"Walt Disney's Three Little Pigs"/"Alouette"/"Polly Polly Doodle"/"Talk Happiness"/"As Beauty Does";** 7/1960 . . . . **20**

LG-711: **"I've Been Working on the Railroad"/"Hail, Hail The Gang's All Here"/"For He's a Jolly Good Fellow";** 6/1960; Mickey and His Gang **15**

LG-712: **"Chip 'n' Dale Chipmunks and Goofy Sing for You"/"I'm a Little Prairie Flower"** (Chip 'n' Dale)/**"Daisy, Daisy" /"Kookaburra"** (Goofy); 6/1960 . . . . **15**

LG-713: **"Music from the Swiss Family Robinson"/"My Monkey and Me"/"The Animal Race Polka";** 11/1960 . . . . **20**

LG-714 **"101 Dalmatians—Dalmatian Plantation"/"Cruella De Ville";** 11/1960 . . . . **20**

LG-715: **"A Song for Your Happy Birthday and for All Your Unbirthdays"/"Happy Birthday"/"The Unbirthday Song";** 11/1960; features Jimmie Dodd, Darlene Gillespie, and Tommy Cole **20**

LG-716: **"Jiminy Cricket, Traffic Cop: Stop, Look and Listen"/"Safety First";** 11/1960 . . . . **15**

LG-717: **"Donald Duck the Milkman"/"Donald Duck the Peanut Vendor";** 11/1960; Jiminy Cricket and Donald Duck **15**

LG-718: **"Walt Disney's Frere Jacques"/"The Little Nut Tree";** 11/1960; France Archer and Beverly Gile **15**

LG-719: **"Donald's Fire Station"/"Donald's Temper";** 11/1960; Jiminy Cricket and Donald Duck **15**

LG-720: **"The Swing"/"Marching Song" (from LP "A Child's Garden of Verses");** 11/1960; France Archer and Beverly Gile . . . **15**

LG-721: **"March of the Toys"/"Babes in Toyland";** 7/1961 . . . . **20**

LG-722: **"I Can't Do the Sum"/"Just a Whisper Away";** 7/1961; Annette **40**

LG-723: **"Barnaby's Songs from Babes in Toyland"/"We Won't Be Happy Till We Get It"/"Castle in Spain";** 6/21/1961 . . . . **15**

LG-724: **"Toymaker's Songs from Babes in Toyland"/"The Workshop Song"/"Just a Toy";** 7/1961; Ed Wynn **15**

LG-725: **"Mary Had a Little Lamb"/"Mother Goose Nursery Rhymes";** 7/1961; Sterling Holloway **15**

LG-726: **"Six Riddles from Mother Goose"/"Riddles and Rhymes";** 7/1961; Sterling Holloway **15**

LG-727: **"Land of Nod"/"Block City"/"Child's Garden";** 7/1961; Frances Archer and Beverly Gile . . **15**

LG-728: **"The Tortoise and the Hare (Parts 1 & 2)";** 7/1961; Sterling Holloway **15**

LG-729: **"I'm Ludwig Von Drake"/"Green with Envy Blues";** 6/1961 . . . . **20**

LG-730: **"Carnival Time with Ludwig Von Drake";** 7/1961 . . . . . **20**

LG-731: **"Jingle Bells"/"From All of Us to All of You";** 7/1961; The All-Mouse Choir **15**

LG-732: **"Silent Night"/"Christmas Carols";** 7/1961; The All-Mouse Choir **15**

LG-733: **"I've Got No Strings—Story from Pinocchio";** 1/1962 . . . . **20**

LG-734: **"When You Wish Upon a Star"/"How the Blue Fairy Brought Pinocchio to Life and Jiminy Cricket Became His Conscience";** 1/1962; Jiminy Cricket **20**

LG-735: **"Give a Little Whistle"/"How Pinocchio and Jiminy Cricket Searched for Gepetto Under the Sea";** 1/1962; Jiminy Cricket **20**

LG-736: **"Hi Diddle Dee Dee—Story from Pinocchio";** 1/1962 . . . . **20**

LG-737: **"ABC's Made Simple: Acting Out the A-B-C's"/"Looby Loo";** 1/1962 . . . . **15**

LG-738: **"Itsy Bitsy Spider"/"Pop Goes the Weasel"/"Ten Little Indians";** 1/15/1962 . . . . **15**

LG-739: **"And They Lived Happily Ever After"/"Someday My Prince Will Come";** 1/1962; MST; Snow White; cover same as WDL-4005 . . **20**

LG-740: **"Heigh Ho, Heigh Ho"/"How the Witch Gave a Poisoned Apple to Snow White";** 1/1962; Seven Dwarfs **20**

LG-741: **"Whistle While You Work"/"How Snow White Found the Cottage of the Seven Dwarfs";** 5/1962 . . . . **20**

LG-742: **"Seven Dwarf's Washing Song (Buddle-Uddle-Um-Dum)"/"How Grumpy Got His Face Washed";** 5/1962 . . . . **20**

LG-743: **"Who's Afraid of the Big Bad Wolf"/"Three Kinds of Pigs' Houses";** 5/1962; The Three Little Pigs **20**

LG-744: **"Casey, Jr."/"Timothy Mouse Tells About Circus Life";** 5/1962 . . . . **20**

LG-745: **"One, Two, Three's—Children's Counting Songs"/"One Potato, Two Potato"/"One, Two, Buckle My Shoe";** 5/1962 . . . . **15**

LG-746: **"The Farmer's in the Dell"/"The Friendly Farmer";** 5/1962 . . . . **15**

LG-747: **"Ten Little Indians (Parts 1 & 2)";** 5/1962; A collection of counting rhymes **15**

LG-748: **"Humpty Dumpty (Parts 1 & 2)";** 5/1962; Sterling Holloway . . **15**

LG-749: **"Old King Cole and Other Nursery Rhymes"/"Old Mother Hubbard";** 7/1962; Sterling Holloway **15**

LG-750: **"Mickey Mouse Club March"/"Mickey Mouse Club Closing Theme";** 7/1962; Jimmie Dodd and the Mouseketeers **25**

LG-751: **"Twas the Night Before Christmas (Parts 1 & 2)";** 5/1962; Jiminy Cricket **15**

LG-752: **"Christmas at Disneyland"/"The Storybook Land Christmas Tree"/"The Futuristic Christmas Tree";** 5/1962; Camarata conducts **15**

LG-753: **"Mouseketunes"/"The Merry Mousketeers"/"Fun with Music";** 5/1962; Jimmie Dodd and the Mouseketeers **20**

LG-754: **"Mousekedance"/"Pussy Cat Polka"** Jimmie Dodd and the Mouseketeers (5/1962) **20**

LG-755: **"He's A Tramp"/"Bella Notte";** 11/1962; from *Lady and the Tramp* **20**

LG-756: **"Siamese Cat Song"/"Home Sweet Home";** 11/1962 . . . . **20**

LG-757: **"Sammy the Way Out Seal"/"Animals and Clowns";** 11/1962 . . . . **15**

LG-758: **"Annette"** (Jimmie Dodd)/**"How Will I Know My Love"** (Annette); 11/1962; Annette on cover. **40**

LG-759: **"The Litterbug Song"/"I'm No Fool";** 1/1963; Jiminy Cricket **15**

LG-760: **"The Story of Hop, the Grasshopper"/"The World Owes Me a Living";** 1/30/1963; Sterling Holloway **20**

LG-761: **"Johnnie Shiloh, The Drummer Boy"/"Dixie";** 1/1963 . . . . **20**

LG-762: **"The Legend of Sleepy Hollow"/"The Headless Horseman"/"Ichabod Crane";** 1/1963 . . . . **20**

LG-763: **"How Paul Bunyan Raced an Engine and a Saw"/"The Paul Bunyan Song";** 1/1963; Thurl Ravenscroft **20**

LG-764: **"Baa Baa Black Sheep"/"Mother Goose Nursery Rhymes";** 2/1963 . . . . **15**

LG-765: **"Three Little Kittens"/"More Pussy Cat Rhymes";** 2/1963 . . . . . . **15**

LG-766: **"Twinkle, Twinkle Little Star"/"All Through the Night";** 2/1963 . . . . **15**

LG-767: **"Higitus Figitus"/"The Legend of the Sword in the Stone";** 7/1963 . . . . **20**

LG-768: **"That's What Makes the World Go Round"/"Mad Madam Mim";** 1963 . . . . **20**

LG-769: **"Most Befuddling Thing"/"Blue Oak Tree";** 7/1963 . . . . **20**

LG-770: **"The Ugly Bug Ball"/"Femininity";** 6/14/1963; from Summer Magic **20**

LG-771: **"Bibbidi Bobbidi Boo"/"Oh Sing Sweet Nightingale";** 7/1963; Ilene Woods **20**

LG-772: **"Sailor Songs"/"Sailing, Sailing"/"Blow the Man Down";** 7/1963; Chip 'n' Dale **15**

LG-773: **"Story of Bambi and Thumper (Parts I and II)";** 7/1963 . . **20**

LG-774: **"The Scarecrow of Romney Marsh"/"Trick or Treat";** 5/1964; The Wellingtons **20**

LG-775: **"It's a Small World Parts I and II";** 5/1964 . . . . **15**

LG-776: **"The Story of Jack and Jill (Parts 1 & 2)";** 6/1964; Rica Moore **15**

LG-777: **"The Story of London Bridge (Parts 1 & 2)";** 6/1964; Rica Moore **15**

LG-778: **"How the Lost Boys Were Captured by Friendly Indians"/"Tee-Dum, Tee-Dee";** 6/1964 . . . . **20**

LG-779: **"Addition Made Easy"/"The Glory Tree";** 6/1964; Jiminy Cricket and Rica Moore **15**

LG-780: **"A Spoonful of Sugar"/"One Man Band";** 6/1964; Marni Nixon **20**

LG-781: **"Supercalifragilistic-expialidocious"** (Marni Nixon and Bill Lee)/**"Step in Time"** (Bill Lee); 6/1964 . . . . **20**

LG-782: **"Jolly Holiday"/"I Love to Laugh";** 6/1964; Richard Sherman . . **20**

D3
Non-Disney Label 78 rpm Recordings

As seen from today's viewpoint, it is interesting to note the issuance of large numbers of "cover" records, i.e., different renditions of the same song by different artists. This was commonplace and popular from the 1930s until approximately 1955. During that time period it was the "song" itself which was popular, not necessarily the rendition by a particular artist.[2] Thus, many different singers or bands could have concurrent "hit" versions of the same song on the music charts of the day, though some, of course, were more popular than others. Many of these appear below in the major label singles catalogs.

The popularity of "cover records" faded out quickly and dramatically in the mid-1950s when the sounds of early rock and roll music began to dominate the popular records charts. Since that time pop hits have been essentially artist-specific, where only a particular rendition of a song becomes popular, identified only with one artist thereafter, and seldom ever later "covered" except in "tribute" compilations by other artists.

---

[2] There were, of course, exceptions. For example, it is difficult to imagine any other version of "Der Fuehrer's Face" except that done by Spike Jones and His City Slickers!

D3.1: ABC-*Paramount* 10" 78 *rpm* *Records*

In 1955, Disney leased masters of some recordings for one year. See the ABC listings in the 45 rpm section as well.

9665: Jimmie Dodd **"The Mouseketeer Theme"/ "Hi to You"** **10**

D3.2: (RCA) *Bluebird* 10" 78 *rpm* *Records*

D3.2.1: Silly Symphony/ Shorts Records and Albums

This was a series of individual original movie soundtrack recordings (MST) from Disney's "Silly Symphonies" (SS) and Mickey Mouse (MM) shorts from the 1930s. The prefix "BK" stands for "Bluebird Kiddie" records. At the time, Bluebird was an independent label produced by RCA. This ended in 1946 when Bluebird became merely a series in the RCA line.

The singles were originally released in England on the "H.M.V." ("His Master's Voice") label in 1936 through Gramaphone Co. Ltd., the RCA affiliate.[3] However, the American (RCA) Bluebirds below were not issued until October 1937. Thus, these are the first original soundtrack recordings ever released on records, albeit they are from cartoon "shorts." As you will see below, Victor's release in January 1938 of the original soundtrack music and songs from *Snow White and the Seven Dwarfs*, makes "Snow White" the first original soundtrack recording *album* of a full-length feature released in the United States. The English release number is listed at the end of the individual American listing. Each American Bluebird release of these records had a paper sleeve for each individual record which depicted Mickey and Minnie. Add $40 for each such picture.

BK-5: **"Who Killed Cock Robin? (Parts I and II)";** (Churchill); SS; (H.M.V. BD-358) **100**

BK-6: **"Lullaby Land (Parts I and II)";** (Harline/Churchill); SS; (H.M.V. BD-370) **100**

BK-7: **"The Pied Piper (Parts I and II)";** (Harline); SS; (H.M.V. BD-375) **100**

BK-8: **"Mickey's Grand Opera"** (Harline)/**"The Orphans' Benefit"** (Churchill); MM; (H.M.V. BD-382) **100**

BK-9: **"The Grasshopper and the Ants"** (Harline), SS/**"Mickey's Moving Day"** (Harline/Malotte), MM; (H.M.V. BD-386) **100**

BK-10: **"Three Little Wolves"** (Churchill)/**"Three Little Pigs"** (Churchill) SS; (H.M.V. BD-387) **100**

Bluebird packaged these six singles into two "BC" three-record sets. "BC" was the designation for "Bluebird Children's" sets. They are each contained in a heavy paper sleeve, probably with an "envelope"-type closing similar to the "Snow White" RCA "J-8" and "Y-6" "Snow White"

[3] While this book lists values for American recordings only, I would be remiss in not informing readers that the British "H.M.V." 78 rpm recordings have beautiful, yellow labels with Disney cartoon drawings on them, and are themselves very collectible and highly sought after. The British "H.M.V." recordings were later released, c. 1945, in a "Specially Decorated Album to Hold Six Records": "Mickey Mouse and Silly Symphonies." There was also a later English (SS) pressing No. H.M.V. BD-910: "Farmyard Symphony—Parts I and II" (Harline). One of the Bluebird "Silly Symphony" singles may have been later released on an American Montgomery Ward (Ward) 78 rpm record. This is unconfirmed.

sets discussed below. The release date for these sets is probably 1940 inasmuch as set BC-3 advertises the availability of "Pinocchio" 78 rpm set P-18 as well. BMG Archives indicates they also appeared in the December 1941 Bluebird Records catalog. The list price for these albums is noted at "$.35 ea.," which would have made the album cost $1.05. It is possible that the records were originally sold only in these packaged sets on their release, as Bluebird listings of the time couple them only as records within the individual sets. The currently known cover graphics to these sets are indicated. Prices include the extremely rare picture sleeve cover to the set!

BC-3: "Mickey Mouse Presents Walt Disney's Silly Symphony Songs"

BC-2: **"Silly Symphony";** three record set contains records BK-5, BK-6, and BK-7; sleeve graphics currently unknown; extremely rare **500**

BC-3: **"Mickey Mouse Presents Walt Disney's Silly Symphony Songs";** three record set contains records BK-8, BK-9, and BK-10; black, white, and red (maroon) cover shows Mickey Mouse pointing to a sign post which reads "Silly Symphony Songs"; back cover contains listings of other available Victor and Bluebird Childrens' records including Victor J-8 (original "Snow White" 78 rpm album) and Victor P-18 (original "Pinocchio" 78 rpm album); extremely rare **500**

D3.2.2: Other Bluebird/ 78 rpm records

Bluebird B-3021: **"Las Tres Chanchitos (Part 1 & 2)" (The Three Little Pigs);** Spanish language version **50**

Bluebird B-3023: **"Quien Mato Al Pechirrojo?" (Who Killed Cock Robin);** Spanish language version . . **50**

Bluebird B-3027: **"El Raton Voladar" (The Flying Mouse);** 1937; Bluebird release in a Spanish language version; from the film short **50**

Bluebird 39-3000 ("Y-1"): **"The Three Little Pigs"** (see Section D3.31.3 under RCA 78 rpm Children's Records as "Y-1")

Bluebird 0019: **"Bibbidi-Bobbidi-Boo"/ ;** Ilene Woods; charted January 14, 1950 . . . . **10**

Bluebird B-5178: **"Who's Afraid of the Big Bad Wolf"/ ;** recorded 9/15/1933; Bill Scotti and Orchestra **20**

Bluebird 7343: **"Whistle While You Work"/ ;** Shep Fields & His Rippling Rhythm Orchestra; charted on Jan. 22, 1938 . . . . **15**

Bluebird 10570: **"When You Wish Upon a Star"/"The Gaucho Serenade"*;** Glenn Miller Orchestra; charted March 20, 1940 . . . . **10**

Bluebird B-11556: **"Love is a Song" (from *Bambi*)/"Tapestry in Blue"*;** Teddy Powell and Orchestra **15**

*Bluebird BY-27: **"A Whale of a Tale"/"Old Betsy"***

*Cadence CCS-1: Bill Hayes **"The Ballad of Davy Crockett"/"Farewell"***

Bluebird B-11586: **"Der Fuehrer's Face"/"I Wanna Go Back to West Virginia"*;** from Disney short of the same name; Spike Jones & His City Slickers; original title for the short was to have been "Donald Duck in Nutziland"; the record, obviously released prior to the film's name change, indicates it was from the film "Nuttsey Land"; charted Oct. 3, 1942 . . . . **25**

D3.2.3: (RCA) Bluebird "Children's Series" 78 rpm Singles

These sold at 49¢ each with picture covers.

Bluebird BY-25: **"The Ballad of Davy Crockett"/"The Graveyard Filler of the West";** Children's Series; Sons of the Pioneers **25**

Bluebird BY-26: **"Lady and the Tramp"/"Siamese Cat Song";** Children's Series **15**

Bluebird BY-27: **"A Whale of a Tale"/"Old Betsy";** Children's Series; Sons of the Pioneers **15**

Bluebird BY-52: **"Johnny Tremain"/"The Liberty Tree";** Children's Series **15**

Bluebird BY-56: **"Wringle Wrangle"/"Westward Ho the Wagons!";** Children's Series; Vaughn Monroe **15**

Bluebird BY-64: **"When You Wish Upon a Star"/"Whistle While You Work"** **15**

D3.3: Broadway 78 rpm Singles

296A: Jack Richards **"The Ballad of Davy Crockett";** Bimbo **20**

D3.4: Brunswick 78 rpm Singles

Brunswick 6651: Victor Young and Orchestra **"Who's Afraid of the Big Bad Wolf"/ ;** charted Sept. 30, 1933 . . . . **20**

Brunswick 8050: Artie Shaw Orchestra **"One Song" (from *Snow White*)/ ;** charted February 19, 1938 . . . . **10**

Brunswick 8074: Horace Heidt Orchestra, vocals by the Kings

Capitol CC-40: ***"Tales of Uncle Remus for Children"***

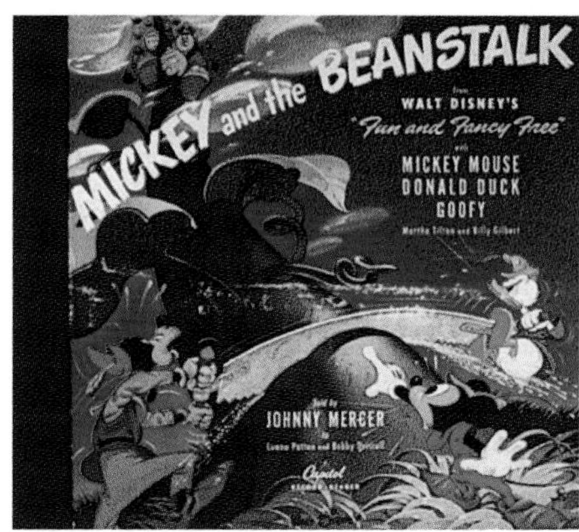

Capitol CCX-67: ***"Mickey and the Beanstalk"***

Men & Glee Club **"Heigh Ho"/ ;** charted March 5, 1938 . . . . **15**

D3.5: *Cadence 78 rpm Singles*

Cadence CCS-1: Bill Hayes **"The Ballad of Davy Crockett" /"Farewell";** 1955; P/S; Cadence Children's Series; yellow picture sleeve, featuring a line drawing of Davy, and a bear running away in the background; very rare sleeve
- Record and sleeve **80**
- Sleeve only **60**

Cadence 1256: Bill Hayes **"The Ballad of Davy Crockett/Farewell";** 1955 . . . . **20**

D3.6: *Capitol 78 rpm Albums and Singles*

D3.6.1: Capitol Children's Series Records

These are similar to the RCA "Little Nipper" 78 rpm sets, and, if two or more records, also have interior booklets and/or picture panels of Disney art. They also have beautiful Disney art covers. These same Capitol covers were reproduced on the 45 rpm, the EP editions and the LP editions. The "CAS" issues sold at 95¢.[4] Many of the covers of the later "CAS" series also contained a small logo of "Bozo the Clown," indicating a Capitol "Bozo approved" record. This is a very collectible series.

---

[4] To the best of my knowledge, Capitol's letter prefix codes can be partially deciphered as follows. The first letter position in the 78 rpms indicates the color of the label: "A"=red; "B"=black; "C"=purple; "D"=blue. The second letter refers to the numbers of records in the set: "A"=1 record; "B"=2 records; "C"=3 records; "D"=4 records, etc.

If there is an "X" in the third letter position, the listing is a Capitol "Record Reader," which has an internal multi-page Disney picture book and story. A letter "S" in the third letter position indicates it was a "picture-folder album." An "N" would indicate a boxed set. The concurrent 45 rpm editions had an "F" in the fourth letter position (see section G5).

As of Feb. 1949, the following retail price schedule was in effect for the other Capitol Disney-related 78 rpm "C" and "D" albums: "CB"-$2.25; "CC"-3.00; "CCX"-$3.75; "CD"-$3.75; "CE"-$4.50; "DAS"-$1.25; "DB"-$2.75; "DBS"-$2.25; "DBX"-$3.50; "DC"-$3.75; "DCX"-$4.50; "DD"-$4.75.

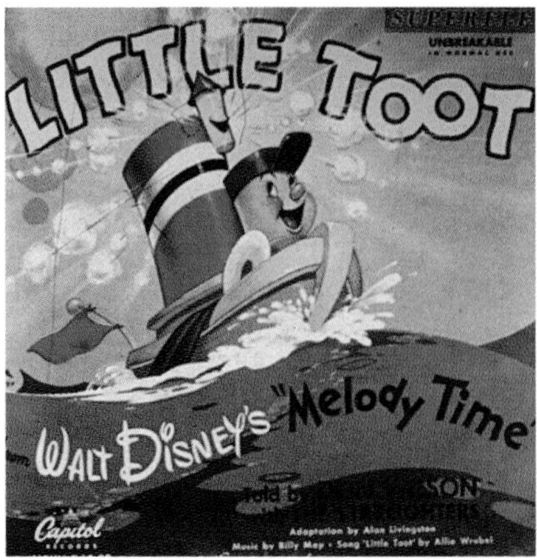

Capitol DAS-80: ***"Little Toot"***

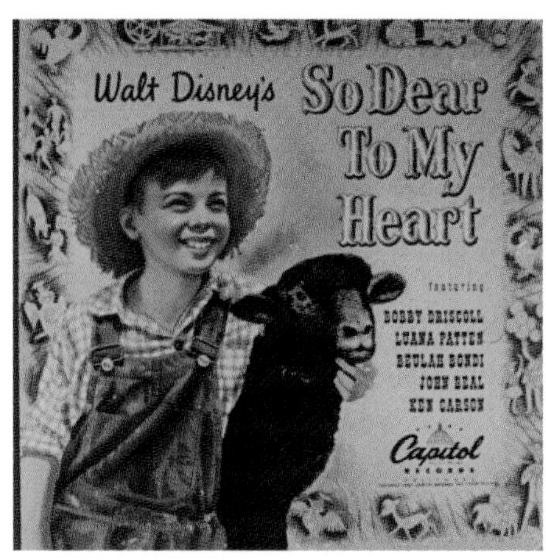

Capitol DD-109: ***"So Dear to My Heart"***

Capitol CC-40: **"Tales of Uncle Remus for Children";** 1947; three record set; from *Song of the South*; Johnny Mercer & Pied Pipers, with "Uncle Remus" and original cast; with interior cover picture panel; purple label records numbered 10069-10071; also appears as DC-116, CC-40 . . . .**50**

DC-116: identical, except it appears on blue label, "Superflex" unbreakable records, #25028-25030; original price: $3.00 . . . . . . **40**

Capitol CCX-67: **"Mickey and the Beanstalk";** 1947; three record set; breakable; from *Fun & Fancy Free*; Johnny Mercer as told to Luana Patten and Bobby Driscoll, with Martha Tilton, Billy Gilbert, and Billy May Orchestra; with 20-page booklet; individual records numbered 10098-10100 on CCX-67; a Capitol Record Reader; original price: $3.75
CCX-67 . . . . **70**

DCX-120: identical "unbreakable" vinyl album, records numbered 25039-25041 . . . . **50**

Capitol DAS-80: **"Little Toot";** from *Melody Time;* Don Wilson with The Starlighters and Billy May Orchestra; GF single with eleven picture panels; one record numbered 25004; original price: $1.25 . . . . **30**

Capitol DD-109: **"So Dear to My Heart";** 1949; four record set; "Superflex" unbreakable records; Billy May and original cast, including Bobby Driscoll, Luana Patten, Beulah Bondi, John Beal,

Capitol EAS-3048: ***"Mr. Toad"***

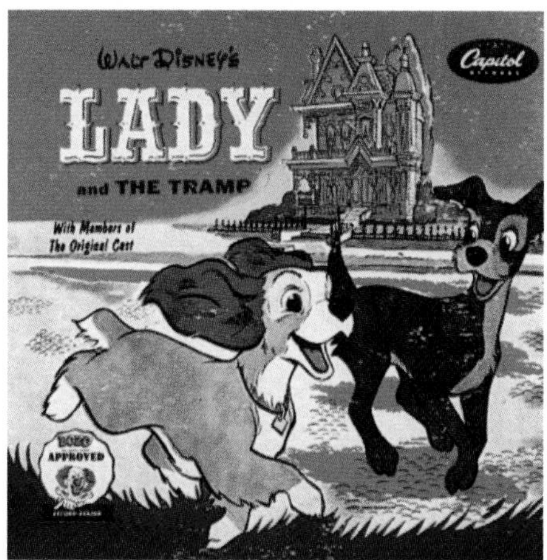

Capitol DBX-3056: ***"Lady and the Tramp"***

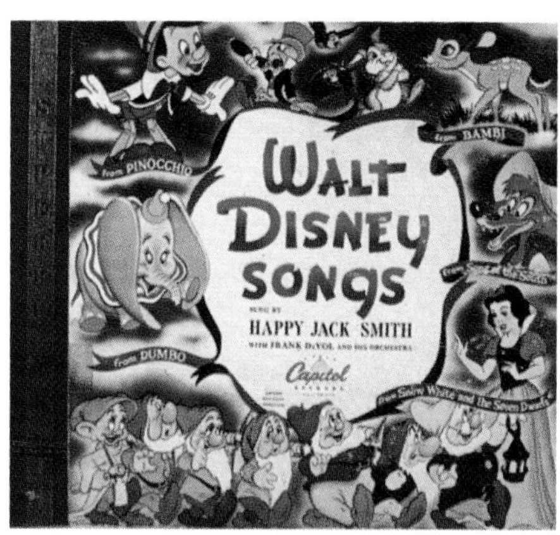

Capitol DC-3057: ***"Walt Disney Songs"***

and Ken Carson; fourteen panel photos from movie (no book); blue label; maroon spine; individual records numbered 25050-25053; also appears on BD-124; covers and interior picture panels are the same for both albums; original price: $4.75
DD-109: **40**

BD-124: regular black label records numbered 20157-20160; black spine; original price: $4.15 .... **50**

Capitol DBX-3013: **"The Three Little Pigs";** 1949; two record set; individual records numbered 30041-30041; Capitol Record Reader **45**

Capitol DBX-3034: **"The Grasshopper and the Ants";** 1949; Don Wilson and original cast; two record set; unbreakable; 21-page booklet; individual records numbered 77-30079 and 77-30080; Capitol Record Reader .. **40**

Capitol EAS-3048: **"Mr. Toad";** Basil Rathbone; 12" 78 rpm single; GF **45**

Capitol DBX-3056: **"Lady and the Tramp";** two record set; individual records numbered 32153-32154; Capitol Record Reader **45**

Capitol DC-3057: **"Walt Disney Songs";** Happy Jack Smith; three record set, includes: "Whistle While You Work," "The Dwarf's Yodel Song," "Hi Diddle Dee Dee (An Actor's Life for Me)," "Little Wooden Head," "Little April Shower," "Give a Little Whistle," "Heigh-Ho," "Bluddle Uddle Um Dum," "When I See an Elephant Fly," "Casey Junior," "Uncle Remus Said," and "Look Out for Mr. Stork"; numbered 32003, 32004 and third number unknown; original price: $3.75 ... **45**

Capitol CAS-3072: **"Little Hiawatha"**; Don Wilson **30**

Capitol CAS-3092: **"The Flying Mouse";** Don Wilson **30**

Capitol DBS-3094: **"The Sorcerer's Apprentice";** Don Wilson; two record set; GF **30**

Capitol CAS-3095: **"Ferdinand the Bull";** Don Wilson **40**

Capitol CAS-3092: ***"The Flying Mouse"***

Capitol DBS-3094: ***"The Sorcerer's Apprentice"***

Capitol CAS-3096: **"Three Orphan Kittens";** Don Wilson **40**

Capitol CAS-3099: **"Elmer Elephant";** Don Wilson **40**

Capitol CAS-3106: **"Brer Rabbit and the Tar Baby";** James Baskett and original cast; this record and the two below are single record editions of the three record album set CC-40 (and DC-116) above . . . **30**

Capitol CAS-3107: **"Brer Rabbit's Laughing Place"** **25**

Capitol CAS-3108: **"Brer Rabbit Runs Away"** **25**

Capitol CAS-3132: **"Bongo the Circus Bear";** Don Wilson **30**

Capitol CAS-3135: **"The Country Cousin";** Don Wilson **30**

Capitol CAS-3136: **"Little Hiawatha";** Don Wilson **30**

Capitol CAS-3096: ***"Three Orphan Kittens"***

Capitol CAS-3099: ***"Elmer Elephant"***

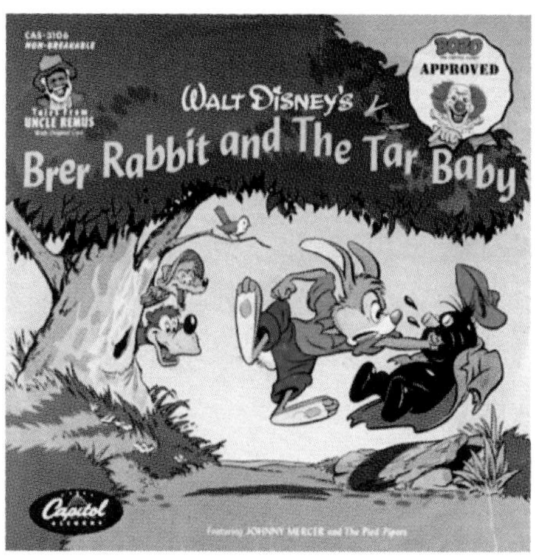

Capitol CAS-3106: ***"Brer Rabbit and the Tar Baby"***

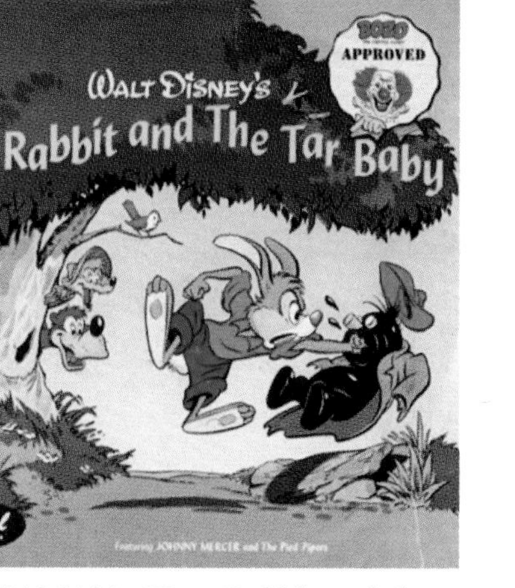

Capitol CAS-3132: ***"Bongo the Circus Bear"***

Capitol DBX-3138: **"Robin Hood";** two record set; 21-page booklet; Capitol Record Reader album **60**

Capitol CAS-3153: **"The Ugly Duckling";** Don Wilson and Stan Freeberg **35**

Capitol CAS-3156: **"You're Nothin' But a Nothin' " (from *The Flying Mouse*)/"Barnacle Bill, the Sailor"** (Candy Candido) **25**

Capitol CAS-3163: **"Never Smile at a Crocodile"/"Following the Leader";** Jerry Lewis **25**

Capitol DBX-3165: **"Mickey Mouse's Birthday Party";** Stan Freeberg; two record set; with booklet; beautiful, blue Mickey Mouse cover; Capitol Record Reader. **45**

Capitol CAS-3198: **"Rob Roy (The Highland Rogue)"** **50**

Capitol DBX-3138: ***"Robin Hood"***

Capitol CAS-3153: ***"The Ugly Duckling"***

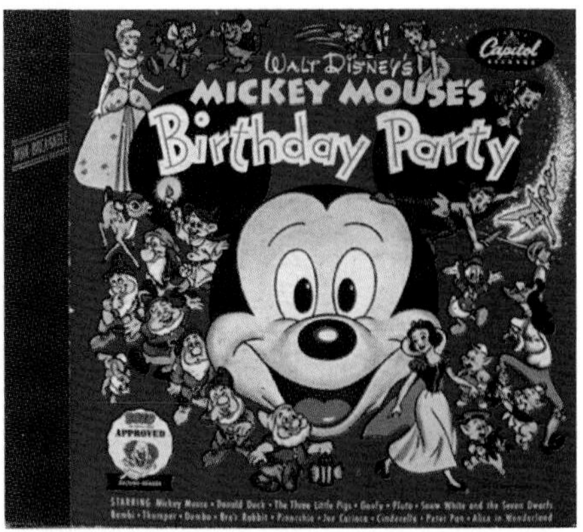

Capitol DBX-3165: **"Mickey Mouse's Birthday Party"**

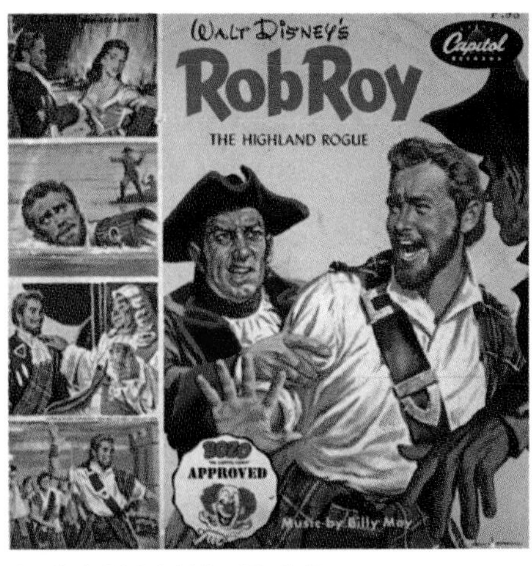

Capitol CAS-3198: **"Rob Roy**

Capitol CAS-3203: **"Pinocchio";** Art Gilmore and June Foray **30**

Capitol CAS-3229: **"The Ballad of Davy Crockett"/"Farewell";** Tennessee Ernie Ford **35**

D3.6.2: Capitol 78 rpm Singles

Capitol 249: Jerry Colonna & Frank De Vol Orchestra **"Casey—The Pride of them All" (from *Make Mine Music*)/"Josephine, Please No Lean on the Bell"*;** 1946 . . . . . **20**

Capitol 305: Pat O'Connor and Billy Butterfield Orchestra **"Sooner or Later (You're Gonna Be Coming Around)" (from *Song of the South*)/"Stardust"*;** 1946 . . . . **15**

Capitol 323: Johnny Mercer, Pied Pipers and Paul Weston Orchestra **"Zip-A-Dee-Doo-Dah" /"Ev'rybody Has a Laughing Place";** charted December 7, 1946; from *Song of the South* **15**

Capitol 461: Margaret Whiting with Frank de Vol Orchestra **"Lazy Countryside"/"So Far"*** **10**

Capitol 690: Jo Stafford & Gordon MacRae **"Bibbidi-Bobbidi-Boo" (from *Cinderella*)/"Echoes"*;** charted December 29, 1949 . . . . . **10**

Capitol 1247: Frank de Vol and Orchestra **"Jing-a-Ling, Jing-a-Ling" (from *Beaver Valley*)/"Sweethearts on Parade"*** **10**

Capitol 1511: The Dinning Sisters **"Very Good Advice" /"Somebody"*** **10**

Capitol 3058: Tennessee Ernie Ford **"The Ballad of Davy Crockett" /"Farewell";** P/S **30**

Capitol 3233: Hal Derwin and Orchestra **"No One But You" (an adaption of "Looking for Romance" (from *Bambi*)/** **10**

Capitol 15063: Andy Russell **"Blue Shadows on the Trail" (from *Melody Time*)/** **15**

Capitol 15225: Jack Smith with Earl Shelton Orchestra **"Lavender Blue (Dilly Dilly)" (from *So Dear to My Heart*)/** ; 1948; charted January 22, 1949 . . . . **15**

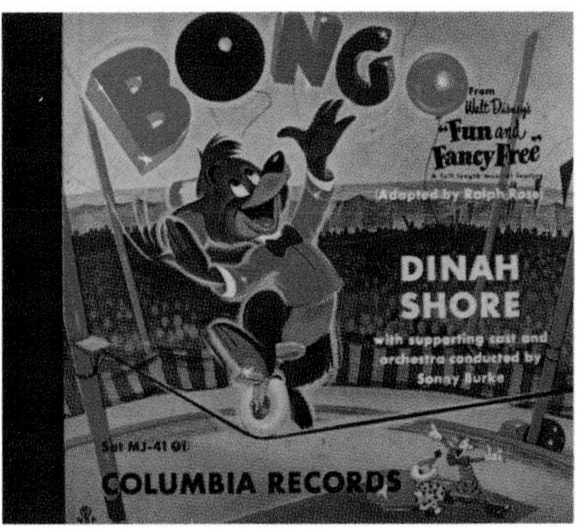

Columbia MJ-41: ***"Bongo"***

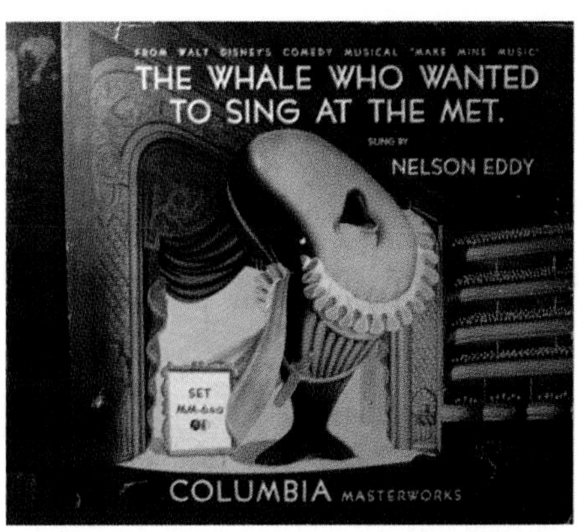

Columbia MM-640: ***"The Whale Who Wanted to Sing at the Met"***

Capitol 15232: Peggy Lee "**So Dear to My Heart"/** **15**

Capitol 15233: Pied Pipers **"It's Watcha Do With Watcha Got"/**Frank Silver **"Yes, We Have No Bananas"*;** 1948 . . . . **15**

D3.7: *Columbia 78 rpm Albums and Singles*

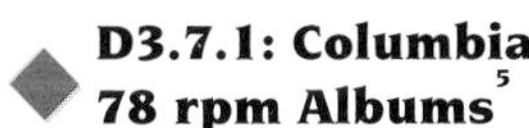

D3.7.1: Columbia 78 rpm Albums[5]

Columbia MJ-41: **"Bongo";** STK; three record set; from *Fun and Fancy Free*; Dinah Shore; Sonny Burke conducts; individual records numbered 37898-37900 . . **75**

Columbia MJV-107: **"Jiminy Cricket and the Sandman";** Paul Peterson and Cliff Edwards **35**

Columbia MJV-112: **"Songs from Alice in Wonderland";** Rosemary Clooney and Percy Faith Orchestra **35**

Columbia MM-640: **"The Whale Who Wanted to Sing at the Met";** c. 1946; MST; three record set; from *Make Mine Music*; Nelson Eddy **100**

[5] In the Columbia letter-prefix codes, "J" designates its "Junior" series. "V" indicates the record is vinyl based.

D3.7.2: Columbia Davy Crockett 78 rpm Albums

Columbia issued these TV soundtrack 78 rpm sets in both individual "Box-set" editions *and* in paper gatefold sleeves. The pictures are the same, as are the numbers. TV photo picture panels appear on the inside of the box-set lid, and in the interior gatefold of the paper-sleeve edition. The box-sets are the rarer of the two, however, both should be considered very rare. Disney had leased the master recordings to Columbia in December of 1954. Columbia's lease expired on February 6, 1958.

The albums derive from the tremendously popular Disney Davy Crockett TV

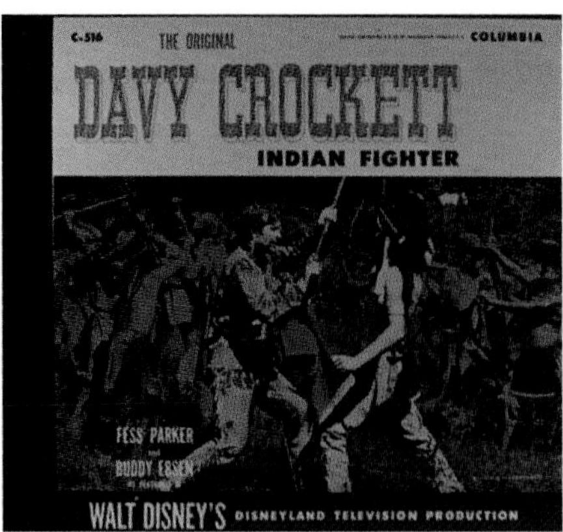

Columbia C-516: ***"Davy Crockett-Indian Fighter"***

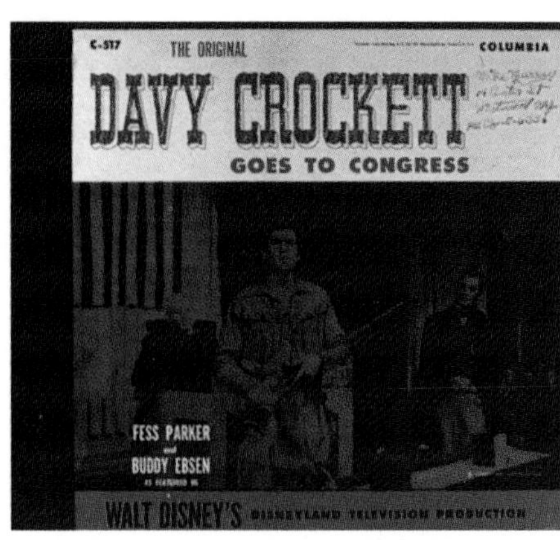

Columbia C-517: ***"Davy Crockett—Goes to Congress"***

Shows from 1954-1955 featuring Fess Parker and Buddy Ebsen. Score and Songs by George Bruns (See also Columbia listings in the Columbia "J" Series below and in non-Disney Columbia LPs and EPs sections).

Columbia C-516: **"Davy Crockett-Indian Fighter";** 1955; TV episode aired on December 15, 1954
Box set **75**
Paper Set **50**

Columbia C-517: **"Davy Crockett—Goes to Congress";** 1955; TV episode aired on January 26, 1955
Box set **75**
Paper set **50**

Columbia C-518: **"Davy Crockett—At The Alamo";** 1955; TV episode aired on February 23, 1955
Box set **100**
Paper set **75**

D3.7.3: Columbia 78 rpm Singles

D3.7.3.1: Columbia "J" (Junior) Children's 78 rpm Records

All have picture sleeves.

Columbia J-107: Cliff Edwards **"Jiminy Cricket and the Sandman"** **25**

Columbia J-242: Fess Parker **"The Ballad of Davy Crockett"/"I Gave My Love";** 1955; P/S **40**

Columbia J-254: Fess Parker and Buddy Ebsen **"Old Betsy"/"Be Sure You're Right";** P/S **30**

Columbia J-260: Fess Parker **"King of the River"/"Yeller, Yeller Gold"** . . **40**

Columbia J-261: **"Davy Crockett and Mike Fink: The Great Keelboat Race and Their Fight with the River Pirates";** 1956; two record set; 78 rpm; GF with picture panels and color cover; Note: "Davy Crockett's Keelboat

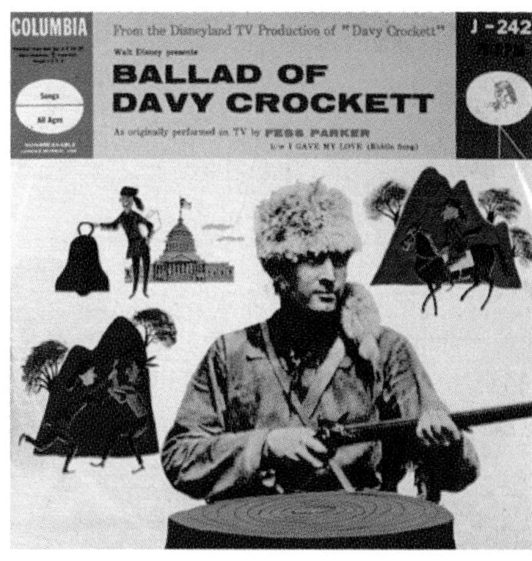

*Columbia J-242: Fess Parker **"The Ballad of Davy Crockett"/"I Gave My Love"***

*Columbia J-260: Fess Parker **"King of the River"/"Yeller, Yeller Gold"***

Race" aired on 11/16/55 and "Davy Crockett and the River Pirates" aired on 12/14/55. These were later combined into a movie *Davy Crockett and the River Pirates* released on 7/18/56; Rare **60**

Columbia J-268: Dotty Evans and Johnny Anderson **"When You Wish Upon a Star"/"When I See an Elephant Fly"** **25**

Columbia J-269: Johnny Anderson and the Merrymakers **"Heigh Ho"/"Whistle While You Work"** . . **25**

Columbia J-270: The Merrymakers **"Who's Afraid of the Big Bad Wolf/Bluddle-Uddle-Um-Dum"** . . **25**

Columbia J-271: Dotty Evans and Johnny Anderson **"Mickey Mouse's Birthday Party"/"Unbirthday Song"** **25**

D3.7.3.2: Columbia Regular Series 78 rpm Singles

Columbia D-213: Jimmie Dodd and the Frontier Men **"Be Sure You're Right"/"Old Betsy"** **15**

Columbia 2824: Ben Bernie Orchestra **"Who's Afraid of the Big Bad Wolf"/ ;** charted October 21, 1933 . . . . **25**

Columbia 35351: Horace Heidt Orchestra **"When You Wish Upon A Star"/ ;** charted April 20, 1940 . . . . **15**

Columbia 36651: Xavier Cugat Orchestra **"Brazil"/"Chiu-Chiu";** charted January 23, 1943 . . . . **15**

Columbia 36799: Tommy Tucker Trio **"Baia" (from *The Three Caballeros*)/ ;** 1943 . . . . **10**

Columbia 36967: Benny Goodman Orchestra with Liza Morrow **"All the Cats Join In" (from *Make Mine Music*)/"Don't Be a Baby, Baby"*;** 1946 . . . . **15**

Columbia 37050: Dinah Shore **"Two Silhouettes" (from *Make Mine Music*)/ ;** 1946 . . . . **10**

Columbia 37147: Modernaires with Paula Kelly & Mitchell Ayres Orchestra **"Zip-A-Dee-Doo-Dah"/ ;** charted January 11, 1947 . . **10**

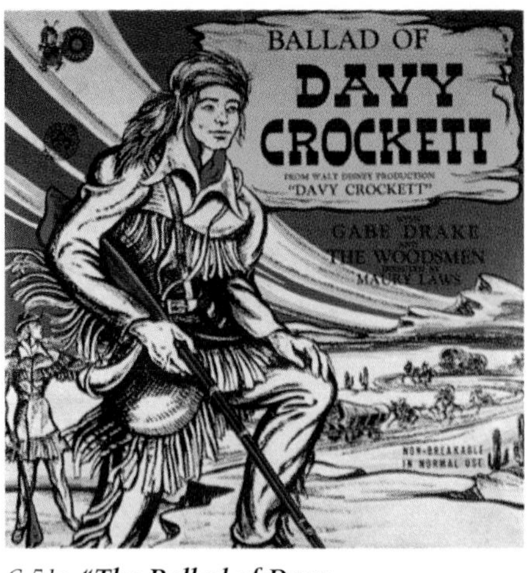

*C-51: "The Ballad of Davy Crockett"/"Cowboy Songs"**

Columbia 37206: Dinah Shore **"Sooner or Later"/** **10**

Columbia 37884: Dinah Shore **"Lazy Countryside"/** **10**

Columbia 38229: Dinah Shore **"Lavender Blue (Dilly Dilly)"/"So Dear to My Heart";** charted December 18, 1948 . . . . **10**

Columbia 38659: Dinah Shore **"Bibbidi-Bobbidi-Boo"/** ; charted February 11, 1950 . . . . **10**

Columbia 4-39295: Doris Day and the Four Hits **"Very Good Advice"/"It's So Laughable"*** **10**

Columbia 39302: Alan Dale **"I'm Late"/"Alice in Wonderland"** **10**

Columbia 40449: Fess Parker **"The Ballad of Davy Crockett"/"I Gave My Love";** 1955; Disney leased masters of this and the record below to Columbia in December of 1954; Columbia's lease expired on February 4, 1960 . . . . **20**

Columbia 40450: Fess Parker **"Farewell"/"I'm Lonely My Darling";** 1955 . . . . **20**

Columbia 40510: Fess Parker and Buddy Ebsen **"Be Sure You're Right (Then Go Ahead)"/"Old Betsy";** 1955; leased to Columbia until April 1, 1960 . . . . **20**

Columbia 40568: Fess Parker **"King of the River"/"Yaller, Yaller Gold";** leased to Columbia until August 5, 1960 . . . . **20**

D3.8: *Cricket* 78 *rpm* Singles

C-51: Gabe Drake and the Woodsmen **"The Ballad of Davy Crockett"/"Cowboy Songs"*;** colorful line-drawn cover of Davy Crockett **25**

C-52: **"Old Betsy (Davy Crockett's Rifle)"/"Davy Crockett March"** . . **25**

C-53: **"Siamese Cat Song"/"Tweedle Dee and Tweedle Dum"** **5**

C-61: The Overtones **"Zippy Doo Dah" (sic)/"Topsy-Turvy Town"*** . . **5**

C-86: **"Wringle Wrangle"/"Barnyard Song"*** **5**

D3.9: *Coral* 78 *rpm* Singles

Coral 60438: Les Brown Orchestra and Lucy Ann Polk **"Very Good Advice"/"T'was Brillig"** **10**

D3.10: *Decca* 78 *rpm Albums and* Singles

D3.10.1: Decca 78 rpm Albums

The Decca 78 rpm albums, while mostly studio tracks, contained beautiful full-color Disney covers. Many of the early albums had interior artwork and/or sepa-

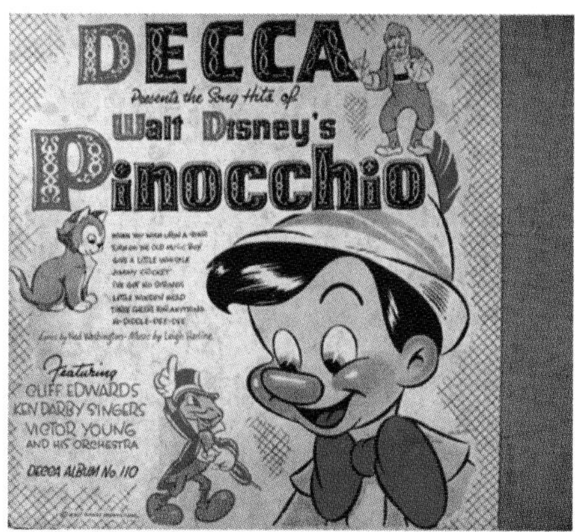

Decca A-110: ***"Song Hits from Walt Disney's Pinocchio"*** *(Back Cover)*

Decca A-368: ***"Snow White and the Seven Dwarfs"***

rate booklet inserts as well. Highly collectible and difficult to find above VG+ condition.

Decca A-110: **"Song Hits from Walt Disney's Pinocchio";** 1940; four record set; features Victor Young Orchestra with Cliff Edwards, Julietta Novis, the Kings Men, and Ken Darby Singers; white cover with multiple line drawings of Pinocchio and other characters from the film; front and back cover are the same; individual records numbered 3000-3003 (See also A-424 below); original selling price: $1.90 . . . . **60**

Decca A-243: **"Walt Disney—Best Remembered Songs from Shorts and Full Length Feature Cartoons";** four record set; Nat Brandwynne Orchestra; individual records numbered 18387-18390; original selling price: $2.50 . . . . **75**

Decca A-368: **"Snow White and the Seven Dwarfs";** 1940; four record set; features Lyn Murray Orchestra and Chorus, with Evelyn Knight, Harrison Knox, Audrey Marsh, Elizabeth Mulliner, and the Andy Love Four; pink "clouds" cover with Snow White, Dwarfs, and castle; individual records numbered 23325-23328; original selling price: $3.50 . . . . **60**

Decca A-369: **"Saludos Amigos";** 1944; STK; three record set; features Charles Wolcott Orchestra with Aloysio Oliveira and Bando da Lua; with 10-page separate booklet insert; individual records numbered 23329, 23330, and 23318; original selling price: $3.00; never transferred to LP; deduct $50 without booklet **150**

Decca A-373: **"The Three Caballeros";** 1944; STK; three record set; features Charles Wolcott Orchestra with vocals by Ray Gilbert and Nestor Amaral; with separate small booklet insert; individual records numbered 23341-23343; original selling price: $2.75; never transferred to LP; deduct $50 without booklet . . **125**

Decca A-373: ***"The Three Caballeros"***

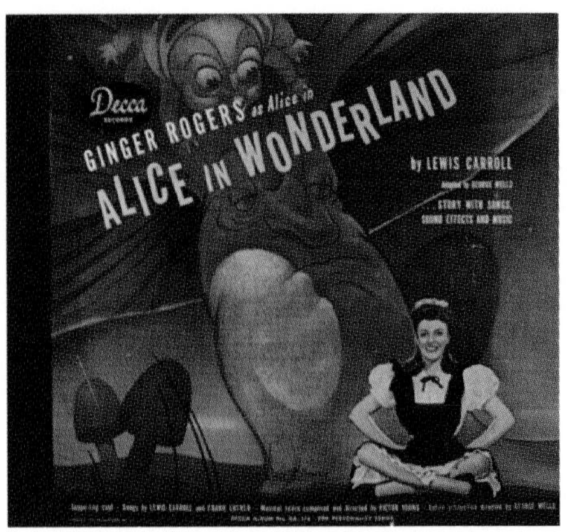

Decca DA-376: ***"Alice in Wonderland"***

Decca DA-376: **"Alice in Wonderland";** 1944; STK; Ginger Rogers & Victor Young Orchestra; non-Disney music but Disney art cover; original selling price: $3.50 . . . . **50**

Also issued in a two 12" 78 rpm set with same number **40**

Decca DA-391: **"Cinderella";** 1945; STK; three record set; Edna Best and others; Victor Young score; non-Disney music but Disney art cover; original selling price: $3.00 . . . . **50**

Decca DA-420: **"The Happy Prince";** 1946; two record set; STK; Bing Crosby and Orson Welles; Bernard Herrmann score conducted by Victor Young; non-Disney music but Disney art cover; adapted from radio show; individual records numbered 40007-40008; original selling price: $2.75 . . . . **50**

Decca DA-391: ***"Cinderella"***

Decca DA-420: ***"The Happy Prince"***

*Decca DA-432: **"Rip Van Winkle"***

*Decca DAU-725: **"Ichabod (The Legend of Sleepy Hollow)"***

Decca A-424: **"Song Hits from Pinocchio";** 1946; four record set; features Victor Young Orchestra with Cliff Edwards and the Ken Darby Singers; Pinocchio and Blue Fairy on cover; also has inner front cover art work; reissue of A-110; original selling price: $3.75 . . . . **50**

Decca DA-432: **"Rip Van Winkle";** STK; two record set; Walter Huston and cast; score by Wilbur Hatch; non-Disney music but Disney art cover; original selling price: $2.75 . . . . **50**

Decca DAU-725: **"Ichabod (The Legend of Sleepy Hollow)";** 1949; Victor Young; Bing Crosby narrates and sings; songs by Gene DePaul and Don Raye **45**

Decca DAU-731: **"Alice in Wonderland";** three record set; Ginger Rogers; individual records numbered 40093-40095; unbreakable records **40**

D3.10.2: Decca 78 rpm "K"(Kiddie) Children's Series Records

Decca K-17: **"Snow White and the Seven Dwarfs";** 1947; three record set; complete musical score featuring Frank Luther with Zora Layman, The Clubmen, and Bob MacGimsey; individual records numbered 1700-1702; original selling price: $1.05 . . . . . . **50**

Decca K-45: **"Whistle While you Work"/ ;** Red Foley **15**

Decca K-58: **"Heigh Ho"/"Whistle While You Work";** features Frank Luther with Zora Layman, The Clubmen, and Bob MacGimsey; record numbered 88087 . . . . **20**

Decca K-63: **"Lambert the Sheepish Lion";** Sterling Holloway **20**

Decca K-64: **"Susie the Little Blue Coupe";** Sterling Holloway **20**

Decca K-65: **"The Little House (Part 1 and 2)";** Sterling Holloway **35**

Decca K-65: "The Little House (Part 1 and 2)"

Decca K-110: **"Walt Disney's Dream Adventure"** 15

Decca K-115: **"Be Sure You're Right (Then Go Ahead)"/"Old Betsy";** Burl Ives 10

Decca K-147: **"The Ballad of Davy Crockett"/"Goober Peas"*;** Burl Ives 25

Decca K-148: **"A Whale of a Tale" (from *20,000 Leagues...*)/"And the Moon Grew Brighter and Brighter"*;** Kirk Douglas and the Mellowmen 25

Decca K-149: **"Siamese Cat Song"/** . . 20

D3.10.3: Decca 78 rpm Singles

Decca CUS-22: Fred Waring and the Pennsylvanians **"Alice in Wonderland";** two records set; individual records numbered 88071 and 88072 35

Decca CU-115: Bing Crosby and Orson Welles **"The Happy Prince";** STK; 12"; Bernard Herrmann score conducted by Victor Young; non-Disney music but Disney art cover; adapted from radio show; a "Children's Unbreakable" long-play 78 rpm record; original selling price: $2.00 25

Decca 280: Victor Young Orchestra **"You're Nothin' But a Nothin' " (from *The Flying Mouse*)/** 10

Decca DU-1011: Fred Waring and the Pennsylvanians **"The Ballad of Davy Crockett";** 12" 78 rpm record; high gloss, red cover of Davy Crockett; with complete unabridged 20 verses of the song 50

Decca 1847: Dick Robertson Orchestra **"Ferdinand the Bull"/"Mr. Wu! Mr. Wu!"*;** 1938 15

Decca 2238: The Merry Macs **"Ferdinand the Bull"/"I Got Rings on My Fingers"*;** 1939 20

Decca 2739: Ted Weems Orchestra **"Jiminy Cricket"/"Monstro the Whale";** 1940 15

Decca 2969: Guy Lombardo Orchestra **"When You Wish Upon a Star"/"Turn on the Old Music Box"*;** charted April 13, 1940 10

Decca 3008: Woody Herman Orchestra **"Give a Little Whistle"/ ;** 1940 10

Decca 3035: Roy Smeck Orchestra **"When You Wish Upon a Star"/ ;** 1940 10

Decca 3050: Frances Langford **"When You Wish Upon a Star"/ ;** 1940 15

Decca DB-3707: Arizona Boys Choir **"The Ballad of Davy Crockett"/"Blue Shadows on the Trail";** c. 1955 20

Decca 3895: Richard Himber Orchestra **"The Reluctant Dragon"/ ;** 1941 . . . . **15**

Decca 3935: The Kings Men **"The Reluctant Dragon"/ ;** 1941 . . . . . . **15**

Decca 4061: Johnny Messner Orchestra **"Baby Mine"/"When I See An Elephant Fly";** 1941; from *Dumbo* **10**

Decca 18134: Fernando Alvarez **"Brazil"/** **10**

Decca 18412: Fred Waring Orchestra **"Brazil"/ ;** 1943 . . . . . **10**

Decca 18445: Guy Lombardo Orchestra **"Love Is a Song" (from *Bambi*)/ ;** 1943 . . . . **10**

Decca 18460: Jimmy Dorsey Orchestra **"Brazil"/ ;** charted December 26, 1943 . . . . **10**

Decca 18606: Andrews Sisters **"Tico-Tico"/"Straighten Up and Fly Right"*;** charted July 8, 1944 . . **10**

Decca 18874: Randy Brooks **"Without You"/** **10**

Decca 23318: Charles Wolcott Orchestra **"Pedro from Chile"/"Tico-Tico";** charted August 26, 1944 . . . . **10**

Decca 23353: Ethel Smith and Bando Carioca **"Tico-Tico"/ ;** charted November 25, 1944 . . . . . **10**

Decca 23364: Bing Crosby and the Andrews Sisters **"The Three Caballeros"/** **10**

Decca 23413: Bing Crosby & Xavier Cugat Orchestra **"You Belong to My Heart"/"Baia";** charted on June 16, 1945; from *The Three Caballeros* **10**

Decca 23474: Andrews Sisters **"Johnny Fedora"/"Money Is the Root of All Evil"*** **15**

Decca 23532: Roy Eldridge and Orchestra **"All the Cats Join In" (from *Make Mine Music*)/"Ain't That a Shame"*;** 1946 . . . . **15**

Decca 23748: Connie Boswell, Bob Crosby and the Bob-O-Links **"Zip-A-Dee-Doo-Dah" (from *Song of the South*)/"Too Many Times"*;** 1946 . . . . **10**

Decca 23799: Guy Lombardo Orchestra **"Uncle Remus Said"/"The Anniversary Song"*** . . **15**

Decca 23819: Bing Crosby **"Blue Shadows on the Trail"/"Easter Parade"*;** 1948 . . . . **15**

Decca 24174: Joe Mooney **"Lazy Countryside"/** **10**

Decca 24547: Burl Ives **"Lavender Blue (Dilly Dilly)" (from *So Dear to My Heart*)/ ;** charted February 12, 1949 . . . . **15**

Decca 24702: Bing Crosby **"Adventures of Ichabod and Mr. Toad/The Headless Horseman"** . . . **20**

Decca 27032: Bando da Lua **"Bibbidi Bobbidi Boo"/"Rag Mop Samba"*** **10**

Decca 27242: Andrews Sisters **"Jing-a-Ling, Jing-a-Ling" (from *Beaver Valley*)/"Parade of the Wooden Soldiers"*** **15**

Decca 27462: Guy Lombardo Orchestra **"The Unbirthday Song"/"The Little White Duck"*** . . **15**

Decca 27314: Sonny Burke Orchestra **"Jing-a-Ling, Jing-a-Ling" (from *Beaver Valley*)/"Mambo"*;** #5 . . . . **15**

Decca 27564: Danny Kaye **"I'm Late"/"The Walrus and the Carpenter"** **15**

Decca 29423: Burl Ives **"The Ballad of Davy Crockett"/"Goober Peas"*** **20**

Decca 29427: Peggy Lee **"Siamese Cat Song"/"He's a Tramp";** STK . . **20**

Decca 29433: Victor Young **"Bella Notte"/"The Medic"*** **15**

Decca 29460: Peggy Lee **"Bella Notte"/"La La Lu";** MST **20**

Decca 29487: Cliff Edwards **"When You Wish Upon a Star"/"Give a Little Whistle"** **20**

Decca 29549: Burl Ives **"Be Sure You're Right (Then Go Ahead)"/"Old Betsy"** **20**

Decca 29642 [29692?]: Gary Crosby **"Yaller, Yaller Gold"/"Give Me a Band and My Baby"*** **15**

Decca 88186: Peggy Lee **"Siamese Cat Song"/"La La Lu";** Children's Series **20**

D3.11: Dot 78 *rpm* Singles

1240: Mac Wiseman **"The Ballad of Davy Crockett"/"Danger! Heartbreak Ahead"*** **20**

D3.12: *Fantasy* 78 *rpm* Singles

526: Dave Brubeck Quartet **"Alice in Wonderland"/"All the Things You Are"*** **20**

D3.13: *General* Mills 78 *rpm* "*Alice in Wonderland*" Set

In 1951, General Mills released a promotional/premium eight record, 78 rpm set of songs from Disney's *Alice in Wonderland*. The records are 5-3/4" in diameter. Each record side has a different illustration of characters from the film. The set came in an envelope mailer jacket featuring a black and white picture of Alice and the White Rabbit. Each envelope held two of the records.

The studiotrack recordings are actually the same as the "Little Golden" record releases numbered RD-18 through RD-25 (See Section F1 below). The mailer indicates they were available from "Wonderland, P.O. Box 776, New York City." They are very rare. In this set, the records were renumbered as follows:

1/3: **"Alice in Wonderland"/"I'm Late (The White Rabbit's Song)"**

2/16: **"In a World of My Own (Alice's Song)"/"The March of the Cards"**

4/12: **"Alice in the White Rabbit's House (and the Dodo's Song)"/"How You Do and Shake Hands (Alice Meets Tweedledum and Tweedledee)"**

5/6: **"Very Good Advice (Alice's Song)"/"The Caucus Race"**

7/8: **"The Walrus and the Carpenter (with Tweedledum and Tweedledee) Pts. I and II"**

9/10: **"All in a Golden Afternoon (The Flowers' Song)"/"Alice in the Garden of Live Flowers"**

11/14: **"Alice Meets the Caterpillar and the Cheshire Cat"/"The Mad Tea Party"**

13/15: **"A Very Merry Unbirthday"/"Painting the Roses Red"**

Complete set with cover **120**

Individual records, each **10**

D3.14: *Hansen* 78 *rpm* Singles

These recordings were leased to Charlie Hansen, who was also a distributor for very early Disneyland records.

102: George Bruns, Tommy Cole, and Quincy Jones Orchestra **"King of the River"/Mike Stewart "Yaller, Yaller Gold";** 1956 . . . . . . **10**

103: Tommy Cole, Darlene Gillespie, Quincy Jones **"I Am Not Now (and Never Have Been in Love)"/"Do Mi So";** 1956 ..... **10**

105: Betty Cox, Quincy Jones **"Hi to You"/"Holly Boy"** (1956) **10**

D3.15: *Hollywood Recording Guild 78 rpm Singles*

2001: Jack Andrews and the Rhythm Boys **"The Ballad of Davy Crockett"/"The Tenderfoot"*** **15**

2005: The HRG Orchestra **"The Mouseketeers March"/"The Piggy Bank Song"*** **15**

2006 The HRG Orchestra **"The Triple R Song"/** **15**

D3.16: *Lightning 78 rpm Records*

17A: Guy Chookoorian **"The Ballad of Davy Crockett"/"The Golden Bracelet"*** **20**

D3.17: "*Little Golden*" 78 *rpm Records—All Sizes*

(See Separate "Little Golden" Section F)

D3.18: *Mattel "Mickey Mouse Club Newsreel" Record and Slides Sets*

This rare series, c. 1956, consists of individual packages, each containing one 6" 78 rpm record and two film strip slides of photos from the named film. Cover sleeve graphics include the Mickey Mouse Club logo, and drawings of Mickey, a camera, and the disc and slides. The series titles appear as well. The records themselves are lettered, not numbered, along with the titles impressed into the center dead wax. The records are black vinyl with no paper labels. The listed prices include the record, cover, and the film strips. Deduct 50% without the film strips. The following are the currently known titles:

Cartoons

Series "A": **"Touchdown Mickey"/"Dance of the Leopard Boys (No Sail)"** **30**

Series "B": **"The Mail Pilot"/"Peculiar Penguins"** **30**

Series "C": **"Two-Gun Mickey"/"Don Donald"** **30**

Series "D": **"Elmer Elephant"/"The Brave Little Tailor"** **30**

Series "E": **"The Tortoise and the Hare"/"The Gorilla Mystery"** **30**

Series "F": **"The Three Little Pigs"/"Ye Olden Days"** **30**

Adventures

Series "J": **"At the Waterhole" (from Walt Disney's *The African Lion*)/"The Buffalo Battle" (from Walt Disney's *The Vanishing Prairie*)** **40**

Series "K": **"Water Birds"/"Bear Country"** **40**

Newsreels

Series "R": **"Frogville, USA"/"On Silent Wings"** **30**

Series "S": **"The Hippo Who Goofed"/"Teen-age Toreadors"** .. **30**

*Series "K": **"Water Birds"/"Bear Country"***

D3.19: Mattel/Rainbo "Davy Crockett" 78 rpm, 7" Picture Disc Set

Stock No. 528:98: This was produced by Mattel, Inc., c. 1955, entitled "The Legend of Davy Crockett on Records." In original, uncut condition, it consists of a six-page, accordion-style fold-out, 14-1/4" x 42-3/4". Across the top of the fold-out are five, one-sided, unnumbered, 7" "cardboard" cartoon picture disc 78 rpm records. At the top of the first page is a painted picture of Davy Crockett. Various other Crockett paintings run across the bottom of the entire spread. When the individual records are cut out to be played, the remaining bottom paintings form an accordion-style booklet. The entire set was packaged in a blue, outer cardboard picture-cover mailer, showing two young children playing the records. A young boy is wearing a Davy Crockett coonskin hat, popular at the time. The cover has a folder flap on the back. No individual record numbers appear on the discs, however, given Mattel's two series below, the records are assumed to be numbered 1-5. Very rare.

The individual records are:

"Davy Crockett—Hunter"

"Davy Crockett—Indian Fighter"

"Davy Crockett—Frontiersman"

"Davy Crockett—Goes to Congress"

"Davy Crockett—Alamo Defender"

Entire set, uncut **125**

Entire set, cut-out records, booklet and mailer **75**

Individual records cut-out, each **15**

D3.20: Mattel/Rainbo "Musical Map" 78 rpm, 7" Disneyland Picture Disc Set

Stock No. 529: This was produced by Mattel, Inc., c. 1955, entitled "Your Trip to Disneyland on Records" ("Walt Disney's Disneyland"). In original, uncut condition, it consists of a six-page, accordion-style fold-out, 14-1/4" x 42-3/4". Across the top of the fold-out are five, one-sided, unnumbered, 7" "cardboard" cartoon picture disc 78 rpm records. At the top of the sixth page are Disney character cut-outs which could be placed on a record player tone-arm (Donald Duck, Tinker Bell, Mickey Mouse, and a crocodile). A six-page map of Disneyland runs across the bottom of the entire spread. When the individual records and characters are cut out to be played, the remaining Disneyland map forms an accordion-style booklet. The entire set was packaged in a blue, outer cardboard picture-cover mailer, showing two young children playing the records. The cover has a folder flap on the back. The individual record numbers are in the dead wax trail-off section of the disc. Very rare.

The individual records are:

"Introduction to Disneyland—#6"

"Tomorrowland—#7"

"Fantasyland—#8"

Stock No. 529: ***"Your Trip to Disneyland on Records"***

Stock No. 537: ***"Your Own Mickey Mouse Club On Records"***

"Frontierland—#9"

"Adventureland—#10"

Entire set, uncut **125**

Entire set, cut-out records, figures and mailer **75**

Individual records, cut-out, each **10**

D3.21: Mattel/Rainbo Mickey Mouse Club Picture Disc Records

Stock No. 537: "Your Own Mickey Mouse Club On Records" is a series of five 7" cardboard cut-out, one-sided, picture disc, 78 rpm records, in a fold-open cover, similar to the above two Mattel sets. The cover picture of two children playing records is the same as D3.18 above, however it has a large, circular Mickey Mouse Club logo at the top.

Individual records are:

11—**"Mickey Mouse Club March and Mouseketeer Song"**

12—**"Cartoon Time"**

13—**"Joe MacDonald Musical on the Farm"**

14—**"Mickey Mouse Club Circus Day"**

15—**"Toot-Toot Talent Roundup"**

Uncut condition with mailer **100**

Entire set, cut-out condition **60**

Individual records, each **10**

Note: There is a one-sided, yellow label, (no-name) D.J. copy EP of these songs. It does not have a P/S, however includes a small note sheet with a message to DJs. The number is RR-23210.
Rare. **40**

D3.22: Mayfair 78 rpm Records

K-128: June Winters **"Alice in Wonderland";** 10" EP; includes "Alice in Wonderland," "I'm Late," "All in a Golden Afternoon," and "The Unbirthday Song"; line drawing of "Alice" on the yellow label **25**

D3.23: Mercury 78 rpm Records

A-89: **"Walt Disney's Alice in Wonderland";** 1950; STK; three

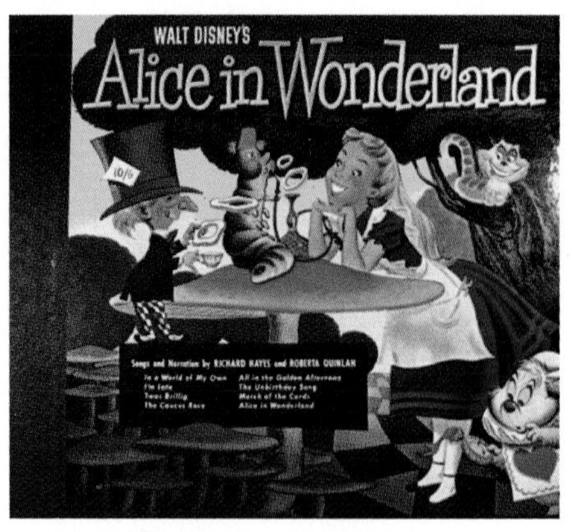

A-89: "Walt Disney's Alice in Wonderland"

record set; cast includes Richard Hayes and Roberta Quinlan; individual records numbered 5627-5619 . . . . **45**

MP-2: Mickey Mouse and Donald Duck **"The Magic Flying Carpet Parts 1 & 2";** 1952; Children's "Playcraft Series" with picture sleeves; Disney character story also appears uncredited on Mercury LP CLP-1210 "A Trip to Adventureland" (Guide price $45) **30**

MP-3: Mickey Mouse and Donald Duck **"Aladdin and His Lamp";** 1952 . . . . **30**

MP-27: Rusty Draper **"The Ballad of Davy Crockett"/"Lazy Mule"*** . . . **25**

5397: Two Ton Baker **"The Work Song"/"Peter Cottontail"*** **15**

5615: Roberta Quinlan **"Alice in Wonderland"/"Gotta Find Somebody to Love"*** **10**

5639: Richard Hayes and Roberta Quinlan **"I'm Late," "The Caucus Race"/"The Unbirthday Song"** . . . **15**

70555: Rusty Draper **"The Ballad of Davy Crockett"/"I've Been Thinking"*** **20**

D3.24: MGM 78 *rpm Records*

11914: James Brown and the Trail Winders **"The Ballad of Davy Crockett"/"He's a Rockin' Horse Cowboy"*** **20**

11967: Kay Armen **"Bella Notte"/"La La Lu"** **15**

K-13316: Johnny Tillotson **"Angel" (from *Those Calloways*)/"Little Boy"*** **20**

D3.25: *Musicraft* 78 *rpm Singles*

15018: Phil Brito **"You Belong to My Heart" (from *The Three Caballeros*)/"I Don't Want to Love You (Like I Do)"***; charted September 2, 1944 . . . . **15**

D3.26: *Pavillion* 78 *rpm Records*

691-A: Ted Maksymowicz Orchestra **"The Ballad of Davy Crockett"/"Sky Chief"*** **15**

D3.27: *Davy Crockett* 7", 78 *rpm Peter Pan Peanut Butter Single*

DF-100: **"Walt Disney's The Ballad of Davy Crockett"/"I'm Lonely My Darling (Green Grow the Lilacs)";** 1955; 7" 78 rpm record; The Sandpipers & Mitchell Miller Orchestra; produced by Derby Foods and sold as a 25¢ premium offer; comes with a mailing envelope depicting Davy Crockett and a Peter Pan Peanut Butter jar printed with the song lyrics; label is printed directly on black vinyl in white ink with song info and a Peter Pan Peanut Butter jar logo. It has also been seen with a paper label; likely manufactured by Little Golden Records

Record and cover **30**

Cover only **20**

D3.28: Peter Pan 7" and 10" 78 rpm Records

This series contains no Disney Art, and is noted for the music only; distributed by James B. Jonathan Co., Kenosha, Wisconsin; manufactured by Synthetic Plastics Co., of Newark, New Jersey; all with P/S; there were also 78 rpm editions, same price

345: **"Little Toot"** **10**

370: **"Hi-Diddle-Dee-Dee"/"Camptown Races-Oh, Susannah"*** **10**

371: **"Someday My Prince Will Come"** **10**

372: **"Who's Afraid of the Big Bad Wolf"** **10**

373: **"When You Wish Upon a Star"** **10**

374: **"Give a Little Whistle"** **10**

375: **"Whistle While You Work"** **10**

376: **"Heigh-Ho"** **10**

377: **"When I See An Elephant Fly"** . . **10**

378: **"Bluddle-Uddle-Um-Dum"/"Pony on the Merry-Go-Round"*** **10**

379: **"The World Owes Me a Living"** . . **10**

380: **"The Dwarf's Yodel Song"/"In the Land of Lemonade and Lollipops"** **10**

377: *"When I See An Elephant Fly"*

381: **"I've Got No Strings"** **10**

403: Bob Towers **"The Ballad of Davy Crockett"/**Jack Arthur **"Red River Valley"*;** 1955 . . . . **15**

416: **"Funnie Little Bunnies"/"Silly Easter Bonnet"** **10**

428: Laura Leslie **"I've Got No Strings"/** **10**

443: **"When I See an Elephant Fly"/"In the Middle of the House"*** **10**

520: Lee Adams **"Someday My Prince Will Come"/** **15**

526: Laura Leslie **"When I See An Elephant Fly"/** **15**

528: Dale Loring **"The World Owes Me a Living"/** **15**

D3.29: Playtime 78 rpm Records

248: **"Mickey Mouse Song"/"The Elephant";** Uncle Don; 7" 78 rpm record; picture label features a witch **30**

Record No. GM-101

Record No. GM-101: **"Happy Mouse"/"It's Great to be Goofy"/"Mocking Bird"/"Fire Fighting Fellow"** **25**

Record No. GM-102: **"Laughing Song"/"Animal Alphabet (A-E)"/"Animal Alphabet (F-J)"/"It's Fun to Whistle"** **25**

Record No. GM-103: **"I'd Rather Be I"/"Donald Duck's Song"/"Mouskeriddle #1"/"Mouskeriddle #2"** **25**

Record No. GM-104: **"Ten Little Indians"/"Mousekartoon Time"/"The Gadget Tree"/"Li'l Davy"** **25**

D3.30: *Rainbo Recard (sic)* "*Wheaties*" *Mickey* Mouse *Club* Picture Disc Cut-Outs—78 *rpm*

Unnumbered: "Mickey Mouse Club: Walt Disney's Mouseketeer Recards"; c.1956; series of eight 5" cardboard cut-out, one-sided, picture disc 78 rpm records from the front of Wheaties cereal boxes.

Individual records are:

Donald Duck—"Donald Duck's Song"

Goofy—"It's Fun to Whistle"

Mickey Mouse—"Happy Mouse"

Mickey Mouse—"The Gadget Tree"

Mickey, Donald, and Goofy—"I'd Rather Be I"

Chip n' Dale—"The Laughing Song"

Chip n' Dale—"Ten Little Indians"

Goofy—"Fire Fighting Fellow"

Box, uncut condition, each **70**

Cut-out condition, each **10**

The back cover of the Wheaties box advertised four other "regular weight" (i.e., normal) 7" 78 rpm EP "Mouseketeer" records available at 25¢ each, with picture sleeves, and orange vinyl:

D3.31: Victor/RCA 78 *rpm Records*

D3.31.1: Victor/RCA 7" Picture Disc 78 rpm Singles

These were recorded on November 3 & 10, 1933, and were issued in 1934 with an RCA listing title as "Silly Symphonies and Mickey the Mouse Songs." These are extremely rare, 7" black and white picture discs! Each record had a non-picture cover, lime-green sleeve with the individual record number stamped at top. The sleeve opened at the top. The sleeves were all printed with a red generic title indicating: "Silly Symphonies Songs—Selections from Mickey Mouse and Silly Symphonies Motion Pictures." While each record was encased in its own flapless sleeve, the Archives' set has one sleeve with a flap at the top in addition to the other three. Thus the possibility exists that the set of three was originally included in an outer flap sleeve. Original price: $1.75. Disney received a 5% royalty from RCA on these recordings.[6]

[6] There are also Canadian RCA 7", non-picture disc pressings of these, with picture labels, black vinyl and with the same numbers.

RCA 224: **"Who's Afraid of the Big Bad Wolf Parts I and II";** (Churchill); Frank Luther and Orchchestra; picture disc **500****

RCA 225: **"In a Silly Symphony/Mickey Mouse and Minnie's In Town";** Frank Luther and Orchestra; picture disc ... **500****

RCA 226: **"Lullaby Land of Nowhere"/"Dance of the Bogey Men";** (Churchill/Harline); Frank Luther and Orchestra; picture disc! **500****

**If accompanied by the original sleeve, add $100 per record!

Note: Frank Luther made a large number of children's records from the 1920s into the 1950s and was often then called "The Bing Crosby of the Sand-Pile Set" (See also his recordings on Decca). Luther's real name was Franklin Luther Crow. He died on November 16, 1980.[7]

D3.31.2: (RCA) Victor 78 rpm Albums

Victor J-8: **"Songs from Walt Disney's Snow White and the Seven Dwarfs";** 1937; MST; cover notes: "With the same characters and sound effects as in the film of that title"); price includes the picture cover for the set **300**

Victor J-8: ***"Songs from Walt Disney's Snow White and the Seven Dwarfs"***

On December 7, 1937, RCA contracted with Disney for a license to record "Snow White" in English and Spanish versions. It was released on or about January 20, 1938.[8] This is the first ever released American, full-feature, soundtrack album. It consists of three 78 rpm records in an "envelope"-type sleeve, opening at the top, with a movie still picture, depicting the Dwarfs crossing over a log, pasted on the cover. A "J" prefix designated Victor's "Juvenile" (or "Junior") Series. In 1940 this first pressing set was selling for $1.50. It is extremely rare! (First reissue as RCA Victor Y-6 below). The individual record numbers and songs (released concurrently as singles) are as follows:

[7] While these Luther records are generally considered to be the first recorded Disney related records, there was an earlier unauthorized foreign pressing. In November 1932, "Count Mazzaglia Custelli 'of Mickey Mouse Fame' " recorded a "novelty cartoon record" on British Decca, F-3175 (a 10" 78 rpm record, blue label). The songs were "Mickey Mouse Discovers a New Island"/"Mickey Mouse On the Island of the Polar Bears." Disney had not given its permission for such a recording, and upon notice British Decca allegedly destroyed all copies in December 1932. Should a copy of this record surface, it would be extremely valuable.

[8] As with the Bluebird "Silly Symphony" records (See Footnote 3, Section D), the "H.M.V." label in England also released a three record set, with a blue cartoon, envelope-type cover of Snow White and the Dwarfs. Each individual record in the set also has a separate picture sleeve with an envelope-type flap at the top. The labels are the same very pretty yellow design, with pictures of Snow White and the Dwarfs.

25735: **"With a Smile and a Song"/"Dig-A-Dig Dig" and "Heigh Ho";** single charted on February 12, 1938

25736: **"I'm Wishing" and "One Song"/"Whistle While You Work";** single charted on February 12, 1938

25737: "**Dwarf's Yodel Song"/"Someday My Prince Will Come Song";** this single became a popular hit for Adrienne Casillotti (a.k.a. Adriana Caselotti—the voice of Snow White); charting on February 19, 1938

Victor P-18: **"Pinocchio";** recorded January 19, 1940, released in February, 1940; MST; three record set; 78 rpm; cover notes: "Recorded from the original sound track of the Walt Disney Production, Pinocchio"; this was the first use of the term "original sound track"; individual records numbered 26477, 26478, and 26479

First issue: Light blue, die-cut front cover with eight color picture panels on the inner jacket and sleeves; internal sleeve artwork is beautiful; initially sold for $2.00 .... **150**

Second issue: Same cover picture but it is not die-cut; without internal pictures; the same cover picture was used when it was later reissued as RCA Y-349 below **75**

Victor P-101: **"Dumbo";** released November 14, 1941; MST; three record set; 78 rpm; individual records numbered numbered 27660-27662; original price: $2.00; the first pressing of "Dumbo" (reissued as Y-350 below) **100**

D3.31.3: RCA 78 rpm Children's Albums—Including the "Little Nipper" and "Youth" Series

These are well-produced 78 rpm albums. Most have gorgeous, high-gloss Disney covers, and either an interior multi-page booklet or picture panels of Disney art as well. RCA also issued many of these in 45 rpm and a few EP versions, and recycled them constantly as LPs on RCA Camden and the Bluebird "Children's Series," depicting the same cover art. However, for pure artwork, the 78 rpm sets are the ones to have! They are difficult to find in nice condition.

While these are listed in numerical order, RCA reissued many in the series in "unbreakable" vinyl when it became available, and utilized earlier unused series numbers. Accordingly, the listing may not be chronological.[9]

Y-1: **"The Three Little Pigs"/"The Orphan's Benefit";** 1944; MST; breakable record; yellow cover, with flap at the top and with a picture of the Three Little Pigs playing a piano; notation on the bottom of the front cover states that it is part of the "Victor Library of Children's Records"; original price: .60¢; extremely rare (Y-1" is actually a "Bluebird" label record number 39-3000. It is noted here to complete the "Y" Disney series in sequence) **75**

---

[9] RCA released Spanish language editions of the Disney versions of two films:

SY-4 **"La Cenicienta" (Cinderella)** **50**

SY-5 **"Alicia En El Pais De Maravillas" (Alice in Wonderland);** Evangelina Elizondo **50**

*Y-1: **"The Three Little Pigs"/"The Orphan's Benefit"***

*Y-6: **"Snow White and the Seven Dwarfs"** (Second issue)*

Y-6: **"Snow White and the Seven Dwarfs";** 1944; MST; three record set; 78 rpm; "envelope"-type sleeve, opening at the top, the sleeve graphics consist of the title panel and circus character drawings on a bright red sleeve; each record in the set also had "Y-6" on the label; this was the second release of the complete soundtrack album by RCA (See Victor J-8 above); original price: $1.80; extremely rare **150**

The individual record numbers and the original "J-8" record numbers are stamped into the dead wax area. The numbers and songs are as follows:

41-0000: **"With a Smile and a Song"/"Dig-A-Dig Dig" and "Heigh Ho"**

41-0001: **"I'm Wishing" and "One Song"/"Whistle While You Work"**

41-0002: **"Dwarf's Yodel Song"/"Someday My Prince Will Come"**

Y-14: **"The Three Little Pigs"/"The Orphan's Benefit";** 1949; MST; One 78 rpm unbreakable single; GF cover which hinges open from the top; cover depicts the Pigs dancing and playing a brick piano; record number 45-5094; first RCA label reissue of Bluebird Y-1 above **35**

Y-17: **"Snow White and the Seven Dwarfs";** 1949; MST; three record set; unbreakable records; cover of Dwarfs crossing over log, same cover picture as "J-8" above; there are no inner pictures; individual records numbered 45-5097,45-5098, and 45-5099; reissue of "J-8" and "Y-6" above **50**

Y-32: **"The Three Little Pigs"/"The Orphan's Benefit";** 1949; MST; same cover as Y-14, but the GF opens from the side; record number is 45-5094; original price: $1.25 . . . . **40**

Y-33: **"Snow White and the Seven Dwarfs";** 1949; STK; two record set; unbreakable records; features Dennis Day, Ilene Woods and Paul Smith Orchestra; yellow

Y-33: "Snow White and the Seven Dwarfs"

Y-345: "Peter and the Wolf"

cover of Snow White dancing with Dopey and Dwarf band with 23-page booklet; individual records numbered 45-5256 and 45-5257; original price: $3.40 .... **60**

Y-323: **"Peter and the Wolf";** 1946; STK; two record set; breakable records; Sterling Holloway; with booklet; individual records numbered 45-0005 and 45-0006; original price: $2.50 .... **40**

Y-345: **"Peter and the Wolf";** 1947; STK; Sterling Holloway; two record set; unbreakable records; inner cover pictures only; without booklet; issued in regular album and in GF; individual records numbered 45-5130 and 45-5131; reissue of Y-323 .... **30**

Y-349: **"Pinocchio";** 1947; MST; three record set; unbreakable records; no inner pictures; individual records numbered 45-5138, 45-5139, and 45-5140; later RCA reissue of Victor P-18 non-die cut cover **40**

Y-350: **"Dumbo";** 1947; MST; three record set; unbreakable records; individual records numbered 45-5141, 45-5142, and 45-5143; RCA reissue of Victor P-101—same cover **50**

Y-368: **"Johnny Appleseed";** 1948; STK; three record set; unbreakable records; Dennis Day; green cover with picture of Dennis Day and Johnny Appleseed; paper GF sleeve; individual records numbered 45-5213,45-5214, and 45-5215 ..... **40**

Y-369: **"Melody Time";** 1948; STK; two record set; features Sammy Kaye Orchestra & Kaydets—"Little Toot," Freddy Martin Orchestra—"Bumble Boogie," Roy Rogers and The Sons of the Pioneers—"There'll Never Be Another Pecos Bill" and "Blue Shadows on the Trail"; GF; individual records numbered 45-5186 and 45-5187 .... **50**

Y-375: **"Pecos Bill";** 1948; STK; three record set; Roy Rogers and Sons of the Pioneers; cover has a picture of a standing Pecos with a lasso which envelops a picture of Roy Rogers; hard-bound album; individual records numbered 45-

Y-375: "Pecos Bill"

Y-385: "Pinocchio"

5216, 45-5217, and 45-5218; may also appear in a box set **50**

Same album number and cover photo appear in a paper sleeve GF edition **40**

Y-382: **"Dumbo";** 1949; STK; three record set; Shirley Temple with cast; without booklet, but has 12 internal picture panels; individual records numbered #45-5246, 45-5247, and 45-5248; original price: $3.85 .... **50**

Y-385: **"Pinocchio";** 1949; STK; two record set; unbreakable; features Sandy Edwards, Jackson Beck, Patsy Campbell, and Frank Milano; Cliff Edwards narrates; 24-page booklet; individual record numbered 45-5253 and 45-5254; original price: $3.40 .... **50**

Y-386: **"Peter and the Wolf";** 1949; STK; two record set; from *Make Mine Music*; unbreakable; Sterling Holloway and Charles Wolcott Orchestra; 24-page booklet; cover depicts Peter and the animals in a forest; individual records numbered 45-5130 and 45-5131; original price: $3.40 .... **40**

Y-389: **"Pecos Bill";** 1949; STK; three record set; from *Melody Time*; Roy Rogers and Sons of the Pioneers; 12 picture panels; tan cover is different than Y-375, and depicts Pecos Bill on a horse, lassoing a picture of Roy Rogers; individual records numbered 45-5216, 45-5217, and 45-5218; original price: $3.85 .... **40**

Y-390: **"Johnny Appleseed";** 1949; STK; three record set; from *Melody Time*; unbreakable; Dennis Day and Ken Darby Orchestra; 12 picture panels; cover is different than Y-368, and depicts Johnny Appleseed in an orchard; individual records numbered 45-5213, 45-5214, and 45-5215; original price: $3.85 .... **40**

Y-391: **"Bambi";** 1949; STK; three record set; unbreakable; Shirley Temple and Paul Smith Orchestra; 12 picture panels; individual records numbered 45-5219, 45-5220, and 45-5221; original price: $3.85 .... **50**

Y-395: **"Bambi";** STK; three record set; green cover and paper GF sleeve **40**

Y-391: ***"Bambi"***

Y-399: ***"Cinderella"***

Y-399: **"Cinderella";** 1950; STK; two record set, unbreakable; features Ilene Woods as Cinderella, Paul Smith Orchestra, and Verne Smith, James MacDonald, Eleanor Audley, Helene Stanley, Lucille Bliss, Verna Felton, John Brown, and Clarence Nash; 24-page booklet; individual records numbered 45-5260 and 45-5261; original price: $3.40; this record album actually hit the number one position on Billboard magazine's "pop" chart list—an unprecedented event at the time . . **50**

Y-416: ***"Treasure Island"***

Y-400: **"The Brave Engineer (The Story of Casey Jones)";** 1950; Jerry Colonna; record number 45-6262; Rare; original price: $1.25 . . **60**

Y-416: **"Treasure Island";** 1950; (Henri Rene); STK; two record set; unbreakable; Bobby Driscoll; non-Disney Music; GF paper sleeve with 12 photos from film; individual records numbered 45-5283 and 45-5284; original price: $2.20 . . . . **40**

Y-430: **"Birthday Fun";** 1951; Dennis Day; includes "Happy Birthday Song" and "The Unbirthday Song"; record number 45-5303; original price: .95¢ **25**

Y-432: **"Mr. Television";** 1951; features Milton Berle and original voices of Donald Duck and Mickey Mouse; record number 45-5314; original price: $1.25 . . . . **40**

Y-433: **"Mr. Animated Cartoon";** 1951; Milton Berle and original voices of Donald Duck and Mickey Mouse; record number 45-5315; original price: $1.25 . . . . **40**

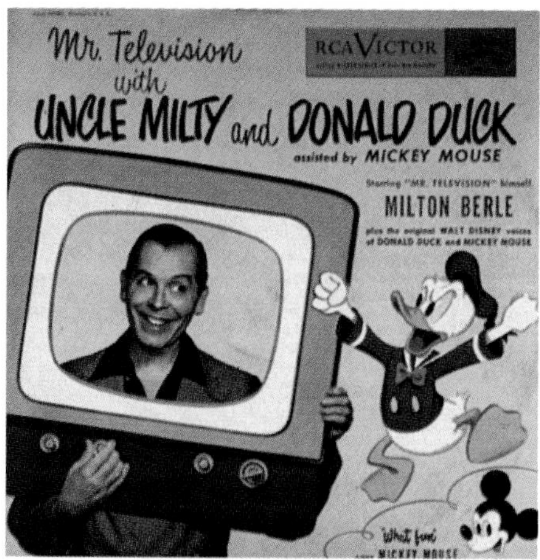

Y-432: "Mr. Television"

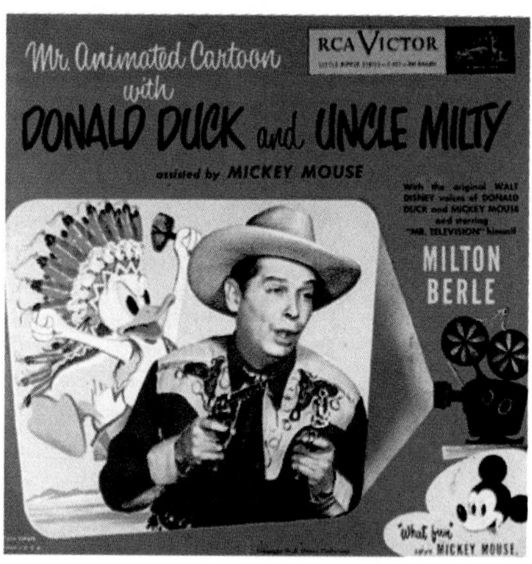

Y-433: "Mr. Animated Cartoon"

Y-434: **"Alice and the White Rabbit";** 1951; STK; features Kathryn Beaumont and others; record number 45-5293 . . . . **30**

Y-435: **"Alice and the Mad Tea Party";** 1951; STK; features Kathryn Beaumont, Arnold Stang, Frank Milano, Naomi Lewis, Todd Russell, Michael King, Merrill Joels, Jackson Beck, and vocal quartet Three Beaus and a Peep; GF; record number 45-5294 . . . . . **30**

Y-436: **"Alice and the Trial";** 1951; STK; features Kathryn Beaumont, Todd Russell, Michael King, Merrill Joels, Jackson Beck, and Three Beaus and a Peep; GF; record number 45-5295 . . . . **30**

Y-437: **"Alice in Wonderland";** 1951; STK; two record set; features Kathryn Beaumont, Ed Wynn, Jerry Colonna, and Sterling Holloway; GF with 24-page booklet; individual records numbered 45-5296 and 45-5297; original price: $3.40 . . . . **40**

Also packaged in folders as part of "A Little Nipper Giant Storybook Record Album" book (10-1/2" x 13-1/4") Alice in Wonderland; Disney notes that this album, and its counterpart 45 rpm edition "WY-437" did not sell well because its extra large size did not allow it to be placed for display in the standard record racks of the day **60**

Y-447: **"Snow White and Sneezy";** 1952; (Leyden); Dennis Day; record number 45-5329; original price: .95¢ **30**

Y-448: **"Snow White and Dopey";** 1952; (Leyden); Dennis Day; record number 45-5330; original price: .95¢ **30**

Y-463: **"Peter Pan";** 1953; Hugo Winterhalter Orchestra; original price: .95¢ **25**

Y-472: **Captain of the Spaceship*/"A Toot and a Whistle and a Plunk and a Boom"** Spike Jones and the Mellomen; P/S **40**

Y-483: **"Cinderella";** single record . . . **25**

Y-484: **"Snow White and the Seven Dwarfs";** single record **25**

Y-472: ***"A Toot and a Whistle and a Plunk and a Boom"*** *(B-side)*

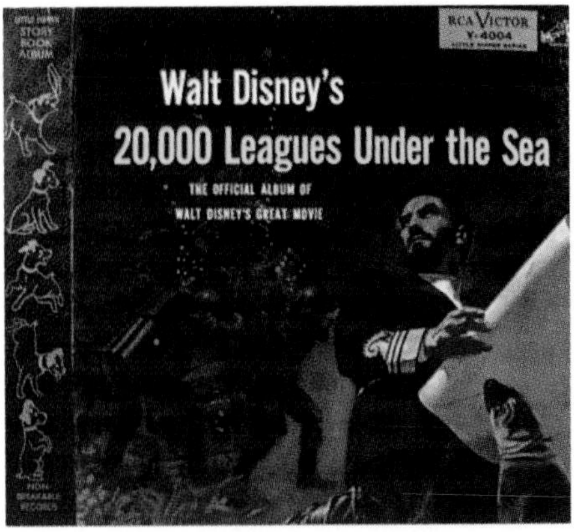

Y-4004: ***"20,000 Leagues Under the Sea"***

Y-485: **"Alice in Wonderland";** single record **25**

Y-486: **"Peter Pan";** single record; no Songs but background music; P/S **25**

VY-2000: **"Trick or Treat";** 1952; two 7" record set; 78 rpm; Donald Duck; Norman Leyden conducts; original price: $1.00 . . . . **25**

VY-2001: **"Mickey Mouse's Candy Mine";** 1952; (Leyden); two 7" record set; 78 rpm; Mickey Mouse and Goofy; with booklet; original price: $1.00 . . . . **25**

VY-2002: **"The What-siz and the Who-siz";** 1952; (Leyden); two 7" record set; 78 rpm; Mickey Mouse and Goofy; original price: $1.00 . . . . **25**

VY-4000: **"Adventures in Music-Melody";** 1952; STK; four 7" record set; 78 rpm; Bill Thompson and Jud Conlon Singers; adapted from Walt Disney Movie; original price: $2.95 . . . . **35**

Y-4001: **"Peter Pan";** 1952; STK; two record set; unbreakable; features Bobby Driscoll, Kathryn Beaumont, John Brown, Bill Thompson, Verne Smith, and Jud Conlon Vocal Group; 24-page booklet; individual records numbered 4001-1 and 4001-2 . . . . **40**

VY-4001: **"Peter Pan";** 1952; STK; four 7" record set; 78 rpm; features Bobby Driscoll, Kathryn Beaumont, John Brown, Bill Thompson, Verne Smith, and Jud Conlon Vocal Group; original price: $2.95 . . . . **30**

Y-4004: **"20,000 Leagues Under the Sea";** 1954; STK; two record set; unbreakable; features William Redfield, Ian Martin, Bernard Lenrow, Arthur Anderson, and William Clauson; 24-page booklet; non-Disney music; individual records numbered 4004-1 and 4004-2 . . . . **75**

D3.31.4: Victor/RCA 78 rpm Singles

Victor 1663: Charlie Spivak Orchestra **"You Belong to My Heart" (from *The Three Caballeros*)/"There Must Be a Way"*;** charted May 26, 1945 . . . . **10**

Victor 24410: Don Bestor Orchestra **"Who's Afraid of the Big Bad Wolf"/"Mickey Mouse and Minnie's In Town";** recorded on September 25, 1933; charted on October 28, 1933; vocals by Florence Case, Charles Yontz, and Frank Sherry **20**

Victor 24616: Raymond Paige & Orchestra **"The Wise Little Hen"/"The Grasshopper and the** Ants"; recorded April 19, 1934 . . . **20**

Victor 25419: Wayne King Orchestra **"Mickey Mouse's Birthday Party"/"Nursery Rhymes"*;** charted October 31, 1936 . . . . **20**

Victor 26455: Sammy Kaye Orchestra "**When You Wish Upon a Star"/"Turn On the Old Music Box"*** **10**

Victor 26466: Kemp's Orchestra **"Give a Little Whistle"/"I've Got No Strings"** **10**

Victor 26477: Cliff Edwards **"When You Wish Upon a Star"/"Give a Little Whistle";** 1940; Victor Young Orchestra and Ken Darby Singers; single from Pinocchio **15**

Victor 26504: Kenny Baker **"When You Wish Upon a Star"/** **10**

Victor 27449: Sammy Kaye Orchestra **"The Reluctant Dragon"/ ;** charted on July 27, 1941; vocals by George Gingell and Maury Cross **15**

Victor 82092: Sinfonia Tonta **"El Raton Volador" (The Flying Mouse);** 1939; Spanish language version **25**

RCA 30-0019: Ilene Wood **"So This Is Love"/"Bibbidi-Bobbidi-Boo"** . . **15**

RCA 30-0020: Ilene Wood **"Cinderella's Work Song"/"A Dream Is a Wish Your Heart Makes"** **15**

RCA EI-VB-1179: Mindy Carson, Three Beaus and a Peep, and Andrew Acker **"I'm Late"/"T'was Brillig";** from *Alice in Wonderland*; issued in the RCA "Special Purpose Series" **10**

RCA EI-VB-1182: Three Suns **"March of the Cards"/"The Syncopated Clock"*;** issued in the RCA "Special Purpose Series" **15**

RCA 20-1663: Charlie Spivak **"You Belong to My Heart"/** **15**

RCA 20-1829: Freddy Martin Orchestra **"Bumble Boogie" (from *Melody Time*)/ ;** 1948 . . . . . **15**

RCA 20-1976: Sammy Kaye Orchestra and The Kaydets **"Zip-A-Dee-Doo-Dah"/"Sooner or Later (You're Gonna Be Coming Around)";** charted December 21, 1946 . . . . **15**

RCA 20-2396: Tony Martin and Earle Hagen Orchestra **"Too Good to Be True" (from *Fun and Fancy Free*)/**Bobby Worth **"Lazy Countryside"*;** 1947 . . . . **10**

RCA 20-2401: Phil Harris and Orchestra **"Fun and Fancy Free"/**Louis Prima and Orchestra **"Say It with a Slap"*** **15**

RCA 20-2780: Roy Rogers and the Sons of the Pioneers **"(There'll Never Be Another) Pecos Bill" (from *Melody Time*)/"Blue Shadows on the Trail"** **20**

RCA 20-2785: Vaughn Monroe **"Melody Time"/"Blue Shadows on the Trail";** 1948 . . . . **15**

RCA 20-3100: Sammy Kaye Orchestra **"Lavender Blue (Dilly Dilly)" (from *So Dear to My Heart*)/"Down Among the Sheltering Palms"*;** charted December 11, 1948 . . . . **10**

RCA 78-3113: Perry Como **"Bibbidi-Bobbidi-Boo"**; charted January 28, 1950; from *Cinderella* **10**

RCA 20-3130: Freddy Martin Orchestra **"It's Whatcha Do with Whatcha Got"/** **10**

RCA 20-3606: Vaughn Monroe and Orchestra with the Moonmaids **"So This Is Love"/"There's No One Here but Me"*** **10**

RCA 20-3607: Mitchell Ayers **"A Dream Is a Wish Your Heart Makes"/"Bibbidi Bobbidi Boo"** . . . **10**

RCA 20-3940: Fontane Sisters **"Jing-a-Ling, Jing-a-Ling" (*Beaver Valley*)/"Silver Bells"*** **15**

RCA 20-4087 Hugo Winterhalter Orchestra **"Alice in Wonderland"/"I'll Never Know Why"*** **10**

RCA 20-4088: Mindy Carson, Three Beaus and a Peep, and Andrew Acker **"I'm Late"/"T'was Brillig"**; from *Alice in Wonderland*

10RCA 20-4089: Fran Allison and Wayne King Orchestra **"All in a Golden Afternoon" (from *Alice in Wonderland*)/"Did You Write a Letter to Your Sweetheart"*** **10**

RCA 20-4090: Three Suns **"March of the Cards"/"The Syncopated Clock"*** **10**

RCA 20-4133: Ralph Flanagan and Orchestra **"Very Good Advice"/"Twilight Rhapsody"*** . . . **10**

RCA 20-4225: Betty Hutton, Dinah Shore, Phil Harris, Tony Martin, and Henri Rene and Orchestra **"How d'ye Do and Shake Hands"/"The Musicians"*** **15**

RCA 20-4769: Beaver Valley Sweethearts **"Jing-a-Ling, Jing-a-Ling" (from *Beaver Valley*)/"Juke Box Diner"*** **20**

RCA 20-6041: Walter Schumann **"The Ballad of Davy Crockett"/"Let's Make Up"*** **20**

RCA 20-6125: Walter Schumann **"Old Betsy"/"Shoeless Joe from Hannibal Mo."*** **10**

RCA 20-6178: Homer and Jethro **"Ballad of Davy Crew-cut" (parody)/"Pickin' and Singin' " (medley)*** **25**

RCA 20-6245: Eartha Kitt **"Sho-Jo-Ji"/"Nobody Taught Me"** **10**

RCA 20-6246: Lou Monte **"Yaller Yaller Gold"/"King of the River"** . . **10**

RCA 20-8429: Fess Parker **"Ballad of Davy Crockett"/"Daniel Boone"*** . . **15**

D3.32: *Talking Book* 78 *rpm* Records

CF-146, 147, and 148: **"Snow White and the Seven Dwarfs"**; 1938; three 12" record set; 78 rpm; by George Kean narrates; includes sound and dialogue from film; recorded on the "Talking Book" label by the American Foundation for the Blind; without cover; one side of each record's label is braille; Rare **125**

D3.33: *Tops* 78 *rpm* Records

R-254-49: The Rhythmaires **"The Ballad of Davy Crockett"/"It May Sound Silly"*** **25**

Section E
Disneyland and Buena Vista 45 rpm Recordings

E1
Original Disneyland 45 rpm 7" Singles

E1.1: "WD-4000" *Series*

This series was on yellow label, with Disneyland name logo at the bottom. "Hansen Records Inc." printed at top of label.

WD-4012: **"The Littlest Outlaw"**/Cliff Edwards **"Doroteo (The Automobile Song)"**; 1956; (Lava) **30**

WD-?: William Lava Orchestra **"El Padre"/"The Moon Won't Let You Tell a Lie"** **30**

E1.2: "F" *Series*

This series comprises the first 45 rpm 7" singles records actually produced by Disney. Early issues initially had yellow labels with the Disneyland logo at the bottom, with "pixie-dust" surrounding it. These "yellow" labels were #34-36 and were actually produced and distributed through "Hansen Records Inc." operated by Charles Hansen utilizing licensed Disney master recordings. Disney took over actual record production at F-037 and it and F-038 retained the yellow label. The labels quickly changed over to a purple color with the standard Disneyland logo at F-039. Not all of this series had picture sleeves, however those that have been confirmed are noted. The series commenced numerical sequence at "F-034" and ran through "F-068." It then jumped numerical sequence to an "F-100" series which ran through "F-130." Finding any of these other than the Annette hits and Fess Parker's hit of "Wringle Wrangle," especially with their picture sleeves intact, is quite difficult.

A very few of these exist in 78 rpm versions also without the "F" prefix, to wit numbers 37, 38, 42, 43, 44, 45, 54, and 63.

E1.2.1: Initial "F" Series "F-034" to "F-069"

F-034: Jeanne Gayle **"Song of the South"/"Sooner or Later"**; 1956; yellow label **30**

F-035: Jimmy Dodd **"Zip-A-Dee-Doo-Dah"/"Everybody Has a Laughing Place"**; 1956; yellow label **30**

F-036: Cliff Edwards **"Song of the South"** (MST)/**"When You Wish Upon a Star"**; 1956; yellow label reads "Hansen Records Inc., New York" at top of Disneyland label . . **30**

F-037: Camarata **"Railroadin' Man"/"Sons of Old Aunt Dinah"** (from ***The Great Locomotive Chase***); 1956; yellow label; P/S; also 78 rpm **30**

F-038: Camarata **"Summer Love"/"Autumn Way"**; 1956; also 78 rpm **20**

F-039: Fess Parker **"Wringle Wrangle" (vocal)/**Camarata **"Wringle Wrangle" (instrumental);** 1956; purple label . . **30**

F-040: Cliff Edwards **"I'm Sorry I Made You Cry"/"Nineteen Twenty-Five";** 1956 . . . . **25**

F-041 Cliff Edwards **"Ja Da"/"How Can I Miss You";** 1956 . . . . **25**

F-042 Jiminy Cricket **"T'was the Night Before Christmas"/"Kris Kringle";** 1956; P/S; also 78 rpm **25**

F-043: Fess Parker **"Wringle Wrangle"/"Ballad of John Coulter";** 1956; back cover has song lyrics; P/S; purple label; also 78 rpm **30**

F-044: Camarata "**Wringle Wrangle"/"Westward Ho the Wagons";** 1956; P/S; also 78 rpm **25**

F-045: Fess Parker **"The Ballad of John Coulter"/"Pioneer's Prayer";** 1956; P/S; also 78 rpm . . **30**

F-046: Frances Archer and Beverly Gile **"Maybe Tomorrow"/"Sinful People";** 1957 . . . . **25**

F-047: Camarata **"Bibbidi Bobbidi Boo"/"Cinderella";** 1957; P/S; 1st pressing **25**

"Bibbidi Bobbidi Boo"/"The Work Song"; 2nd pressing **20**

F-048: Viveca Lindfors **"Bonjour La Vie"/"Viale D'Autunno";** 1957 . . . **20**

F-049: Fess Parker **"A Hole in the Sky"/"Wedding Bell Calypso";** 1957; P/S **25**

F-050: Darlene Gillespie **"Sittin' in the Balcony"/"Too Much";** 1957 . . **35**

F-051: Darlene Gillespie **"Butterfly"/"Seven Days";** 1957 . . **35**

F-052: Darlene Gillespie **"I've Never Been in Love"/"Rockabilly";** 1957 . . . . **35**

F-053: Fess Parker **"Gonna Find Me a Bluebird"/"Catch Me Fish";** 1957 . . . . **25**

F-054: George Bruns **"Liberty Tree"/"Johnny Tremain";** 1957; also 78 rpm **25**

F-055: Tutti's Trumpets **"Trumpeter's Prayer"/"Boy Meets Horn";** 1957 . . . . **20**

F-056: Stan Jones **"Too Young to Marry"/"Creakin' Leather";** 1957 . . . . **35**

F-057: Ukulele Ike (Cliff Edwards) **"June Night"/"Sunday";** 1957 . . . . **25**

F-058: Camarata **"Love Is a Song"/"Little April Shower";** 1957 . . . . **20**

F-059: Jerome Courtland **"The Saga of Andy Burnett"/"Ladies in the Sky";** 1957 . . . . **25**

F-060: Darlene Gillespie and Jimmy Dodd **"Together Time"/**Darlene Gillespie **"Now to Sleep";** 1957 . . **25**

F-061: Jimmy Dodd and Darlene Gillespie **"Perri"/"Break of Day;** 1957 . . . . **25**

F-062: Henry Calvin **"Garcia's Lament"/"Zorro";** 1957 . . . . **25**

F-063: Karen Pendleton and Cubby O'Brien **"Rollin' Stone"/"Bidin' My Time";** 1957; also 78 rpm **25**

F-064: Stan Jones **"Sings the Theme from 'Sheriff of Cochise' " /"Theme from 'Cheyenne' ";** 1958; P/S **35**

F-065: Kevin Corcoran and Jerome Courtland **"Old Yeller"/"How Much Is That Doggie in the Window";** 1958 . . . . **30**

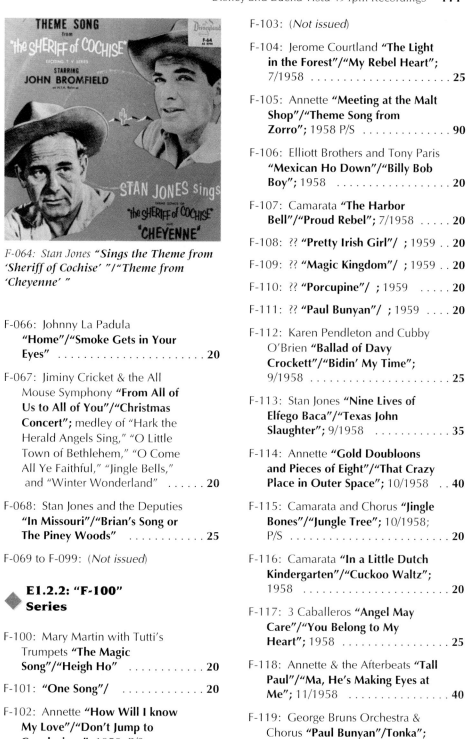

F-064: Stan Jones ***"Sings the Theme from 'Sheriff of Cochise' "/"Theme from 'Cheyenne' "***

F-066: Johnny La Padula **"Home"/"Smoke Gets in Your Eyes"** **20**

F-067: Jiminy Cricket & the All Mouse Symphony **"From All of Us to All of You"/"Christmas Concert";** medley of "Hark the Herald Angels Sing," "O Little Town of Bethlehem," "O Come All Ye Faithful," "Jingle Bells," and "Winter Wonderland" **20**

F-068: Stan Jones and the Deputies **"In Missouri"/"Brian's Song or The Piney Woods"** **25**

F-069 to F-099: (*Not issued*)

E1.2.2: "F-100" Series

F-100: Mary Martin with Tutti's Trumpets **"The Magic Song"/"Heigh Ho"** **20**

F-101: **"One Song"/** **20**

F-102: Annette **"How Will I know My Love"/"Don't Jump to Conclusions";** 1958; P/S; same as LP MM-24 above **75**

F-103: (*Not issued*)

F-104: Jerome Courtland **"The Light in the Forest"/"My Rebel Heart";** 7/1958 . . . . **25**

F-105: Annette **"Meeting at the Malt Shop"/"Theme Song from Zorro";** 1958 P/S **90**

F-106: Elliott Brothers and Tony Paris **"Mexican Ho Down"/"Billy Bob Boy";** 1958 . . . . **20**

F-107: Camarata **"The Harbor Bell"/"Proud Rebel";** 7/1958 . . . . . **20**

F-108: ?? **"Pretty Irish Girl"/ ;** 1959 . . **20**

F-109: ?? **"Magic Kingdom"/ ;** 1959 . . **20**

F-110: ?? **"Porcupine"/ ;** 1959 . . . . . **20**

F-111: ?? **"Paul Bunyan"/ ;** 1959 . . . . **20**

F-112: Karen Pendleton and Cubby O'Brien **"Ballad of Davy Crockett"/"Bidin' My Time";** 9/1958 . . . . **25**

F-113: Stan Jones **"Nine Lives of Elfego Baca"/"Texas John Slaughter";** 9/1958 . . . . **35**

F-114: Annette **"Gold Doubloons and Pieces of Eight"/"That Crazy Place in Outer Space";** 10/1958 . . **40**

F-115: Camarata and Chorus **"Jingle Bones"/"Jungle Tree";** 10/1958; P/S **20**

F-116: Camarata **"In a Little Dutch Kindergarten"/"Cuckoo Waltz";** 1958 . . . . **20**

F-117: 3 Caballeros **"Angel May Care"/"You Belong to My Heart";** 1958 . . . . **25**

F-118: Annette & the Afterbeats **"Tall Paul"/"Ma, He's Making Eyes at Me";** 11/1958 . . . . **40**

F-119: George Bruns Orchestra & Chorus **"Paul Bunyan"/Tonka";** 1958 . . . . **25**

F-120: Camarata **"Sleeping Beauty Medley"/"Sleeping Beauty Theme"**; 1959 20

F-121: Stan Jones **"Song of the Dance Hall Girls"/"The Lilies Grow High"**; 1959 25

F-122: ?? "Lonely Guitar"/ 20

F-123: Roberta Shore **"Shaggy Dog"/"C'est Chiffon"**; P/S 20

F-124: Sean Connery and Janet Munro **"Pretty Irish Girl"/"Bellamaquilty's Band"**; P/S; the record's value is spurred on by singing of Sean Connery, Hollywood's original "James Bond" character in many later films. 50

F-125: Rex Allen **"Swamp Fox"/"Bronco Boogie"** 25

F-126: Jeanne Gayle **"Don't Mention His Name to Me"/"Love One Another"** 20

F-127: Sterling Holloway **"Jingle Bells"/"Mouse Square Dance"** . . . 20

F-128: Jordan Whitfield **"Heaven"/"Let There Be Peace on Earth"**; 1960 20

F-129: Henry Calvin **"Biddle-dee-dee"/"Toby Tyler"**; 1960 20

F-130: Burl Ives **"Chim Chim Cheree"/"Lavender Blue"**; 1964; P/S 20

E2

Buena Vista 45 rpm 7" "F" Series Singles (300-400 Series)

Many with picture sleeves denoted "P/S." However, many were not issued with picture sleeves.

F-330: Darlene Gillespie **"Porcupine"/"Loddy Doddy Doo"**; 1958 25

F-331: Camarata **"Riding West (Theme from Spin and Marty)"** (Lava)/**"Trudie"**; 1958 20

F-332: Mary Martin **"Makin' Believe It's Christmas Eve"/"Motherless Child"**; 10/1958 15

F-333: Clair Hogan and the Commanders **"I Wonder"/"Sing a Smiling Song"**; 1/1959 15

F-334: Commanders **"Once Upon a Dream"/"Sing a Smiling Song"**; 1/1959; Stereo 25

F-335: Camarata **"On the Trail"/"Trumpeter's Prayer"**; 1959; Stereo 20

F-336: Annette **"Jo Jo the Dog Faced Boy"/"Lonely Guitar"**; 4/1959 . . . 35

Same number released as **"Jo Jo the Dog Faced Boy"/"Love Me Forever"** 30

F-337: Tutti's Trumpets **"Flat Foot Floogie"/"Doggone It, It's a Dog"**; 4/1959 10

F-338: Camarata **"From 'The Horse Soldiers' I Left My Love"/"Lover's March"**; 7/1959 15

F-339: Annette **"Lonely Guitar"/"Wild Willie"**; 5/1959; P/S 60

F-340: Roberta Shore **"Happy Music"/"Love at First Sight"**; 7/1959 10

F-341: Rex Allen **"Lazy River"/"Say One for Me"**; 6/1959 15

F-342: Rex Allen **"I Couldn't Care Less"/"Pretty Irish Girl"**; 6/1959 . . 15

F-343: Johnny Johns **"The Heart of an Angel"/"I'm in the Mood for Love"**; 1959 15

F-344: Annette **"My Heart Became of Age"/"Especially for You";** 8/1959 . . . . **60**

F-345: Elliott Brothers Orchestra **"Boo Bam Boogie"/"What Is This Thing Called Love";** 8/1959 . . . . . . **10**

F-346: Kookie Kazoo Band **"Hey Batter Batter"/"Icka Back Soda Cracker";** 9/1959 . . . . **15**

F-347: Rex Allen **"The Little Old Church in the Valley"/"Morgen";** 8/1959 . . . . **15**

F-348: Roberta Shore **"Love at First Sight"/"Take Me Along";** 10/1959 . . . . **10**

F-349: Annette **"First Name Initial"/"My Heart Became of Age";** 10/1959; P/S **60**

F-350: Johnny Walsh **"My Darling,Why"/"So I'll Never Leave";** 10/1959 . . . . **10**

F-351: Rex Allen **"Staying Young"/"Forever and Ever";** 11/1959 . . . . **15**

F-352: Camarata **"Climb the Mountain"/"This I Know";** 11/1959 . . . . **10**

F-353: (*Not issued*)

F-354: Annette **"O Dio Mio"/"It Took Dreams";** 12/1959; P/S **60**

F-355: Rex Allen **"Barefoot Country Boy"/"Conversation with a Mule";** 1/1960 . . . . **15**

F-356: Camarata **"Lost in a Fog"/"Toot Sweet (It's Really Love)";** 3/1960 . . . . **10**

F-357: Larry Green **"Toby Tyler"/Mitchell Boys Choir "Biddle-Dee-Dee";** 4/1960 . . . . . . **20**

F-358: Rex Allen **"The Lillies Grow High"/"I'm the Man";** 5/1960 . . . . **15**

F-362: Annette ***"Pineapple Princess"/"Luau Cha Cha Cha"***

F-359: Annette **"Train of Love"/"Tell Me Who's the Girl";** 5/1960; P/S . . **60**

F-360: Camarata Strings **"Tropical Botiqua"/"A Day Without You";** 7/1960 . . . . **10**

F-361: Gloria Woods & Afterbeats **"Doo Dee Doo Doop"/"Ching Ching";** 7/1960 . . . . **15**

F-362: Annette **"Pineapple Princess"/"Luau Cha Cha Cha";** 8/1960; P/S **40**

F-363: Rex Allen **"Charro Bravo"/"I Love You So Much It Hurts";** 8/1960 . . . . **15**

F-364: Thurl Ravenscroft and Ranger Chorus **"Roll Along (Unto the Sea)"/"Ten Who Dared";** 9/1960 . . **15**

F-365: Camarata **"Golden Years"/"Theme from 'Swiss Family Robinson' ";** 11/1960 . . . . . **15**

F-366: Isle Werner **"Capito"** (English)/**"Capito"** (German); 12/1960 . . . . **10**

F-367: Jerry Colonna **"Cruella De Ville"/"101 Dalmatians";** 1960 . . . **20**

F-374: Annette ***"Dream Boy"/"Please, Please Signore"***

F-368: Camarata Orchestra **"Louis"/"Trumpeter's Prayer";** 1960 . . . . . **10**

F-369: Annette & Paul Anka **"Talk to Me Baby"/"I Love You Baby";** 11/1960; P/S **40**

F-370: Rex Allen **"Dodie Ann" /"Pretty Irish Girl";** 10/1960 . . . . . **15**

F-371: Stan Jones **"Ghost Riders in the Sky"/"Wringle Wrangle";** 1960 . . . . . **25**

F-372: The K-Nine **"101 Dalmatians";** 1961 . . . . . **20**

F-373: Fred MacMurray & Midfield Glee Club **"Flubber Theme"/"Absent Minded Professor March";** 4/1961 . . . . . **25**

F-374: Annette **"Dream Boy"/"Please, Please Signore";** 1/1961; P/S **40**

F-375: Annette **"Indian Giver"/"Mama, Mama Rosa (Where's the Spumoni)";** 1961; P/S **40**

F-376: Hayley Mills & the Afterbeats **"The Parent Trap"/"Cobbler, Cobbler";** 1961 . . . . . **35**

F-377: Camarata Orchestra **"Maggie's Theme"/"Braziliero";** 6/1961 . . . . . **10**

F-378: School Belles **"Whistling at the Boys"/"Whistling Bells";** 6/1961 . . . . . **20**

F-379: (*Not issued*)

F-380: Bob Grabeau **"For Now, For Always"/"Miracle at Lourdes";** 6/1961 . . . . . **10**

F-381: Fred MacMurray **"Flubber Theme"/"Serendipity";** 4/1961; Annette picture on the P/S **30**

F-382: Gary Shortall **"Private Property"/"Talkin' in My Sleep";** 7/1961 . . . . . **10**

F-383: Vonnair Sisters **"Dum Papa Too Tah Tah"/"Beach Love";** 7/1961 . . . . . **15**

F-384: Annette **"Hawaiian Love Talk"/"Blue Muu Muu";** 7/1961; P/S **40**

F-385: Hayley Mills **"Let's Get Together"/"Cobbler, Cobbler";** 8/1961; P/S **35**

F-386: Ludwig Von Drake **"Green with Envy Blues"/"I'm Ludwig Von Drake";** 10/1961 . . . . . **15**

F-387: Camarata Orchestra **"Babes in Toyland Part I"/"Part II";** 10/1961 . . . . . **10**

F-388: Annette & Vonnair Sisters **"Dreamin' About You"/"The Strummin' Song";** 1961; P/S **40**

F-389: Hayley Mills **"Cobbler, Cobbler";** 1961; promo only **35**

F-390: Vonnair Sisters **"Goodbye to Toyland"/"I Don't Want to Play in Your Yard";** 12/1961 . . . . . **15**

F-391: Prof. Ludwig Von Drake **"The Von Drake Quake"/"It Gets You";** 2/1962; P/S **15**

F-392: Annette **"That Crazy Place in Outer Space"**/Dany Saval and Tom Tyron **"Seven Moons (of Batalayre)"**; 2/1962; P/S without Annette **40**

F-393: Camarata Orchestra **"Moon Pilot (7 Moons of Batalayre)"/"When You Wish Upon a Star"**; 3/1962 . . . . **25**

F-394: Annette **"The Truth About Youth"/"I Can't Do the Sum"**; 2/1962; P/S **50**

F-395: Hayley Mills **"Johnny Jingo"/"Jeepers, Creepers"**; 2/1962; P/S **35**

F-396: Camarata Orchestra **"Bon Voyage Waltz"/"Tu Sai"**; 5/1962 . . **15**

F-397: Peggy King **"Bon Voyage"/"I Get a Kick Out of Kissin' "**; 5/1962 . . . . **10**

F-398: Elliott Brothers Orchestra **"Grad Nite at Disneyland"**; includes: "That's All"/"Mexican Hoe-Down"/"Goodnight Sweetheart"; 1962 . . . . **15**

F-399: Vonnair Sisters **"Luscious Lucius"/"See for Yourself"**; 6/1962 . . . . **15**

F-400: Annette **"My Little Grass Shack"/"Hukilau Song"**; 6/1962 . . **35**

F-401: Hayley Mills **"Side by Side"/"Ching Ching & a Ring Ding Ding"**; 6/1962; P/S **35**

F-402: Camarata Orchestra **"Mon Amour Perdu (My Lost Love)"/"Tu Sai"**; 6/1962 . . . . **10**

F-403: Billy Storm **"Puppy Love Is Here to Stay"/"Push Over"**; 10/1962 . . . . **20**

F-404: Camarata Orchestra **"Like Lost"/"Spring Fever"**; 7/1962 . . . . **10**

F-395: Hayley Mills ***"Johnny Jingo"/"Jeepers, Creepers"***

F-405: Annette **"He's My Ideal"/"Mr. Piano Man"**; 10/1962; P/S **40**

F-406: Billy Strange **"I'll Remember April"/"The Mooncussors"**; 12/1962 . . . . **20**

F-407: Annette & Marzocchi **"Bella Bella Florence"/"Canzone D'Amore"**; 10/1962; rare with P/S **120**

F-408: Hayley Mills **"Castaway"/"Sweet River"**; 11/1962; P/S **35**

F-409: Hayley Mills and Maurice Chevalier **"Enjoy It"/"Let's Climb"**; 11/1962; P/S **35**

F-410: Camarata **"In Search of the Castaways"/"Bubbles"**; 11/1962 . . **15**

F-411: ?? **"Bubbles"/** **15**

F-412: Vonnair Sisters **"Golden Rule"/"Watch Out for Don"**; 10/1962 . . . . **15**

F-413: Billy Storm **"Love Theme from El Cid"/"Cee Cee Rider"**; 12/1962 . . . . **20**

F-434: Julie Andrews ***"Super-Cali-Fragil-Istic-Expi-Ali-Docious"/"A Spoonful of Sugar"***

F-414: Annette **"Teenage Wedding"/"Walkin' and Talkin' ";** 1/1963; with extremely rare P/S depicting Annette in bridal gown . . **300**

F-415: Billy Storm **"Double Date"/"Good Girl";** 1/1963 . . . . . **20**

F-416: Vonnair Sisters **"Blame It on My Youth"/"Pretty Little Girl with the Red Dress On";** 2/1963 . . **15**

F-417: Billy Strange **"Johnny Shiloh"/"Day by Day";** 1/1963 . . . **20**

F-418: Billy Storm **"Lonely People Do Foolish Things"/"Deed I Do";** 3/1963 . . . . **20**

F-419: Burl Ives **"On the Front Porch"/"Ugly Bug Ball";** 6/1963; P/S **20**

F-420: Hayley Mills and Eddie Hodges **"Flitterin' "/"Beautiful Beulah";** 6/1963; P/S **35**

F-421: Wellingtons **"Savage Sam and Me"/"Just Say Auf Wiedersehen";** 5/1963 . . . . **20**

F-422: (*Not issued*)

F-423: Maureen Scott **"The Ugly Bug Ball"/"He's So Near";** 8/1963 . . . . **15**

F-424: Billy Storm **"He Knows How Much We Can Bear"/"Motherless Child";** 7/1963 . . . . **20**

F-425: The Ward Singers **"He's Got the Whole World in His Hands"/"Down by the Riverside";** 8/1963 . . . . **20**

F-426: Fess Parker **"The Ballad of Davy Crockett"/"Farewell";** 8/1963; P/S; lyrics on back **25**

F-427: Annette **"Treat Him Nicely"/"Promise Me Anything";** 9/1963; P/S **65**

F-428: Kay Bell and the Spacemen **"Scream Along"/"Surfer's Blues";** 9/1963 . . . . **20**

F-429: Billy Storm **"Since I Fell for You"/"Body and Soul";** 11/1963 . . **20**

F-430: Wellingtons **"Tomisina";** 5/1964 . . . . **20**

F-431: Annette and Tommy Kirk **"Scrambled Egghead"/**Annette and Wellingtons **"Merlin Jones";** 12/1963; P/S **65**

F-432: Annette **"Custom City"/"Rebel Rider";** 6/1964; P/S . . **65**

F-433: Annette **"Muscle Beach Party"/"I Dream About Frankie";** 4/1964; P/S **65**

F-434: Julie Andrews **"Super-Cali-Fragil-Istic-Expi-Ali-Docious"/"A Spoonful of Sugar";** 7/1964; P/S **20**

F-435: Ron Grainer **"Nicola"/"Three Goddesses of Love";** 8/1964 . . . . . **15**

F-436: Annette **"Bikini Beach Party"/"The Clyde";** 9/1964; P/S . . **60**

F-437: Annette **"The Wah Watusi"/"The Clyde";** 10/1964 . . . **35**

F-438: Annette **"Something Borrowed, Something Blue"/"How Will I Know My Love"**; 1/1965; P/S; rare **90**

F-439: Big Ben Banjo Band **"Jolly Holiday"/"Mary Poppins Medley"**; 2/1965 .... **15**

F-440: Annette **"The Monkey's Uncle (with Beach Boys)"/"How Will I Know My Love"**; 3/1965; P/S **40**

F-441: Dick Van Dyke **"Chim Chim Cheree"/"Step In Time"**; 4/1965; P/S **20**

F-442: Annette **"The Boy to Love"/"No One Else Could Be Prouder"**; 5/1965 .... **35**

F-443: Mary Martin and Camarata Orch. **"Bibbidi-Bobbidi-Boo"/"I'm Late"**; 5/1965 .... **15**

F-444: Camarata **"A Dream Is A Wish Your Heart Makes"/"Work Song"**; 5/1965 .... **10**

F-445: Louis Prima and Gia Maione **"That Darn Cat"/"Supercalifragilisticexpialadocious"**; 8/1965; P/S; promo record for Penny's Department Store **20**

F-446: Louis Prima and Gia Maione **"Jolly Holiday" /"Supercalifragilisticespiralidoso"**; 1965; Italian version **15**

F-447: Bobby Troup Trio **"Girl Talk"/"Won't Somebody Please Belong to Me"**; 1965 .... **15**

F-448: Bobby Troup Chorus **"That Darn Cat: Title Theme"/"Winnie the Pooh: Title Theme"**; 10/1965 . . **15**

F-449: Disneyland Boys' Choir **"It's a Small World"/"Silent Night"**; 11/1965; P/S **10**
Special P/S was printed for the Beverly Hill Hadassah for "It's a Small World" track only. **25**

F-450: Annette **"No Way to Go But Up"/"Crystal Ball"**; 3/1966 ...... **35**

F-451: Jack Halloran Singers **"California Angels"/"Take Me Out to the Ball Game"**; 6/1966 . . . **25**

F-452: Jack Halloran Singers **"California Angels A-OK (Official Fight Song)"** (6/1966) P/S **25**

F-453: Louis Prima and Gia Maione **"Winnie the Pooh, Parts I and II"**; 8/1966; P/S **15**

F-454: Louis Prima **"Santa, How Come Your Eyes Are Green When Last Year They Were Blue"/"Senor Santa Claus"**; 12/1966 .... **15**

F-455: Maurice Chevalier **"Joie De Vivre"/"There's a Great Big Beautiful Tomorrow"**; 2/1967; P/S **15**

F-456: Robert F. Brunner **"Theme from 'Monkey, Go Home' "/ "Yolanda's Theme"**; 2/1967; P/S **20**

F-457: Tommy Steele **"Fortuosity"/"I'm a Brass Band Today"**; 6/1967; two different P/S: one features an alligator and Steele, other shows Steele with a guitar; value is the same **20**

F-458: Mary Martin **"Whistle While You Work"/"Heigh Ho"**; 4/1967 . . **10**

F-459: Bullwhip Griffin **"The Adventures of Bullwhip Griffin"**/Carol Lee Lombard **"Good Grief, Griffin"**; 4/1967 . . . **25**

F-460: Camarata Orchestra and Mike Sammes Singers **"Hail, Knight of the Woeful Countenance"/"What Does He Want of Me (What Do You Want of Me)"**; 5/1967 ...... **15**

F-461: Phil Harris **"Bare Necessities"**/Louis Prima **"I Wanna Be Like You"**; 10/1967 . . . **15**

F-462: Camarata **"Beautiful Things"/"Let's Have a Drink on It"**; 12/1967 . . . **10**

F-463: Jungle VIPs **"Vulture Song"**/Vultures **"Whatcha Gonna Do"**; 12/1967 . . . **25**

F-464: Jungle V.I.P.'s **"Bare Necessities"**/Phil Harris **"Bare Necessities"**; 1/1968 . . . **15**

F-465: Louis Armstrong **"Ten Feet Off the Ground"/" 'Bout Time"**; 3/1968 . . . **15**

F-466: Louis Armstrong **"The Bare Necessities"**/Tutti's Trumpets **"Louis"**; 3/1968 . . . **15**

F-467: Anne Shelton **"Family Band"/" 'Bout Time"**; 5/1968 . . . **10**

F-468: Lively Five **"Dakota"/"Lazy Afternoon"**; 5/1968 . . . **10**

F-469: Louis Armstrong **"Bibbidi-Bobbidi-Boo"/"Zip-A-Dee-Doo-Dah"**; 8/1968 . . . **15**

F-470: Louis Armstrong Orchestra **"High Ho"/"When You Wish Upon a Star"**; 8/1968 . . . **15**

F-471: Louis Armstrong Orchestra **"Ballad of Davy Crockett"/"Chim Chim Cheree"**; 8/1968 . . . **20**

F-472: **"Minnie's Yoo Hoo-Excerpts from the Mickey Mouse Fortieth Anniversary Show"**; 12/1968 . . . **25**

F-473: Bobby Russell **"The Ballad of Smith & Gabriel Jimmy Boy"/"Summer Street"**; 4/1969 . . . **15**

F-474: Bobby Russell **"The Ballad of Smith & Gabriel Billyboy"/"Summer Street"**; 7/1969 . . . **15**

F-475: Annette **"Merlin Jones"/"The Computer Wore Tennis Shoes"**; 12/1969; P/S; Stereo . . . **35**

F-476: Anne Shelton **"It Won't Be Long 'Til Christmas"/"The Christmas Star"**; 11/1969; P/S . . . **15**

F-477: Phil Harris **"What! No Mickey Mouse (What Kind of Party Is This"/"Minnie's Yoo Hoo"**; 7/1970; P/S . . . **20**

F-478: Phil Harris **"Ev'rybody Wants to Be a Cat"/"Thomas O'Mally Cat"**; 11/1970 . . . **15**

F-479: Maurice Chevalier **"The Aristocats"**/Mike Sammes Singers **"The Aristocats"**; 12/1970 . . . **15**

F-480: Scatman Crothers **"Ev'rybody Wants to Be a Cat"/"I'm the Scatcat Man"**; 12/1970 . . . **15**

F-481: BD and Company **"He's Gonna Make It"**/Bobby Troup & Trio **"That Darn Cat"**; 2/1971 . . . **10**

F-482: Rod McKuen **"Pastures Green"/"Scandalous John"**; 6/1971; P/S . . . **15**

F-483: Bobby Hammack Orchestra **"It's A Small World"**/Jack Coleman Singers **"It's A Small World"**; 9/1971; Stereo . . . **20**

F-484: Bobby Hammack Orch. **"Age of Not Believing"/"It's A Small World"**; 9/1971 . . . **10**

F-485: Louis Prima **"The Age of Not Believing"/"With a Flair"**; 9/1971 . . **10**

F-486: Angela Lansbury **"Substitutiary Locomotion"/"Age of Not Believing"**; 12/1971 . . . **15**

F-487: Pat Boone **"Little Green Tree"/"The Songs of Christmas"**; 12/1971; P/S . . . **20**

F-488: Shane Tatum **"Moreover and Me"/"Minnie's Yoo Hoo"**; 2/1972; P/S . . . **15**

F-499: Mike Curb Congregation ***"Mickey Mouse March"***

F-489: Louis Armstrong **"Zip-A-Dee-Doo-Dah"/"When You Wish Upon a Star";** 2/1972 .... **10**

F-490: Shane Tatum & Marnie Walker **"Napoleon and Samantha"/"Last Voyage Home";** 6/1972; P/S **15**

F-491: Marvin Hamlisch **"Love Theme from 'The World's Greatest Athlete' "/"Teeny Tim's March";** 3/1973; P/S **25**

F-492: Mike Curb Congregation **"Robin Hood March"/"Oo-De-Lally";** 3/1974 .... **10**

F-493: Roger Miller **"Whistle Stop"/"Not in Nottingham";** 12/1973; P/S **15**

F-494: Mike Curb Congregation **"Winnie the Pooh"/"Zip-A-Dee-Doo-Dah";** 12/1973 .... **10**

F-495: Nancy Adams **"Robin Hood"/"Love";** 2/1974 .... **10**

F-496: Louis Prima **"Phony King of England"/"Robin Hood";** 2/1974 .. **10**

F-497: Louis Prima **"Robin Hood";** 6/1974 .... **10**

F-498: Julie Budd **"Roses and Rainbows"/"Any Fool Can See";** 7/1974 .... **10**

F-499: Mike Curb Congregation **"Mickey Mouse March"/**Jimmy Dodd Mouseketeers **"Mickey Mouse Alma Mater";** 12/1974; P/S **25**

E3
Disneyland and Buena Vista "500" Series— 45 rpm, 78 rpm and 33-1/3 rpm 7" Records

This "500" numbering system for Disney/Buena Vista records is a hodge-podge of various formats issued over the years. It includes a very few 78 rpm records, many 45 rpm, and even some 33-1/3 EPs. There are also many promos included. It is convenient to keep the numbering in sequence and all in one spot for the reader. The only exception is the "LLP-500" EPs which duplicate some of these numbers and which appear above at Section C12.

500: **"It's A Small World";** flexidisc made of pliable plastic **50**

NHP-501: **"Our National and Historical Parks";** 7" EP; may have been a special order or giveaway item; with booklet describing the National Parks **25**

The four "F" numbers directly below were a special 45 rpm "Zorro" series on Disneyland which was derived from LP WDA-3601 above. They also appeared with an "A" prefix on 78 rpm editions. Add $10 if it grades as an M- 78 rpm, otherwise a VG+ 78 rpm is the same value as an M- 45 rpm.

DL-559: "General Electric Carousel of Progress: 'Great Big Beautiful Tomorrow' "

F-501: **"Walt Disney Presents Senor Zorro"** (2/1958) P/S **35**

A-501: 78 rpm edition **45**

F-502: **"Zorro Frees the Indians";** 2/1958; P/S **35**

A-502: 78 rpm edition **45**

F-503: **"Walt Disney Presents Zorro and the Ghost";** 2/1958; P/S **35**

A-503: 78 rpm edition **45**

F-504: **"Zorro's Daring Rescue";** 2/1958; P/S **35**

A-504: 78 rpm edition **45**

F-505: **"Going Quackers"/"Vacuum Cleaner Hoses";** 1980; Willio and Philio and Donald Duck **15**

Note: Numbering skips to 555.

DL-555: **"Flubber Song"/"Serendipity";** 1962; 33-1/3 rpm; Fred MacMurray; Annette verse on Serendipity side; P/S **35**

DL-556: **"Ugly Bug Ball"/"Those Crazy Days of Summer";** 1962; Disneyland Band **20**

DL-557: **"Davy Crockett"/"Whale of a Tale";** The Wellingtons; promo . . **25**

558: **"Monsanto Presents Miracles from Molecules" (Sherman);** 33-1/3 EP; P/S; instrumental on both sides **25**

DL-559: **"General Electric Carousel of Progress: 'Great Big Beautiful Tomorrow' " (and a medley of Disney tunes);** 1968; P/S; from Walt Disney's Carousel of Progress at the 1964-65 NY World's Fair; comes in a cardboard mailer envelope **25**

DL-560: **"The Orange Bird Song"/"Orange Tree";** 1971; Anita Bryant; P/S; indicates "Compliments of the Florida Citrus Industry" **25**

DL-561: **"These Are the Best Times"/"These Are the Best Times";** 1975; Bobby Goldsboro Promo; from *Superdad* film; no P/S **25**

562: **"We Have Love"/"Under the Mistletoe";** 1975; promo from *Dickens' Christmas Tree* **25**

563: **"Winnie the Pooh for President";** 1976; story and song; Sears, Roebuck issue **25**

564: **"Winnie the Pooh for President (Campaign Song)";** 1976; Larry Groce; no P/S **20**

564: **"I'd Like to Be You for a Day"/"I'd Like to be You for a Day";** promo from *Freaky Friday;* Note: same number as above **25**

565: **"Pete's Dragon";** 12/1977; 33-1/3 EP; four song promo; no P/S **25**

566: **"I'd Like to Be You for a Day"/"I'd Like to be You for a Day";** The Osmonds; promo from *Freaky Friday* **25**

567: **"Learning to Tell Time Is Fun";** Grolier; 33-1/3 EP with black and white booklet in the "LLP" style. . . . **20**

568: **"Disco Mouse";** 5/1977; no P/S **15**

DL-569: **"Disco Mouse (Mickey Mouse March)"/"Walking the Dog";** 5/1977 . . . . **15**

570: **"The Rescuers";** promo; P/S **25**

571: **"Mickey's Birthday Songfest";** 5/1978; 33-1/3 EP; no P/S **25**

572-573: (*Not issued ?*)

574: **"Snoopy"/"Flashbeagle";** Desiree Goyette; promo with a "Flashbeagle" P/S and pink "Flashbeagle" logo label **20**

E4
Mickey Mouse Club "LG-600" Series 45 rpm Records (1978)

All have picture sleeves.

601: **"Snow White";** 9/1978 . . . . **10**

602: **"Pinocchio";** 9/1978 . . . . **10**

603: **"Dumbo";** 9/1978 . . . . **10**

604: **"Bambi";** 9/1978 . . . . **10**

605: **"Peter and the Wolf";** 9/1978 . . **10**

606: **"Song of the South";** 9/1978 . . . **10**

607: **"Cinderella";** 9/1978 . . . . **10**

608: **"Alice in Wonderland";** 9/1978 . . **10**

609: **"Peter Pan";** 9/1978 . . . . **10**

610: **"Davy Crockett and Other Heroes";** 9/1978 . . . . **10**

611: **"Lady and the Tramp";** 9/1978 . . **10**

612: **"Mother Goose";** 9/1978 . . . . . . **10**

613: **"Sleeping Beauty";** 9/1978 . . . . . **10**

651: "Mickey Mouse March"

614: **"Babes in Toyland";** 9/1978 . . . . **10**

615: **"Hansel and Gretel";** 9/1978 . . . **10**

616: **"Farmer in the Dell and Other Nursery Rhymes";** 9/1978 . . . . **10**

617: **"Mary Poppins";** 9/1978 . . . . . . **10**

618: **"Winnie the Pooh";** 9/1978 . . . . **10**

619: **"It's a Small World";** 9/1978 . . . **10**

620: **"The Jungle Book";** 9/1978 . . . . **10**

621: **"Winnie the Pooh and the Blustery Day";** 9/1978 . . . . **10**

622: **"Happy Birthday";** 9/1978 . . . . **10**

623: **"Robin Hood";** 9/1978 . . . . **10**

624: **"Disney Marching Songs for Children";** 9/1978 . . . . **10**

625-650: (*Not issued*)

The following are 45 rpm EPs:

651: **"Mickey Mouse March";** 9/1978 . . . . **15**

652: **"Mousekedances";** 19/978 . . . . **15**

653: **"Mouseketeers Talent Roundup";** 9/1978; includes "We're the Mouseketeers"; "Rollin' Stone Talent Roundup"; "Hi to You" **15**

654: **"Spin and Marty"**; 9/1978 ..... **15**

655: **"Jiminy Cricket's Mouse Club Songs"**; 9/1978 .... **15**

656: **"Mickey Mouse Alma Mater"**; 9/1978 .... **20**

E5
Special Issue Promo "700" Series Records

AL-701: **"Walt Disney's Summer Magic"**; 3/1963; 7"; 33-1/3 EP; Burl Ives and Hayley Mills; P/S; probably a giveaway or premium order from Alcoa Aluminum; songs taken from LP BV-4025 .... **25**

OK-702: **"Mary Poppins"**; 9/1964; MST; 7"; 33-1/3; EP; P/S; includes "Mary Poppins Song" and "Jolly Holiday"; a Kraft Foods premium record **35**

E6
Disneyland "LG" 700-800 Series 45 rpm 7" Singles ("Little Gem")

These have yellow labels—all with picture sleeves. Originally sold at 29¢. On LG-701 through LG-712, the covers had a vertical color band on the right side. The sleeves in the earlier numbers opened on the side instead of the top. There were 78 rpm counterparts at least through LG-782. See above at Section D2. See also a separate "800" series below.

LG-701: **"Donald Duck and His Nephews Sing Clementine"/"We Boys Will Shine Tonight"**; 6/1960 .. **20**

LG-702: **"Donald Duck and Uncle Scrooge's Money Rocket (A Fun Story)"**; 6/1960 .... **20**

LG-703: **"Mickey's Band Concert"/"While Walking Through the Park One Day"/"The Band Played On"/"In the Good Old Summertime"**; 6/1960 .... **20**

LG-704: **"Chipmunk Fun with Chip 'n' Dale"**; 6/1960 .... **20**

LG-705: **"Walt Disney's Mother Goose Rhymes"/"London Bridge Is Falling Down"/"Here We Go 'Round the Mulberry Bush"**; Disneyland Children's Chorus; 6/1960 .... **20**

LG-706: **"Walt Disney's Bear Went Over the Mountain"/"Sing A Song of Six Pence"/"Hey Diddle Diddle"/"Misty Moisty Morning"**; Disneyland Children's Chorus; 6/1960 .... **20**

LG-707: **"Walt Disney's Lullabies"/"Rockabye Baby"/"Brahms' Lullaby"**; 6/1960 .... **20**

LG-708: **"Walt Disney's Frog Went A-Courtin' "/"Fiddle Dee Dee"**; Frances Archer and Beverly Gile; 6/1960 .... **20**

LG-709: **"America the Beautiful"** (Hayley Mills)/**"Yankee Doodle"** (Disneyland Chorus); 6/1960 ..... **30**

LG-710: **"Walt Disney's Three Little Pigs"/"Alouette"/"Polly Polly Doodle"/"Talk Happiness"/"As Beauty Does"**; 7/1960 .... **20**

LG-711: **"I've Been Working on the Railroad"/"Hail, Hail The Gang's All Here"/"For He's a Jolly Good Fellow"**; 6/1960; Mickey and His Gang **15**

LG-712: **"Chip 'n' Dale Chipmunks and Goofy Sing for You"/"I'm a Little Prairie Flower" (Chip 'n' Dale)/"Daisy, Daisy"/ "Kookaburra" (Goofy);** 6/1960 . . . . **15**

LG-713: **"Music from the Swiss Family Robinson: My Monkey and Me"/"The Animal Race Polka";** 11/1960 . . . . **20**

LG-714: **"101 Dalmatians—Dalmatian Plantation"/"Cruella De Ville";** 11/1960 . . . . **20**

LG-715: **"A Song for Your Happy Birthday and for All Your Unbirthdays"/"Happy Birthday"/"The Unbirthday Song";** 11/1960; features Jimmie Dodd, Darlene Gillespie, and Tommy Cole **20**

LG-716: **"Jiminy Cricket, Traffic Cop"/"Stop, Look and Listen"/"Safety First";** 11/1960 . . . **15**

LG-717: **"Donald Duck the Milkman"/"Donald Duck the Peanut Vendor";** 11/1960; Jiminy Cricket and Donald Duck **15**

LG-718: **"Walt Disney's Frere Jacques"/"The Little Nut Tree";** 11/1960; France Archer and Beverly Gile **15**

LG-719: **"Donald's Fire Station"/"Donald's Temper";** 11/1960; Jiminy Cricket and Donald Duck **15**

LG-720: **"The Swing"/"Marching Song" (from LP "A Child's Garden of Verses");** 11/1960; France Archer and Beverly Gile **15**

LG-721: **"March of the Toys"/"Babes in Toyland";** 7/1961 . . . . **20**

LG-722: **"I Can't Do the Sum"/"Just a Whisper Away";** 7/1961; Annette **40**

LG-723: **"Barnaby's Songs from Babes in Toyland"/"We Won't Be Happy Till We Get It"/"Castle in Spain";** 6/21/1961 . . . . **15**

LG-724: **"Toymaker's Songs from Babes in Toyland"/"The Workshop Song"/"Just a Toy";** 7/1961; Ed Wynn **15**

LG-725: **"Mary Had a Little Lamb"/"Mother Goose Nursery Rhymes";** 7/1961; Sterling Holloway **15**

LG-726: **"Six Riddles from Mother Goose"/"Riddles and Rhymes";** 7/1961; Sterling Holloway **15**

LG-727: **"Land of Nod"/"Block City"/"Child's Garden";** 7/1961; Frances Archer and Beverly Gile . . **15**

LG-728: **"The Tortoise and the Hare (Parts 1 & 2)";** 7/1961; Sterling Holloway **15**

LG-729: **"I'm Ludwig Von Drake"/"Green with Envy Blues";** 6/1961 . . . . **20**

LG-730: **"Carnival Time with Ludwig Von Drake";** 7/1961 . . . . . **20**

LG-731: **"Jingle Bells"/"From All of Us to All of You";** 7/1961; The All-Mouse Choir **15**

LG-732: **"Silent Night"/"Christmas Carols";** 7/1961; The All-Mouse Choir **15**

LG-733: **"I've Got No Strings—Story from Pinocchio";** 1/1962 . . . . **20**

LG-734 **"When You Wish Upon a Star"/"How the Blue Fairy Brought Pinocchio to Life and Jiminy Cricket Became His Conscience";** 1/1962; Jiminy Cricket **20**

LG-735: **"Give a Little Whistle"/"How Pinocchio and Jiminy Cricket Searched for Gepetto Under the Sea";** 1/1962; Jiminy Cricket **20**

LG-736: **"Hi Diddle Dee Dee—Story from Pinocchio";** 1/1962 . . . . **20**

LG-737: **"ABC's Made Simple"/"Acting Out the A-B-C's"/"Looby Loo";** 1/1962 . . . . **15**

LG-738: **"Itsy Bitsy Spider"/"Pop Goes the Weasel"/"Ten Little Indians";** 1/15/1962 . . . . **15**

LG-739: **"And They Lived Happily Ever After"/"Someday My Prince Will Come";** 1/1962; MST; Snow White; cover same as WDL-4005 . . . . **20**

LG-740: **"Heigh Ho, Heigh Ho"/"How the Witch Gave a Poisoned Apple to Snow White";** 1/1962; Seven Dwarfs **20**

LG-741: **"Whistle While You Work"/"How Snow White Found the Cottage of the Seven Dwarfs";** 5/1962 . . . . **20**

LG-742: **"Seven Dwarf's Washing Song (Buddle-Uddle-Um-Dum)"/"How Grumpy Got His Face Washed";** 5/1962 . . . . **20**

LG-743: **"Who's Afraid of the Big Bad Wolf"/"Three Kinds of Pigs' Houses";** 5/1962; The Three Little Pigs **20**

LG-744: **"Casey, Jr."/"Timothy Mouse Tells About Circus Life";** 5/1962 . . . . **20**

LG-745: **"One, Two, Three's—Children's Counting Songs" /"One Potato, Two Potato" /"One, Two, Buckle My Shoe";** 5/1962 . . . . **15**

LG-746: **"The Farmer's in the Dell"/"The Friendly Farmer";** 5/1962 . . . . **15**

LG-747: **"Ten Little Indians (Parts 1 & 2)";** 5/1962; a collection of counting rhymes **15**

LG-748: **"Humpty Dumpty (Parts 1 & 2)";** 5/1962; Sterling Holloway . . **15**

LG-749: **"Old King Cole and Other Nursery Rhymes"/"Old Mother Hubbard";** 7/1962; Sterling Holloway **15**

LG-750: **"Mickey Mouse Club March"/"Mickey Mouse Club Closing Theme";** 7/1962; Jimmie Dodd and the Mouseketeers **25**

LG-751: **"Twas the Night Before Christmas (Parts 1 & 2)";** 5/1962; Jiminy Cricket **15**

LG-752: **"Christmas at Disneyland"/"The Storybook Land Christmas Tree"/"The Futuristic Christmas Tree";** 5/1962; Camarata conducts **15**

LG-753: **"Mouseketunes:The Merry Mousketeers"/"Fun with Music";** 5/1962; Jimmie Dodd and Mouseketeers **20**

LG-754: **"Mousekedance"/"Pussy Cat Polka";** 5/1962; Jimmie Dodd and Mouseketeers **20**

LG-755: **"He's A Tramp"/"Bella Notte";** 11/1962; from *Lady and the Tramp* **20**

LG-756: **"Siamese Cat Song" /"Home Sweet Home";** 11/1962 . . **20**

LG-757: **"Sammy the Way Out Seal"/"Animals and Clowns";** 11/1962 . . . . **15**

LG-758: **"Annette"** (Jimmie Dodd)/**"How Will I Know My Love"** (Annette); 11/1962; Annette on cover. **40**

LG-759: **"The Litterbug Song"/"I'm No Fool";** 1/1963; Jiminy Cricket **15**

*LG-775: **"It's a Small World Parts I and I"** (with mailing envelope)*

LG-760: **"The Story of Hop, the Grasshopper"/"The World Owes Me a Living";** 1/30/1963; Sterling Holloway **20**

LG-761: **"Johnnie Shiloh, The Drummer Boy"/"Dixie";** 1/1963 . . **20**

LG-762: **"The Legend of Sleepy Hollow"/"The Headless Horseman"/"Ichabod Crane";** 1/1963 . . . . **20**

LG-763: **"How Paul Bunyan Raced an Engine and a Saw"/"The Paul Bunyan Song";** 1/1963; Thurl Ravenscroft **20**

LG-764: **"Baa Baa Black Sheep"/"Mother Goose Nursery Rhymes";** 2/1963 . . . . **15**

LG-765: **"Three Little Kittens"/"More Pussy Cat Rhymes";** 2/1963 . . . . **15**

LG-766: **"Twinkle, Twinkle Little Star"/"All Through the Night";** 2/1963 . . . . **15**

LG-767: **"Higitus Figitus"/"The Legend of the Sword in the Stone";** 7/1963 . . . . **20**

LG-768: **"That's What Makes the World Go Round"/"Mad Madam Mim";** 1963 . . . . **20**

LG-769: **"Most Befuddling Thing"/"Blue Oak Tree";** 7/1963 . . **20**

LG-770: **"The Ugly Bug Ball"/"Femininity";** 6/14/1963; from *Summer Magic* **20**

LG-771: **"Bibbidi Bobbidi Boo"/"Oh Sing Sweet Nightingale";** 7/1963; Ilene Woods **20**

LG-772: **"Sailor Songs: Sailing, Sailing"/"Blow the Man Down";** 7/1963; Chip 'n' Dale **15**

LG-773: **"Story of Bambi and Thumper (Parts I and II)";** 7/1963 . . . . **20**

LG-774: **"The Scarecrow of Romney Marsh"/"Trick or Treat";** 5/1964; The Wellingtons **20**

LG-775: **"It's a Small World Parts I and I";** 5/1964; P/S is yellow at the top and featured the photo of the attraction as had appeared on the second cover to the LP on ST-3925 above **15**

Also came in a cardboard picture mailing envelope as an "Official souvenir record from Walt Disney's 'It's a Small World' at the New York World's Fair." **40**

LG-776: **"The Story of Jack and Jill (Parts 1 & 2)";** 6/1964; Rica Moore **15**

LG-777: **"The Story of London Bridge (Parts 1 & 2)";** 6/1964; Rica Moore **15**

LG-778: **"How the Lost Boys Were Captured by Friendly Indians"/"Tee-Dum, Tee-Dee";** 6/1964 . . . . **20**

LG-779: **"Addition Made Easy"/"The Glory Tree";** 6/1964; Jiminy Cricket and Rica Moore **15**

LG-780: **"A Spoonful of Sugar"/"One Man Band";** 6/1964; Marni Nixon **20**

LG-781: **"Supercalifragilisticexpialidocious"** (Marni Nixon and Bill Lee)/**"Step in Time"** (Bill Lee); 6/1964 . . . . **20**

LG-782: **"Jolly Holiday"/"I Love to Laugh";** 6/1964; Richard Sherman . . **20**

LG-783: **"Chim Chim Cheree"/"Let's Go Fly a Kite";** 6/1964; Bill Lee **20**

LG-784P: **"A Country Coyote Goes Hollywood";** 2/1965; Bill Lee and Rex Allen; promotional **40**

LG-785: **"Winnie the Pooh"/"Little Black Rain Cloud";** 4/1965; Sterling Holloway & Choir **20**

LG-785-S: **"Winnie the Pooh"/"Little Black Rain Cloud";** 8/1965; Sears, Roebuck premium gift record with blue cover **30**

LG-786: **"That Crazy Place from Outer Space"/"Happy Glow";** 7/1965; from *Scarecrow of Oz* . . . **20**

LG-787: **"Mind Over Matter (Parts 1 & 2)";** 8/1966; from *Winnie the Pooh* **20**

LG-788: **"Rumbly in My Tumbly"/"Up, Down and Touch the Ground";** 9/1966; Sterling Holloway **20**

LG-789: **"Puff the Magic Dragon"/"The Loch Ness Monster";** 8/1966; Thurl Ravenscroft **15**

LG-790: **"Black Beauty"/"The Pearlie's Song";** 9/1966; Jack Halloran Singers **15**

Second pressing: **"Black Beauty"** (Jack Halloran Singers)/**"Turn To"** (Robie Lester) **15**

LG-791: **"The Gnome-Mobile Song"/"In My Jaunting Car";** 4/1967 . . . . **20**

LG-792: **"Fortuosity"/"Watch Your Footwork";** 10/1967 . . . . **20**

LG-793: **"I'll Always Be Irish"** (Richard Sherman)/**"What's Wrong with That"** (Bill Lee); 10/1967 . . . . **20**

LG-794: **"Detroit"/"Are We Dancing";** 10/1967; Bill Kanady . . **20**

LG-795: **"The Bare Necessities" /"My Own Home";** 8/1967 . . . . . . **20**

LG-796: **"I Wan'na Be Like You"/"That's What Friends Are For";** 8/1967 . . . . **20**

LG-797: **"Trust in Me"/"Colonel Hathi's March";** 8/1967 . . . . **20**

LG-798: **"Birthday, Birthday"/"Who's at Rabbit's Table";** 6/1967 . . . . **20**

LG-799: **"The Little Engine"/"The Little Streetcar";** 8/1967 . . . . **15**

LG-800: **"Yankee Doodle"** (Rica Moore)/**"Yankee Doodle"** (Disneyland Concert Band and Glee Club); 8/1967 . . . . **15**

LG-801: **"The Story of Little Red Riding Hood Part I and II";** 8/1967; Rica Moore **15**

LG-802: **"The Ugly Duckling (Parts 1 & 2)";** 8/1967; Ginny Tyler **15**

LG-803: **"Old Mother Hubbard";** 8/1967 . . . . **15**

LG-804: **"Simple Simon"/"Riddle Time";** 8/1967; Sterling Holloway . . **20**

LG-805: **"Brother Come and Dance with Me"/"When at Night I Go to Sleep";** 8/1967; Marni Nixon and Sally Sweetland **15**

LG-806: **"Hello! Bonjour!"/"O' Canada"**; 8/1967 . . . . **15**

LG-807: **"Songs from the Enchanted Tiki Room"/"The Tiki, Tiki, Tike Room"/"Elfnchor from Die Rheinnixen"**; 6/1968 . . . . **15**

LG-808: **"One and Only, Genuine, Original Family Band"/" 'Bout Time"**; 4/1968 . . . . **20**

LG-809: **"Drummin' Drummin' Drummin' "/"Let's Put It Over with Grover"**; 4/1968 . . . . **20**

LG-810: **"Ten Feet Off the Ground"/"West of the Wide Missouri"**; 4/1968 . . . . **20**

LG-811: **"Dakota"/"The Happiest Girl Alive"**; 4/1968 . . . . **20**

LG-812: **"A Rather Blustery Day"** (Sterling Holloway)/**"The Wonderful Thing About Tiggers"** (Sam Edwards); 8/1968 . . . . **15**

LG-813: **"Happy Mouse"/"The Mickey Mouse Mambo"**; 8/1968; Jimmy Dodd and the Mickey Mouse Chorus **20**

LG-814: **"Christmas Songs for Children"/"Oh Come All Ye Faithful"/"The First Noel"/"Joy to the World"/"It Came Upon the Midnight Clear"**; 10/1968 . . . . **15**

LG-815: **"Favorite Songs of Christmas"**; 10/1968 . . . . **15**

LG-816: **"The Elegant Captain Hook"/"Your Mother and Mine"**; 5/1969 . . . . **20**

LG-817: **"What Made the Red Man Red"/"Second Star to the Right"**; 5/1969 . . . . **20**

LG-818: **"The Aristocats"** (Mike Sammes Singers)/**"Thomas O'Malley Cat"** (Phil Harris); 9/1970 . . . . **20**

LG-819: **"Everybody Wants to be a Cat"** (Phil Harris)/**"Scales and Arpeggios"** (Mike Sammes Singers); 9/1970 . . . . **20**

LG-820: **"The Age of Not Believing"/"A Step in the Right Direction"**; 4/1971 . . . . **20**

LG-821: **"The Beautiful Briny"/"Portabello Road"**; 4/1971; Mike Sammes Singers **20**

LG-822: **"Substitutiary Locomotion"/"The Old Home Guard"**; 4/1971; Mike Sammes Singers **20**

LG-823: **"The Orange Bird Song" /"Orange Tree"**; 5/1971; Anita Bryant **15**

E7
Disneyland and Buena Vista "800" Series Special Pressings— 45 rpm and 33-1/3 rpm 7" Records

F-801: K-Nine **"Cruella De Vil"/"101 Dalmatians"**; 1961; 45 rpm; Disneyland label **10**

C-801: K-Nine **"Cruella De Vil"/"101 Dalmatians"**; 1961; 33-1/3 rpm; P/S **25**

802: Annette and Tommy Sands **"Let's Get Together"/"The Parent Trap"**; 5/1962; 45 rpm; P/S **30**

802: Annette and Tommy Sands **"Let's Get Together"/"The Parent Trap"**; 5/1962; 33-1/3 rpm; P/S . . . **40**

C-803: Annette and Tommy Sands **"Let's Get Together"/"The Parent Trap"**; 1961; 33-1/3 rpm; P/S; black label **45**

STER-804: **"Great Moments with Mr. Lincoln"** 33-1/3 rpm; P/S; Stereo **25**

Section F
"Little Golden Records— All Sizes and Speeds

F1
Little Golden Disney 6" 78 rpm Singles

The Little Golden Records catalog is very confusing, and a difficult one for collectors. It began in 1948 and was issued by Simon and Schuster.[1] The Disney-related records began in 1955. The records have picture sleeves with Disney art. The regular Little Golden record series consisted of many types of children's records, usually with just an unprefixed number. However, in the beginning there was a "Disney" series which was originally prefixed by a "D" number. The covers on the original series had the Little Golden logo in a strip down the left side of the cover.

Eventually both series were merged. The regular series then got an "R" prefix and the Disney's got an "RD" prefix and the covers then did not have the left side logo. It is currently unknown at what number the original "D" series ended and the "RD" series continued alternately with the "R" series. One source indicates the series merged somewhere in the 100-200 numbered series. All prefixes were eliminated at or about #500. The 45 rpm records used the same numbering as the 78 rpm however, the 45's were 7" records and the 78's were 6". The 45's were on black vinyl, as were most of the 78s, however some of the 78's had orange vinyl pressings.

They are mostly black vinyl with yellow labels, with the same type of line-drawn covers as the regular Little Golden Records. From #1 to approximately #250, the picture sleeves opened at the top and the artwork was "horizontal," i.e., wider than it was high. At approximately #251, the artwork became "vertical," i.e., higher than it was wide, though there were some random "horizontal sleeves." Earlier "vertical" sleeves were probably reissues. From #251 to #500, the sleeve back covers featured black and white photos. After #500, the covers opened on the right side, and the back covers were used for other Little Golden Records listings.

Mitch Miller conducted the orchestra on many of these records, with vocals by "The Sandpipers." The Sandpipers consisted of Bob Miller, Mike Stewart, Ralph Nyland, and Dick Byron.

The list below is likely incomplete with regard to some Disney-related recordings which simply could not be discovered or verified. However, at times Little Golden inserted many non-Disney related records in its numerical

---

[1] For those collectors who are really interested, the final chapter in the Little Golden Record series was apparently written in court in 1991, when owners of the musical rights to the recordings sued the eventual successor-in-interest owner of Little Golden for back royalties and fraud. The case, *Licette Music. Corp. v. A.A. Records Inc.*, was tried in New York State Supreme Court, New York County, resulting in a verdict of over 4-1/2 million dollars in favor of the owners of the musical rights. See *New York Law Journal*, p. 1, May 1, 1991, and the full published decision on May 6, 1991, Aff'd 196 App. Div. 2d 467; Lv den 82 N.Y. 2d 662.

D2: "Whistle While You Work"/"Snow White in the Cottage"

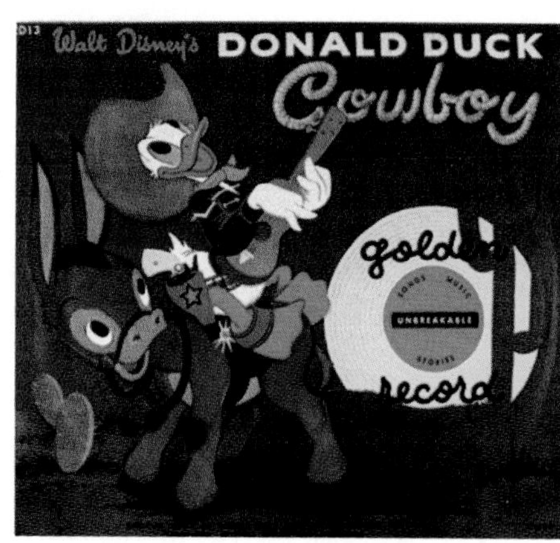

D13: "Donald Duck, Cowboy"/

sequences. Rest assured that most of the missing numbers are non-Disney records. The author would be happy to hear from those of you who may have additions to these listings for future editions of this price guide.

You should note that the Little Golden Records are collectible primarily for their Disney-related covers—abused records without covers (common in the 78s) should sell for no more than $1-$2 tops! Even then, such records are usually bought to complete a run or perhaps in hope of a later sleeve find. As with all records listed, all estimated values for Little Golden records of all sizes and speeds include the record and its cover! Remember, if the format is 78 rpm the values given are for "VG+" copies. Long play 33-1/3 LP albums and 45 rpm values are given for "M-" copies.

D1: **"Hi-Ho, Hi-Ho"/"The Seven Dwarfs";** 1955 . . . . **35**

D2: **"Whistle While You Work" /"Snow White in the Cottage"** . . . **25**

D3: **"Give a Little Whistle" /"Pinocchio & Jiminy Cricket"** **25**

D4: **"I've Got No Strings" /"Pinocchio, the Little Puppet"** **25**

D5: **"Mickey Mouse and His Friends"/"Pluto and His Phonograph"** **25**

D6: **"Donald Duck's Singing Lesson"/"Pluto, the Pup"** **25**

D7: **"Mickey's New Car"/"Donald Duck at the Opera"** **25**

Reissue has "Mr. Mickey Mouse" instead of "Opera" song **20**

D8: **"Donald Duck, Baby Sitter"/"Mickey Mouse and Farmer Rush Rush"** **25**

D9: **"Bibbidi-Bobbidi-Boo"/** **20**

D10: **"Cinderella's Work Song"/** . . . **20**

D11: **"A Dream Is a Wish Your Heart Makes"/** **20**

D12: **"Happy Birthday to You from Disneyville"** **20**

D13: **"Donald Duck, Cowboy"/** **20**

D14: **"Santa's Toy Shop"/"Santa's Toy Shop Song"** **20**

D15: **"Who's Afraid of the Big Bad Wolf"/** **20**

D39: "Trick or Treat and Lambert the Sheepish Lion"

D16: **"Ferdinand"/** **20**

D17: **"Funny Little Bunnies" /"Bouncy-Bouncy-Bally"** **20**

D18: **"Alice in Wonderland"/"In a World of My Own"**[2] **25**

D19: **"I'm Late"/"Alice in the White Rabbit's House"** **25**

D20: **"I Give Myself Very Good Advice"/"The Caucus Race"** **25**

D21: **"The Walrus and the Carpenter with Tweedle-Dum and Tweedle-Dee"** **25**

D22: **"All in a Golden Afternoon"/"Alice in the Garden of Live Flowers"** **25**

D23: **"Alice Meets the Caterpillar and T'was Brillig"/"How D'Ye Do and Shake Hands"** **2**

[2] The "Alice in Wonderland" recordings, RD-18 through RD-25, were utilized by General Mills in 1951 as an eight record premium set in a mailer with picture labels. See Section D3.13 above.

D24: **"A Very Merry Unbirthday"/"The Mad Tea Party"** **25**

D25: **"Painting the Roses Red"/"The March of the Cards"** **20**

D26: **"Bongo, the Circus Bear"** **20**

D27: **"Zip-A-Dee-Doo-Dah"/"The Laughing Place"** **20**

D28: **"Little Toot"** **20**

D29: **"Snow White Yodel Song" /"Doing the Dopey Dance"** **20**

D30: **"Bluddle-Uddle-Um-Um"** **20**

R31-34: (Non-Disney records)

D35: **"Peter Pan Theme Song"/"You Can Fly"** **25**

D36: **"Second Star to the Right" /"March of the Lost Boys"** **25**

D37: **"What Made the Red Man Red"/"Your Mother and Mine"** . . . **25**

D38: **"A Pirate's Life"/"The Elegant Captain Hook"** **25**

D39: **"Trick or Treat"/"Lambert the Sheepish Lion"** **20**

D40: **"Peter Pan's Song"/"Never Smile at a Crocodile"** **25**

D41: **"Donald Duck, Fire Chief"/"Donald Duck Song"** **15**

D42: **"When You Wish Upon a Star"** **20**

RD43: **"Hi-Diddle-Dee-Dee (Song and Story)"** **20**

RD44: **"Melody Time"/"The Bird and the Cricket and the Willow Tree"** **20**

RD45: (Non-Disney Record)

RD46: **"Mr. Chip 'n' Mr. Dale"/"Goofy's Song"** **15**

RD47-RD59: (Non-Disney Records)

RD60: **"Mickey Mouse's Birthday Party"** **20**

RD61: **School Days** 15

RD62: **"Mickey Mouse's Christmas Party";** includes "Jingle Bells"/"Christmas Symphony"; orange wax; Mickey Mouse Club record 20

RD63-RD64: (Non-Disney Records)

RD65: **"Peter and the Wolf"/"Jing-A-Ling";** based on *Beaver Valley* . . 20

Note: No Disney related single issues between "65" and "150."

D150: **"The Tortoise and the Hare"** 15

D151: **"Goofy the Toreador"** 15

D152-D161: (Non-Disney Records)

D162: **"A Toot and A Whistle, A Plunk and A Boom"** 20

D164: **"Bambi: Thumper Song"/"Little April Showers"** 20

D168: **"Johnny Appleseed: Pioneer Song"/"Apple Song"** 20

D169: **"Dumbo"** 20

D172: See F6 below

D174: **"Snoopy the Seal"** 15

D175: See F6 below

D188: **"At the Country Fair";** includes "Donald Duck on the Ferris Wheel"/"Goofy and the Funhouse"/"Chip n' Dale on the Roller Coaster"/"Pinocchio on the Merry-Go-Round" 15

D190: **"Songs from Lady and the Tramp"** 20

D194: **"Disneyland Theme Song: When You Wish Upon a Star"** . . . 20

D195: **"Songs from Lady and the Tramp: Siamese Cat Song" /"What Is a Baby? La La Lu"** 20

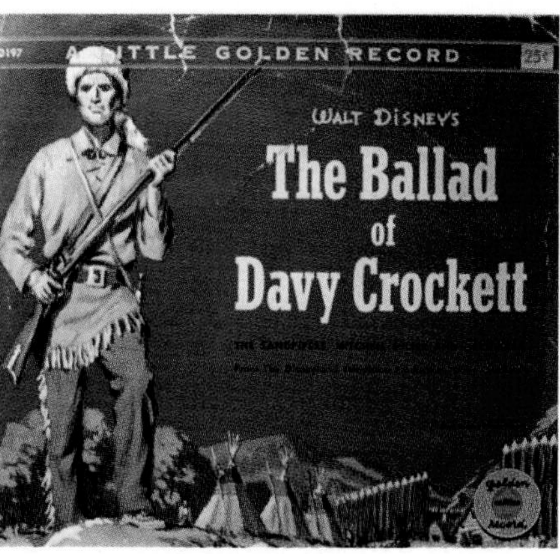

D197: "The Ballad of Davy Crockett, Parts 1 and 2"

D197: **"The Ballad of Davy Crockett, Parts 1 and 2"** 20

D213: **"Be Sure You're Right (Davy's Motto)"/"Bang Goes Old Betsy" (Bruns);** Jimmie Dodd & Frontier Men 25

D214: **"Siamese Cat Song"/"Bella Notte"** 20

F2
Little Golden Mickey Mouse Club and Other 6" 78 rpm Records

Made by Simon and Schuster (Little Golden); Produced by Sandpiper Press. Original Cost: 25¢. These had Mickey Mouse Club logo on the sleeves or the labels.

D222: **"Official Mickey Mouse Club Song"/"Official Mickey Mouse Club March";** features Jimmy Dodd, The Mouseketeers, and Jiminy Cricket 35

D223: **"Mickey Mouse Club Pledge"/"Sho-Jo-Ji (Japanese Play Song)"** 25

D234
songs from Walt Disney's Mickey Mouse Club
25¢
ANYONE FOR EXPLORING? AND
The Mickey Mouse Newsreel Music
JIMMIE DODD, THE MICKEY MOUSE CLUB CHORUS AND ORCHESTRA

D234: "The Mickey Mouse Club Newsreel Song"/"Anyone for Exploring"

D238: "King of the River (Mike Fink's Song)" (Bruns)

D224: **"You, the Human Animal"/"Mickey Mouse Club Book Song"** **25**

D225: **"The Mickey Mouse Club Picture House Song"/"When I Grow Up"** **25**

D226-D231: (Non-Disney Records)

D232: **"I'm No Fool (Safety Song)"/"Frere Jacques"** (Francis Archer and Beverly Gile) **25**

D233: **"Animals and Clowns Song" /"Who Am I?"**; Jimmie Dodd **25**

D234: **"The Mickey Mouse Club Newsreel Song"/"Anyone for Exploring";** Jimmie Dodd and the Mickey Mouse Club Chorus; orange wax **25**

D235: **"The Merry Mousketeers"/"Talent Roundup Rodeo;"** Jimmie Dodd and the Mickey Mouse Club Chorus; orange wax **25**

D238: **"King of the River (Mike Fink's Song)"** (Bruns)/**"Yaller Yaller Gold"** (The Frontier Men); from *Davy Crockett and the River Pirates* **30**

D247: **"Riddle-De-Riddle-De-Day"/"The Robin Hood Ballad";** The Sandpipers **25**

Note: "Vertical" sleeves begin here. Verticals with earlier numbers are reissues.

D251: **"Quack, Quack, Quack"/"Donald Duck";** not Mickey Mouse Club record **20**

D253: **"Hi to You"** (Beverly Gile and Frances Archer)/**"Do-Me-So"** (Jimmie Dodd and Mouseketeers) **25**

D254: **"Mickey Mouse Mambo"/"Pussycat Polka"/"Mousekedance"/ "Mouseketap";** Jimmie Dodd and Ruth Carrell **25**

D280: **"Bibbidi Bobbidi Boo"/ ;** Sandpipers **20**

D281: **"The Work Song" /"Cinderella";** Anne Lloyd and Sandpipers; Micky Mouse Club record **15**

D282: **"A Dream Is a Wish Your Heart Makes";** Sandpipers **15**

D291: **"Huckleberry Finn"/"Painting Aunt Polly's Fence";** Sandpipers; Annette photo on back cover **25**

D292: **"Good Night Little Wrangler"/"The Triple R Song";** Anne Lloyd and Mike Stewart; orange wax; Mickey Mouse Club record **20**

D293: **"Railroadin' Man"/"Son of Old Aunt Dinah";** from *The Great Locomotive Chase*; orange wax . . . **20**

D300: **"Fantasyland"** **20**

D301: **"Frontierland"** **20**

D302: **"Tomorrowland"** **20**

D303: **"Walt Disney's Song of Adventureland"** **20**

D306: **"Play a Polka"/"The Drum Song";** Sandpipers; orange wax; Mickey Mouse Club record **15**

D308: **"Westward Ho the Wagons (Theme Song)";** orange wax **20**

D310: **"Wringle Wrangle"/"I'm Lonely My Darling (Green Grow the Lilacs)";** orange wax; back cover picture of Fess Parker **20**

D311: **"The Ballad of John Coulter"/"Pioneer's Prayer"** **20**

D335: **"The Hardy Boys—Gold Doubloons and Pieces of Eight";** orange wax; Mickey Mouse Club . . **20**

D340: **"Johnny Tremain"** (Parts 1 & 2) **15**

D342: **"Some Day My Prince Will Come"** (Parts 1 & 2) **15**

D344: **"The Liberty Tree";** yellow wax; not a Mickey Mouse Club record **15**

D345: **"Proverbs"/"Do What the Good Book Says";** Sandpipers; Mickey Mouse Club record **15**

D479: "I Wonder"

D347: **"Perri" (Title song)/"Break of Day"** **15**

D348: **"A Mousekethought"/"Smile and Face the Music";** Mouseketeers group photo back cover **15**

D390: **"Old Yeller" (Title Song)** **25**

D394: **"Songs from Perri: Together Time"/"Now to Sleep"** **20**

D448: **"Adventures of Zorro";** yellow wax; not a Mickey Mouse Club record **25**

D449: **"Saga of Andy Burnett";** orange wax; not a Mickey Mouse Club record **20**

D452: **"Snow White"/"Someday My Prince Will Come";** story and song **20**

D454: **"Adventures of Zorro"** **20**

D479: **"I Wonder";** from *Sleeping Beauty*; Darlene Gilespie **20**

RD480: **"Once Upon a Dream"** (from *Sleeping Beauty*)/**"Briar Rose Meets the Prince";** 1958; Darlene Gilespie **20**

D481: **"Hail to Princess Aurora";** from *Sleeping Beauty* **20**

D482: **"Sing a Smiling Song";** from *Sleeping Beauty* **20**

D483: **"Skumps";** from *Sleeping Beauty* **20**

D486: **"Sleeping Beauty Theme Song"** **20**

D496: **"Walt Disney's John Slaughter"** **25**

Note: The "500" series are not Mickey Mouse Club records.

503: **"The Nine Lives of Elfego Baca";** Sandpipers **20**

R531: **"Tonka Theme Song" /"Tomahawk War Dance";** Wayne Sherwood and Sandpipers . . **20**

RD548: **"Disney's Shaggy Dog: Parts 1 and 2"** **20**

R549: **"Chip and Dale Sing Kris Kringle (Parts 1 & 2)";** yellow wax **15**

584: **"Toby Tyler"** **20**

R585: **"The Swamp Fox"** **20**

R605: **"Donald Duck Around the World"/"Donald Duck Theme Song"** **15**

R609: **"The Pollyanna Song"/"America the Beautiful";** 1960; yellow wax **15**

R614: **"Zip-a-dee-doo-dah"/"The Laughing Place"** **15**

RD627: **"101 Dalmatians"/"Cruella de Ville";** story and song **20**

R628: **"Cinderella"** **20**

D664: **"Swiss Family Robinson"** **20**

R648: **"Serendipity"/"Absent Minded Professor"** **15**

F654: **"Triple R Song"** **20**

D661: **"Toyland March"/"I Can't Do the Sum"** **15**

D662: **"Babes in Toyland: March of the Toys"/"Workshop Song"** **15**

D665: **"Swiss Family Robinson"** **15**

R668: **"Here's Ludwig Von Drake"** . . **15**

R669: **"Pinocchio Songs"** **15**

R670: **"I've Got No Strings"/"Pinocchio the Puppet"** . . **15**

R671: **"Hi Diddle Dee Dee"** **15**

R675: **"When You Wish Upon a Star"/"Story of Pinocchio"** **15**

679: **"Winnie the Pooh"** **15**

D684: **"Swiss Family Robinson"** **15**

721: **"Snow White and the Seven Dwarfs"/"Heigh-Ho"** **15**

758: **"The Sword in the Stone: Higitus-Figitus"/"What Did Merlin Ever Do?"** **15**

1067: **"Who's Afraid of the Big Bad Wolf";** reissue of D15 . . . . **15**

1086: **"Snow White and the Seven Dwarfs"/"Whistle While You Work"** **15**

F3
Golden 33-1/3 rpm LPs

GLP-2: **"Walt Disney's Song Parade (25 Best Loved Songs)";** 1957; STK; features Mitch Miller, and including Art Carney, Cliff Edwards and others **30**

GRC-2: **"Walt Disney's Song Parade from Disneyland";** 1956; STK; features Mitch Miller, and including Art Carney, Cliff Edwards and others; 29 songs; great cover **30**

LP-48: **"Favorite Songs from Walt Disney Motion Pictures"** 30

LP-77: **"Pinocchio";** STK; Cliff Edwards and Sandpipers; John Allen narrates 25

LP-93: **"Snow White and the Seven Dwarfs";** STK 25

LP-107: **"Favorite Songs from Walt Disney Motion Picture Hits";** c. 1963; STK; features Cliff Edwards, Billy Bletcher, and Sandpiper Chorus; original price: $1.98 25

198:2: **"Walt Disney's Song Parade (25 Best Loved Songs)";** 1957; STK; features Mitch Miller, and including Art Carney, Cliff Edwards and others; same record as GLP-2 above 25

F4
Little Golden 7" 45 rpm EPs

Original price: 49¢

EP-378: **"Westward Ho the Wagons"/"Wringle Wrangle"** 25

EP-379: **"Bibbidi-Bobbidi-Boo"/"A Dream Is a Wish Your Heart Makes"/"The Work Song";** 1957; Mitch Miller and the Sandpipers . . 25

EP-384: **"Walt Disney's Snow White"** 25

EP-460: **"Pinocchio and Peter Pan Songs and the Three Little Pigs (Disney Movie Favorites)"** 25

EP-465: **"Zorro, Old Yeller and Andy Burnett"** 25

EP-479: **"Walt Disney Songs from Sleeping Beauty"** 20

EP-485: **"Disney Heroes (Old Yeller, Andy Burnett, Zorro)"** 20

EP-488: **"Six Donald Duck Songs"** . . . 20

EP-523: **"Six Songs from Walt Disney's Peter Pan"** 25

EP-525: **"Mickey Mouse Club Favorites"** 25

EP-527: **"Disney Themes";** includes "Mickey Mouse Club" and "Sleeping Beauty"/"When You Wish Upon a Star" 20

EP-528: **"Disney Western Favorites"** 25

EP-530: **"Disney Heroines (Sleeping Beauty, Snow White)"** 20

EP-669: **"Pinocchio Songs and Stories"** 20

2042: **"Songs from Walt Disney's Pinocchio"** 20

2043: **"Songs from Walt Disney's Snow White"** 20

2044: **"Songs from Walt Disney's Cinderella"** 20

2045: **"Who's Afraid of the Big Bad Wolf"** 20

2098: **"The Reluctant Dragon"/"Puff, the Magic Dragon"*** 20

D2348: **"Anyone for Exploring?"** 20

F5
Big Golden Record "DBR" 10" 78 rpm EPs

This 10" 78 rpm EP series was number-prefixed "DBR" for "Disney Big Record." The recordings were compilations of songs from the Little Golden Disney related "D" and "RD" 6" 78 rpm singles above. DBR numbers 1 through 7 were numbers issued only to Disney

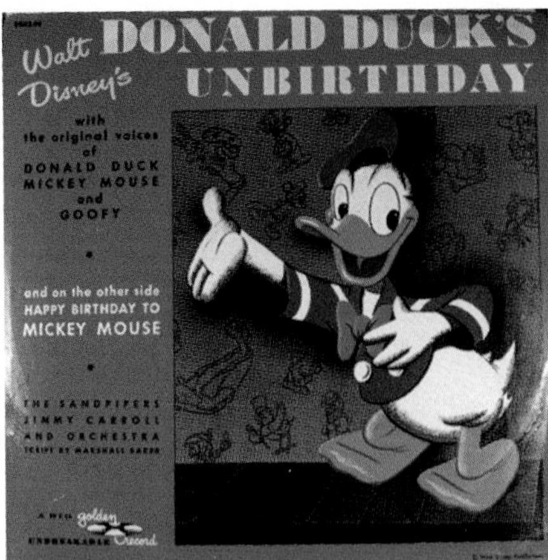

Walt Disney's
DONALD DUCK'S UNBIRTHDAY
with the original voices of DONALD DUCK MICKEY MOUSE and GOOFY
and on the other side HAPPY BIRTHDAY TO MICKEY MOUSE
THE SANDPIPERS JIMMY CARROLL AND ORCHESTRA

DBR-3: ***"Walt's Disney's Happy Birthday to Mickey Mouse"/"Donald Duck's Unbirthday"***

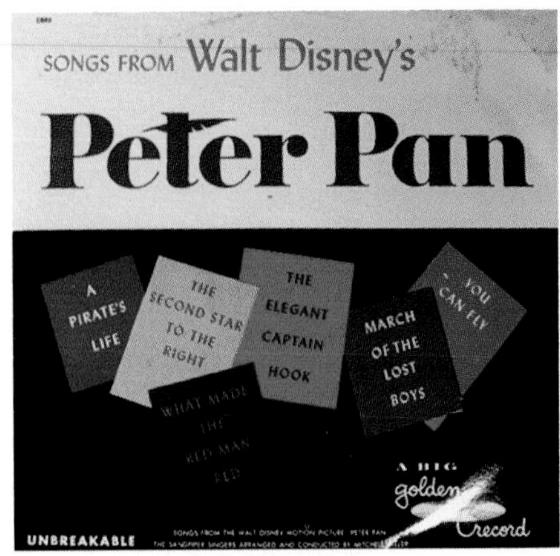

SONGS FROM Walt Disney's
Peter Pan
A PIRATE'S LIFE
THE SECOND STAR TO THE RIGHT
THE ELEGANT CAPTAIN HOOK
MARCH OF THE LOST BOYS
YOU CAN FLY
WHAT MADE THE RED MAN RED
A BIG golden Record
UNBREAKABLE

DBR-6: ***"Songs from Disney's Peter Pan"***

records. Thereafter, Golden used some duplicate "BR" numbers for non-Disney records as well. The series ran to at least number "44" which later resulted in some duplicate numbers with two different titles when Disney produced its own 7" "DBR" EP records which also included the numbers DBR-20 through DBR-44 (See and compare with Section C8 above). Currently known Disney titles are listed. Others may exist. Very Rare. Early numbers were on yellow vinyl.

DBR-13: ***"Walt Disney's Mr. Chip n' Mr. Dale"/"Goofy's Song"***

DBR-1: **"Songs from Alice in Wonderland";** 1955; Mitch Miller; six songs **35**

DBR-2: **"Songs from Alice in Wonderland";** 1955; Mitch Miller; six songs **35**

DBR-3: **"Walt's Disney's Happy Birthday to Mickey Mouse" /"Donald Duck's Unbirthday"** . . . **30**

DBR-4: **"Songs from Disney's Snow White"** **30**

DBR-5: **"Song's from Disney's Robin Hood"** **35**

DBR-6: **"Songs from Disney's Peter Pan"** **30**

DBR-7: **"Walt Disney's 3 Little Pigs and 3 Little Wolves"** **30**

BR-8 to BR-12: (Non-Disney records)

DBR-13: **"Walt Disney's Mr. Chip n' Mr. Dale"/"Goofy's Song"** **30**

BR-14 to BR-15: (Non-Disney records)

DBR-16: **"Walt Disney's The Sword and the Rose";** apparently the only recording of music from this film; black vinyl; Rare **50**

DBR-16: ***"Walt Disney's The Sword and the Rose"***

BR-17 to BR-19: (Non-Disney records)

DBR-20: **"Christmas Mule Train" /"Night Before Christmas"** 25

BR-21 to BR 28: (Non-Disney records)

DBR-29: **"Pinocchio Story and Songs"** 25

BR-30 to BR-44: (Non-Disney records)

F6
Little Golden "SD" 7" 78 rpm EPs

SD-73: "**Disney's Songs of the City";** (Alec Wilder); includes "Mickey Mouse, the Policeman," "Goofy, the Street Cleaner," "Donald Duck Fire Chief," and "Seven Dwarfs, Postmen" 35

SD-78: **"Walt Disney's Little Friends;** (Alec Wilder); includes "The Li'l' Bad Wolf," "Tinker Bell," "Huey, Louie & Dewey," and "Dopey's Whistle" 35

SD-78: ***"Walt Disney's Little Friends***

SD-121: **"The World Owes Me a Living"/"The Grasshopper and the Ants"** 25

SD-172: **"Pecos Bill"** 25

SD-175: **"The Reluctant Dragon, Parts 1 and 2"** 25

F7
Little Golden 6" Albums (78 rpm and 45 rpm)

These are repackages of individual Little Golden releases and originally sold for $3.95. Price includes the box and/or the cover!

DLGR4:100: **"Walt Disney's Mickey Mouse's Christmas Party (Walt Disney's Christmas Album)";** four record set; 78 rpm and 45 rpm editions; GF 40

GRC2 (Golden Record Chest): **"Walt Disney Song Parade: 29 Songs from Disney"** eight records box set; 78 rpm and 45 rpm editions; 48 minutes playing time 60

LGRC1 (Little Golden Record Chest): **"Songs from Walt Disney's Mickey Mouse Club"**; eight 6" records, box set; 78 rpm edition only; 16 Songs; orange vinyl; originally sold for $2.95; repackage of D222-225 and D232-235 with artwork from the P/S of D222; also sold in shrink wrap in toy stores as a Mickey Mouse Club record set **60**

F8
Little Golden 7" "FF" Series (45 rpm and 78 rpm)

These duplicated many titles in the "D" Series above. Original price: 29¢.

FF-448: **"Zorro"** **20**

FF-449: **"The Saga of Andy Burnett"** **20**

FF-454: **"Zorro"** **20**

FF-479: **"I Wonder"**; from *Sleeping Beauty* **20**

FF-480: **"Once Upon a Dream"**; from *Sleeping Beauty* **20**

FF-481: **"Hail Princess Aurora"**; from *Sleeping Beauty* **20**

FF-482: **"Sing a Smiling Song"**; from *Sleeping Beauty* **20**

FF-483: **"Skumps"**; from *Sleeping Beauty* **20**

FF-486: **"Sleeping Beauty Theme Song"** **20**

FF-496: **"Walt Disney's John Slaughter"** **20**

FF-503: **"Elfego Baca"** **20**

FF-531: **"Tonka-The Theme Song"/"Tomahawk War Dance"** . . **20**

FF-548: **"Disney's Shaggy Dog"** **25**

FF-549: **"Disney's Chipmunks"** **15**

FF-605: **"Donald Duck Around the World"/"Donald Duck Theme Song"** **15**

FF-661: **"Toyland March"/"I Can Do the Sum"** **15**

FF-671: **"Pinocchio Story and Song: Hi Diddle Dee Dee (Parts 1 & 2)"** **15**

FF-702: **"Lambert, the Sheepish Lion"/"Pokey Little Puppy"** **15**

F9
Other Little Golden EPs

W3: **"Thumper Song"/"When I See an Elephant Fly"/"Zip-a-dee-doo-dah"/"The Laughing Place"** **15**

W5: **"Peter Pan Theme"/"You Can Fly"/"Second Star to the Right"/"March of the Lost Boys"** **15**

W6: **"Alice in Wonderland"/"I'm Late"/"A Very Merry Unbirthday"/"How Do You Do and Shake Hands"** **15**

W7: **"Ferdinand the Bull"/"The Reluctant Dragon"/"Pecos Bill"/"The Apple Song"** **15**

Section G
Other Non-Disney Label 45 rpm 7" Singles

Note: Songs marked with * are non-Disney selections.

G1
ABC-Paramount 45 rpm Records

In 1955, these records were leased by Disney to ABC for one year

CX-2: Jimmy Dodd **"Mickey Mouse Mambo"/" Humphrey Hop-Pussy Cat"** **20**

9665: Jimmy Dodd **"Mousketeer Theme"/"Hi to You"** **25**

9680: Jimmy Dodd **"Mickey Mouse Mambo"/"Humphrey Hop-Pussy Cat"** **20**

9690: Cliff Edwards **"The Littlest Outlaw"/"Doroteo";** 1956; William Lava conducts. **25**

9691: Jimmy Dodd **"Zip-A-Dee-Doo-Dah"**/Jeanne Gayle **"Song of the South"** **20**

9785: Bill Hayes **"Wringle Wrangle"/"Westward Ho the Wagons"** **20**

G2
Beverly Hills 45 rpm Records

45-9375: Debbie Reynolds **"The Age of Not Believing"/ ;** 1972; from *Bedknobs and Broomsticks* **10**

G3
Brunswick 45 rpm Records

9-55019: Larry Hooper **"Johnny Tremain"/"The Liberty Tree"** **20**

G4
Cadence 45 rpm Records

1256: Bill Hayes **"The Ballad of Davy Crockett"/"Farewell";** 1955; P/S; there were over 200 cover versions of "Davy Crockett" issued around the world, but it was this recording that was the main hit in the United States; see "A Short History of Recorded Disney Music" **40**

CCS-1X: Bill Hayes **"The Ballad of Davy Crockett"/"Farewell";** 1955; P/S; Cadence Children's Series release; exact same record as above with different number;

see same Cadence 78 rpm release above
Record with sleeve **60**
Sleeve only **40**

1349: The Chordettes **"Zorro"/"Love Is a Two Way Street"*;** 1958; Top 40 hit of the theme from TV series; includes "Z" slash picture cover **35**

G5
Capitol 45 rpm Records

All had the same high quality picture sleeve covers as had appeared on the 78 rpm editions. See Section D3.6 above and footnote regarding letter codes. Original prices are listed where known. A very collectible series.

CDF-3000: **"So Dear to My Heart";** four record set; original cast: Luana Patten and Bobby Driscoll; original price: $3.70 . . . . **35**

CASF-3001: **"Little Toot";** features Don Wilson, the Starlighters, and Billy May Orchestra; original price: .95¢ **20**

CCF-3008: **"Brer Rabbit (Uncle Remus: Song of the South)";** three record set; features Johnny Mercer, the Pied Pipers, and the original cast; original price: $2.85 . . . . **40**

CBXF-3018: **"The Three Little Pigs";** two record set; original cast; narrates Don Wilson; a Record Reader with 21-page booklet; individual records numbered F-30048 and F-30049 . . . . **30**

EAXF-3018: **"The Three Little Pigs";** Don Wilson narrates; original price: $2.25 . . . . **25**

CBXF-3034: **"The Grasshopper and the Ants";** two record set; Don Wilson narrates; a Record Reader with booklet **30**

EAXF-3034: **"The Grasshopper and the Ants";** Don Wilson narrates; original price: $2.25 . . . . **25**

KASF-3048: **"Adventures of Ichabod and Mr. Toad";** Basil Rathbone narrates **25**

EAXF-3056: **"Lady and the Tramp";** original price: $2.25 . . . . **30**

CCF-3057: **"Walt Disney Songs";** three record set; Happy Jack Smith Orchestra; includes "Whistle While You Work," "The Dwarf's Yodel Song," "Hi Diddle Dee Dee (An Actor's Life for Me)," "Little Wooden Head," "Little April Shower," "Give a Little Whistle," "Heigh-Ho," "Bluddle Uddle Um Dum," "When I See an Elephant Fly," "Casey Junior," "Uncle Remus Said," and "Look Out for Mr. Stork"; original price: $2.85 . . . . . . **35**

F-3058: Tennessee Ernie Ford **"The Ballad of Davy Crockett" /"Farewell";** 1955 . . . . **20**

CASF-3092: **"The Flying Mouse";** Don Wilson **25**

CBSF-3094: **"Fantasia: The Sorcerers Apprentice";** two record set; Don Wilson **25**

CASF-3095: **"Ferdinand the Bull";** Don Wilson **30**

CASF-3096: **"Three Orphan Kittens";** Don Wilson **25**

CASF-3099: **"Elmer Elephant";** Don Wilson **25**

CASF-3106: **"Brer Rabbit and the Tar Baby";** this record and the two below are single record issues of the three records used in "CCF-3008" above **20**

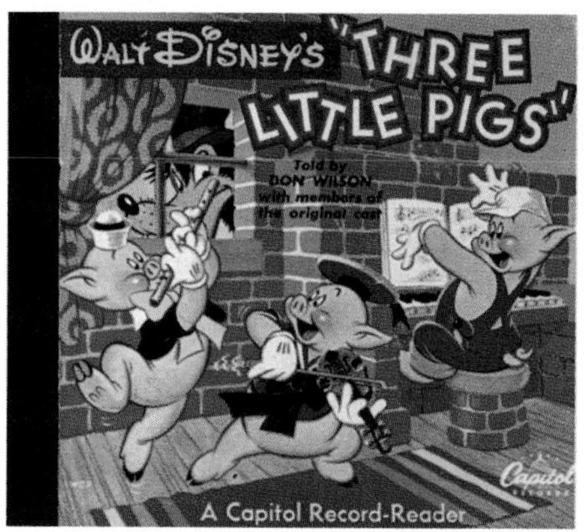

CBXF-3018: ***"The Three Little Pigs"***

CASF-3095: ***"Ferdinand the Bull"***

CASF-3107: **"Brer Rabbit and the Laughing Place"** **20**

CASF-3108: **"Brer Rabbit Runs Away";** original price: $1.05 . . . . . **20**

F-3122: Gordon MacRae **"Bella Notte"/"Follow Your Heart"** **15**

CASF-3132: **"Bongo the Circus Bear";** Don Wilson **25**

CASF-3135: **"The Country Cousin";** Don Wilson **20**

CASF-3136: **"Little Hiawatha";** Don Wilson **20**

CBXF-3138: **"The Story of Robin Hood";** two record set; GF; live action film; Nestor Paiva narrates . . **30**

F-3144: **"The Ballad of Duvid Crockett" (parody)/Tweedle Dee*;** Mickey Katz **25**

CASF-3153: **"The Ugly Duckling";** Don Wilson and Stan Freeberg . . . **20**

CASF-3163: **"Never Smile at a Crocodile"/"Following the Leader"*;** Jerry Lewis **20**

EAXF-3165: **"Mickey Mouse's Birthday";** Stan Freeberg; original price: $2.25 . . . . **20**

CASF-3183: **"Little Hiawatha";** Don Wilson **20**

CASF-3198: **"Rob Roy (The Highland Rogue)"** **35**

CASF-3229: **"The Ballad of Davy Crockett"/"Farewell";** Tennessee Ernie Ford **20**

F-3993: **"Zorro"/"Min Skol-Din Skol"*;** Fred Waring and the Pennsylvanians **20**

G6
Columbia 45 rpm records

4-40449: Fess Parker **"The Ballad of Davy Crockett"/"I Gave My Love";** 1955 . . . . **25**

4-40450: Fess Parker **"Farewell"/"I'm Lonely My Darling"** **20**

4-40467: Lu Ann Simms **"The Siamese Cat Song"/**Mitch Miller **"La La Lu"** **15**

4-40510: Fess Parker and Buddy Ebsen **"Old Betsy (Davy Crockett's Rifle)"/"Be Sure You're Right (Then Go Ahead)"** . . **25**

4-40568: Fess Parker **"King of the River"/"Yaller Yaller Gold";** 1956; from *Davy Crockett and the River Pirates* 30

4-51505: Bobby Lord **"The Swamp Fox"/"Too Many Miles"*** 20

MJV 4-112: Rosemary Clooney and Percy Faith Orchestra **"Songs from Walt Disney's Alice in Wonderland";** two record set 30

J-4-221: The Mariners **"Toot, Whistle, Plunk and Boom"/"The Monkey Band";** Children's Series . . 25

J-4-242: Fess Parker **"The Ballad of Davy Crockett"/"I Gave My Love";** 1955; Childrens's Series . . . 25

J-4-752: The Forty-Niners **"The Ballad of Davy Crockett"/"Windy Bill"*;** Children's Series 20

G7
Coliseum 45 rpm Records

45-2709: Count Basie and Orchestra **"Fortuosity"/"Detroit"** 10

G8
Coral 45 rpm Records

9-60439: Modernaires **"I'm Late"/"Alice in Wonderland";** 1951 10

9-61445: Steve Allen **"Old Betsy"/"Goo-Goo Doll"*** 15

9-61597: Lennon Sisters **"Hi to You"/"Mickey Mouse Mambo"** . . . 20

G9
Cricket 45 rpm Records

CEP-11: **"Dennis Day Sings Songs from Johnny Appleseed"** 25

C-51: Gabe Drake and the Woodsmen **"The Ballad of Davy Crockett"/Cowboy Songs";** colorful colorful line-drawn cover of Davy Crockett 25

C-52: **"Old Betsy (Davy Crockett's Rifle)"/"Davy Crockett March"** . . 25

C-53: **"Siamese Cat Song"/"Tweedle Dee and Tweedle Dum"** 5

C-61: The Overtones **"Zippy Doo Dah" (sic)/"Topsy-Turvy Town"*** . . 5

C-86: **"Wringle Wrangle" /"Barnyard Song"*** 5

G10
Decca 45 rpm Records

2-120: Fred Waring and the Pennsylvanians **"Alice in Wonderland";** two records set; Children's Series 25

9-108: Lyn Murray Orchestra **"Snow White and the Seven Dwarfs"** 25

1-190: Sterling Holloway and Jimmy Carroll Orchestra **"The Little House";** P/S; Children's Series 25

28400: Fred Waring Orchestra **"Bibbidi-Bobbidi-Boo"/"Zip-A-Dee-Doo-Dah"** 15

28401: Fred Waring Orchestra **"When You Wish Upon a Star"/"One Song"** 15

28402: Fred Waring Orchestra **"Lavender Blue"/"Tico Tico"** 15

29427: Peggy Lee **"Siamese Cat Song"/"He's a Tramp"** 20

29433: Victor Young **"Bella Notte"/"The Medic"*** 15

29460: Peggy Lee **"Bella Notte"/"La La Lu"**; STK 15

29483: Bing Crosby **"Farewell"/"Jim, Johnny and Jonas"*** 20

29487: Cliff Edwards as Jiminy Cricket **"When You Wish Upon a Star"/"Give a Little Whistle"** 25

29549: Burl Ives **"Be Sure You're Right (Then Go Ahead)"/"Old Betsy"** 20

29692: Gary Crosby **"Yaller Yaller Gold"/"Give Me a Band and My Baby"*** 15

9-38017: Rex Allen and the Mellomen **"Wringle Wrangle"/"Westward Ho the Wagons"** 15

9-88071-2: Fred Waring and the Pennsylvanians **"Alice in Wonderland"**; two record set 25

9-88186: Peggy Lee **"Siamese Cat Song"/"La La Lu"**; Children's Series 20

G11

Dot 45 rpm Records

1240: Mac Wiseman **"The Ballad of Davy Crockett"/"Danger Heartbreak Ahead"*** 25

G12

Gregar 45 rpm Records

71-0114: New Christy Minstrels **"The Age of Not Believing" (from *Bedknobs and Broomsticks*)/"Love It Along"*** 10

2-120: Fred Waring and the Pennsylvanians "Alice in Wonderland"

G13

Hansen 45 rpm Records

Hansen Records was run by Charlie Hansen, an early distributor for Disneyland Records and music. All records c. 1955.

102: George Bruns, Tommy Cole, and Quincy Jones **"King of the River"/"Yaller, Yaller Gold"** 10

103: Tommy Cole, Darlene Gillespie, and Quincy Jones **"I Am Not Now (and Never Have Been in Love)"/"Do Mi So"** 15

105: Betty Cox and Quincy Jones **"Hi to You"/"Holly Boy"** 10

G14

Kapp 45 rpm Records

242: Bill Hayes **"9 Lives of Elfego Baca"/"Love I Mean"*** 20

K-605: Mary Martin and the Do-Re-Mi Childrens' Chorus **"Feed the Birds"/"A Spoonful of Sugar"**; P/S . . 15

MP-3x45: Mickey Mouse and Donald Duck ***"Aladdin and His Lamp"***

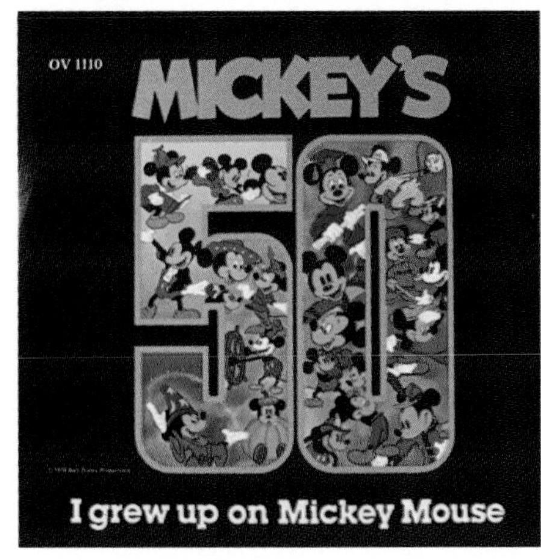

OV-1110: ***"Mickey's 50th"***

G15
Laurie 45 rpm Records

3052: Dion and the Belmonts **"When You Wish Upon a Star"/"Wonderful Girl"***; 1960 . . . **20**
With P/S; Rare **60**

G16
Mercury 45 rpm Records

MP-2x45: Mickey Mouse and Donald Duck **"The Magic Flying Carpet Parts 1 & 2"**; 1952 . . . . **20**

MP-3x45: Mickey Mouse and Donald Duck **"Aladdin and His Lamp"**; 1952; Children's Playcraft series **20**

70555: Rusty Draper **"The Ballad of Davy Crockett"/"I've Been Thinking"*** **20**

71010: Len Dresslar **"Wringle Wrangle"/"Believe in Em"** **15**

G17
MGM 45 rpm Records

10077: Korn Kobblers **"Who's Afraid of the Big Bad Wolf"/"3 Blind Mice"*** **20**

10178: Kings Men **"Little Toot"/"Pecos Bill"** **25**

10657: Judy Valentine **"Cinderella Work Song"/"I'd Like to Wrap You Up"*** **15**

11941: James Brown and the Trail Winders **"The Ballad of Davy Crockett"/"He's a Rockin' Horse Cowboy"*** **20**

11960: Joni James **"When You Wish Upon a Star"/"Is This the End of the Line"*** **20**

11963: Marion Sisters **"The Siamese Cat Song"/"He's a Tramp"** **20**

11967: Kay Armen **"Bella Notte"/"La La Lu"** **20**

G18
Ovation 45 rpm Records

OV-1110: **"Mickey's 50th"**; P/S **25**

G19
Peter Pan 45 rpm Records

45-4000: **"Little Toot"** **10**

G20
Philles 45 rpm Records

107: Bob B. Soxx and the Blue Jeans **"Zip-A-Dee-Doo-Dah"/"Flip and Nitty"***; 1962; actually Bobby Sheen and the Blossoms **30**

G21
RCA "Bluebird" 7" 45 rpm Children's Series

WBY-25: **"The Ballad of Davy Crockett"/"The Graveyard Filler of the West"**; Sons of the Pioneers **25**

WBY-26: **"Lady and the Tramp"/"Siamese Cat Song"** **20**

WBY-27: **"A Whale of a Tale"/"Old Betsy"**; Sons of the Pioneers **25**

WBY-52: **"Johnny Tremain"/"The Liberty Tree"** **20**

WBY-56: **"Wringle Wrangle"/"Westward Ho the Wagons!"**; Vaughn Monroe **20**

WBY-64: **"When You Wish Upon a Star"/"Whistle While You Work"**; Joe Reisman Orchestra . . . **20**

G22
RCA "Little Nipper" and "Youth" Children's 45 rpm Series

These were released as adjunct format recordings to RCA's beautiful 78 rpm "Little Nipper" multi-record albums for children, containing the same music and cover pictures (see above). They usually had gatefold covers, and contained music and a narrative story accompanied by pictures—similar to what Disney would later do with its "ST" LP series. The later "WY" records were listed as part of RCA's "Youth Series."

See the 78 rpm listings for the RCA "Y" series at Section D3.31.3 for expanded artist information.[1] The original selling price of the record is listed where known. Most appeared on clear yellow vinyl.

WY-32: **"The Three Little Pigs"/"The Orphan's Benefit"**; MST; record numbered 47-0206 . . . . **30**

WY-33: **"Snow White and the Seven Dwarfs"**; 1949; STK; two record set; individual records numbered 47-0204 and 47-0205; original price: $2.95 . . . . **30**

WY-382: **"Dumbo"**; 1949; STK; two record set; individual records numbered 47-0194 and 47-0195; original price: $2.15 . . . . **30**

WY-385: **"Pinocchio"**; 1949; STK; two record set; individual records numbered 47-0202 and 47-0203; original price: $2.95 . . . . **30**

---

[1] RCA released Spanish language editions of the Disney versions of two films:
WSY-4: **"La Cenicienta"** (Cinderella) . . . **40**
WSY-5: **"Alicia En El Pais De Maravillas"** (Alice in Wonderland); Evangelina Elizondo **40**

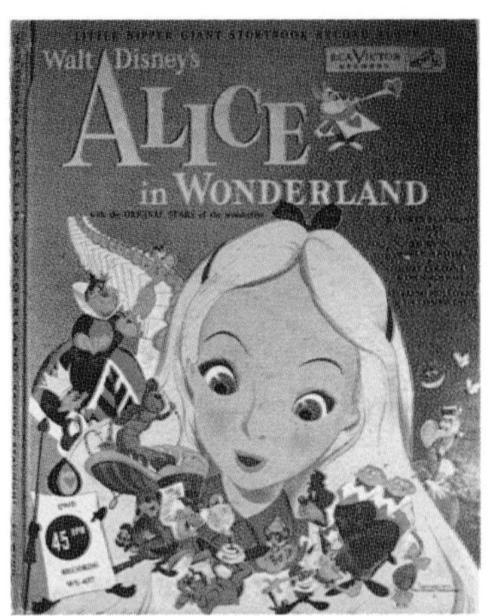

WY-437: "Alice in Wonderland"

WY-386: **"Peter and the Wolf";** 1949; STK; two record set; individual records numbered 47-0190 and 47-0191; original price: $2.95 . . **30**

WY-389: **"Pecos Bill";** 1949; STK; two record set; from *Melody Time*; Roy Rogers; individual records numbered 47-0200 and 47-0201; original price: $2.15 . . . . **30**

WY-390: **"Johnny Appleseed";** 1949; STK; two record set; from *Melody Time*; Dennis Day; yellow vinyl; individual records numbered 47-0198 and 47-0199; original price: $2.15 . . . . **30**

WY-391: **"Bambi";** 1949; STK; two record set; Shirley Temple; yellow vinyl; individual records numbered 47-0196 and 47-0197; original price: $2.15 . . . . **30**

WY-399: **"Cinderella";** 1950; STK; two record set; individual records numbered 47-0210 and 47-0211; original price: $2.95 . . . . **30**

WY-400: "**The Brave Engineer (The Story of Casey Jones)";** 1950; Jerry Colonna; record numbered 47-0212; original price: $1.15 . . . . **40**

WY-416: **"Treasure Island";** 1950; STK; Henri Rene; non-Disney music composed by and conducted by Paul Smith; cast: Bobby Driscoll; two record set numbered 47-0234/47-0235; $2.15 . . . . **30**

WY-430: **"Birthday Fun";** 1951; Dennis Day; features "Happy Birthday Song"/"The Unbirthday Song"; record numbered 47-0274; original price: .85¢ **20**

WY-432: **"Mr. Television";** 1951; features Milton Berle and original voices of Walt Disney's Donald Duck and Mickey Mouse; yellow vinyl; record numbered 47-0284; original price: $1.15 . . . . **30**

WY-433: **"Mr. Animated Cartoon";** 1951; features Milton Berle and original voices of Walt Disney's Donald Duck and Mickey Mouse; yellow vinyl; record numbered 47-0285; original price: $1.15 . . . . **30**

WY-434: **"Alice and the White Rabbit";** 1951 . . . . **25**

WY-435: **"Alice and the Mad Tea Party";** 1951; features Kathryn Beaumont, Arnold Stang, Frank Milano, Naomi Lewis, Todd Russell, Michael King, Merrill Joels, Jackson Beck, and the vocal quartet Three Beaus and a Peep . . . **25**

WY-436: **"Alice and the Trial";** 1951; features Kathryn Beaumont, Todd Russell, Michael King, Merrill Joels, Jackson Beck, and the vocal quartet Three Beaus and a Peep **25**

WY-437: **"Alice in Wonderland";** 1951; STK; two Record set; features Kathryn Beaumont, Ed Wynn, Jerry Colonna, and Sterling Holloway; yellow vinyl; individual records numbered 47-0267 and 47-0268; original price: $3.20 . . **35**

Also packaged in folders as part of "A Little Nipper Giant Storybook Record Album" book (10-1/2" x 13-1/4") "Alice in Wonderland" **60**

WY-447: **"Snow White and Sneezy";** 1952; (Leyden); Dennis Day; yellow vinyl; record numbered 47-0299; original price: .85¢ **25**

WY-448: **"Snow White and Dopey";** 1952; (Leyden); Dennis Day; record numbered 47-0300; original price: .85¢ **25**

WY-463: **"Peter Pan";** 1953; STK; Hugo Winterhalter and Orchestra; original price: .85¢ **20**

WY-472: **"A Toot and a Whistle and a Plunk and a Boom"/"Captain of the Spaceship"*;** Spike Jones and the Mellomen **30**

WY-2000: **"Trick or Treat with Donald Duck";** 1952; yellow vinyl **25**

WY-2001: **"Mickey Mouse's Candy Mine";** 1952; (Leyden); Mickey Mouse and Goofy; yellow vinyl . . . **25**

WY-2002: **"The What-siz and the Who-siz";** 1952; (Leyden); Mickey Mouse and Goofy; yellow vinyl **25**

WY-4000: **"Adventures in Music—Melody";** 1952; STK; two record set; adapted from Walt Disney film; Bill Thompson and Jud Conlon Singers **25**

WY-4001: **"Peter Pan";** 1952; STK; two record set; features Bobby Driscoll, Kathryn Beaumont, John Brown, Bill Thompson, Verne Smith,and Jud Conlon Vocal Group; yellow vinyl; bound with an orange plastic spiral binding; 22-page booklet; individual records numbered WY-4001-1 and WY-4001-2 . . . . **35**

WY-4001: "Peter Pan"

WY-4004: **"20,000 Leagues Under the Sea";** 1954; STK; two record set; features William Redfield, Ian Martin, Bernard Lenrow, Arthur Anderson, and William Clauson; with booklet; black vinyl **35**

G23
Other RCA Victor 45 rpm Records

54-0015: Ilene Woods **"Cinderella's Work Song"/"A Dream Is a Wish Your Heart Makes"** **15**

48-0035: Roy Rogers and the Sons of the Pioneers **"Pecos Bill"/"Blue Shadows on the Trail"** **15**

47-3113: Fontane Sisters **"Bibbidi-Bobbidi-Boo"/** **15**

47-3127: Fontane Sisters **"Cinderella's Work Song"/** **15**

49-3451: Arthur Fiedler and Boston Pops **"Medley from 'Alice in Wonderland' "/** **10**

4087: Hugo Winterhalter Orchestra **"Alice in Wonderland"/"I'll Never Know Why"*** **15**

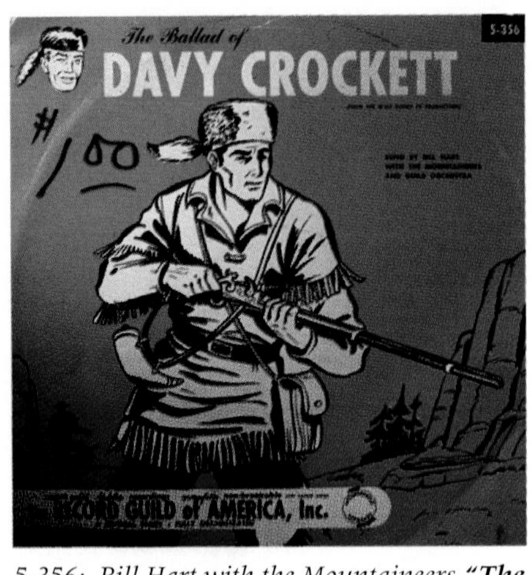

5-356: Bill Hart with the Mountaineers ***"The Ballad of Davy Crockett"***

20-4088: Mindy Carson, Three Beaus and a Peep, and Andrew Acker **"I'm Late"/"T'was Brillig"**; from *Alice in Wonderland* **15**

4089: Fran Allison and Wayne King Orchestra **"All in a Golden Afternoon" (from *Alice in Wonderland*)/"Did You Write a Letter to Your Sweetheart"*** **15**

47-6041: Walter Schumann **"Ballad of Davy Crockett"/"Let's Make Up"*** **20**

6055: Sons of the Pioneers **"Davy Crockett"/"Graveyard Filler of the West"** **25**

6125: Walter Schumann **"Old Betsy"/"Shoeless Joe"*** **20**

47-6178: Homer and Jethro **"Ballad of Davy Crew-cut" (parody) /"Pickin' and Singin' "* (medley)** **25**

6245: Eartha Kitt **"Sho-Jo-Ji"/"Nobody Taught Me"** **15**

6246: Lou Monte and Hugo Winterhalter Orchestra **"King of the River"/"Yeller Yeller Gold"** . . **15**

6276: Sons of the Pioneers **"King of the River"/"Yeller Yeller Gold"** . . **15**

8429: Fess Parker **"Ballad of Davy Crockett"/"Daniel Boone"*** **20**

G24
Record Guild of America 45 rpm Records

5-356: Bill Hart with the Mountaineers **"The Ballad of Davy Crockett" (with story);** 1955; P/S **25**

G25
Royale 45 rpm Records

14581: **"All the Songs from Walt Disney's 'Alice in Wonderland' ";** Bob Dale and Nadia Dore; three record set; GF; red vinyl; P/S; green, line-drawn cover **50**

Appendix A
Record Grading Notations

Over the years the hobby of record collecting has developed a "short-hand" notation system used in the listing of records for sale. It is an attempt to give the potential buyer an accurate description of the record or album cover with respect to its graded condition and other pertinent information about the album.

The actual vinyl record and/or its cover is graded individually. Unless otherwise stated by a seller, records are considered to be visually graded, not play graded. While record grading is always somewhat subjective, the following is an example from DIS*Coveries* magazine of an attempt to further clarify a generally agreed upon grading standard:

SS: STILL SEALED. Still in original shrink wrap. Unopened and in original manufactured condition. Usually sold for a premium. These are the most dangerous investment quality records to purchase. Since it is sealed, visual inspection of the inserts and vinyl cannot be made. SS records with ANY defect such as mildew or discoloration of the cover will not rate the premium SS implies.

M: MINT. The record and sleeve are in original, unsealed condition. They may have been played, but will have no visual or audible deterioration.

EX: EXCELLENT. The record may show signs of wear and use, but will have almost no audible defect. Sleeves in this condition may show marginal deterioration that will keep them from being graded mint, but will not have any repairs, pen, or pencil.

VG: VERY GOOD. Records will be noticeably less than perfect. They obviously have been played, but the damage is not visually or audibly distracting. Minor scuffs and slight surface defects may be present. Background ticks and hiss are minimal. Sleeves may show some slight ring wear and may have minor creases. Seams will be intact unless they have separated due to a failure of manufacturer's gluing agent.

G: GOOD. This record will have both visual and audible distractions, but will still be playable. The record and sleeve will show visual wear and moderate use. Sleeves will show ring wear, but will not be physically damaged.

F: FAIR. This record is visually and audibly distracting. It will still play although obviously damaged and will not have skips, but may have "play through" scratches. It is still usable. Sleeves will show heavy ring wear and some minor physical damage.

P: POOR. This record is one step away from the trash. It may or may not play. The sleeves are faded, torn, holed, marked, or otherwise damaged beyond pleasurable viewing. Anything worse than this condition should be classified as BAD.

(©1996 Antique Trader Publications, Inc.)

As I indicated earlier, you may often see variations in this system, with pluses (+) or minuses (-) attached to the letter grade, e.g., G+, to indicate higher or lower gradations. The grade of EXC is essentially the equivalent of a VG+ grade. The notation for a Mint Minus (M-) record is quite common as well, as many collectors and sellers believe no opened and played record can be higher than M-. If you are in doubt as to the grade of a record you have and want to sell, it's better to downgrade it one notch than to over grade it and have problems with a potential buyer who is disappointed with your grading.

Cover Notations:

Listed below are some of the more common notations in use in conjunction with the overall record "grade" as discussed in the Introduction to this book:

CO: CUT-OUT. A generic description indicating that the album's cover has been either had a "BB" size, or larger hole drilled through it, or has had a corner of the album cover clipped off (CC), or has had a small saw-mark (SM) cut in the edge of the cover. These markings were made either by the manufacturer or distributer to indicate that the record had been "cut-out" of the selling catalog and were being remaindered to the public, usually at a bargain price. Such markers also prevented a customer from attempting to return the album for a full-price refund.

Sometimes the covers were CO and then sealed—at other times the albums were already sealed and then CO. In the 1950s, remainder albums were often ink-stamped on the back cover with an "NR" (No Return), or an "X" or similar notation was impressed directly into the cardboard cover.

BB: See CO above. In the 1950s and 1960s, a very few manufacturers put a small metal rivet in the BB to prevent tearing of the cover. The holes are commonly just given the generic term "CO."

CC: CUT CORNER. A form of CO where the corner of the album cover is clipped off.

DIE-CUT: The cover of an LP or 78 rpm album has been manufactured with a small opening purposely cut into the cover, usually to reveal a picture on the inner booklet. It is not a defect, but is an original special pressing process. Die-cut covers were the hallmark of the early second pressing Disneyland ST-3900 LPs in their "Magic Mirror" variation. They were also used to display the entire picture disc record in the Disneyland "3100" series, and the souvenir picture disc EPs. The first edition 78 rpm album of "Pinocchio" on Victor P-18 also had a die-cut cover.

DJ: DISC JOCKEY COPY. Manufacturers often sent a copy of early pressings of a record to radio stations to encourage air-play. In the 1950s and 1960s, they were often marked on the cover, usually the back cover, by a rubber stamp noting some variation of the phrases, "Disc Jockey Copy" or "Radio Station Copy." It is considered less of a defect than normal consumer writing on a cover. Many do not consider it a defect at all, but a plus due to its indication that the vinyl is an early pressing. See Promo, WOC, and WLP.

Fox; Foxing: This is a term incorporated from comics collectors, and indicates that the cover has rust colored spots in varying degrees, probably a form of mold caused by exposure to dampness in the past.

GF, G/F, Gate: GATEFOLD COVER. See the Introduction. The cover opens up like a book. These often contain an inner booklet, and were the hallmark of the Disney "Story Teller" (ST) series of albums.

#OC: NUMBER ON COVER. A specific variation of WOC/WOBC below, where only a number has been written somewhere on the cover.

Promo: PROMOTIONAL COPY. These were usually also "Disc Jockey" (DJ) copies or trade giveaways. In the 1970s and 1980s, it was common for the manufacturers to stamp a phrase, often in gold print, somewhere on the cover, indicating that it was a promotional copy and "Not for Sale" or resale. This may or may not be considered a defect by some collectors, since these records were literally "first pressings," often pressed on superior vinyl which enhanced the sound, and, in some cases, on colored vinyl other than black. Any colored vinyl pressing is considered highly collectible and commands a premium price.

Often the "Promo" record label may itself have been different than the commercial release, appearing with the normal manufacturer's logo and record information, but often with an overall white background to the label. These are noted as "White Label Promos" (WLP). A separate category of "promo" records were those usually custom-pressed and containing interviews with the stars of the film and/or songs and dialogue with special labels. Often these records were packaged with scripts to be followed by a DJ. These scripts followed stock answers or comments made by the film's star on the record. When played, it allowed the DJ to ad-lib responses or questions and made it appear to a radio audience that an actual on-air interview was taking place. These were known as "open-ended" interviews. See also DJ and WLP.

PS or P/S: PICTURE SLEEVE. See the Introduction. The record, usually a 45 rpm or 78 rpm single, has a paper sleeve cover which is printed with a picture depicting either the record artist, a scene from the movie, or song information. These are highly collectible and difficult to find in nice condition for many of the Disney singles. Some picture sleeves are worth more than the record they contain!

RW: RING WEAR. Denotes that improper storage or improper handling of the record has caused pressure from the vinyl record to wear unevenly against the front and/or the back cover, causing the paper of the outer graphic pictures or writing to flake off, usually in a circular manner reflecting the interior record. It varies in degrees, affects the grade of the cover and should always be noted, indicating its degree, e.g., "slight RW."

SM: SAW MARK. (See CO above). A cut into the edge of the album cover, indicating a remaindered record.

SOC: STICKER ON COVER. Some form of adhesive sticker, either rubber based or glue based, usually a name tag or price tag, has been applied to the cover by a previous owner. Often these can be removed if done so carefully. Glue based stickers (i.e., similar to postage stamp adhesive) can often be removed with the use of a few drops of water. If the sticker has been applied by the manufacturer, noting a particular song, artist or award, it is not a defect and should be left on the record.

Split: SPLIT SEAMS. The album cover seams or edges have worn through, or have been cut through in various degrees, usually by improper insertion of the record over repeated use.

SS: STILL SEALED. See the Introduction. The album is unopened and encased in a very thin, pliable poly clear bag (mid-1950s/early 1960s) or in plastic "shrink-wrap" (late 1960s-1980s). These are considered a big plus, constitute the ultimate record collectible, and command a premium price unless soiled over time by mildew or some other defect. Some of the sealed Disney records had Disneyland or Buena Vista logos embossed on the bags.

TOC: TAPE ON COVER. A previous user has applied some form of adhesive tape to the cover, usually in an attempt to correct an album's split seams. See TS and Split.

TS: TAPED SEAMS. A previous owner has attempted to repair split seams by using adhesive tape. See TOC and Split.

WOC or WOBC: WRITING ON COVER or WRITING ON BACK COVER. The front or back cover has been written or printed on in some manner, with ink, pencil, ball-point pens, crayon—you name it! Often, light pencil markings can be removed. Ink, on the other hand, unless it is water soluble and applied on a glossy cover, is permanent. Ball point pen writing, even if able to be removed, inevitably leaves impressions in the cover. If the writing is small and unobtrusive it is less of a defect. Writing on the back cover is considered a less serious defect than writing on the front cover. Many people felt a need to write their names on the covers or to apply their own numbering systems to their collections. See DJ and Promo.

WS: WATER STAINED. Water damaged cover (WSOC) or label (WSOL). A WS cover often shows evidence of mildew as well.

Label and Vinyl Notations

NAP: NOT AFFECT PLAY. A notation often used with an indication of scratches, indicating that the scratch is light and doesn't effect the playing of the record, i.e., cause it to skip the groove.

SCF: SCUFFS. The vinyl has been scuffed usually by its paper sleeve. Not a serious defect,unless it affects play in any degree.

SOL: STICKER ON THE LABEL. Usually a name tag or record number applied with glue or rubber based sticker. See SOC above.

WLP: WHITE LABEL PROMO. A Disc Jockey or premium record, in which the record label color is white with otherwise normal logos and printing.

WOL: WRITING ON THE LABEL.

Appendix B
Disney's Full-Length Animated Films 1937-1997

Since 1937, the Walt Disney Company has released 35 full-length animated films. Most of the films were periodically rereleased for new generations every six to eight years. Indeed, prior to 1984, it was Disney policy to prohibit any other exploitation of its full-length features in any medium other than theatrical release. This policy changed in 1985 when Disney released *Pinocchio* on videocassette. The listings below indicate the initial theatrical release date for the film and any subsequent rerelease date over the years.

1. *Snow White and the Seven Dwarfs*: 1937, 1944, 1952, 1958, 1967, 1975, 1983, 1987, 1993
2. *Pinocchio*: 1940, 1945, 1954, 1962, 1971, 1978, 1984, 1992
3. *Fantasia*: 1940, 1946, 1956, 1963, 1969, 1977, 1982, 1985, 1990
4. *Dumbo*: 1941, 1949, 1959, 1972, 1976
5. *Bambi*: 1942, 1946, 1956, 1963, 1969, 1977, 1982, 1988
6. *Saludos Amigos*: 1943, 1949
7. *The Three Caballeros*: 1945, 1977
8. *Make Mine Music*: 1946
9. *Fun and Fancy Free*: 1947; film segments of *Bongo* and *Mickey and the Beanstalk* were later individually released.
10. *Melody Time*: 1948
11. *The Adventures of Ichabod and Mr. Toad*: 1949; film segments were later released as *The Legend of Sleepy Hollow* and *The Wind in the Willows*.
12. *Cinderella*: 1950, 1957, 1965, 1973, 1981, 1987
13. *Alice in Wonderland*: 1951, 1974, 1981
14. *Peter Pan*: 1953, 1958, 1969, 1976, 1982, 1989
15. *Lady and the Tramp*: 1955, 1962, 1971, 1980, 1986
16. *Sleeping Beauty*: 1959, 1970, 1979, 1986
17. *101 Dalmatians*: 1961, 1969, 1979, 1991
18. *The Sword in the Stone*: 1963, 1972, 1983
19. *The Jungle Book*: 1967, 1978, 1984, 1990
20. *The Aristocats*: 1970, 1980, 1987
21. *Robin Hood*: 1973, 1982
22. *The Many Adventures of Winnie the Pooh*: 1977
23. *The Rescuers*: 1977, 1983, 1989
24. *The Fox and the Hound*: 1981, 1988
25. *The Black Cauldron*: 1985
26. *The Great Mouse Detective*: 1986, 1992
27. *Oliver and Company*: 1988
28. *The Little Mermaid*: 1989
29. *The Rescuers Down Under*: 1990
30. *Beauty and the Beast*: 1991
31. *Aladdin*: 1992
32. *The Lion King*: 1994
33. *Pocahontas*: 1995
34. *The Hunchback of Notre Dame*: 1996
35. *Hercules*: 1997

Appendix C
Music Composers for Disney Films—Filmography

With the general exceptions of Leigh Harline, Paul Smith and recently, Alan Menken, most of the studio composers of the early Disney films have gone unheralded and uncredited over the years. For whatever reason, many of the Disney label records, and some of the earlier recordings on other labels fail to list composer credits at all. This is surprising inasmuch as Disney was able to use many of the finest composers and musicians available at the time. In the 1970s, the Disney Studios commenced to rely on independent composers to score its films.

I have attempted to note composers, where known, for the various recordings and films.[1] The dates listed are for the film release or initial TV showing. They may not necessarily be the same as the record release date, if a recording was made. There are some films listed which were not Disney productions, but which were released as "soundtracks" on either Disneyland or Buena Vista records, e.g., many of Annette's movies. Inasmuch as Disney ceased making vinyl records in 1988, the score for any film released after that date is available, if at all, only on compact disc (CD). The Composer Index also includes films made for Disney's subsidiaries, Touchstone and Hollywood Pictures, and other later Disney produced films which had non-Disney label soundtracks.

If a composer is listed for "songs only," another composer is usually credited with the underscore. Some notable conductors are indicated by "Cond."

Addison, John
Ride a Wild Pony (1976)

Alwyn, William (1905-1985)
In Search of the Castaways (1962)
Swiss Family Robinson (1960)
Third Man on the Mountain (1959)

[1] For those with interest in learning more about the Disney composers, several excellent articles have been authored by Ross Care, and have appeared in film soundtrack magazines over the years. See: *Funnyworld* No. 18 (Summer 1978), "Symphonists for the Sillies: The Composers for Disney's Shorts," Sight and Sound (Winter 1978), "Cine-Symphony;" *Soundtrack!* Vol. 8, No.31, Sept. 1989, "Melody Time: Musicians for Disney Animation 1941-1955."

Altman, Richard
Funny Bones (1995)

Amfitheatrof, Daniele (1901-1983)
Song of the South (1946) live sequence

Arntson, Bruce
Ernest Goes to Jail (1990) w/Shelstad
Ernest Scared Stupid (1991) w/Shelstad

Ashman, Howard (1951-1991) lyrist
Aladdin (1992)
Beauty and the Beast (1991)
The Little Mermaid (1989) Academy Awards for Best Original Score and Best Song for "Under the Sea"

Baker, "Buddy" Norman D. (1918-)
The Apple Dumpling Gang (1975)

The Apple Dumpling Gang Rides Again (1979)
Aquamania (1961)
The Bears and I (1974)
The Best of Walt Disney's True-Life Adventures (1975) w/Smith and O. Wallace
Charley and the Angel (1973)
The Country Cousin (1967) LP only
Donald and the Wheel (1961)
Donald in Mathmagic Land (1959)
The Gnome Mobile (1967)
The Devil and Max Devlin (1981) w/Hamlisch
The Haunted Mansion (1969) Park attraction music
Hot Lead and Cold Feet (1978)
King of the Grizzlies (1970)
The Litterbug (1961)
The Many Adventures of Winnie the Pooh (1977)
Mickey's Christmas Carol (1983)
Misadventures of Merlin Jones (1964)
The Monkey's Uncle (1964)
Napoleon and Samantha (1972)
Nashville Coyote (1973)
Never a Dull Moment (1968)
No Deposit, No Return (1976)
$1,000,000 Duck (1971)
Rascal (1969)
Run, Cougar Run (1972)
The Shaggy D. A. (1976)
Summer Magic (1963)
Superdad (1973)
"The Swamp Fox" (1959-1961) TV
"Texas John Slaughter" (1958-1959) TV
That Darn Cat (1965)
A Tiger Walks (1964)
Toby Tyler or Ten Weeks with a Circus (1960)
Treasure of Matecombe (1976)

Baker, Michael Conway
One Magic Christmas (1985)

Barry, John (1933-)
The Black Hole (1979)
The Scarlet Letter (1995)

Bartek, Steve
Cabin Boy (1994)

Bass, Jules (lyrist) (1935-)
The Hobbit (songs only)
The Return of the King (songs only)

Bernstein, Elmer (1922-)
The Black Cauldron (1985)
The Cemetery Club (1993)
The Good Mother (1988)
Oscar (1991)
Roommates (1995)

Bernstein, Peter
My Science Project (1985)

Bock, Jerry
A Stranger Among Us (1992)

Box, Euel (1928-)
Benji the Hunted (1987)

Bradley, Scott
Merbabies (1938)

Broughton, Bruce (1945-)
Homeward Bound: The Incredible Journey (1993)
Holy Matrimony (1995)
Honey, I Blew Up the Kid (1992)
Homeward Bound II (Lost in San Francisco) (1996)
The Rescue (1988)
The Shadow Conspiracy (1996)
Tombstone (1993)

Broughton, David
The Rescuers Down Under (1990)

Brunner, Robert F. (1938-)
Amy (1981)
The Barefoot Executive (1971)
The Biscuit Eater (1972)
Blackbeard's Ghost (1968)
The Boatniks (1970)
The Castaway Cowboy (1974)
The Computer Wore Tennis Shoes (1969)

Gus (1976)
Lt. Robin Crusoe U.S.N. (1966)
Monkeys Go Home (1967)
The North Avenue Irregulars (1979)
Now You See Him, Now You Don't (1972)
The Small One (1978)
Smith! (1969)
Snowball Express (1972)
The Strongest Man in the World (1975)
That Darn Cat (1965)
Wild Country (1971)

Bruns, George (1914-)
The Absent Minded Professor (1961)
Adventures of Bullwhip Griffin (1967)
The Aristocats (1970)
Babes in Toyland (1961)
Davy Crockett and the River Pirates (1956)
Davy Crockett, King of the Wild Frontier (1955)
The Fighting Prince of Donegal (1966)
Follow Me, Boys! (1966)
Goofy's Freeway Trouble (1965)
Herbie Rides Again (1974)
The Jungle Book (1967)
Johnny Tremain (1957)
The Horse in the Gray Flannel Suit (1968)
The Love Bug (1969)
101 Dalmatians (1961)
Perri (1957) songs only
Robin Hood (1973)
Sleeping Beauty (1959) Adaption of Tchaikovsky and songs
Son of Flubber (1963)
The Sword in the Stone (1963)
"The Tenderfoot" (1964) TV
Tonka (1958) song only
Westward Ho the Wagons (1956)
"The Wonderful World of Walt Disney" (TV)
"Zorro" (1957-1959) TV

Burke, "Sonny" Joseph Francis (1914-1980)
Lady and the Tramp (1955) songs only

Burwell, Carter (1955-)
Bad Company (1995)
A Goofy Movie (1995)

Butler, Artie (1942-)
The Rescuers (1977)

Camarata, "Tutti" Salvador (1913-)
Babes in Toyland (1961) Cond.
Darby O'Gill & the Little People (1959) Cond.
The Parent Trap (1961) Cond.
Westward Ho the Wagons (1956) Cond.

Carlos, Wendy
Tron (1982)

Churchill, Frank E. (1901-1942)
Adventures of Ichabod and Mr. Toad (1949)
The Army Mascot (1942)
Bambi (1942) w/O. Wallace & Plumb
Barnyard Olympics (1932)
The Bears and the Bees (1932)
The Big Bad Wolf (1934)
The Bird Store 1932)
Birds in the Spring (1933) w/Lewis
Bone Trouble (1940) w/Smith
Bugs in Love (1932)
Building a Building (1933)
The Busy Beavers (1931)
Camping Out (1934) w/Lewis
The Castaway (1931)
The Cat's Out (1931)
The China Plate (1931)
The Clock Store (1931)
Cock O' the Walk (1935) w/Malotte
The Dog-Napper (1934) w/Lewis
Dumbo (1941) w/O. Wallace; Academy Award for Best Musical Scoring of a Motion Picture
Egyptian Melodies (1931)
The Flying Mouse (1934) w/Lewis
Funnie Little Bunnies (1934) w/Harline
Giant Land (1933)
The Grocery Boy (1932)
Gulliver Mickey (1934)
The Fox Hunt (1931)

The Golden Touch (1935)
The Klondike Kid (1932)
Lullaby Land (1933) w/Harline
Mickey in Arabia (1932)
Mickey Plays Papa (1934) w/Lewis
Mickey's Gala Premiere (1933)
Mickey's Mellerdrammer (1933)
Mickey's Man Friday (1935) w/Lewis
Mickey's Pal Pluto (1933)
Mickey's Polo Team (1936) w/Smith
More Kittens (1936)
Musical Farmer (1932)
Old King Cole (1933) w/Lewis
On Ice (1935) w/Harline & Lewis
The Orphan's Benefit (1934 & 1941)
Peter Pan (1953) song only
Playful Pluto (1934)
Pluto's Judgment Day (1935) w/Harline
The Practical Pig (1939)
Puppy Love (1933)
The Reluctant Dragon (1941)
The Robber Kitten (1935)
Santa's Workshop (1932)
Shanghaied (1934)
Sky Trooper (1942)
Snow White and the Seven Dwarfs (1937)
The Steeple Chase (1933)
The Three Little Pigs (1933)
Three Little Wolves (1936)
Three Orphan Kittens (1935)
Thru the Mirror (1936) w/Smith
Toby Tortoise Returns (1936) w/Harline
The Tortoise & the Hare (1935) w/Harline
Touchdown Mickey (1932)
Who Killed Cock Robin? (1935)
The Whoopee Party (1932)
Ye Olden Days (1933)

Clarke, Stanley
What's Love Got to Do with It? (1993)

Colombier, Michel
The Program (1993)
Ruthless People (1986)

Conti, Bill (1942-)
The Adventures of Huck Finn (1993)
Bound by Honor (1993)

Convertino, Michael
Aspen Extreme (1993)
The Doctor (1991)
The Santa Clause (1994)

Copeland, Stewart
Taking Care of Business (1990)

Coppola, Carmine
New York Stories (1989)

Cox, Andy
Tin Men (1987) (w/Steele)

Daniel, Eliot
Fun and Fancy Free (1947) songs only
Make Mine Music (1946) songs only
Melody Time (Pecos Bill) 1948
So Dear to My Heart (1949) song only
Song of the South (1946) songs only

Darby, Ken
Darby served as vocals arranger and music director (*Melody Time*) on several of the Disney films of the 1940s. He worked with the Disney Studios from 1940-1947, scoring the "Willie the Whale" sequence (The Whale Who Wanted to Sing at the Met) in *Make Mine Music* (1946). He had also earlier created the unique voices of the "Munchkins" in *The Wizard of Oz*. His "Kings Men" vocal group was featured in:
Dumbo (1941)
And the "Ken Darby Singers" sang in:
Melody Time (1948)
Song of the South (1946)

Daring, Mason(1949-)
Wild Hearts Can't Be Broken (1991)

Davie, Cedric Thorpe
Kidnapped (1960)
Rob Roy, The Highland Rogue (1953)

Davis, Don
A Goofy Movie (1995)

Debney, John (1956-)
Hocus Pocus (1993)
Houseguest (1995)
Runaway Brain (1995) Mickey Mouse short
White Fang 2: Myth of the White Wolf (1994)

DeLerue, Georges (1925-1992)
Beaches (1988)
Heartbreak Hotel (1988)

DePaul, Gene (1919-)
Adventures of Ichabod and Mr. Toad (1949) songs only
Alice in Wonderland (1951)
So Dear to My Heart (1949) songs only

De Vol, Frank
Herbie Goes Bananas (1980)
Herbie Goes to Monte Carlo (1977)

Dodd, Jimmie (1910-1964)
"Mickey Mouse Club" (1955) TV; March & Alma Mater

Donaggio, Pino (1941-)
Tex (1982)

Doyle, Patrick (1953-)
Shipwrecked (1991)

Dubin, Joseph S.
Bee at the Beach (1949)
Cold Storage (1951)
Cold War (1951)
Corn Chips (1951) w/O. Wallace
Donald Applecore (1952)
Don's Fountain of Youth (1952)
Father's Lion (1952)
Father's Weekend (1953)
For Whom the Bulls Toil (1953)
Hello, Aloha (1952) w/Harry Owen
Home Made Home (1951)
How to be a Detective (1952)
How to Dance (1953)
Man's Best Friend (1952)
Out on a Limb (1950)
Plutopia (1951)
Pluto's Christmas Tree (1952)
Tomorrow We Diet (1951)
Uncle Donald's Ants (1952)

Edleman, Randy (1947-)
Angels in the Outfield (1995)
The Big Green (1995)
The Chipmunk Adventure (1988)
The Distinguished Gentleman (1992)
Tall Tale (1995)
V.I. Warshawski (1995)
While You Were Sleeping (1995)

Eidelman, Cliff
A Simple Twist of Fate (1994)

Elfman, Danny (1953-)
The Nightmare Before Christmas (1993)
Dead Presidents (1995)
Dick Tracy (1990)

Endelman, Stephen
Tom and Huck (1995)

Fain, Sammy (1902-1989)
Alice in Wonderland (1951) songs only
101 Dalmatians (1961) songs only
Peter Pan (1953) songs only
The Rescuers (1977) songs only
Sleeping Beauty (1959) song only

Fenton, George
Born Yesterday (1993)

Fiedel, Brad (1951-)
Straight Talk (1992)

Folk, Robert
Can't Buy Me Love (1987)
In the Army Now (1994)

Foster, David
One Good Cop (1991) w/Ross

Fox, Charles (1940-)
Trenchcoat (1983)

Frizzell, John
The Rich Man's Wife (1996) w/J.N. Howard

Frontiere, Dominic
The Color of Night (1994)

Gibbs, Richard
The Gun in Betty Lou's Handbag (1992)
Passed Away (1992)
Son-in-Law (1993)

Gilbert, Ray (1912-1976) lyrist
Adventures of Ichabod and Mr. Toad (1949) songs only
Make Mine Music (1946) songs only
Melody Time (1948) songs only
Song of the South (1946) 1947 Academy Award with Allie Wrubel for Best Original Song "Zip-A-Dee-Doo-Dah"
The Three Caballeros (1945) songs only

Gilkyson, Terry
The Aristocats (1970) song only
The Jungle Book (1967) song only
The Moon-Spinners (1964) song only
Savage Sam (1963) songs only
The Swiss Family Robinson (1960) song only
The Three Lives of Thomasina (1964) song only

Gimbel, Norman
20,000 Leagues Under the Sea (1954) songs only

Goldsmith, Jerry (1929-)
Angie (1994)
Baby...Secret of the Lost Legend (1985)
Medicine Man (1992)
Night Crossing (1982)
One Little Indian (1973)
Powder (1995)

Goldstein, William
Hello Again (1987)

Goodman, Miles (1949-)
Indian Summer (1993)
The Muppet Christmas Carol (1992)
Sister Act 2 (1993) w/Shaiman
What About Bob? (1991)

Goodwin, Ron (1925-)
The Littlest Horse Thieves (1977)
One of Our Dinosaurs Is Missing (1975)
Unidentified Flying Oddball (1979)

Grainer, Ron (1922-1981)
Candleshoe (1978)
The Moon-Spinners (1964)

Gross, Charles
Country (1984)
Turner & Hooch (1989)

Hamlisch, Marvin (1944-)
The Devil and Max Devlin (1981) w/B. Baker
Three Man and a Baby (1987)
The World's Greatest Athlete (1973)

Harline, Leigh (1907-1969)
The Art of Self Defense (1941)
Baggage Buster (1941)
The Band Concert (1935)
The China Shop (1934)
The Cookie Carnival (1935)
The Country Cousin (1936)
Donald's Camera (1941)
Donald Gets Drafted (1942) Song only: "The Army's Not the Army Anymore"
Elmer Elephant (1936)
Farmyard Symphony (1938)
Father Noah's Ark (1933)
Fun and Fancy Free (1947) song only
Funny Little Bunnies (1934) w/Churchill
The Goddess of Spring (1934)
Golden Eggs (1941)
A Good Time for a Dime (1941)
The Grasshopper and the Ants (1934)
Hawaiian Holiday (1937) w/Smith
Lend a Paw (1941)
Lullaby Land (1933) w/Churchill

Mickey's Amateurs (1937) w/ O. Wallace
Mickey's Garden (1935)
Mickey's Grand Opera (1936)
Mickey's Mechanical Man (1933)
Mickey's Rival (1936)
Mickey's Service Station (1935)
Mickey's Trailer (1938)
Mother Pluto (1936)
Moving Day (1936) w/Malotte
Mr. Mouse Takes a Trip (1940) w/O. Wallace
Music Land (1935)
The Night Before Christmas (1933)
Old MacDonald Duck (1941)
On Ice (1935) w/Lewis & Churchill
The Old Mill (1937)
Pantry Pirate (1940)
Peculiar Penguins (1934)
The Pet Store (1933)
The Pied Piper (1933)
Pinocchio (1940) w/Smith; Academy Award for Best Adapted Score and for Best Song: "When You Wish Upon a Star"
Pluto Junior (1942)
Pluto's Dream House (1940)
Pluto's Judgment Day (1935) w/Churchill
The Sleep Walker (1942)
Snow White and the Seven Dwarfs (1937)
Toby Tortoise Returns (1936) w/Churchill
The Tortoise and the Hare (1934) w/Churchill
Truant Officer Donald (1941) w/Smith
Two Gun Mickey (1934)
The Vanishing Private (1942) w/O. Wallace
Water Babies (1935)
The Wise Little Hen (1934)
Woodland Cafe (1937)
Wynken, Blynken and Nod (1938)

Himmelman, Peter
Crossing the Bridge (1992)

Hirshhorn, Joel
Pete's Dragon (1977)

Hoble, Ray
Fun and Fancy Free (1947) song only

Holdridge, Lee (1944-)
Splash (1984)

Horner, James (1953-)
A Far Off Place (1993)
Honey, I Shrunk the Kids (1989)
The Journey of Natty Gann (1985)
Off Beat (1986)
The Rocketeer (1991)
Something Wicked This Way Comes (1983)
Swing Kids (1993)

Howard, James Newton
Alive (1993)
Pretty Woman (1990)
The Rich Man's Wife (1996) w/Frizzell
Three Men and a Little Lady (1990)
Tough Guys (1986)

Huddleston, Floyd (1919-)
The Aristocats (1970) songs only
Robin Hood (1973) songs only

Isham, Mark (1951-)
Billy Bathgate (1991)
Miami Rhapsody (1995)
Never Cry Wolf (1983)
Quiz Show (1994)

Jackson, Wilfred
Steamboat Willie (1928)
Disney's first sound short was "scored" mostly through public domain songs arranged by Jackson, the film's director.

Jankel, Chaz
D.O.A. (1988)

Jarre, Maurice (1924-)
Dead Poets Society (1989)
The Island at the Top of the World (1974)
The Last Flight of Noah's Ark (1980)

John, Elton
The Lion King (1994) w/Tim Rice; Song only: "Can You Feel the Love Tonight" Academy Award for Best Song

Johnston, Richard O.
The Fox and the Hound (1981)

Jones, Stan (1914-1963)
Jones is perhaps best known for his classic cowboy song, "(Ghost) Riders in the Sky." He also wrote the title song for the acclaimed John Wayne film, *The Searchers*, and songs for other non-Disney films: *Wagonmaster; Rio Grande* and *The Horse Soldiers.* His Disney work appears in:
The Great Locomotive Chase (1956) song only
"Spin and Marty" (1955) TV; song only
Ten Who Dared (1960) song only
"Texas John Slaughter" (1956) TV Theme
"Westward Ho the Wagons (song only)

Jones, Trevor
Arachnophobia (1990)
Blame It on Broadway (1992)

Kamen, Michael (1948-)
Adventures in Babysitting (1987)
Jack (1996)
The Three Musketeers (1993)
101 Dalmatians (1996—live action remake)

Keister, Shane
Ernest Goes to Camp (1987)

Kent, Walter (1911-) lyrist
Melody Time (1948) Johnny Appleseed

Lava, William (1911-1971)
Adventures of Zorro (1957) TV
The Littlest Outlaw (1955)
The Sign of Zorro (1960)
Spin and Marty (1955) TV

Lawrence, David
Camp Nowhere (1994)

Laws, Maury (1923-)
The Hobbit (LP only)
The Return of the King (LP only)

Leven, "Mel" Melville Abner (1914-)
The Adventures of Bullwhip Griffin (1960) songs only
Babes in Toyland (1961) songs only
101 Dalmatians (1961) songs only

Lewis, Bert
Head of Disney Music after Carl Stalling's departure in 1930, and composer of early Disney shorts including:
Babes in the Woods (1932)
The Barnyard Broadcast (1931)
Birds in the Spring (1933) w/Churchill
Camping Out (1934) w/Churchill
The Dognapper (1934) w/Churchill
The Duck Hunt (1932)
Fishin' Around (1931)
The Flying Mouse (1934) w/Churchill
Just Dogs (1932)
King Neptune (1932)
The Mad Doctor (1933)
The Mad Dog (1932)
The Mail Pilot (1933)
Mickey Plays Papa (1934) w/Churchill
Mickey's Fire Brigade (1935)
Mickey's Good Deed (1932)
Mickey's Kangaroo (1935)
Mickey's Man Friday (1935) w/Churchill
The Moose Hunt (1931)
Old King Cole (1933) w/Churchill
On Ice (1935) w/Churchill and Harline
Pioneer Days (1930)
Playful Pan (1930)
Trader Mickey (1932)
The Wayward Canary (1932)

Leyden, Norman
Cinderella (1950)
Peter Pan (1953)

Livingston, Jerry (1915-)
Alice in Wonderland (1951) songs
Cinderella (1950) songs

Malotte, Albert Hay (1895-1964)
Composer of late 1930s Disney Shorts:
Alpine Climbers (1936)
The Brave Little Tailor (1938)
Broken Toys (1935)

Cock O' the Walk (1935) w/Churchill
Ferdinand the Bull (1938)
Little Hiawatha (1937)
Lonesome Ghosts (1937)
Magician Mickey (1937)
Mickey's Elephant (1936)
The Moth and the Flame (1938)
Moving Day (1936) w/Harline
Orphan's Picnic (1936)
Three Blind Mouseketeers (1936)
The Ugly Duckling (1931 and 1939)
The Whalers (1938)

Mancina, Mark
Man of the House (1995)

Mancini, Henry (1924-1994)
The Great Mouse Detective (1986)
Condorman (1981)

Mandel, Johnnie (1925-)
Escape to Witch Mountain (1975)
Freaky Friday (1977)

Manfredini, Harry
My Boyfriend's Back (1993)

Manilow, Barry (1946-)
Oliver and Company (1988) songs only

Manson, Eddie Lawrence (1922-)
Tiger Town (1984)

Marder, Mark
True Identity (1991)

Marks, Franklin
Charlie, the Lonesome Cougar (1967)
How to Have an Accident in the Home (1956)

Marshall, Phil
Noises Off (1992)
Run (1991)

Martin, Peter
Where the Heart Is (1990)

Marvin, Rick
3 Ninjas (1992)

Mathieson, Muir (1911-1975)
In Search of the Castaways (1962) Cond.
Kidnapped (1960) Cond.
Rob Roy, the Highland Rogue (1954) Cond.
The Story of Robin Hood and His Merrie Men (1952) Cond.; live action film
The Swiss Family Robinson (1960) Cond.
The Sword and the Rose (1953) Cond.
Third Man on the Mountain (1959) Cond.
Treasure Island (1950) Cond.

McHugh, David (1941-)
Three Fugitives (1989)

McKuen, Rod (1933-)
Scandalous John (1971)

McNeely, Joel
Iron Will (1994)
Squanto: A Warrior's Tale (1994)
Terminal Velocity (1994)

Menken, Alan (1949-)
Aladdin (1992) Academy Awards for Best Score and Best Song: "A Whole New World"
Beauty and the Beast (1991) Academy Awards for Best Score and Best Song: "Beauty and the Beast"
Hercules (1997)
The Hunchback of Notre Dame (1996)
Life with Mikey (1993)
The Little Mermaid (1989) Academy Awards for Best Original Score and Best Song: "Under the Sea")
Newsies (1992)
Pocahontas (1995) w/Schwartz; Academy Awards for Best Original Musical or Comedy Score and for Best Original Song: "Colors of the Wind"

Mercer, Johnny (1909-1976)
Robin Hood (1973) songs only

Miller, Marcus
A Low Down Dirty Shame (1994)

Miller, Roger (1936-1994)
Robin Hood (1973) songs only

Morey, Larry (1905-1971)
Adventures of Ichabod and Mr. Toad (1949) songs only
Bambi (1942) w/Churchill, O. Wallace, and Plumb
Ferdinand the Bull (1938)
The Reluctant Dragon (1941) songs only
Snow White and the Seven Dwarfs (1937)
So Dear to My Heart (1949) song only

Morris, John (1926-)
Stella (1990)

Mothersbaugh, Mark
It's Pat (1994)

Myers, Stanley (1930-)
Sarafina! (1995)
The Watcher in the Woods (1981)

Newborn, Ira
The Jerky Boys (1995)

Newman, David (1954-)
The Air Up There (1994)
Disorganized Crime (1989)
Duck Tales—The Movie: Treasure of the Lost Lamp (1990)
Fire Birds (1990)
Gross Anatomy (1989)
I Love Trouble (1994)
The Marrying Man (1991)
The Mighty Ducks (1992)
Mr. Destiny (1990)
My Father the Hero (1994)
Operation Dumbo Drop (1995)
Paradise (1991)

Newman, Randy (1943-)
Toy Story (1995)
James and the Giant Peach (1996)

Newman, Thomas
Deceived (1991)
Phenomenon (1996)
Unstrung Heros (1995)

North, Alex (1910-1991)
Dragonslayer (1981) A Disney/Paramount production
Good Morning, Vietnam (1987)

O'Hearn, Patrick
Father Hood (1993)

Owens, Harry
Hello, Aloha (1952) w/Dubin

Parker, Clifton (1905-)
Treasure Island (1950)
The Story of Robin Hood (1952) live-action film
The Sword and the Rose (1953)

Pike, Nicholas
Blank Check (1994)
Captain Ron (1992)

Plumb, Edward H. (1907-1958)
After *Bambi*, Plumb essentially became the Disney orchestrator/arranger on many films:
Bambi (1942) w/Churchill, O. Wallace, and Morey
Donald's Crime (1945) w/Smith
Donald's Diary (1954)
How to Sleep (1953)
Mother Goose Goes Hollywood (1938)
The New Neighbor (1953)
Saludos Amigos (1943) w/Wolcott & Smith
Victory Through Air Power (1943) w/Smith and O. Wallace

Poledouris, Basil (1945-)
Rudyard Kipling's The Jungle Book (1994)
White Fang (1992) w/Zimmer

Portman, Rachel
Emma (1996)
The Joy Luck Club (1993)
A Pyromaniac's Love Story (1995)

Post, Mike (1944-)
Running Brave (1983) Distributed by Buena Vista only

Preisner, Zbigniew
Feast of July (1995)
When a Man Loves a Woman (1994)

PUBLIC DOMAIN:
Many of the very early Disney shorts were scored with music listed as in the "public domain" (PD). Others have "no information available" (NI) for the music in the Disney Archives. These are listed below. Any readers who have further information on the music for these shorts, or the music director or arranger should feel free to contact the author for additions in the next edition of this book.
Arctic Antics (1930) NI
The Barnyard Concert (1930) PD
The Beach Party (1931) NI
Birds of a Feather (1931) NI
The Birthday Party (1931) PD
Blue Rhythm (1931) NI
Boat Builders (1938) NI
The Cactus Kid (1930) PD
Cannibal Capers (1930) NI
The Chain Gang (1930) PD
The Delivery Boy (1931) PD
The Fire Fighters (1930) PD
Flowers and Trees (1932) PD
Flying Jalopy (1943) NI
Freewayphobia No. 1 (1965) NI
Frolicking Fish (1930) NI
The Gorilla Mystery (1930) PD
Home Defense (1943) NI
Just Mickey (1930) PD
Mickey Cuts Up (1931) NI
Mickey Steps Out (1931) NI
Mickey's Orphans (1931) NI
Mickey's Revue (1932) NI
Mickey's Nightmare (1932) NI
Midnight in a Toy Shop (1930) NI
Mother Goose Melodies (1931) NI
Night (1930) NI
The Picnic (1930) PD
The Shindig (1930) PD
The Spider and the Fly (1931) NI
Traffic Troubles (1931) NI
The Village Smithy (1941) NI
Winter (1930) NI

Redford, J.A.C. (1953-)
D2: The Mighty Ducks (1994)
D3: The Mighty Ducks (1996)
Heavyweights (1995)
A Kid in King Arthur's Court (1995)
Newsies (1992)
Oliver and Co. (1988)

Revell, Graeme
The Crow: City of Angels (1996)
The Hand That Rocks the Cradle (1992)
The Tie That Binds (1995)

Reynolds, John
Frank and Ollie (1995)

Rice, Tim
The Lion King (1994) w/Elton John; song only; Academy Award for Best Song: "Can You Feel the Love Tonight"

Rinker, Al
The Aristocats (1970) songs only

Robbins, Richard
Cocktail (1988)
Jefferson in Paris (1995)

Roberts, Andy
Mad Love (1995)

Robertson, Robbie
The Color of Money (1986)

Robinson, J. Peter
Encino Man (1992)

Ross, Bill
One Good Cop (1991) w/Foster

Rowland, Bruce (1942-)
Cheetah (1989)
Return to Snowy River Part II (1988)

Rubinstein, Arthur B.
Another Stakeout (1993)
Stakeout (1987)

Russo, David
Spaced Invaders (1990)

Safan, Craig
Money for Nothing (1993)

Schifrin, Lalo (1932-)
The Cat from Outer Space (1978)
Return from Witch Mountain (1976)

Schreiter, Hans
Emil and the Detectives (1964)

Schreiter, Heinz
Almost Angels (1962) Musical Director—features the music of Schubert, Brahms, and Strauss

Schwartz, Stephen (lyrist)
Pocahontas (1995) w/Menken]; Academy Awards for Best Original Musical or Comedy Score, and for Best Original Song: "Colors of the Wind"

Scott, John
Shoot to Kill (1988)

Shaiman, Marc
Scenes from a Mall (1991)
Sister Act (1992)
Sister Act 2 (1993) w/Goodman

Shelstad, Kirby
Ernest Goes to Jail (1990) w/Arntson
Ernest Scared Stupid (1991) w/Arntson

Sherman, Richard M. (1928-) **& Robert B.** (1925-)
The Absent Minded Professor (1961) songs only
Adventures of Bullwhip Griffin (1967) songs only
The Aristocats (1970) songs only
Beach Party (1963) songs only
Bedknobs and Broomsticks (1971)
Big Red (1962)
Bikini Beach (1964)
Bon Voyage (1962) song only
Follow Me, Boys! (1966) song only
The Gnome-Mobile (1967) song only
Greyfriars Bobby (1961) songs
The Happiest Millionaire (1967)
Hector, the Stowaway Pup (1964) TV
The Horsemasters (1961) TV
In Search of the Castaways (1962) songs only
It's a Small World (1964 NY World's Fair Theme)
The Jungle Book (1967)
The Legend of Lobo (1962) song only
The *Many Adventures of Winnie the Pooh* (1977) songs only
Mary Poppins (1964) Academy Awards for Best Original Music Score, and Best Song: "Chim Chim Cheree"
The Miracle of the White Stallions (1963)
Misadventures of Merlin Jones (1964) song only
The Monkey's Uncle (1965) song only
Monkeys, Go Home! (1967) song only
Moon Pilot (1962) songs only
Muscle Beach Party (1964) song only
The One and Only, Genuine, Original Family Band (1968)
"Orange Bird" (Walt Disney World attraction—Tropical Serenade)
The Parent Trap (1961) songs only
Summer Magic (1963) songs only
The Sword in the Stone (1963) songs only
"A Symposium on Popular Songs" (1962)
That Darn Cat (1965) song only
Those Calloways (1965) songs only
The Ugly Dachshund (1966)
Winnie the Pooh and the Blustery Day (1968)
Winnie the Pooh and the Honey Tree (1966)
Winnie the Pooh and Tigger Too (1974)
Wonderful World of Color (1961-1969) TV Main Theme

Shire, David (1937-)
Return to Oz (1985)

Shore, Howard (1946-)
Ed Wood (1994)
Guilty as Sin (1993)
An Innocent Man (1989)
Ransom (1996)

Silvestri, Alan (1950-)
Father of the Bride (1991)
Flight of the Navigator (1986)
Judge Dredd (1995)
Outrageous Fortune (1987)
Super Mario Brothers (1993)
Tarzan: The Animated Movie (1997)
Who Framed Roger Rabbit? (1988)

Small, Michael
Consenting Adults (1992)

Smith, Paul Joseph (1906-1985)
The African Lion (1955)
Beach Picnic (1939)
The Best of Walt Disney's True-Life Adventures (1975) w/O. Wallace and Buddy Baker
Bone Trouble (1940) w/Churchill
Bon Voyage (1962)
Californy 'Er Bust (1945)
Camp Dog (1950)
Cinderella (1950) w/O. Wallace
Clock Cleaners (1937) w/O. Wallace
Cold Turkey (1951)
Contrary Condor (1944)
Donald and Pluto (1936)
Donald Gets Drafted (1942) includes Harline song "The Army's Not the Army Anymore"
Donald's Crime (1945) w/Plumb
Donald's Off Day (1944)
Don Donald (1937)
Dude Duck (1951)
The Eyes Have It (1945)
Fall Out—Fall In (1943)
Father's Are People (1951)
Father's Day Off (1953)
Fire Chief (1940)
Food for Feudin'
The Fox Hunt (1938)
Fun and Fancy Free (1947)
A Gentlemen's Gentleman (1941)
Get Rich Quick (1951)
Goofy and Wilbur (1939)
The Great Locomotive Chase (1956)
Hawaiian Holiday (1937) w/Harline
Hockey Homicide (1945)
Hold That Pose (1950)
Hook, Lion and Sinker (1950)
How to Be a Sailor (1944)
How to Fish (1942)
How to Play Baseball (1942)
How to Play Football (1944)
How to Swim (1942)
The Light in the Forest (1958) songs only
Lion Down (1951)
The Living Desert (1953)
Lucky Number (1951)
Melody Time (1948)
Mickey's Circus (1936)
Mickey's Pal Pluto (1933) w/Churchill
Miracle of the White Stallions (1963)
Moon Pilot (1962)
Moose Hungers (1937)
Motor Mania (1950)
Nikki, Wild Dog of the North (1961)
No Smoking (1951)
The Old Army Game (1943)
The Olympic Champ (1942)
Out of Scale (1951)
The Parent Trap (1961)
Perri (1957)
Pests of the West (1950)
Pinocchio (1940) w/Harline; Academy Award for Best Original Score
Pluto and the Armadillo (1943)
Pluto's Playmates (1941)
Pluto's Quin-Puplets (1937)
The Pointer (1939)
Polar Trappers (1938)
Pollyanna (1960)
Puss-Cafe (1950)
R'Coon Dog (1951)
Saludos Amigos (1943) w/Plumb & Wolcott
Secrets of Life (1956)
The Shaggy Dog (1959)
The Simple Things (1953)
Snow White and the Seven Dwarfs (1937) Cond.
So Dear to My Heart (1949)
Song of the South (1946) animated score
Switzerland (1955)
Test Pilot Donald (1951)
The Three Caballeros (1945)
The Three Lives of Thomasina (1964)
Thru the Mirror (1936) w/Churchill

Tiger Trouble (1945)
Toy Tinkers (1949)
Trailer Horn (1950)
Trick or Treat (1952)
Truant Officer Donald (1941) w/Harline
True Life Adventures
Bear Country (1952)
In Beaver Valley (1950)
Nature's Half Acre (1951)
Olympic Elk (1953)
Prowlers of the Everglades (1954)
20,000 Leagues Under the Sea (1954)
Two-Gun Goofy (1952)
The Vanishing Prairie (1954)
Victory Through Air Power (1943) w/O. Wallace and Plumb
Westward Ho the Wagons (1956) song only
Window Cleaners (1940) w/O. Wallace
The Worm Turns (1937)

Snow, Mark
Ernest Saves Christmas (1988)

Sondheim, Stephen
Dick Tracy (1990) song only; Academy Award for Best Song: "Sooner or Later I Always Get My Man"

Stalling, Carl
In the late 1920s, Stalling became Disney's first Music Director and composed the first scores for Mickey Mouse shorts and "Silly Symphonies." He later achieved fame as the Musical Director for Warner Brother's Looney Tunes and Merrie Melodies. His Disney films were:
Autumn (1930)
The Barn Dance (1928)
The Barnyard Battle (1929)
El Terrible Toreador (1929)
Gallopin' Gaucho (1928)
The Haunted House (1929)
Hell's Bells (1929)
The Jazz Fool (1929)
Jungle Rhythm (1929)
The Karnival Kid (1929)
The Merry Dwarfs (1929)
Mickey's Choo Choo (1929)
Mickey's Follies (1929)
Minnie's Yoo Hoo (1930) this later became Mickey Mouse's theme song
The Opry House (1929)
Plane Crazy (1928)
The Plow Boy (1929)
Skeleton Dance (1929) includes Grieg's "March of the Dwarfs"
Springtime (1929)
Summer (1930)
When the Cat's Away (1929)
Wild Waves (1929)

Steele, David
Tin Men (1987) w/Cox

Steiner, Max (1888-1971)
Those Calloways (1965)

Stewart, David A.
The Ref (1994)

Styner, Jerry
Muscle Beach Party (1964) song only; AIP Production
Pajama Party (1964) AIP Production

Summers, Andy
Down and Out in Beverly Hills (1986)

Towns, Colin
Robert A. Heinlein's The Puppet Masters (1994)

Usher, Gary (1939-1990)
Muscle Beach Party (1964) songs only; AIP Production

Wallace, Bernie
Blaze (1989)

Wallace, Oliver George (1887-1963)
Adventures of Ichabod and Mr. Toad (1949)
African Diary (1945)
Alice in Wonderland (1951)
All in a Nutshell (1949)
The Autograph Hound (1939)
Bearly Asleep (1955)

Bee On Guard (1951)
Bellboy Donald (1942)
Ben and Me (1953)
The Best of Walt Disney's True-Life Adventures (1975) w/Smith and Baker
Big Red (1962)
The Big Wash (1948)
Billposters (1940)
Bone Bandit (1948)
Bootle Beetle (1947)
Breezy Bear (1955)
Bubble Bee (1949)
Canine Casanova (1945)
Canine Patrol (1945)
Canvas Back Duck (1953)
Casey Bats Again (1954)
Cat Nap Pluto (1948)
Chicken Little (1943)
Chip an' Dale (1947)
Chips Ahoy (1956)
Cinderella (1950) w/Smith
Clock Cleaners (1937) w/Smith
The Clock Watcher (1945)
Clown of the Jungle (1947)
Commando Duck (1944)
Corn Chips (1951) w/Dubin
Crazy Over Daisy (1950)
Crazy with the Heat (1947)
Cured Duck (1945)
Daddy Duck (1948)
Darby O'ill and the Little People (1959)
Der Fuehrer's Face (1943) original title was to be "Donald Duck in Nutziland"
Dog Watch (1945)
Donald Duck and the Gorilla (1944)
Donald's Better Self (1938)
Donald's Cousin Gus (1939)
Donald's Dilemma (1947)
Donald's Dog Laundry (1940)
Donald's Double Trouble (1946)
Donald's Dream Voice (1948)
Donald's Garden (1942)
Donald's Gold Mine (1942)
Donald's Golf Game (1938)
Donald's Happy Birthday (1949)
Donald's Lucky Day (1939)
Donald's Nephews (1938)
Donald's Ostrich (1937)
Donald's Penguin (1939)
Donald's Snow Fight (1942)
Donald's Tire Trouble (1943)
Donald's Vacation (1940)
Double Dribble (1946)
Dragon Around (1954)
Drip Dippy Donald (1948)
Duck Pimples (1945)
Dumb Bell of the Yukon (1946)
Dumbo (1941) w/Churchill; Academy Award for Best Musical Scoring of a Motion Picture
Early to Bed (1941)
Figaro and Frankie (1947)
First Aiders (1944)
Flying Squirrel (1954)
Foul Hunting (1947)
Frank Duck Brings 'Em Back Alive (1946)
Fun and Fancy Free (1947) "Mickey and the Beanstalk"
Good Scouts (1938)
Goofy Gymnastics (1949)
Grand Canyonscope (1954)
The Greener Yard (1949)
Grin and Bear It (1954)
Hans Brinker or The Silver Skates (1962-TV)
Hockey Champ (1939)
Honey Harvester (1949)
How to Have an Accident at Work (1959)
How to Play Golf (1944)
The Incredible Journey (1963)
In Dutch (1946)
Inferior Decorator (1948)
Jungle Cat (1960)
Knight for a Day (1946)
Lady and the Tramp (1955)
The Legend of Coyote Rock (1945)
The Legend of Lobo (1962)
The Legend of Sleepy Hollow (1949) from *The Adventures of Ichabod and Mr. Toad*
Let's Stick Together (1952)
Lion Around (1950)
The Little Whirlwind (1941)
Mail Dog (1947)
Mickey's Amateurs (1937) w/Harline
Mickey and the Seal (1948)
Mickey's Delayed Date (1947)

Mickey's Down Under (1948)
Mickey's Parrot (1938)
Modern Inventions (1937)
Mr. Mouse Takes a Trip (1940) w/Harline
No Hunting (1955)
No Sail (1945)
Officer Duck (1939)
Old Sequoia (1945)
Old Yeller (1957)
Peter Pan (1953)
Pigs Is Pigs (1954)
The Plastics Inventor (1944)
Pluto and the Gopher (1950)
Pluto at the Zoo (1942)
Pluto's Blue Note (1947) w/Wolcott
Pluto's Fledgling (1948)
Pluto's Heart Throb (1950)
Pluto's Housewarming (1947)
Pluto's Kid Brother (1946)
Pluto's Party (1952)
Pluto's Purchase (1948)
Pluto's Surprise Package (1949)
Pluto's Sweater (1949)
Primitive Pluto (1950)
Private Pluto (1943)
Pueblo Pluto (1948)
The Purloined Pup (1946)
Put-Put Troubles (1940)
Rescue Dog (1947)
The Riveter (1940)
Rugged Bear (1953)
Samoa (1956)
"Sammy the Way Out Seal" (1962) TV
Savage Sam (1963)
Sea Scouts (1939)
Self Control (1938)
Sheep Dog (1949)
Sleepy Time Donald (1947)
Slide, Donald, Slide (1949)
Social Lion (1954)
Society Dog Show (1939)
Soup's On (1949)
Spare the Rod (1954)
Springtime for Pluto (1944)
Squatter's Rights (1946)
Straight Shooters (1947)
T-Bone for Two (1942)
Teachers Are People (1952)
Tea for Two Hundred (1948)
Tennis Racquet (1949)
Ten Who Dared (1960)
They're Off (1948)
Three for Breakfast (1948)
Timber (1941)
Tonka (1958)
The Trial of Donald Duck (1948)
Trombone Trouble (1944)
Tugboat Mickey (1940)
Two Weeks Vacation (1952)
Up a Tree (1955)
The Vanishing Private (1942) w/Harline
Victory Through Air Power (1943) w/Smith & Plumb
Victory Vehicles (1943)
Wet Paint (1946)
White Wilderness (1958)
Wide Open Spaces (1947)
Window Cleaners (1940) w/Smith
Winter Storage (1949)
Wonder Dog (1950)
Working for Peanuts (1953)

Washington Ned (1901-1976) lyrist
Dumbo (1941)
Pinocchio (1940)
Saludos Amigos (1953)
Victory Vehicles (1943) song only

Wechter, Julius (1935-)
Midnight Madness (1980)

Wendy and Lisa
Dangerous Minds (1995)

Williams, Paul (1940-)
The Muppet Christmas Carol (1992) songs only

Wolcott, Charles Frederick (1906-)
Wolcott was Disney's General Music Director from 1944-1948
Adventures of Ichabod and Mr. Toad (1949)
The Art of Skiing (1941)
Bambi (1942) partial
Chef Donald (1941)
Goofy's Glider (1940)
Make Mine Music (1946) song only

Mickey's Birthday Party (1942)
Mr. Duck Steps Out (1940)
The Nifty Nineties (1941)
Pinocchio (1940) partial
Pluto's Blue Note (1947) w/O. Wallace
The Reluctant Dragon (1941)
Saludos Amigos (1943) w/Plumb and Smith
Song of the South (1946) song only
Symphony Hour (1942)

Worth, Bobby (1921-)
Make Mine Music (1946) song only
Melody Time (1948) song only
Fun and Fancy Free (1947) song only

Wrubel, Allie (1905-1973)
Make Mine Music (1946) "Johnny Fedora"
Melody Time (1948) Little Toot
Song of the South (1946) song only; Academy Award with Ray Gilbert for Best Song: "Zip-A-Dee-Doo-Dah"

Zimmer, Hans (1957-)
Cool Runnings (1993)
Crimson Tide (1995)
Green Card (1990)
The Lion King (1994) Academy Award for Best Score
Muppet Treasure Island (1996)
The Preacher's Wife (1996)
Renaissance Man (1994)
The Rock (1996)
White Fang (1992) w/Poledouris

INDEX